"A magisterial review of employee voice and participation, combining deep awareness of long-standing debates with critical analysis of topical issues, such as employee engagement. Professor Hyman highlights the threats to employee voice from market-driven performance management, both here and abroad. An essential text for anyone interested in employee participation."
Andrew Pendleton, Professor of Human Resource Management, Durham Business School, UK

"Drawing on an impressive range of political, management, trade union and employee perspectives, this book addresses employee voice but also pressing employment issues, such as precarious work. Its broad-ranging, reflective view is refreshing and engaging. Essential reading for PhD students in HRM/ employment studies, and for senior undergraduates and postgraduates either as a whole or for individual topic chapters."
Dora Scholarios, Professor of Work Psychology, Strathclyde Business School, UK

"An excellent book starting from the position that employee participation is about control and influence at work. Taking a historical perspective and assessing developments from different actor perspectives (state, employers, employees) the author shows how fashions have waxed and waned as well as situating current narratives in the context of the changing world of work. The author argues that whilst labour market flux is by no means new the pluralist structures that underpinned Western economies are threatened by a number of market-driven directions, restricting the ability of workers to express independent voice."
Adrian Wilkinson, Director, Centre for Work, Organisation and Wellbeing, Griffith University, Australia

Employee Voice and Participation

Employee participation and voice (EPV) concern power and influence. Traditionally, EPV has encompassed worker attempts to wrest control from employers through radical societal transformation or share control through collective regulation by trade unions. This book offers a controversial alternative, arguing that, in recent years, participation has shifted direction.

In *Employee Voice and Participation*, the author contends that participation has moved away from employee attempts to secure autonomy and influence over organisational affairs to one in which management ideas and initiatives have taken centre stage. This shift has been bolstered in the UK and USA by economic policies that treat regulation as an obstacle to competitive performance. Through an examination of the development of ideas and practice surrounding employee voice and participation, this volume tracks the story from the earliest attempts at securing worker control through to the rise of trade unions and today's managerial efforts to contain union influence. It also explores the negative consequences of these changes and, though the outlook is pessimistic, considers possible approaches to address the growing power imbalance between employers and workers.

Employee Voice and Participation will be an excellent supplementary text for advanced students of employment relations and Human Resource Management (HRM). It will also be a valuable read for researchers, policy makers, trade unions and HRM professionals.

Jeff Hyman is Professor Emeritus in Employment Relations at the University of Aberdeen, UK and Honorary Professor of Management at the University of St Andrews, UK. His long-standing research and teaching interests are in employee participation and the future of work.

Employee Voice and Participation

Contested past, troubled present, uncertain future

Jeff Hyman

LONDON AND NEW YORK

First published 2018
by Routledge
2 Park Square, Milton Park, Abingdon, Oxon OX14 4RN

and by Routledge
711 Third Avenue, New York, NY 10017

Routledge is an imprint of the Taylor & Francis Group, an informa business

© 2018 Jeff Hyman

The right of Jeff Hyman to be identified as author of this work has been asserted by him in accordance with sections 77 and 78 of the Copyright, Designs and Patents Act 1988.

All rights reserved. No part of this book may be reprinted or reproduced or utilised in any form or by any electronic, mechanical, or other means, now known or hereafter invented, including photocopying and recording, or in any information storage or retrieval system, without permission in writing from the publishers.

Trademark notice: Product or corporate names may be trademarks or registered trademarks, and are used only for identification and explanation without intent to infringe.

British Library Cataloguing in Publication Data
A catalogue record for this book is available from the British Library

Library of Congress Cataloging in Publication Data
Names: Hyman, J. D. (Jeffrey D.), author.
Title: Employee voice and participation : contested past, troubled present, uncertain future / Jeff Hyman.
Description: New York : Routledge, 2018. |
Includes bibliographical references and index.
Identifiers: LCCN 2017057721 (print) | LCCN 2018011840 (ebook) | ISBN 9781315172880 (Ebook) | ISBN 9781138043770 (hardback : alk. paper) | ISBN 9781138043787 (pbk. : alk. paper) | ISBN 9781315172880 (ebk)
Subjects: LCSH: Management–Employee participation. |
Strategic planning–Employee participation.
Classification: LCC HD5650 (ebook) | LCC HD5650 .E466 2018 (print) |
DDC 658.3/152–dc23
LC record available at https://lccn.loc.gov/2017057721

ISBN: 978-1-138-04377-0 (hbk)
ISBN: 978-1-138-04378-7 (pbk)
ISBN: 978-1-315-17288-0 (ebk)

Typeset in Bembo
by Taylor & Francis Books

Printed and bound by CPI Group (UK) Ltd, Croydon, CR0 4YY

To the memory of my parents and Anselm Citron

Contents

List of tables   xi
Acknowledgements   xii
Abbreviations   xiii

Introduction: History and evolution of employee participation   1
Why the need for a new book on employee participation? 1
Problems of definition 3
Measuring EPV 6
Industrial democracy 8
Employee participation 9
Employee involvement 12
Conclusions 12

1 Why does employee participation and voice matter?   14
Introduction 14
Links between EPV and democratic values 15
Associations between discretion and autonomy at work and dignity, satisfaction, employee health and wellbeing 16
Impact of EPV on economic performance and productivity 26
Conclusions 30

2 Political perspectives on employee participation and voice   32
Introduction 32
Coordinated and liberal markets 32
The role and impact of legislation 36
Government intervention in the European Union 41
Conclusions 43

3 Management perspectives on employee participation and voice   45
Introduction 45
The defensive role of EPV 46
Humanisation of work 47
Strategy and human resource management 48
Organisational and human resource management strategy 49
Management and EPV 57
Conclusions 60

4 Employee and trade union perspectives on employee participation and voice   63
Introduction 63
What do employees want? 64
Precarious work 66
A voice for the precarious worker? 69
Voice and silence 70
Employees and trade unions in Europe 72
Conclusions 75

5 Profit-sharing and employee share ownership: Panacea or gimmick?   77
Introduction 77
The range of financial participation 77
Profit-sharing schemes 78
Employee share schemes 82
Employee ownership 87
Conclusions 92

6 High-performance work and its antecedents   95
Introduction 95
Origins of HPWS: lean production 96
The influence of people management 99
Research on HPWSs 100
Conclusions 105

7 Empowering and engaging employees?: Or simply reinventing the wheel?   107
Introduction 107
Employee empowerment 108

Employee engagement 113
Conclusions 119

8 What's not to like about teamworking? 120
Introduction 120
Why teamworking? 120
Types of teams 123
What makes a team? 125
The question of team autonomy 126
Teams and lean 128
Conclusions 132

9 Collective participation 134
Introduction 134
The decline of collective bargaining in the UK 135
Collective bargaining experience in Europe 137
Different directions? Joint consultation in the UK and Europe 139
Works councils and codetermination: the experience of Europe 142
Supervisory boards and codetermination 143
Partnership at work: a tale of two systems 146
Conclusions 150

10 Internationalisation and the impact of European Works Councils 152
Introduction and background 152
Forms and processes of EWCs 153
Early research on EWCs 155
Revision of the Directive and the 2009 Recast 158
EWC experience following the 2009 Recast 161
Conclusions 163

11 Global markets and prospects for employee emancipation 166
The context for globalisation 166
China and voice 167
India and voice 174
Conclusions 179

12 An uncertain future? 182
Introduction: a contested past 182
EPV: a troubled present 183

EPV: an uncertain future? 186
The impact on the UK of leaving the EU 191
Prospects for EPV 193
Closing the participation gap 196
The future of work 197

References   200
Index   238

Tables

3.1 Arrangements for direct two-way communication between
managers and employees, 2004 and 2011   60
4.1 Union density in the six countries, 2004 and 2016 (per cent)   66
4.2 Union densities for selected NMS countries   75

Acknowledgements

At the age of 74, I never expected to write a new book. That I have done so is in no small part thanks to the encouragement and advice offered by a host of friends and colleagues. Without their support this book would probably never have been started, let alone completed. Initially, I must thank the editorial team at Routledge for their encouragement in moving the project from concept to actuality. Once I realised that I actually had to write something, people with whom I discussed the project generously offered sound advice and suggestions. While it would be impossible to mention all who contributed, I would especially like to thank Jane Burgess, Walter Cairns, David Erdal, Mike Hough, Kath Kane, Ali MacDonald, Chidi Ogbonnaya, Ewen Smith and Adrian Wilkinson. Also, thanks to the helpful folk at Partick public library in Glasgow. Can we really afford to jeopardise institutions that offer so much to so many at so little cost?

Numerous colleagues gave of their valuable time to read through and comment authoritatively on draft chapters; their suggestions have been vital in maintaining progress and keeping my feet firmly planted on the ground. I am in special debt to Chris and Heather Baldry, Ian Cunningham, Martin Dowling, Chen Guo, Andrew Pendleton and Dora Scholarios for offering me their time and expertise despite their many other obligations. Responsibility for the final product is, of course, mine alone.

Finally, I am so fortunate to have a supportive, albeit at times critical, family, without whom I probably would not have found the motivation to undertake a stimulating but at times life-consuming undertaking. Much love and thanks to Matthew and Pierre and above all to Sabine, my sternest but most effective support, for her copy-editing and words of wisdom.

Jeff Hyman
University of Aberdeen
University of St Andrews
November 2017

Abbreviations

ACAS	Advisory, Conciliation and Arbitration Service
ACTFU	All-China Federation of Trade Unions
AWG	autonomous work group
BPR	business process reengineering
CBI	Confederation of British Industry
CIPD	Chartered Institute of Personnel and Development
CME	coordinated market economy
EC	European Commission
EEA	European Economic Area
EI	employee involvement
EO	employee ownership
EP	employee participation
EPV	employee participation and voice
ERA	Employment Relations Act
ESO	employee share ownership
ESOP	employee share ownership plan
ETUC	European Trade Union Confederation
EU	European Union
EWC	European Works Council
EWCS	European Working Conditions Survey
FDI	foreign direct investment
HPWS	high-performance work system
HR or HRM	human resource management
ICE	Information and Consultation of Employees
JCC	joint consultation committee
LME	liberal market economy
MNC	multinational company
NHS	National Health Service

NMS	new member states
PRP	profit-related pay
SAYE	save as you earn
SHRM	strategic human resource management
TUC	Trades Union Council
WERS	Workplace Employment Relations Surveys

Introduction
History and evolution of employee participation

Why the need for a new book on employee participation?

Whether as consumers or producers, organisations dominate our everyday lives like at no previous time. Their behaviour and performance affect us all, whether in providing key public or voluntary sector services or as competitive private-sector enterprises, whose reach can extend across continents. Organisational successes are lauded but failures can wreak economic and political havoc, with accompanying personal misery, as was experienced so dramatically following the global financial crisis of 2008. Recent controversial examples of managerial excess in companies such as BHS and Sports Direct have led to (short-lived) UK prime ministerial calls 'to put people back in control' (Gall 2016a, 2016b). Control is a core issue for policy-makers, practitioners and academics. This encompasses systems and cultures of management, and especially questions of corporate social responsibility and the way in which this can be achieved, people management and employee reactions to different styles of management. Highly relevant here is the question of decisions: who makes them, how they are made and regulated, and their impacts and implications on employee behaviour and productivity.

Employee participation (EP) is about control and influence at work, and research and narratives on these topics have a long history, extending from the early days of industrialisation to the present. The past forty years have witnessed vast technological and economic shifts that are stimulating profound change in employment relationships across the world. The competitive impacts of deregulatory neoliberalism, austerity and globalisation are being felt in both mature and newly industrialising countries, leading in turn to unprecedented changes both in labour market relations and within broader society as levels of financial and welfare inequality grow. Conflicts of interest have been heightened as organisations seek to remain competitive or, in public services, attempt to act within budgetary boundaries. These pressures are seen in the suppression of unions, affecting employee access to means of conflict resolution, in closer managerial and technological monitoring, target-setting, performance measurement and surveillance of employees, including many professionals who previously enjoyed autonomy and independent control over their work. Another outcome has been a surge in employment insecurity as organisations aim to reduce labour costs through mergers, acquisitions and diverse employment flexibility programmes. Conversely, employers may seek benefits in terms of output quality by prescribing team working, multilateral communication and consultation procedures, often within an individualised involvement and engagement framework. The argument of this book is that while tensions in labour market relations are not new, protective pluralist structures that have long dominated Western economies are under existentialist threat from a range of market-driven directions, leaving employees and workers less able to express independent voice and more vulnerable to managerial efficiency-seeking strategies.

The prime aim of this book is to examine and assess ideas and practice surrounding and informing employee participation and voice (EPV) through the actions of state, employers and employees. These start from early attempts at securing worker control of the means of production, followed by the rise of trade union attempts to impose regulation on organisational decisions, leading to present-day efforts on the part of management to contain and subsequently suppress collective influence in neoliberal economies such as the UK, while importing diverse initiatives to engage employees in their work as a means to gain and maintain competitive advantage. We identify different trajectories in continental Europe where dominant pluralist political and economic regimes, though under pressure, help to establish and sustain systems of collective participation, expressed visibly through European Union (EU) regulations. The potential impact of Brexit on EP in the UK adds further critical dimensions to the narrative.

The opening chapters examine the history and definitional complexities of EPV before offering an analysis of its development and rationales. The following three chapters examine in turn political, employer and employee perspectives on EPV. With employer practice in the ascendant, and its prime focus on individual performance-orientated involvement, the following three chapters examine respectively the rationale and effects of financial participation (chapter 5), the use of combinations of involvement techniques designed to elicit high performance through employee commitment to the organisation and its objectives (chapter 6) and the meanings and questionable effects of empowerment and engagement (chapter 7). Teamworking, originally constructed as a defence mechanism by employees against managerial incursions, has now become a significant performance-driving tool and its use and effects are assessed in chapter 8. Chapter 9 examines different approaches to collective participation in situations where unions are faced with a decline in numbers and influence. Chapter 10 looks more closely at European Works Councils, established by the European Union to afford protections to workers employed in multinational enterprises, whose operational decisions would otherwise be out of reach of domestic workers and their representative institutions. Chapter 11 extends the analysis to the newly industrialising world, focusing closely on China and India, hitherto largely hosts to corporate globalisation, which provide tentative contemporary evidence of the potential for emancipatory EPV to influence economic and, potentially, political systems. The final chapter brings the various themes together with a summary of the challenges facing employee voice and representative participation, considering how these are being addressed and finally assessing prospects for the future of EPV.

Problems of definition

EPV's long and convoluted history has its roots in countering the alienating character of work in capitalist enterprises. With the rise of large-scale manufacture, it was seen as a progressive advance by and for labour and working class interests, designed to promote democratic values into workplace (and societal) culture and also to offer more humane (and potentially more productive) working conditions in the face of dominant Taylorist and subsequently Fordist assembly-line production. The rise of trade unions was both part of this social movement and an inhibitor to its progress because of their limited economic and sectional ambitions. Early countermovements to union activity by employers saw the development of profit-sharing exercises to promote a unified workplace culture. Increased recognition of the complexities of securing organisational commitment and motivation led to human relations and neohuman relations prescriptions, which subsequently became both blurred and reinforced by Japanese management concepts that emphasised management control through organisational identification and teamworking. Neoliberal market conditions have led employers to encourage employees to optimise their contribution by providing a stimulating working climate through combinations of progressive HR techniques such as high-involvement work systems. Acting as a counterpoint to these initiatives have been trends toward organisational restructuring, delayering and downsizing, accompanied by increasing use of flexible and insecure labour, backed by managerial policies of tight resource monitoring and control. With precarious work becoming more common in both developed and developing economies, the prospect of increasing numbers of marginalised workers, who benefit neither from progressive HR involvement policies and practices nor from the protective activities of representative participation or indeed from representative democracy in civil society, has become very real (Standing 2011, 2014).

With no common agreement on its purpose and with its complex and continuing history, it is easy to see why commentators find it difficult to agree on a definition to EPV. In her classic analysis, Pateman (1970: 67) suggested that EPV is often left undefined or when a definition is provided it is imprecise. Hodson (2001: 176) discusses the diversity and wide variance of EP practice, both within countries and between them; but rather than offering a definition or definitions, he identifies four main categories of practice: team-based systems, formal consultation, joint union-management programmes, and employee ownership (EO). It would be possible to include a range of other practices with equal justification, though his categorisation is useful in signalling potential escalation of EPV from the local and specific to the wider and more generic. Wilkinson et al. (2010a: 4) point to another potential problem: 'the meaning and form that participation can take varies considerably depending on the [academic] discipline' and comprehensively illustrate these differences by contrasting different disciplinary perspectives, including economic, legal, Marxist, management and industrial relations (Wilkinson et al. 2010b: Part II). In his far-ranging and influential book, while not attempting a specific definition, Blumberg (1968) adopts a radical and optimistic purpose for EP involving the elimination of worker alienation and potential societal transformation, although the participative processes he identifies to secure these changes appear more to confront dissatisfaction at work than to directly challenge the deeper tensions of capitalist production identified by Marx and subsequent labour process theory (Braverman 1974; Marks and Chillas 2014). Cotton et al. (1988) identified five dimensions of 'participatory management', namely: formal/informal; direct/ indirect; level of influence; content; and short term versus long term, suggesting that 'many of the conflicting and ambiguous results of the participatory management literature were a function of the different forms of participation resulting in different outcomes' (Collins 1996: 179).

A more restrictive definition is offered by Heller et al. (1998: 6): 'participation describes how people interact with each other in an organisational context', i.e. it focuses on the *process* of participation; but while this does not tell us much about the actual essence or intended *outcomes* of EP, the authors assert that for EP to signify anything meaningful, there must be information provision which can lead (somewhat vaguely) to 'involvement and consultation yielding various degrees of influence'. In summary, and echoing an earlier classification by McGregor (1960), these authors summarise EP 'as a range of influence ... from very little to a great deal', confirming just how difficult it is to arrive at a unified definition of the process. The same authors, however, in recognising the diversity of participative definition (Heller et al. 1998: 42), come out on the side of a process 'which allows employees to exert some influence over their work and the conditions under which they work' (ibid. 15). Nevertheless, they return to the uncertainty, suggesting that a subjective, possibly disciplinary (see Wilkinson et al. 2010b), element is always present: 'Depending on a given author's preoccupation, definitions stress the purpose ... its scope ... or behaviours included or excluded' (Heller et al. 1998: 42).

These complexities and competing processes and objectives make it futile to conceptualise EPV in terms of a single synchronised movement or system. There are some identifiable chronological movements, notably from initial late nineteenth century–early twentieth century association with democratisation of work, under the influence of socialist thinking. Subsequent post-Second World War social-democratic political economic policies, combined with support for trade union intervention in both political and industrial contexts, helped to secure a more pluralist base to employment relationships, with collective bargaining, social partnership and works councils prominent in different countries. As well as these labour-progressive moves, we also encounter continuity in management approaches, from the early simplistic Taylorist prescriptions of carrot-and-stick motivation through monetary reward and various human relations iterations to present-day employee engagement and high-commitment management policies of securing employee endorsement of organisational goals through individual and team task-based involvement in decisions.

From these different perspectives it is possible to identify three principal streams of participative activity, namely: industrial democracy; representative participation; and managerially inspired employee involvement (EI), all of which form foundations for conceptually and practically different approaches to EPV and their outcomes (Hyman and Mason 1995). These streams are reflected in Pateman's dimensions of full, partial and pseudo participation (Pateman 1970) and the two less radical approaches correspond to Marchington's (2005) categorisation of direct and indirect participation.

While participation in its diversity has long been recognised and scrutinised, the prominence of *voice* to articulate employee interests and its association or competition with participation is a more recent development. Its early manifestation is associated with the work of Hirschman (1970), who contended that dissatisfied consumers and citizens may voluntarily exercise their 'voice' to express discontent at their treatment rather than migrate (or 'exit') to other suppliers or even countries (Lewin 2010: 428–29). This analysis has extended to the scrutiny of employee behaviour in the face of discontent, though with little agreement between commentators on the status and implications of relationships between voice, exit through quitting, and loyalty to the employer, which may be due simply to lack of alternative employment opportunities (Allen and Meyer 1990). Also, as Anderson (2017: 56) notes, quitting may be more costly to employees than to an employer, as voluntarily leaving employment may mean loss of unemployment benefits or insurance. Alternatively, employees may opt to express discontent through *silence*, though recent scholarship suggests that silence may not necessarily be a freely chosen form of expression of resistance but rather the consequence of potential manipulation of the 'control dialectic' prevailing between managerial and employee interests (Donaghey et al. 2011: 61; Brinsfield 2014), in turn helping to reinforce the 'representation gap' identified by Towers in 1997. Again, a problem is that voice, or its absence, means different things to different commentators or disciplines. For example, Gomez et al. (2010: 401) define 'formal' voice as 'any institutionalised form of two-way communication between management and employees'. The authors go on to emphasise that 'any form' embraces a wide range of individual and representative means of expression, which suggests very limited differentiation from other classifications of EP.

Further disciplinary constriction is suggested by Barry and Wilkinson (2016) who distinguish between the employee-relations research approach of treating voice as a collective process to express and channel discontent, conducted through trade unions, and the organisational behaviour definition, which focuses on means adopted by individual employees to communicate with management in pursuit of shared interests. A similar interpretation, where voice expresses on the one hand individual and collective interests and on the other conflict and cooperation, has been provided by Dundon et al. (2004). Their typology of voice consists of (a) a means to articulate individual grievance, (b) mechanisms to involve individual employees in contributing to performance, (c) collective representation of employees in defending and promoting their sectional interests, and (d) collective cooperation with management to promote performance (see also Harley 2014). Nevertheless, from these perspectives it is difficult to discern significant empirical or prescriptive cleavage between EP and voice, a perspective shared by Townsend who uses 'the term employee involvement interchangeably with voice' (Townsend 2014: 155). The IPA, as the Involvement and Participation Association is now known, endorse this view by pointing out that 'voice can take many forms and is generally grouped into direct and indirect voice' (IPA 2011: 3), which shows no demonstrable definitional divergence from direct EI and indirect participation though, as with Heller et al.'s EP definition above, the identified approaches seem to emphasise the contribution of *communication* to organisational performance as a central and possibly defining feature of voice, especially as 'employers increasingly have come to see voice as a performance issue' (ibid. 5).

In our view, voice has similarly imprecise attributes as EP, an interpretation in harmony with that of Wilkinson and Dundon (2010: 175), who describe voice as 'the least precise of all participation mechanisms because in theory it can include all forms …'. Notwithstanding, or because of, these shortcomings, we suggest that voice can be defined as a medium for information exchange between managers and individual employees or collectivities of employees with the aim of securing benefit for all parties. This somewhat narrower communicative function of voice is consistent with the view of Strauss (2006), who considers voice to be a less substantial process than other forms of EP 'as it does not denote influence and may be no more than spitting in the wind' (Wilkinson and Dundon 2010: 168). Conversely, the imprecise nature of voice and silence may offer potential to broaden examination of EPV, as diverse groups may have access to different levels and depths of self-expression through informal restriction by employment status (for example in the case of part-time staff) or through oppressive cultures of bullying and harassment (Acker 2006).

Measuring EPV

Before moving on to analyse the different processes and practices of EPV in more depth, it is also worth evaluating another approach for identifying the contours of voice and EP, namely their measurement. We can identify three main directions for measurement, two that examine inputs into participation and one that assesses outcomes. The first approach is based on continuums rising from low-level input and/or influence. McGregor (1960) envisages a continuum ranging from a little to a lot of participation while Likert (1961) and more recently Heller et al. (1998) present a similar but more defined range, with no information provision at one end and joint problem review and resolution at the other (Pateman 1970: 67–68). This approach help to identify the principal methods subsumed under the EP/voice umbrella, but in terms of measuring and evaluating anything tangible, they are unsophisticated classifications, not especially helpful in assessing the influence or outcomes of participation.

Building on the work of Dundon et al. (2004), Marchington (2005) and his colleagues develop a more focused framework designed 'to unpack the purpose, meaning and subsequent impact of employee participation' (Wilkinson and Dundon 2010: 173), drawing on examination of the *depth, level, scope* and *form* of any participative initiative. Depth refers to state of employee or representative influence, ranging from passive receipt of information to mutual interactive impact. The second measure assesses the vertical level at which participation is expressed, ranging from task-centred work group to organisation-wide bodies. Scope concerns the range of topics available for participation under direct involvement and/or representative participation. Form focuses on whether participation emphasises direct manager-employee interaction or whether it operates through representative intermediaries. Wilkinson and Dundon claim that this 'framework allows for more accurate description not only of the type of involvement and participation schemes in use, but the extent to which they may or may not engage employees' (ibid. 173). They consider that the framework provides more than a continuum of practice, in that it explains the power relations underlying expression of participation (Marchington and Wilkinson 2005). Nevertheless, these and other writers are cognisant of the difficulties in revealing and assessing the influence and impacts of power relations, whether generated internally between the parties to the employment relationship or exerted extraneously, for example, through government pressure.

A third approach examines *outcomes* of the participative approach. As the following chapters show, outcomes can be expected to vary according to type of approach adopted. Hence, representative participation is potentially associated with developments in procedural justice and equality and through these, filters indirectly into organisational benefit. Managers might anticipate substantive outcomes from direct involvement or voice applications in terms of employee performance or productivity or through indirect indicators, such as lower absenteeism, labour turnover and more positive engagement with the organisation and its aims. As outcomes may be expected to relate to the specific type of participative intervention, we present a summary review of the impact of EP/voice schemes in chapter 2, and detailed analyses of outcome in subsequent chapters.

We now extend our approach to defining participation through examination of the three-way typology introduced above.

Industrial democracy

Industrial democracy emerges from different historical sources and political traditions. It engages historically with the theorists and activists of German social democracy, with the guild socialist ideas of societal transformation through networks of worker councils spreading upward from the workplace through civil society and closely associated with the work of G. D. H. Cole (1957) and with the ideals of cooperative movements. From a radical or Marxist perspective, the main distinguishing feature of industrial democracy, as Richard Hyman has emphasised, was 'the socialist objective ... to capture the ownership of the means of production, not to democratise their application' (Hyman 2015: 12). Hyman goes on to emphasise that early ideas of democracy at work diverged between different labour movements and between different countries. While distinctive routes from different schools of thought were proposed, the unifying feature was to transform power and authority relations in society through worker control of the means of production. But the means of 'capture' differed: the persistent and unanswered question hovering over achieving democratic participation is summarised in a nutshell: 'Is the central focus the workplace, or the broader economic and social context in which it is embedded? Is the goal to achieve employment participation in management decisions, to impose controls over management policies, or to create systems of self-management?' (ibid. 12).

Viewed through the lens of capitalist society development, Hyman argues that societal democratisation can be seen as a four-stage process involving, first, attaining political democracy through universal suffrage; second, the achievement of social justice coupled with collective and welfare rights; third, rights over strategic enterprise decision-making and employment, and, finally, economic democracy both within the enterprise and over the macroeconomy. Whilst advances in the first two stages have been essentially established in the developed world, progress in the workplace has been restricted largely to rights of information disclosure and consultation whilst the fourth step, 'socialisation of the economy', made initial progress with policies such as post-war nationalisations, Swedish collective wage-earner funds (Meidner 1978) and, in the UK, from the 1960s until the Thatcherite reforms of the 1980s, formal tripartite consultations between government, employers (through the Confederation of British Industry, CBI) and trade unions (through the Trades Union Council, TUC) over reconciling full employment with central macroeconomic policy-making. These advances have been impeded since the 1980s by the rise and domination of free-market economic policies involving the rollback of the state and subsequent privatisation and distancing of trade unions from political and economic decision-making (MacInnes 1987: 166), reinforced through continuing economic deregulation and the advance of globalisation. Hence, the forward march of enterprise-based industrial democracy has not only halted but is in significant retreat. Outposts still exist in cooperatives and some employee-owned companies, but even in these cases, democracy as a 'thorough-going change in the structure, aims and hierarchy of the enterprise' (Eldridge et al. 1991: 144) is questionable, with hierarchical control over work similar to that experienced in conventional enterprises (Edwards and Wajcman 2005: 129).

Employee participation

In contrast to managerially dominated EI, we have previously defined EP as 'state initiatives which promote the collective rights of employees to be represented in organisational decision-making, or to the consequences of the efforts of employees themselves to establish collective representation in corporate decisions, possibly in the face of employer resistance' (Hyman and Mason 1995: 21). With support from other commentators (for example Kessler 2010: 348), there seems little reason to change this definition, other than add that the state itself can also contribute to opposition to representative participation. Conversely, the key positive aspects involving 'state initiatives' usually offer protective or progressive legislation with regard to establishing trade unions or other collective employee bodies, encouraging and guaranteeing their interaction with management through appropriate regulatory systems and possibly acting as supervisors for agreed or negotiated outcomes. These sorts of initiatives are usually associated with social democratic movements in Europe and especially with the notion of shared stakeholding among employers, employees and community (Kluge 2005) or the initiatives of the Roosevelt administration in 1930s America, which gave rise to the National Labor Relations Act of 1935, guaranteeing unions the right to collective bargaining.

The state can involve itself in participative policies for a combination of reasons, though prime among these tend to be: protection of property rights; advancement of a democratic society; dealing with specific or intractable industrial relations problems; and maintenance of economic competitiveness, stability and progress. In terms of property protection, as the first industrialised country, the UK's legally sanctioned protection of propertied privilege and resistance to collective organisation extends back to the anti-union Combination Acts of 1799/1800 and common law safeguards of the rights of property through opposition to collective acts defined as 'restraint of trade' (Hyman 2003: 38). Though the British state gradually relaxed its strictures on union organisation and abstained from overt intervention with the promotion of voluntary determination of procedures and outcomes between employers and employees, since the 1980s resurgent neoliberal ideology has served to provide a substantial legal framework for treating trade unions as obstacles to labour and product market efficiency in the private sector and *in extremis* as 'the enemy within' in the public arena, thereby justifying restrictive legislation against union activity. This strong political neoliberal emphasis, shared with the USA, favours trade union restrictions in support of deregulatory policies to encourage a more vigorous and competitive economy (Rubery and Edwards 2003; Dickens and Hall 2003). So while British governments have in recent years tended not to legislate independently for EP, restrictions on trade union activity, coupled with encouragement of free dialogue between employers and individual employees, have undoubtedly stimulated the growth of direct EI and managerially initiated voice. British and American stances toward governmental non-intervention and their non-statutory or individualistic approaches to EP are consistent with what Hall and Soskice (2001) term liberal market economies in their *varieties of capitalism* thesis.

The second main approach to organised capitalism identified by Hall and Soskice is the coordinated market economy. These economies, typified by Germany and Scandinavian experience, tend to intervene in organisational management through non-market regulatory approaches founded on securing long-term mutual commitment between the parties, which is in turn based on securely founded bargaining and consultative arrangements, often with trade unions performing an established and central role, and rights formally defined and limited by law.

Germany has a coordinated system of national sector collective bargaining supplemented by codetermination at enterprise level. Works councils were legislated for in the 1920s, discontinued in the National Socialist era and fully restored following World War II by the Works Constitution Act of 1952, which set down the rights and obligations of works council employee and manager representatives (Foley 2014). As a second strand of codetermination, worker directors were introduced through legislation for supervisory boards of directors in strategic industries such as steel in West Germany following the end of the Second World War. This was an attempt to ensure a measure of grassroots surveillance over the activities of industries that before the war had helped to fund the National Socialist party and to support German rearmament (Blumberg 1968: 10). Moreover, worker directors are said to have contributed to Germany's lasting post-war economic success; employee representation on boards of directors extended to other sectors in Germany as well as to many other mainly northern European countries (Markey et al. 2010).

While common on mainland Europe, state endorsement for EP is not universal, as demonstrated by the restrictive policies of liberal market economies such as the UK. Nevertheless, initiatives which presiding national governments do not support can of course be implemented through supranational bodies such as the European Union. The UK initially abstained from European Works Councils, whose regulations for informing and consulting employees under the so-called 'social chapter' were originally rejected by the Conservative governments of the 1980s and 1990s (see chapter 10). EWCs provide for participation of employees on representative bodies of transnational enterprises operating in at least two member countries. Hence, principal approaches associated with EP include collective bargaining, works councils, joint consultation, social partnership and worker directors. The common conceptual feature binding these different approaches together is the principle of pluralism, in which different interest groups (such as local community, consumers, employees and their representatives) can share overriding objectives but have legitimate differences of interest. For pluralists, governmental employment relations policy should be directed at providing the means to regulate potential divergences of interest in ways that offer agreed resolution to the conflicting parties. In democratic countries this has often involved joint decision-making over terms and conditions of employment, through a process of negotiation (Hyman 2003). The pluralist approach has been undermined in recent years by the dominance of neoliberal economics, under which trade unions are treated as impediments to the operation of free markets (Kaine 2014).

The other important dynamic underlying EP concerns the efforts of employees themselves to secure representation. The history of conflict in achieving collective employee recognition in industrialised countries is well recognised and there have been few instances in which pluralist industrial systems have been introduced without struggle between nascent collective employee associations and employers and/or with the state itself. In the UK and USA, the nineteenth and early twentieth-century doctrine of laissez-faire, with its emphasis on free trade, sovereignty of private property and legal support for voluntarism, were associated with trade union repression or at least channelling union activity in directions that offered little serious challenge to the status quo. Often then, trade unions established themselves in the face of physical or legal challenge. As Ciulla remarks in the context of the USA, 'unions struck fear into the hearts of industrialists and the twentieth century became a pitched battle for control of the hearts and minds of the American worker' (Ciulla 2000: 91). A dramatic example of the struggle for union rights in the 1930s is provided by the Ford Motor Company, whose Service Department, headed by chief of security Harry Bennett, was notorious for the way in which it dealt with anyone suspected of union sympathies, let alone membership or activity (Beynon 1973). Threatened with possible accommodation with the United Auto Workers in the mid-1930s through the union-supportive Labor Relations Act, Henry Ford's reaction was uncompromising in its resistance to unionisation by turning 'the Rouge [car plant] into an industrial concentration camp overseen by Bennett's army of Service Department men' (Collier and Horowitz 1989: 160). Workers were spied upon, belongings searched for union material, leading to summary dismissal if any were found; legitimate distribution of union publicity outside the plant was met by extreme violence from Bennett's thuggish enforcers (Collier and Horowitz 1989: 163). Nevertheless, eventually the rule of law prevailed and Ford and other recalcitrant employers were forced to the negotiating table.

While developed industrialised countries today do not forcibly deter union association and organisation, the re-emergence of free-market neoliberal economic policy has helped to reverse decades of pluralist progress and by so doing, impacted negatively on collective participation, specifically in the form of a 'representation gap' (Towers 1997; Heery et al. 2004). In present circumstances of a globalised free-trade economy, these retreats present new and formidable obstacles facing unions and labour sympathisers, whether in the workplace or within the broader national and international political economy. The universal erosion or suppression of worker rights and participative representation has contributed to the so-called 'race to the bottom' in minimising operating costs. In many newly industrialising countries today, collective employee action can be heavily circumscribed or prohibited in ways reminiscent of the physical suppression of trade unions and persecution of their leaders that took place in the earlier days of Western industrialisation.

Employee involvement

Unitarism, founded on belief in shared interests, unified unopposed executive authority and absence of conflict, provides the conceptual foundations for management-inspired EI (Fox 1974; Kessler and Purcell 2003). Previously, we defined EI as 'practices and policies which emanate from management and sympathisers of free market commercial activity' aimed at offering employees some influence over their tasks and immediate workplace environment (Hyman and Mason 1995: 21). This definition stands today and includes the principal communicative dimensions of worker voice. EI is typified by three distinct but linked processes, which will be considered in depth in subsequent chapters. The first is exchange of information, the second provides employees with limited autonomy over tasks through job redesign, empowerment and teamworking, and the third concerns financial involvement and the ideological and somewhat mystical underpinning of the EI project, which can be summarised under the general rhetoric of 'engagement'. Under free market austerity-directed economic and political policies and with highly competitive markets in the ascendancy, it is not surprising that EI initiatives have proliferated whilst legal and market restrictions on trade union activity have served to create the spaces in which EI can be consolidated.

Conclusions

In this chapter, definitions and measurement of voice and participation have been shown to be complex and in some cases unresolved. As demonstrated in the following chapters, a defining feature of EPV is the level of control contained in its exercise. Indeed, the philosopher Joanne Ciulla notes that 'the struggle for freedom and power or control is the central problem of work' (Ciulla 2000: 70). Nevertheless, the issue of control focuses on a question that remains pertinent a hundred years after its exposition in a classic study by Carter Goodrich, namely: 'how many workers do want control, and how much control do they want' (1920: 4). Founded on previous classifications, we suggest three different routes for participation, based primarily on who controls the process and outcomes but also on who is intended to be the major beneficiary.

Nevertheless, benefits may be shared. For example, representative approaches designed to offer a measure of countervailing influence to employees in dealing with their more economically powerful employers may also enhance employee commitment to the enterprise through offering a genuine stake in it (Doellgast and Benassi 2014: 242). Similarly, voice-orientated projects and forms of management-initiated EI may enhance performance by encouraging positive contributions from informed or empowered employees.

However, significant questions remain to be addressed. These include the effects of the representation gap. Arguably, the more diverse and internationalised that organisational operations are, the wider the potential becomes for the existence of a representation gap. We also examine in more depth the links between participative arrangements and the changing workforce, with its increasing precarity and insecurity. Third, and related to the previous point, there is the question of equality: if control is the essence of participation, to what extent do potentially marginalised groups such as part-time workers have the voice and means to address their interests through participative arrangements? Even if these arrangements are formally available, there arises the question of whether cultures of bullying and harassment can act as invisible barriers against effective participation, for example by silencing women and other groups who may not occupy dominating or influential positions in organisational hierarchies. Fourth, and not unrelated to the previous point, the question of whether global multinational power and concomitant growing inequality among nation states increasingly constrains meaningful ways for employees to demonstrate and protect their interests.

Chapter 1

Why does employee participation and voice matter?

Introduction

The previous chapter identified the various – and often conflicting – sources, rationales and effects of EPV. The present chapter focuses on the potential beneficiaries of different EPV formulations. Based on a wealth of reported research, both classical and contemporary, this chapter examines in greater depth:

a   links between EPV and democratic values
b   associations between discretion and autonomy at work and employee dignity, health, wellbeing and satisfaction
c   impact of EPV on economic performance and productivity

From these different perspectives it becomes clear why EPV is today such contested terrain.

We first examine the potential beneficiaries of EPV and through this preliminary analysis enquire if participation advantages more than one party in the employment relationship and, following the seminal work of Ramsay, ask whether a zero-sum situation exists in which only one party benefits from participative exercises, to the detriment of others. The chapter demonstrates difficulties inherent in directly associating participation and effects. First, because participation takes different forms and meanings, it is likely to exert different behavioural effects depending on the intentions and actions of its initiators and the contexts in which they operate. Second, it can be difficult to ascribe specific effects to individual initiatives, as these may have positive, negative or contrasting consequences for employees depending on the context, the prevailing state of employment relationships, in terms of levels of trust and perceived fairness, and the intended outcomes. Third, the definition and operationalisation of concepts such as 'satisfaction' add complexities to the analysis and possible prescriptions. But, with these caveats in mind, we attempt to differentiate between different approaches to participation and thereby to analyse links between them and their effects.

Links between EPV and democratic values

Our initial claim of positive and discernible links between EP and democratic values, expressed in the workplace or potentially in broader society, is examined initially here and its public policy foundations explored further in chapter 2. The first proposition is deceptively simple: organisations that encourage participation are considered more democratic, thereby offering stakeholder citizenship or procedural justice to their employees. These attributes in turn offer benefits to employees, in terms of self worth and personal actualisation, as well as to the organisation, in that participating workers can be expected to be more efficient and productive. This deceptive simplicity is exposed when one questions the nature and objectives of the participation exercise and the extent to which power relations between the parties are affected. Pateman (1970) identified the looseness and variability of definition, though in seeking more precision, she stipulates that participation has to be directed *specifically* toward decision-making; but even here we face difficulties as managers may introduce participative initiatives such as 1980s quality circles to promote 'organizational efficiency', implementing 'techniques used to persuade employees to accept decisions that have *already* been made by the management' (ibid.: 68, emphasis in the original). As shown in the introduction, Pateman describes this process as *pseudo-participation*, while Hyman and Mason (1995: 21) call it employee or direct involvement, namely low-level, individualised and communicative practices and policies that emanate from management and are not intended to impact upon managerial decision-making other than to lubricate its exercise.

In other words, if we think of participation in terms of control over work, initiatives which arise from organisational pursuit of efficiency are likely to be participative in name only for employees, with limited means to influence or redirect management decisions, though they may provide non-participative benefits such as more fulfilling tasks. Ramsay, in fact, went further, arguing that managers' concern to involve employees in limited exercises in autonomy or profit-sharing is only triggered when their interests are threatened at times of economic growth and potential trade union incursions into managerial decision-making. Once threats to managerial prerogative diminish, the involvement techniques either fall into disuse or are rescinded unilaterally by management (Ramsay 1977). In the contemporary economy, there is considerable evidence that managerial involvement or 'empowering' techniques may well accompany or follow organisational restructuring and downsizing to compensate for lower staff numbers (see Beirne (2013) for an excellent summary of tensions inherent in empowering employees in recessionary times). Hodson comments that 'the underlying rationale for employee involvement programs put forward by management is almost always the "stick" of job loss rather than the "carrot" of greater meaning and dignity in work. Workers are thus asked to participate in the context of heightened job insecurity and reduced corporate commitment to workers' (Hodson 2001: 173–74). Approaches under the pseudo involvement banner include various communication procedures, such as briefing groups and the use of company social media to inform employees of specific issues and developments, and limited extensions to task autonomy provided by empowerment and teamworking. Nevertheless, some studies (such as van Wanrooy et al. 2013; Hodson 2001) suggest that employees feel they can derive some benefit even from these limited and potentially manipulative exercises in terms of information provision and enhanced task discretion.

Pateman identifies a second approach, namely *partial participation*, in which authority relations remain essentially undisturbed but in which the subordinate partner has the means to influence decisions but not 'equal power to decide' their outcome (Pateman 1970: 70). Hyman and Mason term these processes employee or representative participation and argue, that unlike involvement, they are associated with collective employee attempts to influence management, typically through collective bargaining and works council membership (Hyman and Mason 1995: 22). Again, as demonstrated in subsequent chapters, there is mixed evidence for the impact of partial participation in democratising work as such exercises include diverse practices ranging from worker directors, domestic and European Works Councils (EWCs) and continental styles of social partnership to the more adversarial approach of collective bargaining. These initiatives have been introduced and maintained, sometimes in the face of continuing employer obstruction or opposition, with the intent of benefiting employee interests, but they can also be associated with positive effects for employers, notwithstanding their employee and trade union provenance (Freeman and Medoff 1984).

Reflecting on the studies of Almond and Verba (1965), Pateman suggests that as effective political democracy in the wider society depends on citizen participation, exercises in partial participation which promote practical citizenship in the workplace can contribute to what she terms political efficacy (i.e. a more democratic society) through their educational and confidence-building impacts (Pateman 1970: 49), though evidence for the effects of these practices has been mixed (Burkitt 1981; Martin 1968). The evidence for a democratising effect of participation in offering greater decision-making influence, whether in the workplace or in broader society, is questionable, any impact being dependent on a coalition of factors, including type and depth of participation, organisational context, wider political traditions, and the state and direction of the economy.

Associations between discretion and autonomy at work and dignity, satisfaction, employee health and wellbeing

Dignity

A second claim is that participation at work proffers greater dignity and self-worth to employees. Dignity is linked to having stable employment but also to being able to exert control over one's work. Ciulla provides an interesting example of the nineteenth-century 'workingman's control code' involving refusal to work whilst being observed by the supervisor as a gesture of defiance and hence maintaining and protecting one's dignity (Ciulla 2000: 92). Dignity also involves the need to find genuine *meaning* in what one does: as we can see with emotional labour, considered below, imposed meaning can and does lead to personal loss of dignity. Nevertheless, as an early study by Herzberg et al. (1957) demonstrates, satisfaction at work can be positively derived from behavioural factors such as consideration and fairness, summarised by Blumberg (1968) in his classic study of industrial democracy as comprising *decency* of supervisory treatment.

Hodson provides a comprehensive exposition and analysis of dignity at work and for our purposes identifies four main challenges to workplace dignity: 'mismanagement and abuse, overwork, limits on autonomy, and contradictions of employee involvement' (Hodson 2001: 5). Mismanagement and abuse are found in pressurised and competitive conditions where workers are primarily blamed for shortfalls in meeting objectives. Workers compensate by attempting to find their own informal means to impose control and meaning, whether negatively through disobedience, subversive humour and even acts of sabotage (Ackroyd and Thompson 1999: 38–41) or more positively through bypassing supervisors and importing their own improvised creative problem-solving methods. Overwork or work intensification can be matched – albeit with some difficulty – through oppositional worker solidarity and occasional practical ingenuity (ibid.: 60). Examples of challenges to autonomy can be found below in the section on professions where managers (often themselves without professional qualifications) aim to control highly skilled or specialised work by deconstructing it into a series of measurable and enforceable targets. Finally, the contradictions of EI are based on the premise that employees can be manoeuvred into self-exploitation, along the lines of the pseudo-participation described above, by contributing to productivity through transforming the corporate culture into one of espoused shared values. In one such case, drawing on a study of a financial institution that eerily prefigures the financial crash of 2008, a company targeted employees as the reasons for poor organisational performance and expected them to accept task intensification rather than undertaking a critical examination of the 'questionable managerial decisions resulting in a history of risky high-stakes loans' (Hodson 2001: 13). Nevertheless, even within these limitations, on the basis of comprehensive meta-analysis, Hodson is able to conclude that 'employee involvement, whatever its forms, results in more meaningful, creative, and positive work-life experiences. These differences are large, consistent, and statistically significant' (ibid.: 181), though as we show later both internal and environmental factors need to be taken into consideration before arriving at this definitive conclusion. Nevertheless, there does appear to be a positive relationship between employee voice, no matter how circumscribed, and dignity at work.

Satisfaction

The study of satisfaction at work and its relations to job quality and performance has a long history. Blumberg (1968: 119) is unequivocal in his view that 'any survey of the literature reveals that far up on the list of factors making for satisfaction at work is the desire, among all groups, for autonomy, responsibility, control and decision-making power on the job'. Another noted authority on the sociology of work, Robert Blauner (1960: 346), maintained that control 'over one's time and physical movement ... control over the environment ... and control as the freedom from hierarchical authority' was one of the main contributory factors to satisfaction at work. From these and recent major studies (e.g. Walton 1985; Huselid 1995; Appelbaum et al. 2000), it would be easy to conclude that job control expressed in forms of participation that provide job satisfaction are intimately associated with quality of performance.

Nevertheless, satisfaction is an elusive concept to capture empirically as it can be highly subjective (Brown et al. 2012), difficult to measure (Rose 2003) and may be influenced by personal factors such as age and gender (Anleu and Mack 2014). Satisfaction as an *outcome* will depend on *inputs* – and these can vary. For example, if expectations from work are low, then a high reported level of satisfaction might simply reflect that low expectations have been exceeded. Also, some commentators argue that different groups of workers may have different expectations from their work, leading to expressions of satisfaction emerging from ostensibly poor quality working conditions. In their study of female care workers, Hebson et al. (2015) demonstrated that high job satisfaction for women can exist alongside objectively poor material working conditions and low extrinsic reward. Work-life contexts need also to be accommodated in models of job satisfaction, but rarely are. However, echoing Hodson above, there do appear to be positive associations between EPV and indicators of satisfaction (Walton 1985). Another fundamental question is whether there exists an identifiable explicit relationship between job satisfaction and work performance. Frequently, one encounters the proposition that 'a happy worker is a productive one' and this proposition has also received some critical research scrutiny. In their study of employee share ownership (ESO), Pendleton et al. (1998) concluded that positive attitudes toward ESO are not necessarily manifested in more positive attitudes to work. Similar doubts about putative associations between satisfaction and performance have also been raised by Guest et al. (1993).

One empirical approach that has been adopted to analyse workplace satisfaction is to apply the same criteria longitudinally to examine whether trends emerge over time. For the UK, annual surveys of social attitudes are undertaken where workers (from senior to junior levels) have been asked how satisfied they are with their main job. In 2015, most report high or reasonable levels of satisfaction, little changed from 2005. There is also the problem of identifying causality: the authors of this survey point out that following the years of recession and austerity, job satisfaction might be reported to be high irrespective of job quality because respondents are relieved to be in employment at all (British Social Attitudes 2015). A more comprehensive range of questions was posed for the UK 2011 Workplace Employment Relations Study in which three dimensions of wellbeing were introduced, namely: job-related contentment, job-related enthusiasm and job satisfaction (van Wanrooy et al. 2013: 127). While the categories of using initiative, the work itself and sense of achievement all received more than 70 per cent in terms of high/medium satisfaction, this proportion dropped markedly to 43 per cent for satisfaction with involvement in decision-making (ibid.: 129). Positive factors supporting higher satisfaction include: greater job control, flexible working practices, recent provision of training, job security and supportive management. The extent to which these variables interact with employee voice is not revealed but if overall satisfaction has remained steady, despite relatively low satisfaction with involvement in decision-making, it would appear that other factors have contributed to satisfaction. Other quantitative studies show mixed results for job satisfaction, some indicating increases *despite* the onset of recession (McManus and Perry 2012), while others show decline in job satisfaction through recession-induced work intensification and reduced task discretion. Interestingly, those reporting higher satisfaction point to the role of employers in raising the quality of work with 'good' jobs replacing 'bad' ones (van Wanrooy et al. 2013: 134), though more nuanced qualitative studies may be required to determine what is meant by 'good' jobs.

Good jobs and the quality of working life

Defining good jobs can be problematic. Academically, definitions tend to vary according to discipline. Economists tend to point narrowly to so-called 'hygiene' or extrinsic factors, such as good pay, social insurance and retirement pensions as underlying good work. Psychologists and health specialists recognise on one hand the negative effects of insecurity, lack of control over the temporal or demand parameters of work and their impacts on mental and physical wellbeing and on the other, the positive influence of social relationships at work (HSE 2009). Sociological perspectives broadly examine the status of jobs, the dynamics of deskilling or upskilling, and especially power and control relations (Dahl et al. 2009).

Two interrelated factors are intrinsic to sociological interest in work: alienation and control of the labour process. Interest in the nature of work under capitalist production and its potentially debilitating effects on those responsible for doing the producing extends back to the Marxist concept of alienation, which describes and explains the exploitation and isolation of workers both from the processes of work and, through task specialisation, from the outcomes of their labour. From an economic perspective, these emotional and physical constrictions are associated with dysfunctional labour behaviours (such as high labour turnover and high rates of sickness absence) and consequential failing economic performance (Blauner 1964). Similar considerations underpin Braverman's labour process analysis of the 'degradation of work' (Braverman 1974) that divides, fragments and secures tight managerial and technological control of both skilled and white-collar tasks. These actions also form the basis of Ritzer's later 'McDonaldization' thesis (Ritzer 1996), under which job fragmentation is extended to contemporary service sectors and potentially to higher added-value occupations. All these accounts point to the dehumanising effects of fragmented Taylorised labour on the human psyche and physical wellbeing. Even within capitalist enterprise, though, these injurious effects may be mitigated through participative practices that offer genuine opportunities for greater individual and collective worker autonomy and control (Gallie 2003; Green 2006), but in the contemporary neoliberal political economy, initiatives in this direction are both limited and subject to constant infringement (Martinez Lucio 2010).

While different academic disciplines might analyse workplace deprivations in different ways or advocate alternative remedies for their effects (Dahl et al. 2009: 8), a range of practically and policy-orientated institutions have an interest in promoting worker wellbeing through quality work, in particular trade union organisations and government agencies like the UK Health and Safety Executive charged with safeguarding employee welfare. The TUC (2010) identifies a broad range of factors that can promote worker wellbeing. These include: creativity, control, workplace culture, fair treatment and reward, job security, hours of work and intensity of effort. Employee control, as ever, appears to be the common dominating factor in different models, but how this and its contingent factors can be achieved in the modern competitive and short-term cost-focused workplace will be a matter of serious debate in this book. One well-meaning but simplistic approach is to offer a desirable and often extensive checklist of items without indicating the means or feasibility of implementing these items; in this context, see Green's (2006) critique of the European Commission's extensive measures of job quality. A similar critique could be aimed at Taylor's well-publicised review of contemporary working practice in the UK, which identifies six key indicators of quality work, including pay and conditions as well as task discretion and autonomy, teamworking and collective relations, but falls short of offering the means to convert these indicators into effective policy (Taylor 2017: 13).

Another influential factor concerns the different histories and traditions of participation enjoyed by different countries. Even states that have enjoyed long and successful regulatory participation regimes have latterly come under pressure from the twin threats of austerity and globalisation (Frege and Godard 2010: 543). These issues will be covered in depth when examining the scope and depth of participation in the EU, but it is clear, for example, that demands for job quality and positive responses to these demands are found in Scandinavian countries with high union densities and in established pluralist states like Germany and the Netherlands.

EPV that offers measures of control for employees and contingent expressions of satisfaction clearly has a place in defining a good job. But a key question concerns the extent of control that is being delegated under participative regimes. Numerous studies demonstrate the ubiquity of relatively low-involvement approaches adopted in the UK and USA in particular. Many of these can be included under the umbrella title of high involvement/participation/commitment/ performance work systems (for convenience, henceforth HPWS, see chapter 6) and include individualistic exercises such as performance appraisal, performance-related pay, suggestion schemes and technologically supported communicative approaches. Conversely, HPWS can also conceal the restrictive parameters of emotional labour associated with increasing aspects of service work and articulated so persuasively by Hochschild (1983) in her studies of flight attendants. For emotional labour, commitment is internalised and separated from true feelings, leading to mental strain and alienation (see also Frayne 2015). Indeed, with the growth of the service economy, and despite a rhetoric of involvement, many negative indicators of workplace experience such as stress and stress-related absence, low satisfaction or morale and early retirement have been reported over the past few years (Wood et al. 2016) as well as pressures toward routinisation and deskilling (Ikeler 2016). These negative manifestations could emerge because EPV systems only exert limited effect, are not being applied or that involvement exercises that are limited to the provision of information and marginal task enhancement are being outweighed by other structural features, such as work intensification or embedded insecurity, linked in turn with lack of trust of managerial motives in demanding employee loyalty and commitment alongside corporate pursuits of downsizing and restructuring. As Ciulla so aptly comments: 'Loyalty is a reciprocal concept' (Ciulla 2000: 153; Thompson 2003).

While there are serious issues over whether EPV is associated with employee satisfaction at work, or how, there are other questions as to whether any increases in satisfaction are causally linked to productive efficiency through enhanced loyalty, greater effort ('going the extra mile') or being more engaged with the enterprise. Interestingly, we *can* see the discordant effects of *tightening* control conditions – when discretion and autonomy are reduced or subject to tighter managerial scrutiny. Professional workers such as doctors, teachers, pharmacists, university and college lecturers provide clear examples of the calamitous drop in job satisfaction and rise in workplace strain that occur when previously autonomous professions are subject to the calculative processes of 'McDonaldization' as described by Ritzer. Twenty years ago he illustrated the negative emotional impacts on USA physicians of 'quantified productivity', a regime which measures 'required number of visits, number of patients seen', accompanied by 'an incentive system tying physician salaries to productivity' (Ritzer 1996: 68). Ritzer's deskilling focus on productive rationality, derived from efficiency, calculability, predictability and technological control, may be seen in contemporary sectors and activities including fast food, call centres, supermarket checkouts with electronic point of sale (EPOS) surveillance, parcel delivery, distribution warehouses with electronic monitoring and bakeries where computer-controlled baking means that 'bakers no longer actually know how to bake bread' (Sennett 1998: 68); here, workers are alienated from both process and product.

But rationalised and depersonalised control is also increasingly the basis of a *new managerialism* defined by Klikauer (2013) as an 'application of managerial techniques to all areas of society on the grounds of superior ideology, expert training, and the exclusive possession of managerial knowledge necessary to efficiently run corporations and societies'. In short, public institutions, such as hospitals, schools and universities, are increasingly defined and managed like commercial organisations. As 'production' in these public services is largely in the hands of specialist workers, under the managerialist regime, McDonaldization aims to extend its control reach to these high-added-value occupations and professions. Direct physical or technological control is difficult to apply over professional activities, but indirect control is increasingly maintained through a panoply of metrics, target setting, key performance indicators (KPIs), appraisal, individual performance-related pay and 'through bureaucratic rules [that] present alternative logics of control to professional autonomy' (Hodson 2001). Hence, Thursfield (2012: 133) argues that conflict exists between 'the professional model of autonomy and the bureaucratic control associated with managerialism'. She adds that through increasing pressures, 'the traditional ideology of professionalism is becoming infected with commercial logic'.

Professionalism can be defined in many ways but would be expected to comprise control of a large body of abstract, formal knowledge; substantial autonomy in regulation and performance guided by ethical principles (Western et al. 2006); authority over clients and subordinate occupations; and a claim of altruism as guiding principle for professional behaviour (Hodson 2001; Pollock 2004: 115). Increasingly, professions *are* losing their autonomy in both private and public sectors. Managerial demands are often based on marketised or business models of service provision and the public sector is emulating competitive private sector models through the following: targeting numbers of patients (doctors), specifying numbers of clients to be seen, alongside a tightening of performance controls (social work and probation: see Gale 2012; Preminger 2016); performance competitiveness in teaching and schools (Carter and Stevenson 2012); bed turnover in hospitals and work intensification pressures on nurses (Hart and Warren 2015); and a growing range of metric targets in universities (number and quality of publications; external research funding obtained; student satisfaction, etc.). Increasingly, organisational culture is becoming dominated by an ethos of 'if you can't measure it, you can't manage it'. Lack of control and growing despair over reduced autonomy among professionals can easily be demonstrated. In 2014 in the UK, 50,000 teachers left the profession, many through the strain of imposed 'never-ending paperwork, to a constant changing regime of exams' and most of all, the fear of bad reviews from government inspectors *(Guardian* 2016a). According to government figures, almost four out of ten teachers quit within a year of qualifying while record numbers are giving up mid-career, leading the general secretary of the Association of Teachers and Lecturers union to comment that 'teachers [are] exhausted, stressed and burnt out in a profession that was being 'monitored to within an inch of its life" *(Guardian* 2015). As Carter and Stevenson (2012: 484) point out, the professional autonomy of teachers needs to be subdued as 'control strategies are central because the state needs to convert the purchased labour power of teachers into realised labour and, under conditions of neo-liberal globalised competition, to contain its costs'.

A similar picture is seen in universities.[1] In a survey reported in 2016 in the *Times Higher Education* (THE 2016) of 3,000 staff in 150 UK universities, there were common complaints from academics that they did not feel they had a voice or that their voice was heeded; there was a distrust of joint consultation (see chapter 9) as a mere process; an increasing use of metrics to define performance and 'ill-fitting managerialism, imported from outside academia is stifling the collegiality that actually makes universities tick'. Managerialism can also lead to highly questionable practices aimed at preserving and inflating the image of university success at the expense of professional autonomy and integrity. Further reflections reported in the same magazine (*THE* 2015) by a necessarily anonymous senior manager in a university's employability department are revealing. The role included gathering data for the annual survey of *Destinations of Leavers from Higher Education*, an important instrument in measuring university league table success. The manager was told to focus heavily on those courses with the best employment and earnings prospects in order to present the most favourable picture of the university's 'success'. The author of the piece was 'instructed to make any salary below £10,000 "disappear" because they were bringing the average down' (*THE* 2015: 44). The article cites other examples of 'fraudulent' practice with which staff were expected to comply, with the result that 'the relentless drive resulted in a disturbing level of control and bullying from senior management positions' (ibid.: 45). Non-compliance could lead to 'implied threats to my job security'; good results could result in unhindered career progress.

A further dimension to the managed erosion of professional identity in higher education is provided by Baldry and Barnes (2012) in their examination of the impact of open-plan offices in universities, where many respondents contrasted the 'contribution of traditional individual offices to professionalised identity and academic culture' (ibid.: 239) with open plans to subsume 'HE to the demands of the market and a concomitant intensification of workload and effort for academics'. The authors' conclusion is stark: 'what is also significant is the evidence for a common managerial offensive that aims to replace the professional autonomy and internalised "craft control" of research and teaching with adherence to externally defined performance standards' (ibid.: 243).

Managerial pressure on professional autonomy is also well captured by the following exchange reported by a colleague, Walter Humes *(Scottish Review* 2016). On a suburban train, he overheard two further education (FE) lecturers, a man and a woman, complaining about the situation in their college. Humes took out his notebook to capture the flavour of their conversation. The man says that senior managers have succeeded in alienating every section of the workforce. Their aim is to impose total control. Staff are threatened with formal disciplinary procedures for minor infringements and are given no recognition for work they do above and beyond their contractual duties. The woman states that managers don't care about people (staff or students): they are only interested in rules and numbers. She gives an example of a long-serving member of support staff, well regarded by colleagues, who had to apply for his own job and was not even given the courtesy of an interview. An atmosphere of suspicion and lack of trust prevails. Employees keep their heads down for fear of becoming the next target. As the train reaches its destination, the man, in an interesting phrase, says that managers have 'an entrepreneurial conception of professionalism', suggesting that corporate rather than educational values have come to dominate. An ironic coda occurs when the woman acknowledges that, bad though the climate is in their college, it is not as toxic as that in another similar establishment.

Humes points out that he is in no position to judge how valid these particular comments are. The managers would no doubt tell a very different story. But these comments are expressed against a background of serious concern about recent developments in the FE sector, with mounting research evidence that this was no isolated incident. In a study involving in-depth interviews with 40 managers and lecturers in two colleges, Mather and Seifert (2014: 100) found a 'range of mechanisms in place for observing, measuring, checking and watching what lecturers actually did in the classroom with a traffic light system designed to publicly highlight (and humiliate) alleged poor performers, electronic checks and student "voice" routinely deployed against them'. The whole system was designed to control the work of lecturers 'with the emphasis being on deskilling in the classic Taylorism sense of removing decisions from professionals at the point of production' (ibid. :108). As background to this assertion of managerial control, across the sector there have been funding problems, major restructuring, reductions in staff and student numbers, closure of a number of courses, complaints about generous leaving packages for some college principals, and threats of industrial unrest. Despite all this, exaggerated claims about the virtues of 'strong leadership' and 'performance management' continue to be peddled (Mather et al. 2009).

It is not just in the public sector that professional autonomy is perceived to be under attack. An article in the Guardian (2016b) described how the biggest pharmacy chain in the UK, once recognised as a traditional paternalistic employer, changed to an overtly performance-driven culture following acquisition by a private equity group for £11bn in 2007. The new business model was described as aiming to 'stretch company finances and staff as far as they can go – then extract profits'. Following the buy-out, staffing has been cut, with pharmacists increasingly required to 'self-check' and meet imposed performance targets. Reported accounts indicate that pressure on pharmacists to meet targets are 'relentless': 'if you miss any target they [managers] want to know the nth degree why ...'. Another complained that the company had changed from 'family-run professional firm to Big Brother, a giant profit-seeking monster ... there's such a culture of fear'. In 2012, a male pharmacist asserted: 'the pressure to meet targets was relentless ... area managers ringing on a daily basis ... told continuously that he was letting the store down'. Concern for professional discretion and autonomy was apparent: 'if my bonus is dependent on the business targets I've been set, you are taking away ... my ability to practice my profession for the patient'. Indeed, in a survey of 624 Boots pharmacists, 60 per cent were concerned that commercial incentives and targets compromised the health, safety or wellbeing of patients, the public as well as the professional judgement of staff.

Similar disquiet over professional or expert autonomy can be witnessed in other areas of high-level work, such as journalism (Aldridge and Evetts 2003) and finance, where expert judgement and decision-making are increasingly displaced through technology via feed inputs from which the computer 'decides', for example, whether loans should be offered (for further discussion of negative welfare effects associated with reduced control in professional work, see Green 2006, 2008). Under the influence of austerity, managerialist incursions into professional work are being reported in other countries, for example among nurses in Canada (Hart and Warren 2015), social workers in Israel (Preminger 2016), and doctors in Germany (Nowak 2006) and the USA (Ritzer 1996: 43).

Health and wellbeing

EPV, as we have seen, is concerned about the degree of control afforded to employees over their work and work environment. Based on the analyses of writers such as Pateman and Hochschild and a range of empirical studies, we suggest that there are different levels of influence on decision-making and control, extending from the low influence provided by individualised management initiated EI to the deeper influence potential of representative participation. We have suggested that these two approaches could have different implications for employees; involvement exercises associated with downsizing, job restructuring and work intensification may not necessarily have beneficial impacts on employee wellbeing and could well have adverse ones. On the other hand, recent studies point to a positive relationship between task-based involvement and worker welfare when the work environment is also positive (Boxall and Macky 2014).

We saw above that reducing professional or specialist autonomy can have a negative impact on job satisfaction and, through pressurised working, on issues such as stress. Moreover, there is solid evidence that offering employees more control over their work lives can have a positive impact on health, including morbidity. Robert Karasek has been one of the most influential and prolific researchers into links between job control, wellbeing and health. He is largely credited with the demand control model of job redesign, which basically shows that high task demands, linked to personal autonomy over work, are positively associated with job satisfaction, psychological wellbeing and health benefits. The model derives from his long-standing research into links between work design and health. In an early 1981 longitudinal study he and colleagues found a direct association between work factors such as low discretion and restriction in scheduling work routines and subsequent heart disease (Karasek et al. 1981). In later research based in Sweden, Karasek studied more than 8,000 full-time employees, of whom a quarter were employed in companies that had recently introduced job reorganisation. Workers in the job reorganisation group who had influence in the reorganisation process and obtained increased task control had lower levels of illness symptoms for most health indicators. For men, a measure of coronary heart disease was significantly lower in circumstances of increased job control. Absenteeism and depressive feelings were also lower. All illness indicators confirmed that job reorganisation was associated with significantly higher stress symptoms. However, for men, symptom levels when reorganisation was accompanied by increased control were often as low or lower than symptom levels for no reorganisation at all (Karasek 1990). In collaborative work with Theorell (Karasek and Theorell 1990), analysing data from both the USA and Sweden, the authors confirm the desirability of redesigning jobs to offer greater employee control, and thereby promote psychological wellbeing, lower stress, reduction in potential cardiac illness and also enhanced productivity.

Similar positive results are reported by Wilkinson and Pickett in their influential book *The Spirit Level,* in which they present findings from a series of studies of job control and health in the UK civil service, concluding that 'having control at work was the most successful single factor explaining differences in death rates between senior and junior civil servants' (Wilkinson and Pickett 2010: 256).

Impact of EPV on economic performance and productivity

So far, our examination has focused on the implications of different forms of EPV for employees, potentially to enable them 'to influence events' and thereby enhance 'procedural justice'; Wood also points out that a key objective of participation, however, is to provide 'fairer substantive returns' (Wood 2010: 407). In other words, the prospect of enhancing performance in tight competitive conditions is an understandable inducement and objective for managers to introduce forms of participation that favour their interests. As management involvement or voice initiatives currently dominate employment relationships (van Wanrooy et al. 2013: 191), a prime objective of this section is to review associations between participation and substantive outcomes such as labour performance. The impact of specific approaches will be analysed in greater depth in subsequent chapters.

It is not realistic to talk of performance without first making reference to productivity, which is itself founded largely on labour performance. A recent report by Ussher for the Joseph Rowntree Foundation (2016) reviews major issues relating to productivity. One problem is that productivity can be assessed in different ways. Basically though, productivity can be defined as the output produced per unit of input. At organisational level this can be measured as 'the value produced (either profit or sales) per unit of labour cost (either per person, or per person full-time equivalent or, more simply, per hour worked)'. These calculations can be aggregated to provide comparable measures for different countries. Productivity measures can also be used to compare different sectors within the same country, though

> it is important to understand the specific definition of productivity that is used ... The productivity of the UK retail sector, for example, could equally be defined as profits per person employed, or sales per hour worked; if it is the efficiency of the technological capital that is more of interest, it could separately be defined as the sales per unit of capital for a fixed number of man-hours. In this sense it can also be thought of as a 'return on investment'.
>
> (Ussher 2016)

Nevertheless, productivity linked to labour inputs is of highest policy interest.

However defined, productivity in the UK has fallen seriously behind other major economies in recent years. The Office for National Statistics (ONS) estimates that output per hour worked in the UK in 2015 was 18 per cent below the average for other advanced G7 economies, a figure little changed from previous years (ONS 2016). In more graphic terms, in his 2016 autumn statement, the UK Chancellor of the Exchequer pointed out that 'it takes a German worker four days to produce what we make in five; which means, in turn, that too many British workers work longer hours for lower pay than their counterparts'. This deficiency is important because 'an increase in productivity translates into an increase in output (amount and quality) without any increase in input (labour and materials)' (ibid.). In other words, there is a direct link between productivity, standards of living and national prosperity.

So how can productivity be enhanced? A number of suggestions have been made. First, employers need to invest more in machinery and technology. Second, workers need to be able to adapt quickly to changes in technology and process, which means more and better education, training and skill development, a demand directed crucially at management. Third, it is contended that higher pay motivates employees to work more efficiently and compels employers to look for more productive methods of working (Ussher 2016). Finally, recommendations from the Rowntree report, while focusing on the retail sector, have implications for other sectors, and these emphasise flatter organisational structures (or delayering), which allow employees to take on a wider range of responsibilities. Other studies point to the importance of EPV in supporting higher productivity (Summers and Hyman 2005; Kalmi et al. 2005). These studies indicate that there does appear to be a direct link between offering employees more control over their working lives and improving performance and productivity.

However, the picture may not always be conclusive because identifying substantive returns from a participative intervention can be problematic. Moreover, it should be borne in mind that managers introduce forms of participation through a complex of motives or combination of influences: (a) because they anticipate tangible returns from their participative investment, (b) because they are required to do so by law or regulation or (c) through workforce, trade union or possibly governmental pressure. Outcomes from these different scenarios may be expected to be sensitive to a complex amalgam of context, economic conditions, organisational history and national culture (Frege and Godard 2010). In other words, 'returns' from EPV may not necessarily be in the form of measurable performance. A further problem in measuring substantive outcomes is that of identifying the prime causative factors; for example, offering employees more responsibility through empowerment or high commitment practices may be associated with improved productivity, but the main and possibly disguised contributory factor could be fear of job loss following downsizing rather than any beneficial consequence of empowerment (Ramsay et al. 2000). A further potential problem is that in aiming for higher productivity, managers may want to monitor and control the quantity and quality of the contribution of professionals, which, as we have shown above, can lead to tensions between professional autonomy and managerial authority, and even to potential loss of productivity.

Basically, as indicated above, we can identify three main avenues for managerial intervention. The first includes those voice-focused involvement approaches devised and introduced by management, specifically to provide direct communication channels between managers and employees in the expectation of enhanced performance or productivity. Central to these initiatives are: downward communication, upward communication, task restructuring through empowerment or teamworking and a variety of procedures involving combinations of these activities. Downward communication involves forms of electronic communication such as emails from senior management, newsletters, regular progress updates, and communal workforce meetings addressed by senior executives. Upward communication includes suggestion schemes and regular staff attitude surveys. Two-way communication includes performance appraisal, team briefing and problem-solving groups and feedback to and from group meetings. Task restructuring, based on concepts of enriching jobs, includes individual empowerment and team formation. Combination or hybrid procedures include employee share schemes, which are intended to act as means of communication and provide employees with a material stake in the company, and high-involvement work systems. As surveys confirm, in the UK and across Europe, many of these initiatives are introduced or conducted in combination (Eurofound 2015a).

The second participation approach comprises steps that employers are required to take in order to comply with the law or through legally derived regulations. As we will see in chapters 9 and 10, these representative initiatives often derive from EU law and include the requirement for companies operating in more than one European country to inform and consult through a representative European Works Council. Also deriving from EU law, at the domestic UK level, these arrangements are mirrored through the 2005 Information and Consultation of Employees (ICE) regulations, which provide for the right of employees to request that companies with 50 or more employees formally inform and consult them about issues in the organisation. For specific sectors in some European countries there is also the requirement to establish worker directors (Markey et al. 2010). In all these cases, the regulations usually provide some scope for employers to interpret and apply the provisions according to their own legal systems, traditions and culture (Frege and Godard 2010).

The third approach to participation, namely representative participation, may result from pressure imposed on employers in the form of union recognition, though sometimes recognition may be granted without major resistance from employers when actively promoted by government. As far back as 1894 the UK Royal Commission on Labour advocated strong worker and employer organisations as the basis for jointly securing and regulating terms and conditions of employment, without undue interference from the state, a philosophy and process known as voluntarism (Hyman 2003: 40). Nevertheless, recognition and accompanying collective bargaining rights might only be granted after sustained pressure, as we saw in the American vehicle manufacturing plants in the 1930s and as we are seeing today, for example, in modern China (China Labour Bulletin 2014). There are also collective participative initiatives that are not necessarily specifically employer- or employee-instigated, though they may be encouraged by either side and also through government policy. These initiatives can include joint consultation and social partnership.

The specific impacts of direct and representative participation and voice interventions will be examined in the following chapters. At this stage, we can offer a more general overview of links between participative initiatives and organisational performance. As might be expected, findings for effect vary and depend vitally on contextual features – such as organisational history and culture, high added value versus low added value, levels of trust and security – and, of course, on the intentions and ambitions for the initiatives themselves. Nevertheless, the performance record for direct involvement appears to be mixed and even positive research findings tend to be qualified (Richardson and Nejad 1986; Bell and Hanson 1987).

Some important observations do, however, emerge. First, a number of quantitative studies tend to demonstrate, though not exclusively, positive associations between forms of EPV and performance outcomes. However, there are potential shortcomings to survey-based studies that should serve to alert us to their possible limitations in directly linking practice to outcome. Importantly, they 'tell us very little about the impact or extensiveness of such techniques within a particular organization', which can limit their usefulness in relating them to the performance of specific organisations (Wilkinson and Dundon 2010: 178). Case studies that undertake a deeper and potentially more comprehensive examination of labour relations in individual organisations often report more nuanced findings on the impact of different EPV initiatives. It can be argued that in order to examine closely and critically the effects of power imbalance between capital and labour, the views, behaviours and interactions of the principal actors can best be revealed through in-depth and possibly comparative or long-term case studies. These lack the benefit of generalisability to a broader population but may better capture the dynamics of social relations and organisational behaviour. Case studies also serve to reveal underlying factors that are not detectable in surveys but that may help to explain workplace responses to EPV initiatives, factors deriving from organisation, employees or state (Yin 1994; Flick 2002).

A second common finding, following the influential studies of Walton (1985), is that for a management initiative to be successful requires a supportive background of trust and security for employees (Brown et al. 1993; White et al. 2003). Where there is a sympathetic background embracing trust, respect and security, there is evidence of positive reciprocal effect, irrespective of type or combination of initiative (Pfeffer 1998). Other research, though, suggests that the *type* of participation can also be a relevant factor. Defourney et al. (1985) found that productivity growth was more evident in cooperatives converted from conventional firms compared with purposely created cooperatives. Other studies indicate that productivity showed a small improvement in labour-managed enterprises but a negligible growth in conventional firms that had introduced participatory practices (Doucouliagos 1995). Another important element, and one to which we shall return later, is the combination effect, i.e. that direct and indirect forms of participation can act synergistically and, notwithstanding the doubts of some analysts (such as Ben-Ner and Jones 1995), contribute to performance enhancement (see e.g. Guest and Peccei 2001; Pendleton 2001; Bryson 2004).

Conclusions

One common theme recurring throughout this chapter is the notion of control as a critical element in supporting and defining EP. We noted that advances in workplace and potentially societal democracy were linked to employee confidence in self-expression gained through their contribution to processes of shared decision-making. Discretion and autonomy at work as expressions of worker control were also linked to employee health, dignity, wellbeing and satisfaction. We also suggested that management-initiated direct or pseudo-participation interventions are not designed specifically to extend worker control over their work environment, though there may be additions to task- and team-based autonomy that potentially exert favourable effects in terms of positive orientations to work, job satisfaction and performance. However, these attributes may be outweighed by more constricting management manoeuvres through work intensification and extensification of hours of work and the application of Taylorist management regimes. We also examined the psychical and behavioural implications of forfeiting control among professional workers exposed to management regimes whose criteria and objectives serve to displace professional authority with commercial values and techniques.

The relationship between control and participation is therefore a crucial one. Control, unlike power, is divisible in that employees can possess and utilise varying aspects of control, from the narrow discretion attached to management-initiated EI to the dominant strategic control associated with full democracy at work. This suggests that in contradistinction to Ramsay's (1977) zero-sum thesis, in which one party exclusively benefits at the expense of other parties, more broadly dispersed control may secure benefits to both employees and managers, though the distribution of benefits would be expected to vary according to the depth and scope of the participative exercises. Thus, while EI might be expected to confer benefits to management, this does not preclude some advantage accruing to employees. Similarly, representative participation would be expected to offer employees greater control, for example through joint determination of terms and conditions, but (and despite hostility from some employers) could also be beneficial to employers. The following chapters will examine in depth the main participative and voice approaches to determine the extent to which the evidence supports these propositions.

Note

1 An interesting and highly revealing picture of the changing culture of even elite universities is presented by Cambridge University academic Stefan Collini (2012) in his examination of the effects of current commercial directives of universities, emphasising efficiency measurements and productivity drives. Rather than motivate, he finds that these control-centred models lead to staff demoralisation and hopelessly *inefficient* deployment of highly educated and dedicated personnel. Control and silencing of academics even follow their departure from employment. According to data obtained by THE (2017a) under UK Freedom of Information laws, 3,722 employees at 48 universities have signed confidentiality clauses, binding them not to disclose details of their departure.

Chapter 2

Political perspectives on employee participation and voice

Introduction

In our opening chapters we argued that it is difficult to conceptualise the development of EPV in linear, temporal or unidirectional terms. This is because EPV policies derive and gather strength from a range of different influences, both structural and processual, which themselves may be subject to broader or transient pressures. Political factors are a major influence on employment relations and these help to explain different transnational trajectories of EPV (Poole et al. 2001). In this chapter we first outline these influences and their effects, and then examine in greater detail the specific contributions of different forms of legislation.

Coordinated and liberal markets

Relatively fixed philosophies or values define and inform government actions that underpin approaches toward EPV. One value system includes the aim to pursue social justice or to address inequality through establishing forms of employment citizenship. An alternative approach, more dominant at present, is for governments influenced by neoliberal free-market thinking to use EPV in order to address economic performance and its deficiencies. Within this broad framework we can identify Hall and Soskice's (2001) well-known varieties of capitalism model, which presents two principal 'broad characterisations rather than robust distinctions' (Edwards and Wajcman 2005: 224) for coordinating and regulating commercial activity. Coordination can be conducted in what Hall and Soskice term *liberal market economies* (LME), associated with labour regulation through market mechanisms promoting unobstructed freedom for employers to hire and deploy workers and in *coordinated market economies* (CME), founded on models of longer-term stakeholder partnership between capital and labour. Coordination for either approach is maintained through governmental institutions such as the law.

Germany is frequently identified as a long-standing exemplar of a CME (Edwards and Wajcman 2005), embracing 'institutional balance of power between labour and capital that has promoted economic growth and adaptation to changing circumstances' (Wailes and Lansbury 2010: 575). Sometimes referred to as the 'Rhine model' or 'stakeholder economy' in contrast to its Anglo-Saxon variant, it has offered shared influence (or codetermination) between unions and management with a governmental welfare structure 'which provides a comparatively tightly woven safety net of pensions, education and health benefits' (Sennett 1998: 53). In Germany, codetermination through two-tier boards of directors, formalised systems of collective bargaining and domestic works councils are regulated by legislation but these and other coordinating institutions have been put under strain and underwent consequent mutation because of recent global and national economic tensions (Marsden 2015; Addison et al. 2014), though the basic model of coordination through 'patient capital' appears to have remained intact (Frege and Godard 2010). Other Northern European countries have introduced similar government-backed regulatory systems (TUC 2015).

Conversely, the USA and UK can both be cited as examples of LME. Following the Wagner Act of 1935, American regulation has largely been limited to support for trade union recognition and free collective bargaining with recognised unions, though, as noted by Foley (2014: 69), low union density coupled with a preference for 'business unionism' has meant that there has been little pressure on successive administrations to extend EPV. In the UK, policy subsequent to the election of Margaret Thatcher's Conservative government in 1979 has been directed at promoting the free and flexible movement of labour, supported by restrictive collective legislation and weaker and less representative trade unions (Heery et al. 2004), gradual erosion of protective legislation for workers (Smith 2015), and a more fragmented, individualised and precarious labour force (Standing 2011, 2014). Though the overall picture is dominated by restrictive statutory regulation of labour relations, there have also been legislated concessions in support of union recognition (van Wanrooy et al. 2013: chapter 4) and adoption of legally endorsed minimum pay, leading eventually to successful campaigns for a 'living wage' (Hirsch and Valadez Martinez 2017). Also, the previous Labour government reversed earlier Conservative opposition to European models of information disclosure and consultation (van Wanrooy et al. 2013), though these reforms may become vulnerable following the UK's June 2016 referendum vote to leave the EU.

In the case of both Germany and the UK, while we can distinguish broad cleavages in the political economies of both countries, the actual mechanisms of coordination are rather more nuanced and sensitive to changes in a country's economic fortunes and to political fluctuations than those suggested by a decontextualised bipolar model. These evolving shifts have led some commentators to argue that gradual convergence of labour market regulation and employment relationships may be occurring (Vos 2006), though others argue for distinctive national systems based on fundamental differences in underlying ideologies, domestic circumstances and the ways in which these are interpreted and acted on (Mills et al. 2008).

Therefore, in addition to being influenced by relatively fixed national systems constructed on ideological as well as prescriptive platforms, EPV is also impacted by domestic environmental factors, such as national economic performance and competitiveness or levels of employment and the ways in which governments choose to interpret and deal with these factors. As we saw above, for the UK, competing in a global economy, an enduring problem has been its productive performance relative to that of other developed economies; governments have established many EPV initiatives on the basis of their diagnoses of productivity deficiencies. Conservative ideology to maintain managerial prerogative and offer limited and exhortative remedies accompanies a readiness to blame and punish collective union responsibility for inadequate performance. This approach contrasts with the policies of Labour governments, which traditionally, though less so recently (Waddington 2003a), have aimed for more pluralistic resolutions to address economic failings. The UK's approach to EPV has therefore been more volatile than those of countries that have adopted less adversarial and more consensual political systems. Nowhere is this volatility more visible than in the advance of unitarist and individualistic EPV policies, at the expense of pluralist and collective representation as union membership and influence, once so strong in the UK, continue to diminish.

The effects of political divisions can be demonstrated by the UK's stance towards the policies and actions of supranational bodies such as the EU and their influence on national-level expressions of EPV. An example of these differences is presented by the UK's attitude towards EU intervention in employment affairs. In 1994, as part of the Social Chapter, a specific protocol attached to the Maastricht Treaty set out common social policy objectives for EU countries, with the aim of preventing 'social dumping' through improved and common working conditions in member states. Integral to the Social Chapter, the EU passed the directive on establishing EWCs. The then Conservative government's response was to opt out of the Chapter on the basis that it was inimical to business competitiveness; EWCs therefore initially enjoyed no formal statutory standing in the UK. It was only with the change to a Labour government in 1997 that the opt-out was rescinded and the UK became subject to the EWC Directive, notwithstanding residual political hostility from the right wing of the Conservative Party to EU intervention, a hostility that found its ultimate expression in the 2016 referendum on EU membership.

While countries have different traditions, conventions and histories of political intervention, these are not immutable but subject to the dynamics inherent in today's rapidly changing global environment and circumstances (Bauman 2000). Derived from the doctrine of laissez-faire, the UK, for example, had a long tradition of governmental non-intervention in legislating for or against EPV, though this tradition shifted significantly under the revived neoliberal economic emphasis that emerged during the 1980s, under the doctrinaire political leadership of Margaret Thatcher in the UK and President Reagan in the USA. The prime objective of this shift was to remove perceived obstacles to competition, both in product and labour markets, where trade unions were specifically targeted as being corruptive of market responsiveness and flexibility (MacInnes 1987). Political backgrounds and allegiances that influence EPV can and do mutate, even in relatively stable and egalitarian countries like Sweden, where, following many years of social democratic rule supported by a strong and politicised trade union movement, the socio-economic climate shifted with conservative political ascendancy, bringing with it significant changes in direction in EPV policy and practice (Rhenman 1968; Baccaro and Howell 2011).

The advance of globalisation and the spread and influence of international enterprise have also impacted on national EPV policies. Many host countries wish to attract inward investment and are therefore prepared to offer terms and conditions deemed to be attractive to potential inward investors. Also, successful EPV approaches adopted in one country may be used as a template for governmental encouragement elsewhere. After the Second World War, Germany implemented a system of worker directors; initially these were restricted to key sectors but eventually the practice became more widespread and remains firmly established in other large enterprises and also spread to other European countries such as the Netherlands, Scandinavian countries and France (EIRR 1991; TUC 2015). Short-lived worker director projects were even introduced in the UK in the then nationalised British Steel Corporation and the publicly owned Post Office. Parity representation of worker directors on unitary boards formed the controversial basis of the majority report of the Bullock Committee (1977), established by the soon to be displaced Labour government along with board representation for employees. The report had met fierce opposition from virtually all sides, from executives fearing loss of prerogative to trade unions concerned at losing their traditional oppositional role and of course from the Conservatives who were preparing their radical neoliberal economic programme for implementation following the anticipated and achieved electoral victory in 1979 (Brannen 1983).

Finally, short-term stimuli or crises, such as public-sector labour disputes, may prompt governments to take remedial but reactive action, though the type of action depends on the complexion of the government in charge and the nature of the challenges it faces. An early and far-reaching example is provided by the establishment of Joint Industrial Councils (JICs) following the deliberations of the Whitley Committee, established in 1917 in response to widespread industrial unrest. The committee recommended that within each major industry, joint councils, comprising representatives of trade unions and employers, be set up to provide employee voice at workshop, regional and national levels, with the prime intention of promoting participation through industry-wide collective bargaining (England and Weekes 1981). While the response from the private sector was unenthusiastic, the JIC model was successfully developed in public service sectors such as the civil service and education and after World War II in nationalised industries and the newly established National Health Service system, creating public sector consultative and negotiating structures that continue in modified forms today (MacInnes 1987: 13–14).

The role and impact of legislation

Having examined underlying motives for political intervention in EPV and their diversity, we are in a position to identify the main instruments through which government interest in EPV can be expressed and channelled. Basically, two routes may be identified, legislation and exhortation. Legislation, in particular, can be problematic. With characteristic directness, Kahn-Freund (1983: 18) contends that the object of labour law 'has always been, and we venture to say will always be, to be a countervailing force to counteract the inequality of bargaining power which is inherent in the employment relationship'. Gollan et al. (2014: 363), however, adopt a broader position, stating that 'legal regulation is a key determinant of workplace democracy, organisational efficiency and employee well-being'. One immediate difficulty emerging from this statement is the challenge of evaluating the role and impact of legislation as it can attend to different and not necessarily compatible objectives. It can serve to:

a   protect employees
b   ensure that common and fair terms of employment are adopted
c   preserve managerial prerogative
d   act in pursuit of political economy objectives, such as restricting industrial action deemed to be damaging to civil society or to wider economic goals
e   prevent perceived undemocratic or threatening behaviour, e.g. in issuing specific and restrictive arrangements for picketing or in requiring formal ballots to be conducted before industrial action
f   provide rules that govern the processes of collective bargaining

For example, in the USA, the National Labor Relations (or Wagner) Act of 1935, as subsequently amended, was designed to prevent unfair labour practices and in particular to encourage recognition of independent trade unions and the exercise of free collective bargaining (Patmore 2010).

Examples of these diverse objectives are readily apparent: for example, in the UK, the Health and Safety at Work Act (1974) was passed to protect employee health, safety and welfare through the appointment or election of workforce safety representatives who can also request the establishment of a health and safety committee. Union presence and involvement in health and safety matters may lead to greater awareness of potential workplace risks (van Wanrooy et al. 2013: 118). Other EU countries have similar jointly monitored protective arrangements (European Agency for Safety and Health at Work 2012). Similarly, antidiscrimination laws aim both to protect employees and to ensure fair terms of employment, irrespective of race, gender, disability, etc.

(Gollan et al. 2014; Patmore 2010). Also serving to protect employees, the Information and Consultation of Employees Directive 2002 (ICE) requires employers to provide information to employees and to discuss with them issues relevant to their employment (see chapter 9). On the other hand, successive UK Employment Acts passed in the 1980s aimed to strengthen management's freedom to act at the expense of trade unions, with the putative objective of making labour markets more responsive to market signals. At the same time these legislative actions represented a not very subtle attempt to shackle trade union influence through enactments that made it increasingly difficult for trade unions to organise or to successfully prosecute industrial action by imposing a series of increasingly restrictive measures on their activities (MacInnes 1987: 54–59). An alternative factor that can inform legislative action, as Kahn-Freund (1983) points out, is the recognition that employees and their unions are economically weaker than employers; so many countries have introduced legislation to either encourage or require employers to recognise trade unions, providing such recognition is desired by the workforces concerned, examples being the Wagner Act in the USA and more recently, in the UK, the Employment Relations Acts (ERA) of 1999 and 2004. Among a number of permissive provisions, such as protections against discrimination for union membership or activities, the 1999 act provided that trade unions can seek legislative support for recognition for collective bargaining purposes from employers with a minimum of 21 employees. The 2004 act aimed to fine-tune provisions and add some further protections.

It is clear from the above that legislation can be contentious for the simple reason that it aims to directly influence the interests and activities of different parties and, through this, can generate different degrees of acceptance or hostility. The fate of the legislation may well depend on the relative strengths of the parties and the depth of hostility expressed, and, of course, on environmental factors such as the state of the economy. Again, examples of failure and success are readily available. The Industrial Relations Act (1971) was passed by a Conservative government intent on improving procedures regulating relations between employers and unions through direct intervention in their activities at a time when voluntarism, the doctrine of state abstention from private sector employment relations, was dominant and fiercely defended. The legislation derived from the need to improve competitiveness through productivity and to reduce industrial action by removing the historical restraint of trade immunities from unions. As the party most directly affected by the legislation, unions resisted the provisions of the act; managers wishing to maintain continuity of production colluded with unions and the TUC, whose cooperation in disciplining its member unions was essential, failed to comply. The act rapidly collapsed (Hyman 2003: 51; MacInnes 1987: 27–29).

Conversely, the 1980s series of Employment Acts, which also aimed to curtail trade union influence and activities by restricting their bargaining strength, have been judged by some to be successful in achieving their intention of reducing industrial action (Dunn and Metcalf 1996). The political and economic context had become increasingly hostile toward trade unions, especially following the failure of the miners to win their protracted and bitter 1983/4 dispute; there is little doubt that this unfavourable environment, restrictive legislation and employer confidence combined to reduce union influence and assurance, and subsequently membership (Dickens and Hall 2003). When legislation is not seen to be sufficiently damaging to the interests of any one party, it is less likely to be resisted, but if it is only benign in intent, it may not necessarily exert any significant impact. This is certainly a charge that has been made, for instance, against provisions established to inform and consult with employees, though some commentators argue that these provisions may in some cases have catalytic effects in enhancing employee voice (Hall et al. 2013) or may conversely surreptitiously act to reinforce management authority, as under ICE provisions, trade unions may no longer provide the single channel of participation with employers which they previously enjoyed and wished to protect (Hall and Terry 2004).

In light of these dynamics, it is worth examining the impact of the 1999 and 2004 ERA in more detail, as these were introduced by the Labour government at a time when union membership and influence in the UK were in serious decline and collective participation through unions remained under considerable threat. The rubric of the legislation was to offer 'fairness at work' by encouraging collective representation of worker interests and protection of individual rights against discrimination by employers. An official review of the 1999 act was published in 2003. In a foreword to the review, Patricia Hewitt, then secretary of state for trade and industry was unequivocal in her support of the legislation's accomplishments: "Despite predictions to the contrary, the Act has been a resounding success … . A new culture at work is appearing.' The controversial central aim of the act was to encourage voluntary settlement of union recognition claims, and the review found that while the Central Arbitration Committee (CAC), which is charged with deliberating over disputed claims for recognition, had made just 52 formal awards by December 2002, more than 700 voluntarily agreed deals had been secured since the introduction of the legislation (DTI 2003: 24).

A review of employment relations legislation conducted by Dickens et al. (2005) also arrived at some tentative positive conclusions. Citing work by Gall (2004a), the review indicated that since 1995, when employers were anticipating the new regulations, there had been some 2,331 recognition agreements, affecting nearly three-quarters of a million workers. Dickens and her colleagues also noted possible positive shifts in employer attitudes toward recognition, as well as the confidence given to unions to launch recruitment campaigns. Nevertheless, they conclude their review with the caution that it was 'too early to assess definitely the quality of resultant union-management relationships' and that there was a 'mixed picture as to whether the existence of statutory recognition has led to adversarial or co-operative employment relations'. They also cite further research by Moore et al. (2004), indicating that bargaining topics were often limited to 'pay, hours and holidays'.

Moreover, subsequent analysis casts some doubt over these early optimistic claims. Later research by Moore (2013) showed a declining trend in applications to the CAC and in voluntary agreements since 2004. Though the overall picture is one of relative stability in terms of union recognition, it should be remembered that only about one-fifth (22 per cent) of all workplaces now recognise trade unions. While the new procedures probably helped to slow the decline in union recognition (van Wanrooy et al. 2013: 58), this proportion compares badly with the 66 per cent recorded in 1984 (Waddington 2003b: 218). As trade unions have long been a central feature of collective participation in developed industrial countries, any decline in their bargaining capabilities casts a shadow over their representative potential, a point which is reviewed in more depth in chapter 9. Early governmental claims that 'a new culture at work is appearing' may well be correct, but the emergent culture is perhaps not what the architects of the recognition procedures were envisaging, especially as recent government initiatives have aimed to further weaken individual and collective employee protections on the grounds that these deter employers from hiring labour, leading one analyst to conclude that 'in portraying employment protections as barriers to job creation and competitiveness, the government has echoed the arguments of its predecessors since 1979, whilst seeking to eliminate the modest improvements in employment rights introduced by the Labour governments after 1979' (Heyes 2013: 78). Further restrictive legislation aimed to protect people from 'undemocratic industrial action' by making it more difficult for unions to engage in disputes with employers was passed with the 2016 Trade Union Act, though a number of its more controversial elements remain under review following strong opposition from a number of sources.

The above accounts demonstrate that legislation can and does impact on EPV (Hall and Terry 2004: 226). Much of the UK's restrictive trade union regulation derived from the 1980s is still in place, albeit in modified form, reinforced by the provisions of the 2016 act, and while legislation is not solely responsible for decline in trade union numbers, density and influence, many authorities recognise that the various legislative actions taken since that time have helped to undermine union collective voice and potency (Hyman 2003: 54). We can also see that legislative impact is very much influenced by underlying contextual factors such as the state of the economy and levels of employment and their associations with dominant political ideologies that inform employment relationships. One further point arises: as the ERA shows, it is not easy to analyse the impact of legislation because of the presence and influence of a multitude of extraneous factors and the empirical problem of directly attributing long-term change to specific stimuli.

An additional factor that can affect legislative impact is its method of implementation: a directive or enforced approach *requires* the parties to follow statutory law, for example, the requirement for unions to organise formal secret ballots and to follow designated procedure in support of industrial action. Requirements can be expressed through proscription – namely identifying or prohibiting specified activities, such as discrimination, as unlawful or illegal – or through promotion, for example requiring companies to establish formal recognition procedures. A second approach involves legally endorsed *enabling* policies which stipulate provisions designed to encourage parties to follow specified actions, for example by offering tax relief to encourage companies to introduce employee share schemes (see chapter 5). By nature, enabling legislation is likely to be less threatening to either party than required legislation and consequently it may be implemented on a voluntary basis, with the expectation of little negative effect or potential bilateral positive effects, as is suggested in the case for share schemes and profit-sharing. A further factor also needs to be included when considering the impact of legislation: the law may govern the need to comply with a specified practice but may not regulate or monitor how that compliance is operationalised. Examples include the suggested weak impact in some countries of EWCs, in which legally constituted committees can comply with the letter of the law but be treated by enterprises largely as vehicles for conveying management information and intentions, rather than as forums for substantive employee representative input (see chapter 10). The effects of specific legally supported EPV activities will be assessed in greater depth in the following chapters.

In addition to legislation, further governmental interventions may be established by the state in exhorting or encouraging the parties to adopt preferred forms of EPV and in setting, with its treatment of its own employees, a good example of employee relations practice for private sector employers, workers and their representatives. An example of direct encouragement with long-term consequences dates from the era of tripartite economic policy in the 1960s when the then Labour government persuaded various (reluctant) employer bodies that they needed a unified voice comparable to that of the TUC in order to discuss and set the terms for economic policy, laying the foundations for the establishment of the CBI, which has subsequently acted as the principal and highly influential mouthpiece of employers (Middlemass 1979: 452). Advice and assistance have long been provided by the state to employers and employee representative bodies. Richard Hyman (2003: 40) reminds us that as long ago as 1893, a labour department was established 'primarily to provide statistical information, the better to inform the decisions of employers and unions' and that in 1898, a government conciliation service was established, which in 1974 became a constituent part of the independent Advisory, Conciliation and Arbitration Service (ACAS) and continues to offer these services to the present day. The state can also provide an ethos of being a 'good employer', setting standards for private enterprises to follow. In the UK, the good employer ethos was demonstrated by providing employment security, fair recruitment policies, secure pensions and a publicly stated willingness to recognise and deal with trade unions (Bach and Winchester 2003). Under pressure from governments to offer public accountability and value for money in a period of austerity, positions have reversed and it is now the competitive and cost-sensitive private sector that serves as the model for the public sector, as demonstrated with the rise of 'new public management' and its emphasis on lean production, efficiency targets, appraisal and outsourcing of peripheral activities.

Government intervention in the European Union

The tradition in many Anglo-Saxon countries has been for limited intervention by the state in employment relations generally and in EPV specifically; the emphasis has tended to be on encouraging rather than enforcing dialogue between employers and employees. As we have seen, this has been the case in the UK and can be observed, among other countries, in the USA, where managerial prerogative is strongly endorsed (Freeman et al. 2007; Patmore 2010), Australia, where voluntarism and a free market approach to employee relations tends to dominate policy (Patmore 2010; Stewart 2012), though less so in Canada, where the 'legal regime ... is more "union friendly"' through its support of collective employment relations and protection of worker rights (Campolieti et al. 2007), and New Zealand, where legislation has both freed up the labour market and encouraged collective bargaining (Boxall et al. 2007a). Nevertheless, these studies also indicate evidence of a substantial and growing 'representation gap' in the same countries (see also Campolieti et al. 2011).

European experience has been more varied. In Germany, legislation for works councils extends back many decades (Streeck 1995). But in many countries, long-standing interventionist policies were interrupted and adversely affected by civil unrest, for example in France in 1968 (Fenby 2015), by civil war, as in the former Yugoslavia (Blumberg 1968; Pateman 1970: chapter 5) and by continental conflicts, of which the Second World War was the most devastating but also most far-reaching in leading initially to the European Common Market and subsequently to the EU, whose legislated directives on employment relations are typically transcribed into national domestic law (Patmore 2010).

The majority of EU countries have formal procedures for worker participation in corporate governance derived from European Commission (EC) directives. According to a TUC report written by European Trade Union Institute researcher Aline Conchon (2015), participation, supported by the EC, can take place through different mechanisms, worker representation with decision-making power in boardrooms being the most common in the EU. Two main factors influence this approach, namely, acknowledgement that the 'shareholder-value approach to corporate governance' may be seen as a prime cause of financial and economic crisis and that worker involvement in setting long-term strategy is contended to be a viable route to help prevent further crises (Conchon 2015: 8). Three main groups are identified in the report:

- 13 countries with widespread rights to worker representation at board level in both the public and the private sectors (Austria, Croatia, Denmark, Germany, Finland, France, Hungary, Luxembourg, the Netherlands, Norway, Slovenia, Slovakia, Sweden)
- Six countries with limited participation rights, mainly found in state-owned or privatised companies (the Czech Republic, Greece, Ireland, Poland, Portugal, Spain)
- 12 remaining countries with no rights at all (Belgium, Bulgaria, Cyprus, Estonia, Iceland, Italy, Latvia, Liechtenstein, Lithuania, Malta, Romania and the UK)

This report also points out that, contrary to popular belief, board-level representation is not restricted to supervisory board participation in two-tier systems, but is also found in unitary boards. The other vital point, which is considered further below, is that representation rights 'are not static and are evolving, especially in recent years under the double effect of the recent financial crisis and political circumstances'. Worker directors are most at risk in countries such as Ireland, Greece and Poland, whose governments are undertaking privatisation programmes, and where statutory board representation is provided principally in state-owned enterprises (ibid.: 36).

The volatile economic environment has left many European countries in a state of flux. According to Eurofound (2014: 11), governments in many member states seem 'to have moved to the forefront as a major industrial relations actor'. While retaining some stable structures based on ideologies favourable toward regulation, the European project has been profoundly affected by the financial crisis since 2008, amid growing instabilities emerging from globalisation and financialisation.[1] There are signs that some Central and Eastern European states are shifting to openly liberal economic positions in the wake of these pressures (Eurofound 2014). The UK's response to the crisis, as we have seen, has been to stimulate recruitment by loosening employment protections and security of tenure. This is an approach that has been echoed in different ways throughout the EU under the pressure of neoliberalism and the influence of international finance 'to introduce new types of flexible contracts and to weaken or eliminate the regulatory effect of organised industrial relations systems' (Hyman 2016: 3). The effect has been a pan-European increase in precarious work, especially for labour market entrants, and the downgrading of the EC's integrated strategy of providing security with flexibility, through the so-called 'flexicurity' agenda (Heyes 2013). However, the impact across Europe has not been uniform, largely as a consequence of different governmental responses to the accumulating tensions caused by recent global economic events and their impact on employment and employment relations. Two of the principal economies in Europe are Germany and France and it is worthwhile noting the current role of the state in these two countries to show what pressures economies are exposed to and how these pressures are being absorbed.

Notwithstanding tensions, it does appear that Germany's coordinated market approach has been sufficiently robust to withstand labour market shocks precipitated by the financial crisis; the institutions of centralised sectoral collective bargaining and codetermination through works councils and board representation have remained largely intact (Frege and Godard 2010: 543), allowing the social partners to cooperatively adjust their stances in response to the new threats. According to Glassner and Keune (2012), in member states including Germany, 'provisions allowing for greater flexibility and/or decentralisation of wage settings have been widely used during the economic turndown', with the objective of protecting competitiveness and employment (Eurofound 2014: 21).

The history of EPV in France has been dominated by the mobilising powers and influence of Communist-backed trade unions, and, although union density in France was estimated at only 7.9 per cent in 2010, there is high collective bargaining coverage. Bargaining at sectoral and company level have been considered stable during the crisis and, although union membership was in decline from the mid-1970s to early 1990s, it has since stabilised, concentrated in the public sectors. Legislation is complex, with frequent modifications, but is generally supportive of collective bargaining at different levels, backed by mandatory works committees of employee representatives and management. The system of workplace employee representation in France is also highly complex; structure and procedure depend on the size of the establishment and are subject to a range of statutory regulations, many of which deal with the roles of employee representatives (worker-participation.eu, undated). Since the financial crisis, local-level employment relations in France have been volatile and occasionally explosive, especially over employer plans for delocalisation, outsourcing and closure. Tensions with unions also rose when the socialist government attempted to introduce greater flexibility into the labour market to reduce high levels of unemployment, especially among young people, a liberalising approach that French employers are urging on French president Emmanuel Macron (Financial Times 2017c; L'Obs 2017a).

Conclusions

This chapter demonstrates that government ideology and action through legal and exhortative intervention strongly determines the shape and actions of EPV. We have seen that while ideology in the binary forms of LME and CME help to mould stable approaches to state intervention, under global competitive pressures, some flexibility becomes manifest, with governmental shifts to privatisation (and possible reductive effects on worker presence in corporate governance), reduced regulation and more flexible employment regimes, involving lowered employment security, which in turn can contribute to reduced levels of trade union membership, a phenomenon witnessed throughout Europe and in the industrialised world generally. Lower union density can put further pressure on collective participation as union negotiating capacity becomes compromised in terms of influencing governmental policy and in defending employees at sectoral and enterprise levels. One consequence of these changes is undoubtedly the present precarious state of social democratic political parties throughout Europe. The other consequence is the pressure exerted on collective participation in the form of declining negotiating power for employee representatives, in whatever organisational forums decisions are reviewed or discussed. In these pressurised circumstances it is possible to see fertile grounds for the consolidation of individualised EI, potentially at the expense of meaningful representative dialogue. In other words, the much-discussed 'representation gap', rather than narrowing, could be maintained or even broadening.

Note

1 Financialisation 'involves the economic and broader social ascendancy of the financial services sector' in recent years but its relevance to EPV lies in its alleged influence across national economies in fracturing 'systems of industrial relations in Europe, with downward pressure on working conditions, labour protection legislation and wage cuts' (Prosser 2014: 351–352). In other words, Europe's social model of regulation has been put in jeopardy by the dominance of the finance sector in its pursuit of short-term competitive advantage. Research has suggested that trade union participation has become more fragile and that financialisation can be linked to downsizing and downgrading of worker terms and conditions of employment (ibid.: 353). A useful comment on the potential restrictive impact of financialisation on labour relations in productive sectors is provided by Cushen and Thompson (2016).

Chapter 3

Management perspectives on employee participation and voice

Introduction

An intriguing question concerning EPV is why employers should express an interest in it. Several explanations have been offered, most of which engage with employers' expressed performance-related needs, but also one law-related factor that involves imposition on employers. According to the UK law of contract, employers and employees are equal contracting parties with mutual rights and responsibilities that, providing they are fulfilled, secure their formal contractual relationship. Therefore, one obligation of employees is to obey the legitimate orders of the employer, usually discharged through its delegated agent, the manager. However, as Huse and Eide (1996: 211) point out, 'Given their size and power, business organizations have an impact on all other institutions of society above and beyond their economic spheres', thus making the idea of contractual equivalence between individual employer and individual employee a fiction in the view of eminent employment lawyer, Otto Kahn-Freund (1983: 18), who contends that

> the relation between an employer and an isolated employee or worker is typically a relation between a bearer of power and one who is not a bearer of power. In its inception it is an act of submission, in its operation it is a condition of subordination, however much the submission and the subordination may be concealed by that indispensable figment of the legal mind known as the 'contract of employment'.

One reason for employer interest in EPV is therefore, as we saw in the previous chapter, that the law can demand it in order to provide a measure of balance between unequal parties, for example, in helping to maintain a healthy and safe workplace, or to ensure that employees are consulted and informed about decisions that immediately affect them. Though employer compliance to laws aimed at protecting employees is mandatory, the level of commitment required in fulfilling these responsibilities may leave them room for manoeuvre or interpretation. One frequently observed example is the difficulty for women to achieve equal pay with men, though equal pay legislation has been on the statute books in the UK for nearly fifty years (DCMS 2014). However, in favourable circumstances, leverage offered by employer shortcomings can be exploited by employee representatives and their trade unions through extending joint regulation to disputed areas, as Goodrich noted in his classic study almost a century ago (Goodrich 1920).

As we saw earlier, the legal system can influence employers' interest in EPV in other ways, notably through non-intervention, as in the voluntarist approach, which offers primacy to the contracting parties themselves to establish their own systems of employment governance. Political arguments for, and encouragement of, voluntary employer involvement initiatives on the basis that individual employers are capable of adopting the most suitable approaches for their own organisation have been mobilised as a barrier against statutory imposition of EPV (MacInnes 1987: 104). Conversely, the law can provide opportunities to encourage employers to establish forms of EPV by promoting union recognition or by introducing statutory directives that define and support the rights of employees to be informed and consulted about workplace matters that affect them.

The defensive role of EPV

Management may express interest in EPV for defensive reasons, a key motive identified by Harvie Ramsay in his celebrated cycles of control thesis (Ramsay 1977, 1983). Writing at a time when it appeared that a positive climate for social justice was gradually encouraging EP toward modifying managerial control, Ramsay, covering over a hundred years, suggested that rather than evolving out of 'the humanisation of capital', EI schemes are introduced by management at times of threat in the economic cycle. When employment is high and union confidence strong, management offer inducements such as profit-share bonuses to employees, often as a means to deter union membership or recognition (see also Hunt 1951; Church 1971).

Once the threat passes, incentives fall into disuse or are abandoned. Ramsay analysed employee relations within a conflictual zero-sum framework, with managers arguably intent on imposing a unitarist culture in their relations with employees. Not surprisingly, this radical rereading of EI motives has met with considerable critical reaction, notably from Marchington and colleagues, who pointed out that involvement growth in the 1980s occurred at a time of almost unprecedented union weakness.

They also argued that involvement schemes are not introduced simply to reinforce control over labour but established in pursuit of objectives related more to the performance aims and culture of the organisation. Their preferred model was one of waves, in which one participative practice is introduced in support of performance objectives and, as its impact subsides, another practice is introduced, presenting a succession of EPV initiatives in wave-like formation (Ackers et al. 1992; Marchington 2005; for a response to cycles critiques see Ramsay 1992). Nevertheless, under firm management control, cyclical movement has diminished in recent years, possibly irrevocably, seriously undermining labour ambitions for enhancing collective workplace control.

Humanisation of work

While maintaining control can be seen in defensive terms, employer interest in EPV is typically portrayed more positively through practices that promise to provide mutual benefit to both managers and employees. This school of thought developed from Elton Mayo's famous 1930s experiments at the Hawthorne plant in Chicago and his critique of FW Taylor's ideas on motivation. These posited that industrial workers were motivated chiefly by money and were willing to surrender task control and provide extra, management-directed effort in exchange for the promise of additional pay (Wilson 2004: 27; Sennett 1998: 41). Mayo's findings have, in turn, been heavily criticised for manipulating both the conditions under which the research was undertaken and the conclusions: a number of commentators see little distinction between Taylor and Mayo's managerial affiliations or sympathies (Wilson 2004 gives a useful summary). Nevertheless, this message of 'be good to your employees and they'll be good to you' took root and found active EPV expression in employer encouragement of group working and of supportive rather than disciplinary supervision. Practices derived from humanistic thinking about motivation were subsequently taken up and developed in the USA by both business popularisers and work psychologists, who together contributed to the emergence of the neo-human relations school in the 1960s and subsequently the Quality of Working Life movement, which embraced employee motivation with teamworking (Procter and Mueller 2000: 5). The main proponents of neo-human relations included established manager favourites Abraham Maslow and his heavily flawed but ever popular hierarchy of needs (Cullen 1997; Watson 1996) and Herzberg's also seriously questioned theory of hygiene factors and motivators (Herzberg 1968; Wilson 2004: 149). Motivators are intrinsic to the job and include span and depth of responsibility, work content, recognition and potential for growth. These factors form the foundation for Herzberg's job enrichment, in which he firmly distinguishes vertical loading involving devolved responsibility from lateral approaches to job redesign, such as rotation or enlargement, which could simply add more boring routines to already tedious work.

These regimes and their neo-human relations derivatives emphasise individual EPV factors such as encouraging the formation of natural work groups, with task-based decision-making responsibilities, individual autonomy, links with customers and clients and opportunities for upward and downward communication (Huczynski and Buchanan 2013: 308). Any hints at collective participation in the neo-human relations framework are either unspoken or not encouraged, with their underlying assumptions being implicitly or explicitly unitarist. At the explicit end, Mayo was of the opinion that 'membership of a trade union was a sign of mental illness' (Grey 2009: 48).

Nevertheless, many employers (and indeed, governments) recognise that as social partners, trade unions can have a positive role to play in preserving harmony and preventing conflict at work. This is partly a validation of the pluralist model of employment relationships, which recognises that conflicts of interest between contracting parties are a reality and that identifying and establishing the constitutional parameters whereby conflict can be contained and resolved is a preferable option to conforming with the questionable unitarist assumption of natural harmony operating under paternalistic rule (Fox 1974). The pluralist model can take different forms (see chapter 9), but the foundational one is of negotiation over terms and conditions of employment between employer or group of employers and recognised trade unions. Negotiation can be supplemented or even substituted by other procedures such as social partnership or works councils, but the basic pluralistic model that offers means of conflict containment and resolution is one embraced by many employers in industrialised countries and encouraged, as we saw in chapter 2, by their governments. However, as we also saw, this model has been severely tested in recent years owing to the combined impact of globalisation, austerity and election of governments with liberal market-orientated agendas.

Neo-human relations models have also been instrumental in the development of contemporary employer interest in EPV, in the following manner: through their role in the pioneering Tavistock Institute focus on socio-technical systems (Miller and Rice 1967); in contributing to practical programmes for advancing EPV, such as the international *Quality of Working Life* network from the 1970s (Brödner and Latniak 2002); through informing alternative team-based production methods such as those established at the Volvo Uddevalla plant (Berggren 1993); and through the subsequent genesis of human relations thinking into progressive or strategically 'soft' human resource management (Hendry and Pettigrew 1992), with its focus on employee empowerment and engagement (Beirne 2013). Further, it has been contended that, bolstered by commitment-seeking ideas imported from Japan (Walton 1985), strategic human resource management (SHRM), in which EPV elements feature heavily, has emerged from twin tracks of progressive people management, represented on one hand by job enrichment and teamworking and on the other by resource-focused management concentrated on maximising efficiency and minimising cost.

Strategy and human resource management

In the previous chapter we examined the roles and directions of state intervention in EPV, focusing on two prime motives, namely offering employees means of protection from unilateral management decision-making and unfair or risky conditions at work and, second, the obligation for governments to act with economic competence to promote high productivity and competitiveness in an increasingly challenging commercial environment and to offer efficiency and value for money in the provision of public services. The role of management is to translate these policy ambitions into functional models of product and service delivery (Beer et al. 1984). With human qualities considered as the mainspring of competitive advantage (Porter 1985), clearly the ways in which people manage and are managed will have implications not only for organisational performance but also for wider issues of corporate responsibility and of optimising human potential and aspiration. In seeking their performance objectives, management face a range of potential constraints: legal requirements, which have been reviewed in the previous chapter; market constraints, based on minimising cost and optimising quality; technological constraints, based on available expertise and means to invest; also, there are social factors that need to be considered, such as worker wellbeing and equality of opportunity; and, finally, pressures to get the most or best out of people, which may suggest different management strategies.

It is not surprising then that American and British management texts and journals are dominated by the idea of business strategy (e.g. Porter 1985; Saloner et al. 2001; Strategic Management Journal) and the ways that effective management of people can relate to business strategy. It is also clear that the concept and operationalisation of strategy are problematic, as testified by the continuous stream of books, academic articles and opportunistic departure lounge publications directed at the hard-pressed executive. If, though, organisational strategy itself is a problematic and contentious concept, then, of course, any derived people strategy may also be disputed owing to the expectation for human resource management (HRM or HR) to contribute to an organisation's strategic direction. At the same time, the HRM function is likely to be highly relevant as an influence on organisational EPV policy and its development.

Organisational and human resource management strategy

The immediate problem can be clearly stated: 'the notion of strategy is subject to a confusing variety of interpretations' (Boxall and Purcell 2016: 31). According to these authors, it is necessary first to distinguish between strategic problems (such as deciding which market to enter) and then to identify the appropriate operational strategy for survival and growth in that market. This approach is similar to that of Kay (1993) who argues that business strategy focuses on the ways an enterprise can operate most effectively within its environment; but of course, as witnessed by Brexit and unexpected presidential victories, the environment is never static and forever dynamic. While there are fundamental interdependent activities such as marketing, finance, production and people management, these will be deployed to fit specific contexts: in other words, the strategy will vary according to a range of identifiable contextual factors, or the ways in which these are determined (Boxall and Purcell 2016: 35–36). Some authors identify two different approaches: the deterministic approach, whereby the context in terms of size, technology, competition, etc., is given and 'determines' the strategic approach to be adopted, and the strategic choice approach, which proposes that executives can identify different directions and consciously choose the combinations which they calculate to be most effective in achieving their objectives (Child 1972).

Of course, these actions presuppose that organisations actually do act strategically, a point that has been authoritatively questioned, based on the complex problem of actually ascribing meaning to the concept of strategy. Whittington (1993) provides a detailed analysis of the problems, identifying different perspectives based on critical structural factors, such as the influence on decision-making of the short-term profit-seeking capital markets typified by the USA and UK, contrasted with the patient capital markets of Japan and Germany, as well as shorter-term contextual factors, such as responding to the impact of low-cost entrants to the food retail sector (Legge 2005: 138). This fluidity leads Boxall and Purcell (2016: 40) to identify *strategy* as a series of choices in responding to or anticipating market conditions and *strategic management* as involving a complex network of scoping, analysis, policy debates and 'scenario planning' exercises (ibid.: 46), aided by effective leadership, well-informed guesswork and good fortune (Grint 2000).

Potential fluidity of business strategy leads to problems for HRM. Strategy has typically (in the 'classic' model) been associated with long-term purposive behaviour with consequences 'fateful for a firm's survival' (Boxall and Purcell 2016: 53; Mintzberg 1990; Paauwe and Boon 2009), in contrast to HRM in its earlier personnel management manifestation, which was regarded more in terms of short-term, reactive behaviour and dependent status (Collings and Wood 2009: 5). Many academic analysts and practitioners agree that HR in its strategic form is expected to integrate with and derive from an organisation's business strategy, in other words to offer 'strategic fit'. However, the suggested fluidity of business strategy could have implications for notions and exercise of HR strategy, which could again face accusations of superficiality and reactivity or, in the famous words of Drucker (1961: 269–70), comprise 'a collection of incidental techniques without much internal cohesion'. An added problem is the extent to which management functions are united in pursuit of performance. As the Chartered Institute of Personnel and Development or CIPD (2017) reluctantly recognises, line management may be in a stronger position than HRM to assert its policies and HRM may in turn adopt a deferential approach to more authoritative or aggressive managerial colleagues subject to the tight constraints of market disciplines (Thompson 2011). Hence, there may be a critical and influential role for line managers in either supporting or subverting designated HR policies, including those derived from offering voice to their subordinates. These questions take on added significance when considering the lack of agreement on what constitutes SHRM and the consequent range of approaches associated with its exercise. These models all have direct associations with and implications for EPV. The four principal SHRM models are: best fit, best practice, resource-based view, and strategic partner.

The best-fit approach basically postulates that HRM policy and practice should be designed to fit an organisation's specific context. The first problem of course is identifying the dominant features of the context and assessing their relative stability. HR specialists tend to agree that the foundations for this approach were laid through the much reproduced Harvard model presented by Beer et al. (1984). This feedback model identifies broad situational factors, such as the legal system, and organisational factors, such as workforce characteristics. These link with potential stakeholder interests in the formulation of appropriate HR policies, whose outcomes are assessed through short-term performance evaluation and longer-term consequences, with both short- and long-term elements feeding back and informing the contextual factors and stakeholder interests. This dynamic model helps to ensure that performance objectives are supported by people management policies appropriate to the identified needs of the organisation. Subsequently, variations of the basic best-fit theme of matching context, interests and HR have been advocated (Bamberger and Meshoulam 2000; Schuler et al. 2001), but the fundamental contingency model parameters are retained.

Two questions stand out: what sort of HR practices and policies are contained within the proposed strategies and in what ways do these relate to EPV? The first question is possibly easier to answer than the second. The immediate problem with the best-fit approach is that it can be examined at different levels. Boxall and Purcell (2016) carefully analyse research on societal, industry and organisational fit, and recognise that with so many potential variables, where cross-cultural elements may also need to be factored in, findings at these levels can be indicative rather than definitive. At organisational level, though, there is evidence that matching appropriate HR policies to a desired competitive strategy can improve performance (ibid.: 68). Boxall and Purcell cite Michie and Sheehan's (2005) thorough study of 362 private sector firms, which found that it is those 'adopting a high-road approach to innovation or quality that gain from a high level of investment in employees' (Boxall and Purcell 2016: 70). Thompson (2011) points out the corollary of this approach: that it could be 'economically rational' to pursue 'low-road' choices, with the expectation of offering limited participation or voice opportunities to employees. Fombrun et al. (1984) identify four key HR processes of selection, appraisal, rewards and development and relate these to a hierarchy of organisational strategies ranging from single product to multiple products in multiple countries, noting ascending levels of HR practice sophistication and investment in people across all four processes. Schuler and Jackson (1987) examined HR practices that align with Porter's (1980) three-level competitive strategy model of cost containment, quality enhancement or innovation, and concluded that the cost model, not surprisingly, is linked to tight managerial control, while innovation is linked with group-working, skills development, employee share schemes and developmental opportunities. Finally, quality enhancement is linked specifically to high levels of task-based participation, training and fair treatment of employees.

From these studies a best-fit approach appears to signify a place for EPV in a strategy to serve high added-value organisational performance, though it is rather more difficult to find evidence for its actual deployment or to specify those EPV approaches that have demonstrably integrated with best-fit HR strategies. This is possibly because, as Paauwe and Boon (2009) correctly point out, measuring strategic fit against performance has been beset by a variety of methodological, temporal and operational problems.

A second strategic model asserts that it is possible to identify suites of universal HR practices that act systematically as 'best practice' to serve organisational performance. Evidence for a positive performance impact through best practice appears to be stronger than that for best fit (Paauwe et al. 2013), though the mechanisms linking practices to performance are still not clear, with a number of studies indicating that ostensibly 'soft' commitment-seeking policies may mask 'hard' objective-seeking practice implementation and be informed by these. This implies that EPV practices commonly associated with the model, such as teamworking, appraisal and performance-related pay, may be more about contemporary processes of management resource control than about developing people in shared endeavour. A full review and critique of the high-performing work systems and their component EPV practices can be found in chapter 6. Important questions posed by Boxall and Purcell (2016: 77) are whether organisational managers do actually follow a best-practice route and secondly, whether they should. Their review of the evidence gives a negative reply to the first question and a conditional one to the second. They report, following Kaufman (2010), that policies that appear to offer choice of approach are highly contextual. When employers pay high salaries to recruit and retain rare skills and optimise expensive technology, then a best practice approach could be economically efficient and worthwhile, but this calculation clearly would not apply in *all* organisational settings. In these circumstances, the use of best practice EPV instruments would be highly contingent upon individual organisational rather than universal circumstances.

A third identified strategic approach is the so-called resource-based view (RBV), which derives from Barney's (1991) assertion that sustained competitive advantage can be secured through development and protection of a firm's internal resources. Principal resources have been characterised as value, rarity, inimitability, non-substitutability and organisation, the latter defined as 'the appropriate management systems and processes to fully exploit the value embedded in internal resources' (Kaufman 2015: 519). Boxall and Purcell add 'appropriability' to these resources on the grounds that they need to be 'capable of capture to the benefit of the firm's shareholders' (Boxall and Purcell 2016: 86). Together, these resources or 'core competencies' (Hamel and Prahalad 1994) can be nurtured and developed within a supportive cultural context to provide a unique resource combination capable of offering competitive advantage to the organisation. For the HR specialist, the RBV approach has the special attraction of justifying management focus on non-tangible assets, namely people and their creativity, skillsets, ideas and energies, all of which can be mobilised to the organisation's competitive advantage. Imitation by competitors would take time, expense, potentially cultural change and managerial qualities and experience, which together may present insurmountable barriers to entry (Boxall and Purcell 2016: 85).

The main critique aimed at the resource-based view is that its inward-looking focus risks neglecting external market features that would also help determine optimum deployment of resources (Chowhan 2016). Kaufman (2015) takes a more complex view, arguing that the true value of an RBV approach can only be examined through the perspective of economic theory. Through an economics paradigm, shortcomings in the current theoretical treatment and analysis of RBV-performance linkages may be identified, shortcomings which together could undermine the practical utility of RVB for managers. Kaufman (2015: 534–535) argues that an economics approach enjoys four large virtues, namely:

a   an explicit focus on the profit/loss … consequences of HRM
b   a concrete and operational measure of value for guiding HRM choices
c   an actionable managerial decision-making model
d   concrete conceptual framework for identifying observable/manipulatable determinants of HRM choices … and their predicted effects

It is also noticeable that there is little explicit or specific reference to EPV in the resource-based literature, though its deployment is sometimes implied. In reviewing barriers to imitation, however, Boxall and Purcell point out that the firm is not just an economic entity but also a social one (Boxall and Purcell 2016: 100). They identify barriers erected through intrinsic 'social complexity', 'social capital' and 'social architecture', which embody sustained and profound patterns of shared community founded on teamworking, mutual trust and cooperation that, through not explicitly codified, can confer significant competitive advantage. Many commentators (e.g. Legge 2005: 20–23) point out that continuous learning and adaptability are the key resources giving competitive advantage and that they can be acquired both individually and collectively through teamworking, suggesting that voice has an unscripted part in providing internal cohesion to the RBV schemata. Legge (2005: 22–23) also provides a prescient warning based on employers' responses to the UK's persisting liberal market approach to economic policy. Citing Keep and Rainbird (2000), she points out that the UK economy tends to be short-termist and underinvested and have a preference for low added-value, low skill, low price goods and services, all inimical to the 'collaborative learning' that forms one of the pillars of the resource-based view.

The fourth identified strategic approach, and one that has been adopted and disseminated enthusiastically by the UK's HR establishment, is the *business partner* approach advocated by American HR specialist David Ulrich (1998). Keen to demonstrate the strategic value to the organisation that HR had previously been unable to provide, Ulrich presented an aspirational model comprising four key roles, namely strategic partner; change agent; administrative expert and employee champion. It is easy to understand the attraction of this framework to HR specialists keen to establish equal status and influence to that enjoyed by their managerial peers. Unfortunately for adherents, Ulrich now describes his earlier business partner model as comparable to 'a cell phone in the 1990s' (Ulrich 2017: 40).

A number of influential voices have condemned this attempt to gain greater partnership legitimacy as a failure. Kochan (2007: 599) argues that 'the two-decade effort to develop a new 'strategic human resource management' (HR) role in organizations has failed to realise its promised potential of greater status, influence, and achievement'. In his coruscating review of contemporary HR trends, Thompson (2011) is perhaps even more disparaging of this role for HR, describing the function as being 'seduced by the glittering prize of becoming a "business partner"' and in the process further diminishing its claim to independent professional – and potentially authoritative – status.

More generally, surrounding the rhetoric concerning SHRM, a persistent stream of publications casts doubt on it as a concept or as practice, an outcome or a process (Bratton and Gold 2012: 51). Legge (2005) is a prominent critic in contrasting HRM rhetoric (or theory) with reality (i.e. practice). So what do we mean when we say that HRM acts strategically? If we ignore, for the moment, the entire complexity of defining and operationalising corporate strategy, the first and generally agreed assumption of SHRM is that an organisation sets goals for the immediate and longer term and utilises labour power in a purposive and integrative manner in order to achieve these goals and to secure competitive advantage (Ulrich 1997). As an occupation, personnel management has a history that has not been conducive to achieving a strategic organisational presence; clearly it is difficult to act and contribute strategically when occupying a marginal managerial position. Hence Bratton and Gold (2015: 51) point out that HRM has been positioned by some commentators along a continuum of reactive (non-strategic) to proactive (strategic), with the important stipulation that in order to act proactively, 'the HR professional has a seat at the strategic table and is actively engaged in strategy formulation', a status which historically has not always been available to HR specialists. Perhaps not surprisingly, achieving board status has been described as the 'holy grail' for HR practitioners (Caldwell 2011). A major obstacle to achieving this ambition is that, in the UK at least, HRM's service and advisory roots lay severally in offering welfare provision, acting as clerical support, interpreter of legal requirements and industrial relations specialist at the sharp end of organisational life, dealing with negotiations with trade unions (Holbeche 2009). One significant historical constraint that emerges from these important but essentially mid-level functions and impinges on assuming strategic responsibility has been the absence of HR specialists on executive bodies (notably the main board of directors) where organisational goals are formulated and directed. Guest and Bryson (2009) estimated that between 1980 and 2004, private sector board-level representation for human resources remained fairly constant at 56 per cent. The Workplace Employment Relations Surveys (WERS) in 2004 and 2011 indicated a similar proportion (van Wanrooy et al. 2013: 53). In other words, during the HR metamorphosis from personnel management, the proportion of HR specialists achieving senior positions has scarcely shifted. Other studies showed similar or even declining levels of HR representation as boards of directors became smaller and at the same time encouraged to increase proportions of non-executive directors (Nixon and Penfold 2011). Cranet research (Cranet 2006) showed that between 1990 and 2004, HR boardroom representation declined from 63.1 per cent to 45.8 per cent (reported in Caldwell 2011: 42). Caldwell also reports HR boardroom presence of less than 4 per cent of FTSE 500 companies, a similar figure to that in large publicly trading companies in the USA. According to the ONS, in 2011 there were 77,000 HR directors working in the UK, compared with 207,000 finance directors, who, unlike HR board members, frequently ascend to chief executive position (Caldwell 2011: 49). With the HR function adopting a more subordinate or passive role in organisational affairs, the danger exists that any desire they may have to promote voice for employees will be overridden by more immediate or cost-driven imperatives.

Nonetheless, it has been suggested that board membership, while offering symbolic status to HR, is not essential for strategic influence. Kelly and Gennard (2007) were strong proponents of this view, arguing, on the basis of their survey interviews with senior HR personnel, that executive committees that deliver direct and regular contact with CEOs provide an appropriate vehicle for HR influence. Caldwell (2011) points out that in the UK, while this representation does appear to be on the increase, there is limited evidence for its strategic impact. A more favourable finding is shown by the management think-tank Korn/Ferry Institute, whose survey of 765 executives indicated that 43 per cent agreed that the influence of the HR function had increased significantly over the past five years, though no details of this increase were given to indicate where in the organisation this influence is generated or how it is expressed (Nixon and Penfold 2011). Another mark of significance for the evolution of HR would be whether it is treated as a key specialist function or as an activity that can be shared by managers with other responsibilities, such as supermarket store managers who have direct responsibility for managing their staff, possibly acting with support from a small cadre of personnel advisors based at head office (Bozkurt and Grugulis 2011). From this point of view, the latest WERS findings are not encouraging: only 14 per cent of workplaces had a job title that indicated a specialism in human resources. In over three-quarters of workplaces, a general manager or owner was responsible for employee relations matters (van Wanrooy et al. 2013: 51). Many of these workplaces were small, however, and 71 per cent of workplaces with more than a hundred employees employed a manager with specific (but not necessarily dedicated) responsibility for HR.

If securing executive authority has been a problem for HR, an alternative route for strategic involvement could be through asserting specialist or expert authority (Etzioni 1959; Scarbrough 1996). As the above figures indicate, responsibility for HR can be adopted by managers with other duties, so an alternative route to influence for the occupation has been to seek expert authority by attaining independent professional status. Since securing chartered status in 2000, the representative body for human resource practitioners in the UK, the CIPD (of which the author is a member), has constantly stressed its 'professional' standing, though when contrasted against the accepted criteria of professionalism (see chapter 1), there remain some doubts, for example concerning its independence, when its identification with and dependence on organisational objectives, for example as a 'business partner' (Ulrich 1998; Ulrich and Brockbank 2005), could undermine professional objectivity and freedom of action. Moreover, the exercise of HRM is not formally restricted to chartered members of the CIPD (in contrast to other professions with organisational interests, such as chartered accountants, engineers and actuaries) and, again in contrast to most professions, the CIPD has no barriers to entry or disciplinary powers against non-members and few available sanctions against its own members. Further, unlike other professions, HR does not possess a monopoly of knowledge or expertise, especially in comparison with similar occupational groups (Ashburner and Fitzgerald 1996: 191). Indeed, in headline critical examples of poor business practice in recent years, it is hard to find evidence of HR specialists acting as an authoritative or independent dissenting voice.

In some cases, we find the opposite in fact. In chapter 5 we examine the disastrous consequences of the Enron stock option scheme, leading to the bigger question of whether the massive earnings differentials enjoyed by senior executives can be justified, either in terms of their effect as an incentive or in terms of corporate social responsibility. It has also been alleged that HR at Enron were complicit in not resisting the toxic ultracompetitive culture that ultimately contributed to its collapse. Lewis (2002) pinpoints HR's 'inherent conflict' – to be 'responsible for corporate ethics, yet seemingly powerless to enforce them at the highest level'. Though the Enron culture was highly individualised and risk-centric, it was supposed to be formally guided by heavily publicised ethical principles embracing respect, integrity, communication and excellence, espoused voice principles that were ignored or rarely monitored in the prevailing gladiatorial atmosphere. This toxicity was most visible in the performance evaluation system, which former CEO Jeff Skilling described 'as the glue that holds the company together' (Lewis 2002) but which in reality formed the basis for the notorious 'rank and yank' system, leading either to individual enrichment or ignominious sidelining or worse. This in turn led to a 'mercenary' dog-eat-dog culture in which the formal policy of teamworking was effectively abandoned in favour of temporary individual glory but eventual corporate dysfunctionality. Whatever the role of HRM in a disaster that affected so many, it was clear that the function was unable or unwilling to offer a viable dissenting or guiding voice for employees.

A more recent example of HR's apparent lack of strategic influence is the (ongoing) case of the retail giant, Sports Direct. According to the company's website: 'We have a fantastic HR department that are responsible for the care and attention of 30,000 Employees across the UK and Europe. And looking after them is our number one priority' (Sports Direct website 2017). Again, this is an example of the distance between rhetoric and reality. Following a number of adverse media and trade union reports, the UK's parliamentary Business, Innovation and Skills Committee conducted an enquiry into the company's policies and practices, concluding that they presented a 'disturbing picture' with staff 'not treated as humans' (House of Commons 2016; see also *Personnel Management Online* 2016). The enquiry focused largely on the main distribution warehouse for UK operations where temporary and zero-hours contracts were common and disciplinary working practices included deducting non-proportionate pay for minor punctuality infringements, threats of and actual dismissal for minor 'offences' such as being absent through sickness, chatting or being too long in the toilet, all enacted under the infamous 'six strikes and you are out' policy described by the committee as a 'punitive measure, which denigrates the workers at Sports Direct and gives management unreasonable and excessive powers' (House of Commons 2016: 9). The company also breached legal minimum wage levels by enforcing unpaid compulsory searching after employees had clocked out. Serious health and safety breaches and issues were also reported, including 110 visits by emergency vehicles between 1 January 2010 and 19 April 2016. The committee commented that the company was 'treating workers as commodities rather than human beings with rights, responsibilities and aspirations' (ibid.: 12). As with Enron, it is difficult to see any positive employee-centred contribution by HR at Sports Direct.

We have reported on just two cases, and while these are not isolated examples of organisational misbehaviour,[1] clearly not all companies are run in such dehumanising and cavalier manner. However, both companies enjoyed a very high national and international profile, whose performance, corporate culture and treatment of stakeholders has been of considerable interest to policy-makers as well as practitioners. Nevertheless, the actions of these companies show that the reality can be a far cry from their policy statements as well as from those socially conscious, commitment-enhancing companies regularly portrayed by popular HRM publications and social media as representing current practice. Weaknesses in HR's ability to implement what many regard as good practice lead to the question of whether voice and participative influence may, for many workers, be more apparent than real.

Management and EPV

Whether HRM has become more strategically orientated or not – and the question remains open – in terms of practice, specific trends of management-directed

EPV are clear. In a previous volume (Hyman and Mason 1995) we remarked on the growth of employer-initiated EI techniques alongside (and potential contributors to) the decline of more collective participative approaches. The growth of EI has often been linked to a belief in the business case for its establishment, in that EI can help to improve employee performance (Procter and Benders 2014). A Slovenian study of managers in 225 companies indicated that management's positive attitudes toward participative practices encourage the implementation of EI. Moreover, perception of positive links with organisational performance tends to motivate managers to implement EI (Franca and Pahor 2012). The decades since the publication of the book have seen a consolidation of involvement practices across both developed and developing economies, underpinned by combinations of liberal market-based policies, globalisation, austerity and union frailty. For more details for the EU, see Eurofound (2015b); for the USA, see Kaufman and Taras (2015); for China, studies conducted by the Center for Advanced Human Resource (2010).

EI is typified by a number of characteristics that have gained prominence in the contemporary environments outlined above. First, EI is management inspired and controlled. Second, it focuses on involvement in designated tasks and on stimulating individual employee or team efforts for these tasks. Third, there is strong emphasis on communication: employees may be passive recipients of management information and consultative procedures but some schemes also encourage upward communication or dialogue between employees and their managers. Fourth, the emphasis is unitarist, encouraging a culture which aims to promote greater employee understanding of and responsiveness to market conditions. A number of generic approaches to EI have been identified, namely:

a   downward communication to individual employees
b   downward communication to groups of employees
c   upward communications
d   two-way communications
e   individual superior–subordinate involvement (e.g. performance appraisal, performance-related pay)
f   job restructuring (such as empowerment, see chapter 7)
g   financial involvement through profit-sharing and employee share schemes (see chapter 5)
h   combination initiatives in the form of high-performance work systems (see chapter 6)

Effective communication has always formed an essential element of unitarist thinking and practice, with the underlying assumption that any conflict at work can be associated with failure to communicate management intentions or decisions clearly. So it is not surprising that communication provides a central and 'almost ubiquitous' (van Wanrooy et al. 2013: 191) place in contemporary patterns of EI, as shown for the UK by the Workplace Employment Relations

Surveys, the most recent of which were conducted in 2004 and 2011. Figures are based on responses from at least 2,283 (2004) and 2,674 (2011) workplace managers. Adapted findings are shown below in Table 3.1.

These surveys covered workplaces with five or more employees, while in earlier WIRS[2] and WERS studies the minimum workplace size was 25, so direct comparisons with earlier surveys (Hyman and Mason 1995: 28) need to be treated with caution. Larger establishments are more likely to have formal direct communication procedures. Among workplaces with more than 20 employees, the incidence of either whole-workforce meetings or team briefings was in excess of 95 per cent (van Wanrooy et al. 2013: 64). It is also relevant to the unitarist project that in 2011, managers in 80 per cent of workplaces preferred to consult directly with their employees rather than through trade unions (ibid.: 63).[3]

Individualised relations are also emphasised through dealings between managers and their immediate subordinates. These relations are clearly visible in the rise of performance appraisal and the closely linked performance-related pay. While these techniques often form part of a high-performance system, they are also used on a stand-alone basis. WERS surveys showed a massive increase in the use of performance appraisal for specified employees, from 43 per cent in 2004 to 70 per cent in 2011 and from 38 to 63 per cent for *all* employees in 2011. Direct links with pay were reported for a quarter of all workplaces, up from 16 per cent in 2004 (van Wanrooy et al. 2013: 93–94). What these figures do not tell us, of course, is the organisational culture in which appraisals and appraisal-based pay are rooted or the purposes for which they are deployed. Formally, appraisal had been described as a central catalytic component of the overall cyclical HR system (Fombrun et al. 1984), offering a positive developmental role through two-way communication to enhance individual performance, motivation and potential. As can be seen from the notorious Enron case, appraisal can have a darker, more disciplinarian side (Townley 1999), as demonstrated in that company's infamously competitive and ultimately destructive 'rank and yank' system, in which annual appraisals were manipulated to openly expose and remove lower-ranked performers. Nevertheless, similar systems of forced ranking have been reported in up to a fifth of American companies, including Sun Microsystems, Ford, Microsoft and Conoco (Time Magazine 2001; Economist 2013). Many employees are reported to be in favour of individual performance-related pay, owing to its direct identification with personal effort and input and distributional justice (Thompson 2009). But studies also show strong employee dissatisfaction and possible wider dysfunctionality as performance is usually linked to and measured by individual target achievement, which can lead to damage to cooperation and collaboration, decline in morale, as witnessed, for example in banks (Laaser 2016), raised stress levels (Carter et al. 2013), problems of favouritism and discrimination (Wilson and Nutley 2003), as well as the issue of quantitative target achievement at the expense of qualitative organisational goals (Edwards and Wajcman 2005: 98).

Table 3.1 Arrangements for direct two-way communication between managers and employees, 2004 and 2011

	All workplaces (%)	
	2004	2011
Meetings between senior managers and all employees	46	46
Team briefings	37	40
Any face-to face group meetings	57	58
Problem solving groups	18	14
Employee survey in past two years	35	38
Suggestion schemes	25	25
Regular use of email to all employees	35	49
Any two-way written communication	58	69

Source: van Wanrooy et al. (2013: 65); reproduced with permission of Palgrave Macmillan.

Where these restrictive perspectives apply, it is probably more accurate to describe performance appraisal or performance-related pay more as a source of employee voice suppression rather than of voice expression.

Conclusions

We have identified and analysed multiple sources for potential employer interest in EPV. These sources can be summarised as: (a) stimulation by (or against) legal requirement, (b) defence against union incursions, (c) humanisation of work, (d) part of strategic HRM, and (e) business case for EI as a reflection of growing emphasis on individualism and response to market pressures.

Voluntary employer interest in EPV focuses largely on what we term EI. Nevertheless, there are numerous other factors that help to shape patterns of deployment of EPV. We have mentioned that employers are required to abide by legal codes, whether of domestic or external origin, as, for example, in the case of EU directives. Employers may also erect voluntary and independently constructed involvement procedures as a defence against threatened blanket legislation or, as Ramsay (1977) argued, against threats posed by coordinated employee actions. Alternative arguments have queried Ramsay's thesis, insisting that employers design and implement forms of involvement to meet a spectrum of objectives broader than labour control and that specific initiatives flourish and fade, to be replaced according to need and impact, not according to perceptions of a collective threat. The various manifestations of work humanisation have been another influence, with the belief that it is simply more productive for managers to engage employees in task-based decisions and to treat them as collaborators rather than as assets to be manipulated and controlled. With organisations under competitive or, in the case of the public sector, budgetary threat, interest in developing strategies to confront market volatility has grown and with it, interest in human resource strategising, although the conceptual foundations of both business and HR strategy have been exposed to rigorous critical interrogation.

With this proliferation of vaguely progressive developments, it would be easy to suggest that the days of control-dominated Taylorist thinking among employers and managers are well behind us, though many analysts would strongly dispute such assertions. Notwithstanding the multitude of publications, university courses and popular sloganising promoting humanistic management, an important question is that of the impact of these approaches on management thought and action. A number of influential critics have conceptually and empirically examined the contrast between rhetoric and action, and found the former wanting. An early refutation was voiced by Harry Braverman (1974) in his comprehensive and sophisticated rebuttal of humanistic capitalism, where he details the successful attempts by management to exploit technological advances to deskill work and to extend this reductionist process from craft workers to the growing ranks (at the time) of clerical and administrative employees. The theme was taken up with renewed vigour in the 1990s with the publication of Ritzer's *McDonaldization of Society*, in which he argued that service workers, including increasingly those at specialist and professional levels, were becoming exposed to management doctrines of efficiency, calculability, predictability and control (Ritzer 1996: 9). Our later examination of 'popular' processes such as lean production (chapter 6) demonstrates the ways in which these standardising dimensions have entered into modern management terminology, policy and practice, leaving diminishing scope for employees to exercise discretion or control over their work. These fundamental concerns have been strongly emphasised in different ways in powerful narratives by American authorities Richard Sennett, Airlie Russell Hochschild and philosopher Elizabeth Anderson, who describes private sector management as nothing less than a 'dictatorship' (Anderson 2017: 38). Sennett (1998: 9–10) refers to contemporary capitalism as 'changing the very meaning of work' by introducing new digitally and technologically informed controls to present an 'often illegible regime of power' in which worker flexibility and insecurity are demanded, but also one in which 'most labor remains inscribed within the circle of Fordism', i.e. exploited by those dehumanising assembly-line techniques which evolved from FW Taylor (1998: 44). Moreover, hovering above all workers is the 'specter of uselessness' (Sennett 2006) as productive capital becomes increasingly flexible in timescale, location and in its vulnerability to the cost-optimising demands of finance.

Hochschild (1983) examined control over work from the perspective that in the modern service economy, demonstrated feelings become central to the value of exchanges between workers and their clients or customers. In other words, employees are expected to manage and deploy emotions as part of the 'commercial logic' of their service as a form of 'emotional standardization or Taylorism' (Frayne 2015: 54). The concept of managing 'emotional labour' through appraisal, monitoring and surveillance is now well established and has been empirically confirmed among flight attendants (Hochschild 1983), call-centre workers (Taylor 1998) and in office work (Gregg 2011), among others.

All this means that today's dominant narrative of employer-instigated and employer-controlled EI can in practice mean very little in terms of extending discretion and autonomy to employees. If anything, this narrative serves, in diverse ways, to reinforce management legitimacy and authority. Even SHRM, with its catalytic promise of closer integration between business objectives and employee management, appears to offer little significance for EPV. Meta-analysis of nearly one hundred studies, covering nearly 20,000 organisations, revealed that added use of high performance work practices leads to 'benefits in increased productivity, decreased employee turnover, and greater financial returns' (Liu et al. 2007, in Kaufman 2015: 519–20). The prime human resource investments, though, are listed as: HR planning, compensation, internal promotion, security and flexitime, with no mention of employee voice. Moreover, as subsequent chapters demonstrate, those elements of EPV that are contained in high-performance work systems (HPWS, see chapter 6) are often tainted with managerial control overtones.

Notes

1 The collapse of the world's financial sectors post-2008 provides an illuminating example of low HRM visibility in organisational strategy. The frantic competitive management culture of the banking and finance sector worldwide is increasingly being implicated in the disastrous losses experienced following the 2008 crash. The multinational Swiss bank, UBS, lost billions of dollars investing in increasingly risky ventures, putting its reputation for prudence in jeopardy. According to the Telegraph (2008), the bank's failure was 'the result of a banking culture that managed to combine a predilection for risk-taking with an overestimation of its own ability'. Similar accusations of arrogance and disassociation from reality were also directed at the Royal Bank of Scotland, another of the global elite of financial institutions (House of Commons 2012). Writing in HR Magazine (2013), Jacobs identifies little subsequent change in financial sector culture and values that reward any sort of profit-seeking behaviour; she accuses financial sector HR of culpability in 'sticking their heads in the sand, pleading ignorance or powerlessness in the years leading up to the crash'. She then cites Andre Spicer, from the Cass Business School, who claims that 'it is HR issues that are at the heart of the problem'. A failure by central HR to establish a genuine participative and open workplace in which subordinates felt free to challenge or even question decisions was clearly part of the dysfunctional culture at these, and other, free-wheeling enterprises.
2 Earlier national UK surveys were termed Workplace Industrial Relations Surveys or WIRS. The change to WERS in 1998 reflected the shift from examining primarily manufacturing-based collective relations and their associations with trade unions to the evolution of more heterogeneous and broader forms of relationships and the inclusion of employee surveys.
3 While team briefings retain their popularity with employers, their intended employee subjects can view them more sceptically. Stewart et al. (2009: 74) quote the conclusions about team briefing by Sandra, a shop steward in the trim section of a Vauxhall car plant: 'It's not a two-way thing. It's just the team leader talking to the team … . That has happened anyway and it's just absolute rubbish … . The lads are not turning up and no one is bothering and the team leader is talking to himself or his best blue-eyed guy is talking.'

Chapter 4

Employee and trade union perspectives on employee participation and voice

Introduction

Preceding chapters examined different dimensions of voice and EP and the roles of employers and government in implementing EPV. But important questions remain – do we know how much access workers have to EPV or what employees are looking for from EPV? Do they, for instance, prefer individual or task-based expression of voice (such as performance appraisal); or collective but not necessarily union-based approaches, such as through works councils; or collective single-channel union representation; or, potentially, any combination of these? Following on from these issues, another question concerns the strength of commitment or indifference on the part of employees towards different forms of EPV.

These questions are important because workers constitute the party with the closest interest in EPV as they rely on diverse forms of participation for information on and contribution to issues, ranging from the individual to the organisational, from knowledge about individual performance and reward at one level to codetermination at another. Even in forward-thinking companies such as John Lewis, according to an internal survey the main employee grumble concerns quality of communication (personal correspondence). At the same time, employees are usually expected to respond to management directives and are rarely in a position to initiate or develop programmes of EPV of their choosing, though of course they may be able to challenge or subvert the *consequences* of management decisions in diverse ways (Ackroyd and Thompson 1999). Until the recent past, many employees could rely on trade unions to provide the means for challenge and representation of collective interests, not just at work but also in broader sociopolitical circles, through engagement in economic planning, in pressure-group activity and through association with sympathetic political parties, for whom unions provide funding in return for ideological and policy support.

Trade unions are confronted with profound structural problems. In the face of global monetarist ideology and policy, which presents market rigidities as the major obstacle to economic efficiency, the governments of many countries have taken an aggressive line on expenditure for public services through privatisation and outsourcing. In developed countries, switches from manufacturing to service work, intense international competition and individualistic employment policies by management, along with the growth in precarious work, have combined to put pressure on trade union activity, membership, finances and influence. Management policies emphasising cooperation rather than conflict have helped to reinforce trends toward reduced trade union profiles across the developed world. Combined, these dynamics lead to the fundamental question: 'Is there a perceived need for trade unions?' (D'Art and Turner 2008).

In this changed landscape of employer ascendancy, employees as employers' 'most precious resource' face significant difficulties: first, in identifying what they actually want, in contrast to what they have (Freeman and Rogers 1999), then in assessing how they might get what they want. We also need to consider how 'voice' and 'silence' can be interpreted and deployed and to evaluate means available to overcome the so-called 'representation gap' in those countries where it has been identified. Finally, we need to look at the past, present and potential roles for trade union and non-trade-union representation in rapidly evolving political, commercial and employment circumstances.

What do employees want?

First we need to identify what employees actually *have* and contrast this with what they *would like* from their relations with managers and then to determine what sort of gaps exist between their aspirations and the reality with which they are confronted. The important question that follows is how then to bridge any identified gaps. It is important to recognise that countries have different histories, traditions and cultures of labour market relations which influence types, depth and expectations of management–employee interaction. In developed economies, three principal systems can be identified: the market-focused Anglo-Saxon system, the social-dialogue dominated or coordinated market European Union system, and the strongly collectivist Scandinavian model (Freeman et al. 2007: 5–13). Developing countries such as India appear to be conforming to a market-based Anglo-Saxon approach, while China's orthodox communist political economy is increasingly being affected by international developments, leading to closer integration with Western companies and ideas (see Chapter 11). Notwithstanding these distinctive models, we cannot specify, for example, that employees in Anglo-Saxon countries all enjoy an identical EPV experience, nor do they have the same aspirations, but we can at least hope to identify common themes. For this analysis, we are first indebted to the seminal cross-national research on six Anglo-American economies (Australia, Canada, Ireland, New Zealand, UK, United States), coordinated by Freeman et al. (2007). Their aggregated union density findings are summarised below and developed or updated where appropriate.

This research identified uniform union decline in density (Boxall et al. 2007b: 208), a process that has subsequently continued across all six countries, as shown in Table 4.1.

Density decline has been most pronounced in the private sector in all countries, even in those like Ireland, where until 2009, unions were invited to actively participate in national economic policy formulation (Roche and Teague 2014).

The individual country surveys conducted for the 2007 study indicate that sizeable minorities of workers in non-union establishments would welcome union representation if it were offered, though it is of course not possible to determine the strength of this support or the conditions under which such ambitions might be encouraged. One important finding was that highly paid and skilled workers are 'relatively indifferent to what unions offer' and that most private sector employees 'favor self-reliance in the labor market' (Boxall et al. 2007b: 213). These conclusions are matched by findings from other studies of high added-value employees. In a UK study of software engineers, national private sector union density for these workers was reported to have fallen from 13 per cent in 1996 to 8 per cent in 2000, with most software engineers in the companies surveyed confirming their strong adherence to individualistic values and bargaining strength based on personal value and contribution (Hyman et al. 2004) and on access to professional networks (Bergvall-Kåreborn and Howcroft 2013). But there is clearly a sector effect here as union density for software workers in the public sector was 40 per cent in 2000, a minimal decline from 1996.

On the other hand, recent official UK data indicate a more nuanced picture of union membership (DBIS 2016). In 2015, professional occupations accounted for 20.4 per cent of employees but 37.3 per cent of union members. Also, employees with degree-level qualifications or equivalent were far more likely to be union members than employees without formal qualifications. Part of the explanation for these figures is that union density is far higher in the public sector (54.8 per cent) than in the private sector (13.9 per cent) and that designated professional workers, such as teachers and nurses, are more likely to be employed in the public sector. For the same reason, women are now more likely than men to be in a trade union (27.1 per cent vs 21.7 per cent). Highest union density was found in education, public administration and in the utilities, which were previously in public ownership, and the lowest density in private-sector hospitality. It would appear that the representation gap is most pronounced in the private sector. Further, the 2007 research indicates that, in contrast to private sector occupationally secure employees, confident in their individual abilities to negotiate the labour market, the union representation gap is highest for vulnerable workers, including the young, low-income earners and those facing adverse working conditions. It is relevant that in 2015, only 5 per cent of employees in the 16–24 age group were in a union and that union

Table 4.1 Union density in the six countries, 2004 and 2016 (per cent)

	Australia	Canada	Ireland	New Zealand	UK	USA
2004	22.7	30.4	34.6	21.1	28.8	12.5
2014	15.5	26.4	27.4	18.7	25.1	10.7
2016	14.5	-	-	17.9*	23.5	10.7

Sources: Boxall et al. (2007b); OECD.Stat (2016); DBIS (2016); DBEIS (2017a); Australian Bureau of Statistics (2017); New Zealand Centre for Labour, Employment and Work Survey (2015); U.S. Bureau of Labor Statistics (2016).

Note: * December 2015.

membership was low for poorly qualified (and hence low paid) employees (DBIS 2016).

The Boxall et al. study also indicated that, compared with the union representation gap, lower proportions of respondents across the six Anglo-Saxon countries expressed a lack of satisfaction with *overall* influence (Boxall et al. 2007b: 210). The authors attribute the smaller gap in satisfaction to the growth of complementary, or possibly substitute, management informative and consultative forums. These developments appear to be consistent with those of the 2011 WERS, which found a 'continuation of growth in the prevalence of direct methods of consultation'. A sizeable minority of employees seem satisfied with these alternative arrangements, with 35 per cent stating that managers were good or very good 'at allowing them to influence decisions', an increase from 32 per cent in 2004. Levels of employee satisfaction with their amount of involvement in workplace decision-making also rose, from 40 per cent in 2004 to 43 per cent in 2011. When employees do not have representation, the findings indicate that they do have a desire for more workplace influence (van Wanrooy et al. 2013: 74–75). Despite these promising findings, it should be noted that well over half of employees were not able to express satisfaction at their levels of involvement or of influence, suggesting that a meaningful representation gap or participation gap (van Wanrooy et al. 2013: 66) remains to be filled, especially for sizeable groups of young, underskilled and vulnerable workers unable to draw upon their labour market human capital.

Precarious work

The extent and effects of labour flexibility in response to changing market circumstances have been much debated over the past thirty years (e.g. Atkinson and Meager 1986; Purcell and Purcell 1998; Anderson 2010) but the publication of Guy Standing's influential book, *The Precariat: A New Dangerous Class* in 2011, presented a wider and more disturbing picture of the pernicious nature of precarious work. In his examination of insecure work across different countries, he argues that the gains made by labour and social democratic policies in the post-war period have been increasingly threatened by neo-liberal policy-making and globalisation. Especially affected are the young, poorly educated and migrants. Among other factors, he argues that labour security has been undermined through lack of effective representation and that, worldwide, increasing numbers of workers – up to a quarter in some countries – are becoming, or have become, disenfranchised, with the potential to form a new and radicalised class.

There is clear evidence that in many Anglo-Saxon countries, representative participation through independent trade unions is at risk of marginalisation, if not elimination, as the incidence of union recognition declines (ILO 2015) or as the scope for bargaining over terms and conditions narrows in private sector organisations (van Wanrooy et al. 2013: 81). Ongoing privatisation and outsourcing programmes are expected to enhance these downward shifts (Herrman and Flecker 2012). One consequence of the swing towards a more management-dominated EPV system is apparent: despite these largely direct approaches, a sizeable representation or participation gap can be identified, which has not narrowed in recent years (van Wanrooy et al. 2013: 66). The same period has witnessed considerable growth of insecure or precarious work, typified by technological control of the labour process, non-employee 'self-employed' status and the risk of discriminatory or abusive treatment (Taylor 2017). For such workers, we may be able to identify a 'representation chasm' due to lack of resources to express their interests. Some workers, though, are seeking redress through independent trade unions, for example through the 'Justice for Janitors' campaign in the USA, and innovative attempts in both Australia and the USA to secure employee status for haulage workers designated imaginatively by employers as self-employed (Kaine 2014: 177). In the UK, trade unions – and other groups – are attempting to organise workers in the so-called gig economy, usually defined as temporary casual work sought by people through mobile phone apps. Precarious work, by often denying employment status, ensures that *employee* voice is minimal. There is little doubt that this kind of work is growing in the UK (Working Lives Research Institute 2012) and USA (Kalleberg 2011). Precarious work has been linked with the following aspects of work casualisation and informalisation (Rossman 2013; Taylor 2017: 24):

- term contracts
- seasonal contracts
- agency work and similar forms of outsourced, indirect third-party relationships that act to obscure the relationship with the real employer
- bogus self-employment disguised as independent contractors
- discriminatory apprenticeships, internships and training schemes
- transformation of employment relationships into commercial contracts, for example in South American agricultural sectors
- part-time work, often in association with self-employed status
- zero-hours contracts.

A comprehensive investigation of working practices across the EU also shows dramatic increases in many of the above forms of precarious working (Working Lives Research Institute 2012).

Kalleberg (2014) provides a conceptual framework for precarious employment, which he describes as primarily insecure, unstable and uncertain, with high risk of job loss and irregular and unpredictable schedules on the job. It may also offer restricted economic and social benefits, such as a living wage, health insurance or retirement benefits. Most relevant for our review, it may only provide limited statutory entitlements provided by labour laws, regulatory protection, and worker rights. Kalleberg (2014: 2) emphasises that 'to a large degree, this results from precarious workers not possessing a collective voice in the labor market, through, e.g., independent unions'. Union decline or restriction is cited as one of the key drivers of precarious work. Further, precarious work may offer little potential for advancement to better jobs, with limited prospects for future work security and life chances, as well as for expectations of continued employment and income. Finally, it can expose workers to dangerous and hazardous conditions, with limited protection against accidents and illness at work or domestic emergencies, and few limits on working time and unsociable hours.

Owing to the diversity, elasticity and lack of visibility of forms of work precarity, data for its prevalence are not easy to compile, though one union estimates that 15 per cent of those working in the UK labour market are now self-employed. According to the ONS, this amounts to nearly five million workers (ONS 2017), of whom just under two million may be freelance professionals, according to the Centre for Research on Self-Employment. The CIPD estimates that within 12 years, freelance workers could make up half the workforce (People Management 2017). The New Economics Foundation (NEF) estimates that London's gig economy has expanded by 72 per cent since 2010 and research conducted by the NEF suggests that only 61 per cent of the labour force has a secure job that pays at least the minimum wage (Devlin 2016). It has been estimated that nearly a million workers in the UK in 2016 were on zero-hour contracts, a rise of 13 per cent from the previous year (ONS 2017), notwithstanding considerable critical publicity and calls to outlaw the practice. A similar picture is emerging in the USA. Katz and Krueger (2016) interrogated data from the American Life Panel and found a 'significant rise in the incidence of alternative work arrangements'; these are defined as temporary help agency workers, on-call workers, contract workers and independent contractors. These arrangements grew from 10.1 per cent in February 2005 to 15.8 per cent in late 2015, with professional workers accounting for much of the increase (Hart-Landsberg 2017). Across Europe similar patterns emerge: in 2015, 15 per cent of workers in 35 European countries were designated as self-employed and a further 12 per cent as temporary employees. The proportion of part-time workers rose from 18 per cent in 2005 to 20 per cent in 2015 (Eurofound 2016a). Precarity through short-term temporary contracts has been associated with strongly negative feelings of wellbeing (Eurofound 2011), with Dawson et al. (2017) identifying a substantial 'wellbeing gap' predicated on employment insecurity. Perhaps not surprisingly, precarious work has been linked to risks to health and safety (Underhill and Quinlan 2011). Also, of course, it means that for a high and expanding proportion of the workforce, employee voice, other than expressed through potentially self-damaging exit, is a virtual mirage.

A voice for the precarious worker?

Standing (2011: 196) confirms that 'the precariat Voice [sic] in the sphere of work and labour is weak', but questions whether established trade unions would be prepared to act for these vulnerable workers on the grounds that their principal role is to defend narrow, sectional and economistic interests of existing members. On the other hand, unions recognise the increasing fragmentation of work and the growing numbers of people locked into precarious work, and are taking steps to extend their reach and ambitions to organise groups such as part-time workers, many of whom are women (TUC 2016).

Nevertheless, for precarious workers to have a voice, an early priority is for them to be recognised as employees, and several notable attempts in this direction have recently been reported, often with the assistance of trade unions supported by social media campaigns, some of which have been established to help organise precarious workers into trade unions. Other campaigning groups such as the Better than Zero network, which acts against abuses in the hospitality sector in Scotland, have achieved success in both encouraging young people to support trade unions, and by using apps to alert potential consumers of employer exploitation of workers. A notable success has been achieved by the GMB union (which organises drivers). A test case brought on behalf of two Uber drivers had their work status confirmed as employees; this reassignment from self-employment has important implications for pay and benefits for approximately 40,000 drivers throughout the UK. The GMB is actively campaigning and recruiting members at Uber as well as at other delivery companies. The New Economics Foundation (2016) also reports that drivers from food delivery service Deliveroo are attempting to achieve 50 per cent membership of their drivers from one London borough into the Independent Workers of Great Britain (IWGB) union,[1] thereby triggering formal union recognition from the company. If successful, this would be the first instance of union recognition by an app-based employer in the UK.

Another noteworthy example of a union providing a voice where there might otherwise be silence has been the success of the Unite union in confronting the controversial Sports Direct company to obtain employment terms for some 3,000 casual workers. During the campaign, the union highlighted questionable working practices at the company's massive distribution warehouse and, as well as the transfer of these workers to established employment contracts, the union gained a commitment from the company to end zero-hour contracts (TUC 2017a). Growing acknowledgement of the vulnerability of many workers stimulated the UK government to launch a widespread investigation into the provision of 'decent jobs' and the scale and impacts of the gig economy (Taylor 2017; see chapter 12). Further afield, among a number of identified proactive union cases, Rossman (2013) cites the example of the largest poultry producer in Australia, the Baida Poultry plant in Victoria, where among approximately 430 workers regularly working at the plant, only 284 were directly employed by Baida, with the remainder working under inferior terms and conditions, leading to an indefinite strike in their support by the National Union of Workers.

Can these possibly unanticipated expressions of union-backed voice herald a shift in employee orientations to collective representation? It should be recalled that in the public sector, levels of union density and presence have typically been maintained, usually because public sector employers remain relatively receptive to trade unions and, indeed, managers can find benefits in dealing with them (D'Art and Turner 2008). It will also be recalled that while highly qualified employees in the private sector tend to eschew trade unions, the same does not apply to similar workers in the public sector, confirming that the roles of employer and state are vital in preserving and promoting collective representation. It should also be recalled that women, who now represent a majority of UK workers, are not averse to joining trade unions, many of which have established campaigns specifically directed at recruiting women. Indeed, many women have now established senior positions within trade unions, while others have graduated to prominent political activism through their trade unions. An excellent review of women's progress in union membership and governance is provided by Kirton (2015). Nascent collective organisation can even be found in institutions where union recognition is difficult to establish, such as the National Domestic Workers Alliance in the USA. This was founded in 2007 from a movement to protect the human rights and dignity of domestic and care workers, women migrants and their families. Domestic workers are excluded from American labour legislation that provides fundamental protection such as the minimum wage.

Voice and silence

We have argued that voice is a flexible term, broadly synonymous with EP, of which there are many manifestations, though for analytical purposes, we divide these into collective or representative forms, initiating from employee concerns to project employee interests against those of employers, and direct forms, which are part of management's HRM policies to inform and consult, with the objective of enhancing employee commitment and performance (Dundon et al. 2004). While emerging from different interests, neither form need necessarily injure the other party: for example, in a supportive environment, works councils can provide bilateral benefits (see Chapter 9). Nevertheless, it does imply that voice is not simply de facto a neutral facet, but is a control-based resource that can be manipulated to favour some interests at the possible expense of others. The corollary of this is that denial of voice, by either party, can also be used to promote or protect interests. We have seen above that employers can deny voice simply by not recognising workers as employees. Another aspect of voice, or its suppression, can be demonstrated through state deprivation. The UK government required that workers seeking tribunal redress for alleged breach or denial of employment rights by employers needed to pay up to £1,200, a sum most low-paid workers were unable to afford, leading to a 70 per cent collapse of employment tribunal applications. In this instance, though, workers were not silenced. On 26 July 2017, following a sustained and costly campaign by the UNISON trade union, the Supreme Court ruled that the tribunal fees imposed since 2013 were unlawful and discriminatory. Moreover, it ruled that fees paid since their introduction, estimated at some £30 million, must be refunded to claimants. Dave Prentis, the union's general secretary, pointed out that 'the Supreme Court has righted a terrible wrong and sided with those that the government sought to silence' (UNISON 2017).

For workers, the uncontested ability to establish preferred formal employee voice mechanisms may be an inaccessible policy choice, but the capacity to undermine managerial initiatives may be feasible, for example through poor response rates to suggestion schemes and attitude surveys, which could signal a lack of engagement to managers. Townsend (2014: 164) points out that subordinates' dissatisfaction with a line manager's responsiveness to employee attempts to communicate could lead to their unwillingness to engage in subsequent communication.

The principal argument of this book is that control lies at the heart of EPV; from this perspective, silence should be seen as part of the control dynamic or, as Cullinane and Donaghey term it, control over the contractual 'relational exchange' between the parties (Cullinane and Donaghey 2014: 404). Hence, silence may be instrumental to either party: for example, one subprocess of negotiation has been identified as 'attitudinal structuring' or 'structuring the bargaining climate', in which control over information and its disclosure is used to give support to one's side and undermine the other in order to influence bargaining outcomes (Walton and McKersie 1965). Sending non-participants 'to Coventry', i.e. refusing to talk with them, was a classic disciplinary action used in order to cajole or force people to join a trade union or to maintain collective discipline in an industrial dispute. Ackroyd and Thompson (1999: 160), citing Collinson (1994), point out that withholding information from management may also serve as a key resource in resistance to management and in maintaining work-group identity. In their study of a games company, Hodgson and Briand (2013) revealed expressions of resistance through silence by animators and artists who were reluctant to provide essential information in project team meetings. Passive resistance to management may also be displayed by 'playing dumb' (Hodson 2001: 60). Briefing groups, or team briefing, have become very common vehicles for downward-cascaded communication by line managers to subordinates. Van Wanrooy and colleagues found that 66 per cent of all workplaces used team briefings in 2011, an increase of 6 per cent from the 2004 survey (van Wanrooy et al. 2013: 64). While part of the thinking behind these interventions is undoubtedly to improve employee awareness of management intentions, they have also been designed to reinforce direct managerial control over communication by sidelining and devocalising union representatives, especially shop stewards. In a study reported by Danford in the aerospace sector (Danford 2005: 181), a senior steward emphasised this: 'We were worried about the employee communications. We saw the shop stewards as a key communicator … . By circumventing the steward you were going to damage that relationship and become reactive … .'

Silence may therefore also be encouraged by employers as part of a unitarist employment relations ideology that labels outspoken employees as 'troublemakers', especially if connected to trade unions (Fox 1966) or in organisations where 'whistleblowing' may be tacitly discouraged (Callahan et al. 2002). Conversely, recent research from Norway, where whistleblowing without employer retaliation is supported through legislation, shows high levels of employees raising concerns (Skivenes 2017). Based on ideas of psychological contract (Turnley and Feldman 2000) and equity theory (Adams 1963), in which employee inputs into the labour process are voluntarily adjusted to match the perceived fairness of their received outcomes, it is conceivable that perceived injustice would be matched by reduced inputs, including denial of information that could be of potential organisational benefit (Donaghey et al. 2011). A study focusing on the roots of equity by Greenberg (1990) found that employee pilferage in manufacturing plants following management announcements of pay cuts was higher when reasons for the cuts were poorly or insensitively explained, compared to those where full justifications for the cuts were explained to the employees (Wilson 2004: 152).

Employees and trade unions in Europe

It should be noted that while trade union membership has been in precipitous decline in Anglo-Saxon economies over the past thirty years, this decline has slowed and even been marginally reversed in the past two or three years, at least in the UK (DBIS 2016). Also, patterns of union interest, membership and activity in mature continental European economies differ somewhat from those in the market-led economies.

It would clearly not be feasible to deconstruct employee attitudes towards EPV across individual European countries, though some distinctions may be made between established European economies and those new member states (NMS) that joined the EU from Central and Eastern Europe between 2004 and 2007. D'Art and Turner (2008) have undertaken a large-scale survey of worker views toward trade unions in 15 established EU states, involving interviews with nearly 30,000 respondents in 2002/3. Based on their review of socio-economic and employment trends, they presented five key hypotheses:

1. Employees are likely to hold negative views of the utility of trade unions.
2. Service sector employees will report weaker need for trade unions.
3. High-level, high-autonomy employees are less likely to perceive the need for a union.
4. High income satisfaction will be associated with reduced need for a union.
5. Women employees are less likely than men to perceive the need for strong trade unions.

The authors also hypothesised that young people would be more union-adverse and that union membership would be higher for respondents holding left-leaning political orientations.

The results were surprising. Nearly three-quarters of respondents agreed that employees need the protection of trade unions, including 69 per cent of non-union respondents. Longitudinal analysis suggested that over 20 years, proportions 'agreeing with the need for strong unions increased from 53 percent to 70 percent' (D'Art and Turner 2008: 178). A clear majority of higher level, professional workers and those with high task autonomy also agree with the need for a union. As hypothesised, dissatisfaction with income was associated with greater need for trade unions but, more surprisingly, four-fifths of under-25s perceived a need for unions. Three-quarters of women also affirmed support. From an individual country perspective, two countries with low union density, Greece (89 per cent) and Portugal (85 per cent), showed highest sympathy for trade unions, with Germany, at 66 per cent, the lowest, pointing to a 'substantial representation gap or an unfilled need for union representation' in these low-density countries (ibid.: 184). These findings indicate that demand for union protection, latent though it may be, is still substantial across established EU states 'despite the protection that may be afforded by individual employment law or the existence of alternative voice mechanisms' (ibid.: 185).

This study, along with others (e.g. Toubøl and Jensen 2014; Schnabel 2013), shows that trade unions continue to hold some attraction for employees in established EU countries, and signs of membership stability or revival have also been exhibited (Waddington 2014), a trend that may strengthen as recognition of the insecure plight and poor conditions of vulnerable workers grows. Also, for mainstream employees, awareness of unions and of their contribution to social dialogue is high in countries like Germany and France, irrespective of low and diminishing density (see chapter 9). Employee perception of unions in new EU member states is more difficult to interpret. Since the collapse of state socialism in the centralised economies of eastern Europe and subsequent accession to the EU of many Central and Eastern European countries, it is apparent that, with little governmental or employer support, trade union membership in many of these countries has dropped significantly (Meardi 2007). As in the West, membership is appreciably higher in the public sector than in the private sector. It has been estimated that employees in the public sector in Poland were three times as likely to be in a union than private sector workers (Fulton 2015).

Recent density figures for NMS are not encouraging, as can be seen from Table 4.2.

Reviewing surveys conducted in 2005 for the European Foundation for the Improvement of Living and Working Conditions, Eurofound, Meardi (2007: 511) reports that in terms of work satisfaction, NMS employees were less satisfied than their Western equivalents, a situation that appears to have altered little in subsequent surveys (Eurofound 2012), suggesting that accompanying union frailties, opportunities to express 'voice' at work in these countries are restricted. Meardi argues that in these situations, workers' response to grievances is frequently through 'exit', presenting figures of high migration from NMS countries to the UK and Ireland as evidence (Meardi 2007: 511). Migration has been a major factor in Poland but, despite union membership density declining from 28 per cent in 1991 to between 12 and 15 per cent in 2010 (Czarzasty et al. 2014), Polish unions have taken vigorous and successful steps to halt decline, though in response, employers have adopted intimidation, discriminatory pay and restricted employment status to discourage workers from joining unions (ibid.). In these circumstances, it is difficult to be confident about categorising Polish worker attitudes toward trade unions, though in a more sympathetic and less aggressive political and institutional environment, higher numbers would undoubtedly be attracted into them.

Conclusions

In a context of globalisation, financialisation and pressurised economic conditions, employer policy initiatives have contributed to declines in union membership across the world. It might appear that employees are no longer attracted to trade unions as their preferred means of expressing voice. Nevertheless, the picture is complex. Decline has been most pronounced in the private sectors of liberal market economies, where management has often introduced complementary or substitute voice arrangements. Alternatively, as in parts of Eastern and Central Europe, employers have acted directly to deter or suppress union membership and activity. Despite the presence of these alternative or suppressive arrangements, research regularly reveals pronounced representation gaps, whether in market-orientated Anglo-Saxon or coordinated European economies. Surveys also demonstrate continuing interest in union membership, even in non-union establishments (van Wanrooy et al. 2013: 100). Perhaps unexpectedly, young people are also expressing interest, though this has not yet been reflected in union recruitment growth. Women, traditionally (and often inaccurately) portrayed as less likely to be attracted to union membership, are also joining unions and becoming active within them, helped by the feminisation of the workplace and union understanding of wider employee needs.

Though there is evidence that management-initiated programmes of consultation and communication are helping to divert employee interest from union membership, it is questionable whether the majority of workers feel that their influence at work has advanced as a consequence. Moreover, as Chapters 3 and 6 demonstrate, management involvement programmes can become associated negatively with work intensification and stress, leading to expressions of 'virtual exit', through lack of commitment and through disinterest, or manifest exit, through absence and quits. We have also noted that EPV and silence are expressions of control; both managers and employees, whether individually or collectively, can draw upon silence in diverse ways to protect or advance their interests or to damage those of the other party.

Most analyses of EPV assume some sort of access to organisational voice programmes, whether representative or direct. But increasing numbers of precarious workers face major obstacles in voicing their interests, notably through their lack of employment status. These workers are faced by what we term a 'representation chasm'; nevertheless their situation has led to innovative union efforts to support and organise vulnerable workers, with some success.

Notwithstanding union membership losses over the past thirty years, there are signs of stabilisation or even revival in a number of countries as latent interest, combined with active union campaigns for recognition, is beginning to show an impact. A recent study indicated that strike action can be followed by growth in union membership and that new members are encouraged to join if there are perceived workplace injustices and a belief in union effectiveness to remedy them (Hodder et al. 2017; see also Kelly 1997). For migrants,

Table 4.2 Union densities for selected NMS countries

Country	Proportion of employees in union (%)
Romania	33
Slovenia	27
Bulgaria	20
Czech Republic	17
Slovakia	17
Latvia	13
Hungary	12
Poland	12
Estonia	10
Lithuania	10

Source: Fulton (2015).

institutional embeddedness can influence their decision on whether to join a trade union (Kranendonk and du Beer 2016). However, much depends, as Bain and Elsheikh (1976) demonstrated many years ago, on the state of the economy. Slow economic growth and low rates of inflation tend to be associated with both greater management assertiveness and diminished union attraction as unions fail to secure high pay awards; conversely, trends toward higher inflation, coupled with the acknowledged union premium, in which higher pay awards are associated with union intervention, can stimulate latent interest in unions into active recruitment. Also, supportive government and employers can be a significant influence in encouraging union membership (Bain and Price 1983), as evidenced in a number of Scandinavian countries (Sandberg 2013), where post-crash decline in union density and activity has been limited. Though prediction is difficult in volatile economic and political conditions, there is significant evidence that employees do want their voice to be heard through meaningful representation and that in many countries workers recognise that adequate provision for influencing organisational affairs or for protecting collective interests is not at present forthcoming, issues that are examined in further depth in chapter 10.

Note

1   The IWGB is a small independent trade union, recently established to support mainly low-paid migrant workers. It is a campaigning union, for example pursuing a living wage at a number of prominent employers, but also increasingly acting to support specific disadvantaged and unorganised worker groups, such as security guards and, most publicly, couriers and delivery workers; the union has organised well-supported and publicised stoppages at companies such as Deliveroo.

Chapter 5

Profit-sharing and employee share ownership
Panacea or gimmick?

Introduction

Preceding chapters demonstrate that in many countries, and specifically in liberal market economies, recent developments in voice and participation have been primarily management-led, often as an integrated part of a systematic or strategically labelled approach to employee management. The following three chapters examine the background and details of high-profile approaches assumed under these managerial initiatives and assess their impact on employees, on their relations with management and on employee and enterprise performance. This chapter focuses on profit sharing, employee share ownership (ESO) schemes and employee ownership (EO), representing the oldest managerial approaches to EPV but still among the most visible in the contemporary global economy.

The range of financial participation

We should note at the outset that *financial participation* covers a wide area of performance-linked remuneration policy and practice. There are various individual and task-based *performance related schemes*, in which monetary supplements to salary are provided in return for meeting previously established targets (Thompson 2009). This chapter focuses on initiatives designed to offer employees a financial stake in the organisation. First we consider *profit-sharing* or, as it is also called, *profit-related pay* (PRP), which does not involve the release of equity to employees, but instead provides a monetary bonus to be distributed to all or a selection of staff, triggered through achievement of designated levels of profitability or group performance. A second approach comprises ESO schemes, which operate by allocating shares to employees, or by offering shares for purchase at discounted rates, to act as a tax-efficient incentive or benefit. Less common is EO, located in companies like the John Lewis Partnership and in worker cooperatives, where employees who own the enterprise, or substantial parts of it, might anticipate a meaningful governance role.

We have previously noted a lack of precision when defining EPV and in describing its scope. Most individual activities functionally linked to EPV are similarly boundary-fluid and hence difficult to define or measure with confidence, whether in terms of inputs or outcomes. However, financial participation does offer tangible and measurable inputs into EPV and for this reason is worthy of closer examination. Equity-based schemes also share one other characteristic – they are often supported by enabling legislation (which provides for voluntary adoption by companies) or, as in the case of profit-sharing in France, are required by law to be established by companies. Further, some outcomes of share schemes, such as retention of shares and equity allocated as a proportion of remuneration, are also quantifiable. We can also ask questions relevant to their distribution. For example, are share schemes offered as an incentive to perform in certain desirable ways or are they offered as a reward for having done so? Are they offered to all employees or restricted to specific groups? Measuring their impact on employee behaviour and productivity can be problematic because they are unlikely to be offered in isolation from other initiatives, and enterprise performance may also be influenced by a range of extraneous factors unrelated to the provision of equity or monetary bonus to employees. Nevertheless, bearing these caveats in mind, there is a corpus of research covering different enterprises, sectors and countries that does enable us to evaluate the ways in which ESO schemes and profit-sharing are used and their possible links with attitudinal and organisational outcomes.

Profit-sharing schemes

Profit-sharing provides a payment linked to profits or to some other measure, often paid annually, triggered if a target level of profit or performance is achieved. These schemes are something of a misnomer because income supplements may be related to outcome criteria other than profits, with the intention of relating bonuses more directly to aggregate employee inputs, such as productivity gains or ratios of labour costs to net revenue. These schemes, which embrace long-standing Scanlon and Rucker Plans in the USA, are also known as gainsharing. Potentially, therefore, these types of scheme could be extended to non-profit and public-sector organisations, though in the UK at least, they rarely are (van Wanrooy et al. 2013).

Three main potential stimuli for employers to introduce profit-sharing have been identified: first, to link remuneration directly to performance, thereby encouraging higher productivity. Second, if the scheme is broadly based in staff coverage, an objective could be to encourage closer cooperation and possible unitary identification of interests through communal effort and reward. A third potential benefit is to offer a more flexible pay regime, varying compensation in line with overall performance, and thereby potentially stabilising employment. However, there has been little evidence to support these latter effects (Blanchflower and Oswald 1986). A deferred group-sharing emphasis could work to a scheme's disadvantage as it may become difficult for employees to identify their individual efforts with communal outcomes, especially in larger enterprises. This lack of visibility may constrain individual commitment and contribute to 'free-riding', where some employees fail to respond positively to the incentive of profit shares on the grounds that they will receive a monetary bonus irrespective of individual contribution (Cahill 2000).

Profit-sharing has a long history, with its deployment noted as far back as the 1860s in the UK (Ramsay 1977) and the USA (Bureau of Labor Statistics 1916: 46–48). Profit-sharing schemes are also common in Japan and Northern Europe, notably France, where the practice is compulsory for companies employing at least 50 people. In France, benefits from a scheme can be made available immediately or be held in employee savings accounts. Profit-sharing is becoming increasingly common in developing countries such as China. Deferred profit-sharing is the most common form of retirement plan for employees in the USA (Coates 1991: 21). In these plans, an employer credits monetary shares and accrued investment earnings derived from company profits to participating employees' accounts. These accrued earnings are normally only distributed following retirement and provide a measure of superannuation pension.

The US Bureau of Labor Statistics currently estimates that plans are open to about 57 per cent of workers. In the USA, though it is already a common organisational feature, profit-sharing returned briefly to the top of the political agenda recently when Hillary Clinton proclaimed in a presidential debate that she wanted 'to see more companies do profit-sharing. If you help create the profits, you should be able to share in them, not just the executives at the top.' A financial commentator suggests two explanations for renewed American interest in profit-sharing: first, owners of financial assets have been the biggest beneficiaries of the economic recovery that followed the 2008 crash, rather than wage-earning employees. Second, the gap between senior executive compensation and average employee pay has widened massively in recent years, a phenomenon also found in the UK (*Guardian* 2016c). These developments stand in stark contrast to expressed political aspirations for profit-sharing. UK Conservative governments of the 1980s and 1990s encouraged profit-sharing in order to loosen pay rigidity and promote labour market flexibility through tax incentives on schemes. However, these arrangements led to lost tax revenue and claims that the main beneficiaries were designated senior executives and that schemes were failing to provide an incentive or reward open to all employees. In consequence, the tax exemptions were removed.

Despite large divergence in allocation of profit-shares and their benefits, profit-sharing appears to have lost little of its popularity in the UK. Notwithstanding the intervening removal of tax exemption, successive WERS surveys in 1998 and 2004 showed only a slight decrease in the proportion of commercial enterprises offering profit-sharing, standing at 36 per cent (Kersley et al. 2006: 192–93), dipping subsequently to 33 per cent in 2011. It should be noted, though, that the proportion of workplaces offering PRP to *all* employees only rose from 7 to 10 per cent, suggesting that the majority of companies still operate selective schemes (van Wanrooy et al. 2013: 96–97).

So as profit-sharing continues to be a popular compensation mechanism, we need to seek evidence for its effects. More specifically, we examine the following issues: first, what are the objectives actually sought by employers for profit-sharing? Second, to what extent are these objectives fulfilled and especially what is the impact of profit-sharing on employee attitudes, behaviour and through these 'intermediate effects' (Fibírová and Petera 2013), on productivity? Third, is it possible to identify specific conditions under which profit-sharing can exert positive effects? Questions over conditions could include the levels of bonus allocated to stakeholders, whether schemes are skewed to benefit senior managers or all employees, and whether allocations are seen as equitable. Linked to this, we should look for evidence of whether profit-sharing works in synergy with other participative initiatives, such as teamworking. We can also examine whether there are differences in approach and impact between sectors or countries.

According to Kessler (2010: 344), managerial objectives for PRP are to influence employee attitudes and to improve economic performance. Citing a broad European survey of 500 companies, he adds that the most common management motive was to encourage positive interest in the fortunes of the company and the unitarist pursuit of common goals. Though productivity might not be cited as the prime objective, numerous other studies suggest that it does provide an underlying motive for PRP adoption (Pendleton et al. 2003; Kruse 1996). Legislative factors could also be instrumental. Nevertheless, tax-exempt PRP schemes established by the UK government in 1987, mainly to encourage wage flexibility, remained popular among employers even after withdrawal of tax exemption in 2000.

There is certainly a belief shared among many economists that PRP is positively linked with productivity. Long and Fang (2013) argue that PRP has the capability to enhance productivity through (a) more flexible pay regimes, (b) attracting and optimising high-quality human capital, and (c) aligning worker and firm interests. Some studies affirm these benefits unequivocally: for instance, one American longitudinal study indicated higher productivity by profit-sharing firms in 13 out of 15 years between 1971 and 1985 (Coates 1991: 21). However, as Long and Fang (2013: 2) point out in their extensive review of the literature: 'while the research evidence is quite clear that employee profit sharing does increase company productivity on average … the evidence is equally clear that it does not do so in all cases'. D'Art and Turner (2004) conducted a comprehensive review of 2,827 private sector enterprises in 11 European countries, and while finding some evidence of positive links between profit-sharing and performance, they concluded that these links were not definitive. These findings reflect the circumspection of earlier researchers whose reservations were expressed as: '*Most* managers we have met in profit-sharing companies have said that, at least to a *modest* extent, profit-sharing as *part* of their total employee participation arrangement, has had *some* effect' (Bell and Hanson 1987: 6; emphasis added).

Despite these concerns, a number of quantitative and econometric studies do point to positive productivity consequences associated with profit-sharing (Kruse 1993; Green and Heywood 2011; Weitzman and Kruse 1990; OECD 1995). These effects are, however, also subject to reservations based on methodological differences and possible shortcomings, lack of understanding of the mechanisms through which PRP exerts its effects on productivity and the extent to which positive consequences can be attributed to the combined inputs of PRP and other participatory initiatives (Fibírová and Petera 2013: 11; Robinson and Wilson 2006). Two linked studies demonstrate the complexities of associating productivity directly and uniquely with profit-sharing. A UK study conducted by Cable and Wilson in 52 British engineering companies in 1989 did indeed find productivity gains, in the region of 3 to 8 per cent among profit-sharers, but concluded that while profit-sharing contributed to higher productivity, it did not act alone, arguing that 'accompanying changes in other dimensions of organizational design are likely to be required'. The authors cited the quality of interaction between managers and unions, utilisation of capital equipment, choice of technology, internal organisation, and labour force characteristics as potential intervening variables. They also identified another important contributory factor when assessing the impact of EPV: 'profit-sharing was introduced as part of a package involving new technology and negotiated with the workforce' (Cable and Wilson 1989: 371). Many of these same issues were highlighted in a companion study (Cable and Wilson 1990) of 61 (West) German metalworking companies, where Cable and Wilson found a differential of between 20 and 30 per cent in favour of companies practicing profit-sharing. But again, these findings were heavily influenced by 'important interactions with other aspects of firms' organization and operation'. The possibility exists, of course, that the presence of profit-sharing facilitates the introduction of productivity-enhancing new technology and positive interactions. The researchers also made the point that comparing the impact of arrangements in different countries is difficult as profit-sharing is articulated in different ways and firms' differences in important characteristics, such as size, skill levels, employment relations and technology, are also important influences on productivity outcomes.

The above analysis indicates that intervening or combining factors are essential to optimise the potential for PRP to enhance productivity performance. This point was also demonstrated in Long and Fang's (2013) study, which investigated whether teamworking plays a role along with profit-sharing in influencing productivity. The research used longitudinal panel data from a large sample of Canadian workplaces, comparing those workplaces that have introduced PRP alone, those without and those that introduced PRP but with team-based operation. The summary results show that teamworking did have an important catalytic effect 'in the success of employee profit sharing – at least in terms of labor productivity'. Long and Fang also found that establishments without teamworking 'that adopted profit sharing showed no significant growth in productivity' (ibid.: 18). A further significant finding was that 'establishments with teams but that did not adopt profit-sharing showed a substantial decrease in productivity', explained by the contention 'that team-based work needs to be combined with some type of group or organizational performance pay in order to ensure that teams are working towards organizational goals' (ibid.: 20).

In another in-depth Canadian study by Long (2000), interviews were conducted with 108 CEOs of companies operating all-employee profit-sharing, using multiple regression analysis to examine the mechanisms or 'moderators' through which profit-sharing can lead to productivity gains. Other research had previously indicated that bonus size links directly with productivity (Kruse 1993), that lower labour turnover and absenteeism can result from PRP and that these effects in turn impact on overall performance (Wilson and Peel 1991). Nearly all the CEOs in Long's study were convinced of the positive impact of profit-sharing on overall company performance, citing improved employee motivation and performance and the ability to attract and retain staff as important contributors. Three structural factors in particular were also implicated in the success of profit-sharing: the amounts of bonus allocation, communication about the scheme, and managerial philosophy, including integration of profit-sharing with other progressive HR policies (Long 2000: 498–99).

When combined with other participative forms, profit-sharing has a positive impact on employee work orientations and performance that has been noted in a number of studies. For example, Macduffie (1995) conducted research in the global automobile industry and concluded that contingent reward systems, including profit-sharing, integrate best with 'a team-oriented, high commitment workplace' (Long 2000: 497; see also Levine and Tyson 1990). Another relevant observation on profit-sharing is made by Hanson and Watson (1990: 180), who point out in their study that 'only relatively successful companies tend to introduce such schemes'.

Clearly then profit-sharing has the potential to improve productivity, but the above accounts demonstrate that there is no simple formula for its success and neither is success guaranteed. Profit-sharing can exert a positive influence by encouraging employees to adopt favourable attitudes to their work; these attitudes are reinforced by information provision and recognition by employees that their combined efforts can lead to enhanced performance and, by extension, to higher rewards. From the literature it seems that any positive effects of profit-sharing are likely to be furthered when they are combined with other progressive people management practices, as has been suggested, for example, with high commitment work systems.

Employee share schemes

Employee share schemes assume diverse forms and practice, both within and between countries. Basically though, there are three universal kinds of schemes:

shares that are issued free to all employees who satisfy eligibility requirements; shares that employees can purchase, usually at a discount; and schemes where employees are given the option to convert savings into company equity. With governmental support inclined towards different objectives, it is difficult to generalise causality of effect or to make valid cross-national comparisons of aims and outcomes (Knyght 2010). Some schemes can be selective, aimed specifically at executive or high added-value employees, but these have narrower objectives in favouring well-rewarded senior staff and have consequently received wide criticism or even condemnation for their potentially divisive effects (Knyght 2010). Policy encouragement at both governmental and enterprise level now tends to favour all-employee systems, where we will focus our examination.

Many countries offer tax incentives to encourage companies to adopt schemes that offer broad employee coverage. The basics of these share schemes are straightforward: employees either receive or can buy shares in their own company, often at preferential rates, thereby obtaining a concrete 'stake in the firm' in which they are employed. The prime intention for most government-backed schemes is that employees as shareholders will behave as self-interested 'owners' and this behaviour will manifest itself in greater commitment, loyalty, engagement and hence performance (d'Art and Turner 2004). A secondary performance expectation may be that hierarchical relations will become more orientated toward consensus rather than control as both managers and their subordinates are equally favoured as owners and may be assumed to share the same corporate values and expectations, thereby reducing costs of monitoring and supervision (Beirne 2013: 71). This has also been a factor in the opposition to share schemes from some trade unions, fearful that signalling common interests between employees and managers undermines union representative functions and hence potentially membership (Pendleton 2005a). A further political and, some say, cynical motive for ESO can be to lubricate and overcome objections to the privatisation of nationalised assets such as utilities (Nichols and O'Connell Davidson 1992). This movement was especially pronounced in the years of and following the Thatcher governments in the UK in the 1980s and 1990s, when gas, electricity, telecommunications and bus transport, among others, were privatised, despite strong objections and warnings from recognised trade unions about the loss of socialised services and jobs in these sectors.

Typically, government-sponsored schemes are not aimed at structural transformation of companies into social enterprises and tend to offer only limited stock allocations to employees, which raises the question of how recipients (or employee purchasers) respond to their allocation and how successful schemes are in meeting their expressed objectives. In the UK, all the major political parties have given exhortative and legislated support to limited ownership forms of equity provision. Kaaresmaker et al. (2010: 318) identify three main ways in which employees can acquire shares: donation by the enterprise; purchase of shares by employees through a *Share Incentive Plan* (SIP) in the UK, or in the USA, an ESO plan (ESOP), which can be matched by employer contributions (Kruse et al. 2010); and share options, whereby employees enter a designated saving scheme under which they have the option to convert savings into equity at an identified date in the following few years; in the UK, these are called save as you earn (SAYE) or *Sharesave* plans. Often, companies run more than one scheme, so that employees may be offered shares, but also have the option to enter an SAYE scheme run by the employer. These limited ownership schemes are typically employer-initiated and in companies where trade unions are recognised, plans have usually been introduced with little or no trade union input, even at a time when unions enjoyed more influence than today (Baddon et al. 1989; Pendleton 2005a; Kalmi et al. 2004).

ESOPs, now known as share incentive plans, are by far the most common form of employee ownership in the UK, with over two million employees holding shares or options through a government-approved scheme. While the number of schemes declined five years ago, the most recent figures show a steady increase in numbers of the four approved schemes, two of which are for selected employees and two for all eligible employees (HMRC 2017). While the ESOP Centre (2012) suggests technical reasons for the earlier decline, there seems little doubt that commercial uncertainty following the financial crisis also contributed to the temporary volatility of share-provision schemes. Share schemes are still common in the USA, where in 2014 some 14 million employees participated in 6,717 companies operating ESOPs, including the retirement plans known as 401(k). Participating companies included some of the biggest and best known in the USA, such as Starbucks, South West Airlines and high-tech software company Cisco (National Center for Employee Ownership 2015).

The main managerial objectives of share provision in these broad-coverage but limited-ownership schemes appear to be driven by unitarist values, aimed at securing supportive behaviour through engendering favourable employee attitudes. A pan-European survey of 500 companies found that a prominent objective for ESO among management respondents was to encourage employee interest in the fortunes of the company and the pursuit of unity and common goals (van den Blucke 1999). Comparable motives were identified by Morris et al. (2006) in their study of a major UK retailer. Similarly, in their case-study examination of five companies, Baddon et al. (1989: 81–82) identified four linked objectives based on: motivation; promoting positive attitudes that emphasise unity of purpose and harmony; acting as a defensive and deterrent shield against collectivism; and promoting the virtues of ownership as an inherent 'good'. Research by SenGupta et al. (2006) investigating the relationships between ESO and organisational performance did not find raised employee commitment to the organisation to be a principal mediating factor. The research makes an important distinction between different forms of commitment: affective commitment (managers' 'normal' view of the concept), represented by an emotional identification with the organisation, and continuance commitment, as an exchange-based concept founded on a perceived need by employees to stay with an organisation owing to the high costs of leaving (Meyer and Allen 1997). In their comprehensive analysis of the 1998 WERS findings, SenGupta et al. (2006) found that levels of affective commitment are actually *lower* in workplaces with ESO. Positive impacts on productivity can be explained by lower labour turnover linked to continuance commitment to the organisation and anticipated income losses consequent on quitting. They therefore raise the concept of employee shareholding acting as 'golden handcuffs'.

A major question concerns the impact of allocating limited provisions of equity. It is well established that under these government supported schemes, share allocations to employees rarely exceed 5 per cent of remuneration (Baddon et al. 1989; Pendleton 2005a: 87), with the effect that employees, rather than feeling themselves to be part-owners in their enterprise, simply treat share allocations as a bonus, welcome as long as they do not intrude on their gross pay or pay negotiations (Baddon et al. 1989: 275; Kaaresmaker et al. 2010: 330–31). This bonus question can be tested by asking employees whether and for how long they intend to or actually do retain their share allocations. Research shows that many employees do dispose of their shareholdings quickly, especially those occupying lower positions in the organisational hierarchy (Baddon et al. 1989: 206–15). Managers also often demonstrate opportunistic behaviour. Findings show that senior managers in one of Germany's largest companies 'exercised their options early. A large majority of option recipients sold the shares acquired on exercise' (Sautner and Weber 2009: 147). Similar behaviour has been observed among executives in the finance sector, where large allocations of shares have been quickly disposed of, thereby reinforcing the risk of short-term or dysfunctional decision-making over long-term investment planning (Financial Times 2015).

Two more neglected but related areas need to be considered if we are to attempt an evaluation of ESO. First, what impact does the approach have on decision-making and, by extension, does the practice indicate any positive shift toward reducing inequality (distributional effect) or on democratic decision-making (juridical effect). In the first case, we have indicated that many employees receive only small supplements to remuneration and that shares are often quickly disposed of, especially in the case of lower paid workers. Moreover, as Kaaresmaker et al. point out, the voluntary nature of many schemes heavily favours the better-paid and more secure employees, and in particular managers and men generally, casting 'doubt on the claim that employee share ownership *per se* will lead to more equal distribution of wealth' (Kaaresmaker et al. 2010: 324–25).

There is the additional argument, often put forward by trade unions suspicious of employee share plans, that holding equity in the company in which one is employed represents a migratory shift in risk from investors to workers, who, in the case of company failure face multiple jeopardy through loss of job, earnings and savings. That this is not just a theoretical risk is dramatically demonstrated by the collapse of Enron, which had adopted a contributory savings plan for its employees. Enron was a Texas-based energy-trading conglomerate that was one of the largest companies in the USA before filing for the country's biggest bankruptcy in 2001 as the organisation's culture became increasingly competitive and toxic. In the shadow of major corporate scandal, senior managers compounded its financial problems by attempting to obscure the scale of its failure (Thomas 2002) while stock values plunged in freefall from $80 a share to virtually nothing. Thousands of employees lost their jobs and all employees and pensioners who had invested heavily in the company through share purchase saw their savings decimated. According to *NPR News* (2002), estimates of pension losses amounted to $1 billion: a married couple who were both employed and lost their jobs at the company at the same time lost some $600,000 in retirement savings. Most employees had their retirement savings tied up in a 401(k) retirement savings plan sponsored by the employer. In these plans, workers invest a portion of their salary tax-free at time of investment to support their future retirement, often complemented by a contribution from the employer. In order to spread risk, most of these funds offer a broad spread of equity and other investment vehicles, but Enron managers encouraged heavy self-investment in the company. For employee protection, it is difficult to withdraw invested money, with heavy penalties in the case of pre-retirement withdrawal of funds. In other words employees are largely locked into the scheme, which in the case of Enron had disastrous consequences for employee savers. Richard Oppel Jr., writing in the New York Times (2001), described how the precipitous decline in Enron's stock value 'devastated its employees' retirement plan which was heavy with company stock', a situation made worse as employees 'were prohibited from changing their investments as the stock plunged', as their assets in the company plan were frozen. At Portland General Electric, an Oregon utility owned by Enron, some workers nearing retirement, many of whom also independently invested in the company, saw virtually all their savings plans wiped out. Not everyone lost out though: the then chairman was able to exercise stock options of $180 million in the three years prior to the crash and even made some $20 million through selling overvalued stock in the first seven months of 2001, the year of the company's collapse.

It will be recalled from earlier chapters that one interpretation and objective of EP is its promotion of democratic values and process. The mainstream approaches most often found in liberal market economies described above offer only limited stock ownership to employees, but those who retain their shares are nevertheless assumed to enjoy the same rights and responsibilities as other shareholders. It appears, though, that means to exert corporate influence are severely limited: in over 100 all-employee schemes studied by Baddon and her colleagues, over half offered less than 1 per cent of *aggregate* equity to employees (Baddon et al. 1989: 65). Further, as shareholders, employees make no observable difference to organisational governance. A survey by Pendleton (2005b) of 6,000 employee shareholders found that only 2.3 per cent regularly attend their company's AGM and 92 per cent never attend. Even if they were present, attendance at AGMs of individual shareholders does not, of course, imply any influence, with most decisions controlled through institutional shareholders such as pension funds (Gillan and Starks 2003). With major institutional investors holding the majority of shares, even if all employees were to act collectively, through their equity holdings alone, they would exert minimal influence at corporate level in domestically based companies and even less in global enterprises (Knyght 2010). With regard to workplace control, there is little evidence that limited-ownership share schemes provide opportunities for more participation in decisions at any level. As Strauss (1998: 20) has noted, 'employees have few control rights' and, with share allocations viewed as a gratuity to be disposed of opportunistically, as a stand alone initiative, employee shares do not lead to meaningful advances in employee decision-making participation. Baddon et al. (1989: 262) asked respondents whether SAYE provides greater participation in the company; 60 per cent of SAYE participants disagreed with the proposition, compared with 30 per cent who agreed.

Employee ownership

ESO and EO are often conflated, but despite commonalities, there are significant differences between the two approaches. The most clear-cut is in the allocation of equity, and thereby, the assumption of control: some firms, such as worker cooperatives, are fully owned by their employees (Pencavel 2001). Broad-based share ownership can also be found in a number of well-known companies, from the consistently successful retailer John Lewis in the UK to the telecom giant Huawei in China and Spain's Mondragon cooperative collective. Another option is for a company to be owned (in full or partly) by employees and equity to be held indirectly in trust for employees, either collectively or for individual distribution, for example to provide retirement income. A variation of this sort of scheme is found in the USA, where private occupational pension funds are less common than in the UK, for example.

Proponents of financial participation argue that under propitious conditions, such as complementing shareholding with progressive employment policies, employees can gain some influence on decisions and advance their interests in ways that can promote social harmony. One factor does appear to command common agreement: that participation in company affairs and outcomes seems to be positively related to equity allocations. Positive organisational consequences, including higher productivity, greater flexibility and lower staff turnover, have been reported when share ownership is more evenly distributed and in companies where the majority of shares are employee-owned (Doucouliagos 1995). Kramer (2010) examined sales per employee in 300 firms and found that individual sales were significantly higher in employee-owned companies than in traditional companies. Further, there was a positive association between higher levels of stock and sales per employee. The most advanced employee-owned structures occur when companies are fully owned by employees and/or operate as worker cooperatives. Findings consistently show that those companies with high, majority or complete EO perform well across a range of performance criteria (for comprehensive reviews, see e.g. Blasi et al. 2013 and Freeman 2015). Nevertheless, these companies have conventional management structures and objectives and equity-based participation is encouraged for its contribution towards performance and profitability.

Recent UK findings on EO were provided by the 2012 Nuttall Review, chaired by the adviser on EO for the 2010–2015 Conservative–Liberal Democrat coalition government. This report presented a number of reported favourable outcomes for mainstream share schemes, such as increased commitment and dedication (Nuttall 2012: 13), closer engagement with the company and its objectives (MacLeod and Clarke 2009) and enhanced business performance and employee wellbeing (Nuttall 2012: 14; McQuaid et al. 2012). Nevertheless, care needs to be taken in interpreting the conclusions drawn from various studies used in the Nuttall Review. First, from the government adviser charged with promoting ESO, the case studies tend to be selective and the rhetoric positive, with 'employee ownership is a great idea' providing the opening statement, notwithstanding subsequent reservations raised by the report's own findings.

In the Nuttall Review, Lampel et al. (2010) are cited in their survey of UK enterprises as saying that smaller EO companies (with fewer than 75 staff) perform better on profitability and employment growth than larger ones, where wider distribution of shares has the potential to dilute any ownership effect. Other reservations and qualifications are evident throughout the Nuttall Review. While 'driving innovation' appears to be a positive outcome, 'the evidence is partial and requires further development' (Nuttall 2012: 27). Also, in citing Blasi et al. (2010), the authors state 'shared capitalism [*i.e. combinations of financial participation*] reduced absenteeism, as long as it was also accompanied by supportive forms of human resource policies' (Nuttall 2012: 28). The most consistent factor appears to be, as with profit-sharing above, the relationship between EO and other contingent HR and organisational factors. One potential link is with employee engagement, which is seen as both a facilitator (ibid.: 24; MacLeod and Clarke 2009) and an outcome of ESO. The review rather confusingly argues that benefits 'are best achieved when employee ownership is integrated with ensuring employee engagement' (Nuttall 2012: 14). However, one unstated problem and one that we discuss further in chapter 7 is the problematic definitional and operational status of engagement. This is well demonstrated by two successive paragraphs in the review, the first derived from MacLeod and Clarke (2009) states unequivocally that employee engagement has a positive correlation with an impressive series of organisational and employee benefits, whereas 'on the other hand, while emphasising the correlation, studies also recognised that there has not been a definitive study which has unequivocally established causation between employee engagement and higher employer participation, performance or productivity' (Nuttall 2012: 27). In other words, if the direction of causation is unclear, the status and role of engagement becomes equally unclear.

A contrasting hope held out for 'democratic employee-ownership' expressed by Wilkinson and Pickett (2010: 255) is to help to reverse societal inequality, which, as we saw above, has continued to accelerate over recent years. How this deficit can be remedied is problematic, however, as most conventional companies operating in neoliberal economies are unlikely to be persuaded by arguments for the social and egalitarian benefits of either comprehensive EO or of cooperative enterprise.

There have been more radical schemes that, although operating under market conditions, can assume wider, more societal objectives of securing narrow income differentials, providing a broader ownership base and strategic and democratic decision-making roles for employee representatives. One of the best known of these schemes was the wage earner fund established in Sweden in the early 1980s, following the system devised by trade union economist, Rudolf Meidner, with the aim of grafting 'an element of socialism' onto capitalist production, 'as a step on the road towards more democratic ownership of industry and economic democracy', located between private and state nationalised production (Meidner, quoted in Lansley 2015). The fate of the Meidner plan demonstrates both the pressure and forces that capital owners can bring to bear against radical intervention in the economy and in reforming society more broadly. According to Lansley, the original plan for companies to issue new shares each year, equivalent to 20 per cent of profits, to support a regional funds network, met with considerable opposition from employers and their political allies, largely over fears of enhanced union influence in corporate and political policy-making, leading to political defeat for the Swedish social democratic government (Lansley 2015: 12). Eventually a much revised scheme, less threatening to the established order, was introduced that only lasted a few years and was withdrawn in 1992 by the incoming Conservative government, 'at a time when the Right was beginning to seize the intellectual ascendancy with their belief in the encouragement of free markets' (ibid.: 13). From the 1980s, neoliberal dominance became even more pronounced in Anglo-Saxon countries under the influence of economists such as Friedrich Hayek and Milton Friedman and their political supporters, leading to legalised trade union restrictions, expansion of deregulation, privatisation programmes and encouragement of free-trade globalisation (MacInnes 1987: 46–61), a process which has subsequently spread to other countries (Glyn 2006).

One concern is the impact of these unregulated market forces on fully employee-owned businesses and worker cooperatives: successful ones may be tempted to become conventional businesses, especially if they are in need of developmental capital that cannot be generated internally. Those confronted with market uncertainties and overseas competition could face bankruptcy and potential employee shareholder emiseration. The case of two established UK companies illustrates these potential problems.

Loch Fyne Oysters is a Scottish institution, bought by its employees in April 2003, proudly projecting itself following the sale as 'a company owned and run by its employees' (Erdal 2008: 3). The trajectory of the company is detailed in Erdal's book, its title playing on the Scottish self-sufficiency theme first raised in the film *Local Hero*. Following its conversion, Erdal entertained few doubts: 'Employee-ownership works. It is more productive and spreads wealth more widely than capitalism or socialism ever did and it gives people the opportunity to live their working lives more fully than has ever seemed possible under any system' (ibid.: 7). And yet, a mere nine years later, the company was sold, with unanimous employee support, jointly to a private equity investor and a salmon company. In retrospect, viability threats were always present: the availability and price of salmon can vary dramatically and seafood sales can be highly sensitive to external shocks and events (ibid.: 225–27). Moreover, the company was facing debts following a £1.6 million operating loss in 2011 and had little financial scope to expand into new and lucrative markets.

The case of internationally respected paper-maker Tullis Russell was different as a combination of factors contributed to its demise. These included the insolvency of a major customer, the market for its paper products evaporating with the emergence of digital media, escalating costs of wood pulp and unfavourable exchange rates, contributing to uncompetitive price quotations. More darkly, some industry sources considered high staff costs and problems in making staff reductions in an employee-owned company as contributing to its insolvency. Initially some 500 jobs were in danger of being lost at the Fife plant (PrintWeek 2015). Erdal (2015) is insistent, however, that the company's employee ownership since 1994 was not to blame for the receivership, identifying the external factors noted above, rather than internal ownership problems, for the collapse. Indeed, he comments on the company's longevity in a sector where most UK paper mills have long ago vanished and cites the company's consistently high productivity performance and long-standing staff cooperation as factors that have maintained the plant.

The point is that, as a number of writers have affirmed, employee-owned enterprises and cooperatives always face problems in generating investment funds, which at times of austerity, can make them especially vulnerable to takeover or collapse. Pendleton et al. (1998) found that many of the bus cooperatives established in the 1980s experienced difficulties through their inability to purchase new and expensive stock. Pencavel's review of worker cooperatives of the Pacific Northwest arrived at similar conclusions (Pencavel 2001). When the cooperative is well established and has access to secure internal funds or external finance, as is the case, for example, for the extensive Mondragon networks in the Basque region of Spain, the chances of survival are much greater (Jefferis and Mason 1990). Also, in this special case, risks can be spread through a group consisting of more than 250 different cooperatives and associated businesses, employing altogether some 100,000 people (Arando et al. 2010). A further risk to cooperative ideals has been exposed by studies that reveal the extent to which business models and decision-making structures in cooperative companies actually parallel those of conventional practice (Welford 1990: 305).

There is little question that, despite formal moves to democratic control, internal power relations in producer cooperatives and employee-owned companies can continue to favour managerial elites, potentially leading to tension, possible degeneration of cooperative principles (Ben-Ner 1984) and reversion to a conventional business structure (Carter 1990). Maintaining democratic principles has been an essential contributor to Mondragon's longevity: 'it is the essential democratic nature of the Mondragon setup that enables measured and effective adjustments to be continuously undertaken and at lower costs than competitors in conventional firms' (Arando et al. 2010: 4). Nevertheless, despite possible threats in volatile markets, employee-owned firms in the UK can flourish, as demonstrated by the continuing success of John Lewis.

The John Lewis Partnership currently has nearly 90,000 employees or partners, as they are termed. The company has been in operation since the mid-nineteenth century. In 1929 the founder's son transferred ownership to employees through a partnership trust established to distribute a share of the profits as a bonus, which has subsequently been delivered on an annual basis, often accompanied by considerable media publicity. The annual staff bonus has averaged about 15 per cent of pay for the past twenty years, varying between 9 and 22 per cent over the past ten years, calculated according to salary level (Cathcart 2013). Alongside ownership, voice for employees has been provided by a system of representative councils and an open communication network, accompanied by a wide range of benefits not usually found in the retail sector. The Partnership has maintained sales and profitability throughout the recession and its success as a business model has attracted the attention of UK centre-left political parties sympathetic to its participative approach.

For the past 50 years the John Lewis model has attracted both support and a degree of scepticism from authorities such as Pateman (1970), who presented the company as an example of pseudo-participation in which putative ownership of the enterprise does not bestow meaningful control, and Ramsay (1980), who accused the company's paternalism of directing employee representatives toward 'apathy and triviality', underpinned by their organisational impotence. While generally supportive of the Partnership, Cathcart (2013) warns that the potential for degeneration of democratic principle and practice under tight economic conditions is always present. Whether the extensive participation arrangements at the Partnership can be diagnosed as 'pseudo' is questionable, however, for at least two reasons. First, they satisfy Pateman's condition that participation involves 'a modification … of the orthodox authority structure' (Pateman 1970: 68). Second, bearing in mind that Pateman acknowledges that, while profit distribution 'accentuates the prevailing hierarchical structure of remuneration' (Flanders et al. 1968: 42), the 'Partnership has gone some way to meeting the condition of economic equality regarded as necessary for participation by the theorists of participatory democracy' (Pateman 1970: 77).

Nevertheless, it is also clear from the authoritative study by Flanders et al. that employees do not have the same power resources as management for decision-making: 'the decision process itself was basically the normal one of management deciding what it wanted to achieve, and preparing the ground in such a way that orders issued were likely to be obeyed' (Flanders et al. 1968: 177). On the other hand, advocates for the Partnership argue that it has to operate within the rules of a competitive capitalist economy and that while employer and employees necessarily have different and potentially colliding agendas, there are participative mechanisms available to reconcile surface differences. Rather than pursuing 'triviality', it is argued that representatives prefer to seek 'participation on operational rather than strategic concerns' that remain the province of the executive board (Cathcart 2009; 2013). It is, however, noticeable that for such an enlightened enterprise there has been no trade union presence. One important development that might be expected to provoke friction has been noted by Cathcart (2013) and helps confirm the characterisation by Flanders et al. of control relations. This was the tripling of the maximum pay ratio between senior managers and junior partners in London, from 25 times the pay of a partner to 75 times. This considerable constitutional change received little internal adverse comment and has not appeared to alter levels of employee satisfaction or support in annual attitude surveys conducted among employees throughout the Partnership. A second point of friction in recent years has been the exclusion of adjunct workers, such as cleaners, from the participatory programme. Nevertheless, anecdotal evidence suggests that the range of benefits offered to partners, including annual bonuses, allied to the co-ownership culture, in which employment security features strongly, has been instrumental in maintaining high levels of employee support. For John Lewis, share ownership as an integral element of a wider participative philosophy appears to play a positive role on employee attitudes, though managerial control over strategic organisational affairs is safeguarded by the constitutional structure and by the dominant culture, in which there is 'a push by management to redefine democracy in ways which privilege business interests and managerial prerogative' (ibid.: 617). It is perhaps for the above reasons that the Partnership continues to be successful.

Conclusions

In this chapter we have identified a number of attributes of profit-sharing, ESO and EO. While profit-sharing offers none of the claimed property-derived benefits of capital ownership, many studies do report a positive link between it and desired outcomes, such as productivity. Often, though, these findings come with reservations: positive outcomes are often reported when profit-sharing and employee share schemes interact with other financial participation practices, as well as with a variety of voice mechanisms. Hence, drawing on WERS data, Pendleton and Robinson (2015: 1) found that 'productivity effects of individualized incentives are enhanced by profit-sharing' that also 'enhances the effect of collective PBR'. In other words, the standalone status of profit-sharing as a performance stimulant is questionable. Further, care has to be taken in interpreting results, as comparative studies are difficult to construct because of the different ideologies and policies that inform practice across countries and consequent diversity in available schemes and practices (Kaaresmaker and Poutsma 2006). Also, while there is anecdotal evidence that schemes that benefit senior staff exclusively or unequally are looked on with disfavour by less advantaged employees, there is little hard evidence to confirm these assertions; in the meantime, the equality gap between higher and lower paid staff continues to grow, often levered through the use of profit-related bonus schemes and selective equity provision schemes, leading to the suggestion that senior managers are more concerned about their own remuneration than that of their employees.

A more specific and arguably self-serving argument for rewarding senior executives generously was the concern that, without direct performance-related rewards, senior management may fail to aim at maximising profits and opt instead for satisficing or for following 'their own sectional interests' (Beirne 2013: 76). Under these market-orientated conditions, so-called 'fat cats' have continued to thrive (Erdal 2011), feeding off a generous mix of profit shares, substantial deferred equity schemes and salaries determined by executive remuneration committees composed largely of fellow executives (Conyon 1997; Conyon et al. 2009). Earning ratios between chief executives and average salaries have increased eightfold between 1980 and 2010 in the USA and from a ratio of 20 to one to 150 to one in the UK (Beirne 2013: 77–78). According to the High Pay Centre, a FTSE 100 chief executive earned 47 times as much as the average employee in 1997, in contrast to 2012, when the ratio had risen to 133 times (High Pay Centre 2014). In monetary terms, the average FTSE 100 CEO earned over £5 million in 2016, compared with the average worker's £27,645. Not surprisingly, these startling revelations have received critical media and social media comment on the potential negative impact of short-term profit and individual wealth-seeking at the expense of longer-term investment and even of organisational survival, as witnessed by companies such as Enron in the USA and financial institutions everywhere.

We have seen earlier that income inequality can be associated with community and social problems. For example, the examination by Wilkinson and Pickett (2010) of 170 academic papers revealed a clear associative pattern between inequality and mental and physical health and wellbeing. As we have seen above, income inequality is growing in many societies but those with lower levels of inequality, such as Scandinavian countries, tend to present fewer social and health problems, as well as higher economic growth (Freeman 2015). Clearly, the workplace can be an important source of generating and exacerbating inequality. From the organisational perspective, research shows that 'unequal workplaces experienced higher levels of discontent and lower levels of employee well-being' (High Pay Centre 2014: 6). A survey of 1,923 workplaces, covering 21,981 employees, was conducted for the High Pay Centre and pointed to several areas where high unequal pay ratios are associated with organisational dysfunctionality in the form of workplace conflict, higher stress levels, and lower satisfaction and commitment, signalled by higher labour turnover rates (High Pay Centre 2014). We can recall that the attraction and objective of employee participation is to provide both procedural and distributive justice at work and it can be argued that these considerable and growing pay inequalities are representative of neither and could contribute to the negative behaviours and outcomes identified by the High Pay Centre research. While we do not have precise figures on the proportion of executive remuneration consisting of profit-related supplements, we do know that about three-quarters of the pay of top CEOs is linked to performance in the USA, and about 70 per cent in the UK; with the popularity of PRP being maintained in both countries, it seems likely that a sizeable proportion of executive income consists of profit-related monetary supplements that are inaccessible to the majority of their employees. While trade union attitudes to financial participation can be formally hostile (though less so in practice) or at least indifferent (Baddon et al. 1989: 45) and schemes do tend to be established in unionised enterprises, there is little reported evidence that collective influence has been undermined, notwithstanding union fears that profit-sharing and limited share ownership could weaken or replace pay negotiations or distance union negotiators from collective bargaining generally (Kaaresmaker et al. 2010: 330). Fears of adverse effects on union membership of schemes whose underlying aim may be to offer a more unitarist relationship between employees and managers have also not been confirmed. While financial participation is often established in unionised environments, which by their nature are likely to be large, it is in smaller, especially employee-owned, establishments that the influence of schemes on employee attitudes and performance seems to be more pronounced, possibly because free-riding is less likely to be an intervening negative factor (ibid.: 321; Kramer 2010). Finally, while financial participation, whether through profit-sharing or equity provision, is likely to continue to be desirable for employers, especially when government tax incentives add to the attraction, we should note that in addition to the reservations noted above, researchers urge caution about the impact of such schemes, especially because causality can be problematic. Hence, Kaaresmaker and Poutsma (2006) issue a number of methodology-based warnings: these have been summarised by Knyght (2010) to include the question whether positive effects are attributable to 'ownership structure or other factors such as leadership', lack of focus on the relationship between share provision and individual wellbeing or indeed other major dimensions of workers' dispositions at work (see also SenGupta et al. 2006). A study by Kakabadse and Kakabadse (2008) of leadership in transnational organisations intimated that, rather than share schemes or profit-sharing alone, factors such as effectively trained and capable managers, progressive HR policies, embracing work–life balance and effective subordinate support, and implemented corporate social responsibility policies could all be instrumental in promoting positive employee attitudes and performance.

Chapter 6

High-performance work and its antecedents

Introduction

Although mechanisms have not always been clear, management EPV initiatives, when used in combination, appear to exert some positive effects on employee behaviour and performance. It has proven difficult to isolate the identity or contribution of specific components of the combination – what Ramsay et al. (2000) termed 'the black box'. However it is important for policy-makers, employers, employees and academics to know what initiatives have been commonly included in the combinations and what their effects have been. These combinations, or systems, of work practices may be found under different headings, the common ones focusing on high-performance work systems (HPWS), high-involvement work systems (HIWS) and high-commitment work systems (HCWS). To avoid confusion and unnecessary terminological duplication we shall use the single acronym HPWS to describe and analyse these combinations of individual human resource practices. Legge (2005: 19), however, while acknowledging that the terms may be used interchangeably, does distinguish between HCWS and HPWS, the former focusing on job-intrinsic factors such as security, job design and development as routes that can lead to high performance through enhanced commitment, while HPWS can potentially bypass commitment by including 'harder' HR elements, such as loosened job security and concern *'only* with high productivity/profits' (emphasis in the original). Boxall and Purcell (2016: 189) state their preference for the HIWS label because it is more descriptive in 'signaling a shift away from the low-involvement characteristics of traditional factory work'. On the other hand, as the end-objective of these initiatives is to enhance performance and are promoted on a wider sectoral platform today than in factories alone, and as the rhetoric tends to support commitment as the foundation for enhanced performance, we incline toward using the term HPWS as offering a generic and representative coverage of the range of practices and systems under review. Nevertheless, as we show later, and, *pace* Legge, this broad designation can conceal a number of tensions and differences in interpretation (Angelis et al. 2011).

Origins of HPWS: lean production

We start this stage of our enquiry by investigating the influences on HPWSs and their origins, which as a combined set of practices only came to prominence in the 1990s (Harley 2014). We can identify a number of mutually reinforcing routes to the current prominence of HPWSs. First among these has been the impact of successful Japanese methods, notably lean production, on Western, specifically American and British, management thought and practice. Second is the purported elevation of personnel management to HRM and its focus on the formulation of best practice. Third, we can identify a raft of influential research projects and publications that have done much to raise the profile of HPWS among practitioners.

The oil shocks of the early 1970s, followed by the subsequent slow decline of the American auto industry and the rise of high-quality but inexpensive Japanese cars, led to increasing academic and employer interest in the work design and operating methods employed by Japanese manufacturing companies. At the same time comparisons between Japanese productivity and competitor countries indicated big and growing advantages to Japan (Wood 1993), leading both management researchers and employers to closely examine Japanese production methods in the hope of being able to emulate them (Jürgens 1989). A concurrent influence was that domestic production by Japanese companies in the UK was expanding, with inward-investing companies like Nissan and Honda being prime examples. Though the aggregate proportion of British workers employed in Japanese subsidiaries operating in the UK was and remains only small, these companies nevertheless received considerable policy and academic attention, typified by Oliver and Wilkinson's (1992) admired, if rather grandiloquently titled, examination of the Japanese transfer experience, *The Japanization of British Industry*. The salient features of the Japanese approach basically centred around offering more responsibility to workers by involving them in task determination and allocation through quality-focused teams and consensus management in exchange for employment security and a system of pay and advancement based on seniority (Ouchi 1981). The whole system was infused with the doctrine of *kaizen*, the drive for continuous improvement and, importantly, underpinned by an established supportive social system of 'welfare corporatism' (Dore 1973), not found in the UK or USA. Though not specifically referring to Japan, Richard Walton strongly articulated the argument for a commitment-based and quality-driven approach in his influential 1985 article in which he critiqued the rigidly control-centred, manager-directed and less productive methods associated with Fordist and Taylorised production in the USA. A parallel commitment- or involvement-driven approach was advocated at the same time by Lawler (1986). Both Walton's and Lawler's analyses and prescriptions were clearly strongly informed by Japanese practice.

Further, an enthusiastic and openly evangelistic approach toward Japanese 'lean' and quality-based production methods heavily informed the account given by Nissan's personnel director Peter Wickens of people management at the company's UK subsidiary (Wickens 1987). However, a more universal impact and call for action was made by Womack et al.'s (1990) evaluation of Toyota's lean production system. When this best-selling book describing the system was first published, Toyota was half the size of America's General Motors. Within 20 years it had become the world's largest car manufacturer, with lean production cited as the principal reason for its success. The principles behind lean production were straightforward: establish and nourish semi-autonomous multiskilled teams with direct production responsibilities and make the teams accountable for output quality, thereby removing unnecessary slack, stripping out waste, maintaining just-in-time stock levels and promoting *kaizen* at all stages of production. Womack and Jones (2003) later expanded their prescriptive 'lean' exhortations from the manufacturing sector to embrace other sectors, including services. Lean production (or 'lean' as it became simply known) clearly has close links with HPWSs, whether as a freestanding management practice that can feed into HPWSs or as an integral part of the HPWS process itself (Boxall 2012; Angelis et al. 2011). In either case, there is often the unstated assumption of a positive contribution to a more rewarding workplace experience and, through this, to performance and client satisfaction. In this sense, though it was first introduced in high-volume auto manufacturing, lean was subsequently portrayed by its supporters as a radical departure from fragmented, individualised and tightly controlled jobs anywhere, irrespective of whether control was secured through direct supervision or by means of technological surveillance, to the dedicated teams that define lean today (Carter et al. 2011, 2016). On the basis of their extensive international research in car plants, Womack et al. (1990) argued that creative teamworking could moderate the alienating effects of assembly-line work and, through involvement in task-based decision-making, enhance team productive performance, to the mutual benefit of all stakeholders. These assumptions and their implications have subsequently been challenged to the extent that 'lean production … has strong elements of continuity with Taylorism' (Wilkinson and Dundon 2010: 178). If this is indeed the case, its positive associations with HPWSs and their impact on workplace behaviour are also questionable.

An initial problem, and one that has parallels with earlier enthusiasm for the transfer of Japanese modes of working generally, included attempts to transfer aspects of the Toyota lean production experience to manufacturing in the different economic and cultural contexts presented either by neoliberal-dominated governmental policies (Delbridge 1998) or to cultures in which lean might be confronted by social values and attitudes antithetical to its success. An example of the latter was presented when a lean system was unsuccessfully introduced in a Swedish plant acquired by a Japanese company. Existing operations based on a Swedish sociotechnical systems approach reliant on team autonomy, in which 'operators built a complete product' with high levels of self-management, were replaced by a lean process where 'operators only build a small part of the product along assembly lines' (Oudhuis and Olsson 2015: 276). The operational aftermath was disastrous, leading to increased labour turnover, loss of interest in performing tasks and a reduction in 'operators' pride as craftsmen' (ibid.: 275). These differences in approach were attributable to cultural differences between Sweden and Japan. The authors conclude that a production system such as lean that is 'based on one particular cultural system' cannot be transferred successfully without 'taking into account culturally based presumptions and differences' (ibid.: 279).

Nevertheless, there is little doubt that some lean innovations in manufacturing have been successful in raising performance (de Menezes et al. 2010), but whether this is through positive transformative effects of lean or through increased pressure on workers through a form of evolved or 'team Taylorism' triggered through workforce reductions has been the subject of considerable research attention (Baldry et al. 1998; Willmott 1994). This attention, in the UK and USA especially, has intensified through the extension of lean principles to the service sector, and specifically to the public arena, where budgetary pressures and an austerity-dominated tightening of service delivery have provided fertile ground for lean implementation. In the USA, Esbenshade et al. (2016) made a study of business process reengineering (BPR) in a California welfare agency. The researchers claim that BPR has much in common with lean, in that they are both customer-driven and aim 'to improve customer service via rationalized workflow and increased process control' (ibid.: 78). The case study involved a survey of 342 welfare workers, followed by in-depth interviews with 24 of the staff. BPR consisted of three integrated elements: computerised case management, shift from casework to a task-based system and the establishment of a call centre, all leading to elements of confusion and stress, compounded by variable and inconsistent practice, despite the programme's intention to both increase customer satisfaction and 'enhance the performance and job satisfaction of the … staff'. The results were conclusive: intensification and reduced autonomy for staff and deteriorating service quality for clients (ibid.: 90). While not assigning direct blame to the middle and lower levels of management charged with introducing and managing the process, the authors found that, under contemporary neoliberal pressures, there was 'strong evidence that quantitative efficiency was prioritised over service quality' by senior management in a process in which little autonomy was offered throughout the California welfare agency (ibid.: 92).

Carter and his colleagues have published a number of important articles examining the application and effects of lean in UK public services (Carter et al. 2011, 2013, 2016). One case study used a combination of methods to examine health problems of clerical workers in six tax processing centres consequent to staff reductions and imposition of government efficiency savings, with special focus on lean (Carter et al. 2013). The findings revealed 'significant social malaise that national-level statistics merely gesture towards', all indicative of heightened stress through increased work pressures. Declining health especially affected female employees. The study concludes that 'lean's transformation of work bears most responsibility for the increased ill-health' (ibid.: 762). An earlier paper by Carter et al. (2011) also investigated the consequences of lean introduced into the government's tax-collecting service. The authors contend that, rather than offering greater discretion, work reorganisation post-lean embraced strong Taylorist controls, which reduced work that had previously held high skill content to that resembling routine and fragmented semiskilled assembly line operations, in a process termed by Sennett (2006: 127) as 'disempowerment'. Moreover, the teamwork that existed prior to lean and that purportedly lies at its core was seriously undermined following the introduction of lean. Though there have been a number of research studies indicating the pressures faced by employees under lean (Carter et al. 2016), there have also been others that point in more positive directions. Research by Procter and Radnor (2014) is of especial interest because it focuses on the same agency that provides the locus for Carter et al.'s critical analysis, though Procter and Radnor's conclusions on the role of lean tend to be more favourable in offering teams 'indirect autonomy'. Their study and its conclusions provoked a robust response from Carter et al. (2016) who contended that it suffers from a range of definitional, logical, methodological and evidential deficiencies that obscure the oppressive impact of lean on clerical workers, and also on their clients.

Positive findings for lean, from Womack et al.'s pioneering work and subsequently, tend to focus on the outcomes of lean in terms of 'gaining more for less', while the more critical papers focus on the actual processes through which these objectives may be achieved. The uncomfortable truth is that lean as it has been interpreted and practised in the UK and USA can be associated with higher output or better quality, whether in manufacturing or services, but serious questions remain as to whether these changes are linked to tighter and more oppressive management regimes, which in themselves originate from imposed targets set amidst budgetary constraints and staff reductions, or with a genuine enhancement in skills and team-based decision-making autonomy. At present, the balance of research opinion appears to be in favour of tighter regimes. It should also not be forgotten that many of these schemes have been introduced in the era of the new public management, the application of which, even for professional workers (Carter et al. 2016), is scarcely compatible with widening and deepening employee autonomy.

The influence of people management

A second major influence on the emergence and profile of HPWS has been the putative evolution of people management from the largely formulaic and administrative function of personnel management to its current if questionable SHRM status. The roots of this development and subsequent shift to different strategic models of HRM have been considered in Chapter 3; at this stage we focus on reported links between strategic HRM and HPWSs or, in Legge's words (Legge 2001: 25), HRM operationalised in terms of HPWS. As we show above, American – and subsequently, British – management thinking, influenced by the threats and challenges of Japanese efficiency and quality in the 1980s, shifted toward more effective utilisation of worker skills and aptitudes through offering and rewarding individual and group responsibility, summarised in the 'work smarter, not harder' sloganising of management writers and consultants. Probably the most successful of these proselytising writers were Peters and Waterman, whose book *In Search of Excellence*, first published in 1982, has gone on to achieve sales in the millions. The two consultants examined 43 high-performing American companies and identified eight common reasons which attributed to their 'success'. These include: identifying people as the prime source of quality to achieve high productivity; operating a lean system minimising waste; and offering ground-level autonomy founded on strong organisational cultural values. Despite pointed critical questions about methodology, analysis and the poor subsequent performance and even failure of some of the companies (Guest 1992; Legge 2005: 118), the book's messages have provided considerable and lasting food for thought for its management audience. Notwithstanding the proliferation of popular but less than robust analyses, the success of Japanese companies and those American enterprises that pursued progressive routes to higher labour productivity led to a more rigorous assessment of people management approaches, from which the principal strategic management models emerged. As we saw in chapter 3, four main schools of thought have been identified, all of which focus on the effective utilisation of human resources, though the best practice approach, which endeavours to identify and apply the key universal components of an effective people management policy, irrespective of context or sector, clearly has the closest affinity with HPWS (Legge 2005; Boxall and Purcell 2016: 72–79).

Research on HPWSs

Over the past 20 years there has been a stream of influential publications examining HPWS, and reviews and recommendations from these have found their way into standard and rightly highly-regarded HR textbooks, such as, for the UK, Bratton and Gold (2012), Boxall and Purcell (2016) and, internationally, Briscoe et al. (2016); into college and university courses aimed at undergraduate and postgraduate students; and intensive courses directed at executives. This interest has largely been stimulated by heightened attentiveness to company performance in response to increasing global competitive pressures, which in turn has prompted a series of high-quality, if contested, cross-sectional studies, principally of practice in the USA and to a lesser extent in the UK. The empirical core of these studies has been the attempt to identify key contributory people management features of high performance, often defined, as Legge points out, in terms of financial improvement (Legge 2005: 27). Described by Boxall and Purcell (2016: 76) as 'one of the most influential papers ever written in HRM', and certainly one of the most cited, Huselid (1995) is a useful reference point for examining dominant components of an HPWS-based strategy. Huselid drew on 13 nominated 'high performance' practices, including attitude surveys, performance appraisal and performance related pay, profit-sharing and quality-of-life initiatives. He investigated the deployment of the designated practices in surveys conducted among HR managers in some 1,000 companies and then compared utilisation with various performance measures, concluding that greater use of the practices was associated with higher levels of performance. Huselid's empirical studies were complemented by a number of methodologically similar approaches, both in the UK (e.g. Patterson et al. 1997) and the USA (e.g. Macduffie 1995, whose study also included car plants in Europe and Japan; Pfeffer (1994)), with all claiming to identify key stimulators of performance. Arising from these and other studies emerged the contemporary policy, practitioner and research interest in HPWS.

Having briefly scanned the main factors contributing to the development of HPWS, and before scrutinising their impact in more depth, we first attempt to define the concept and its significance. After many years of research on HPWS, Harley (2014: 83) points out that, although disagreements over the identities of component practices persist, there is 'broad agreement' about its meaning and intent. Based on his own earlier work (Harley 2005) and that of Appelbaum (2002), he identifies HPWS as delegated work organisation that encourages teamworking and high-scope jobs with task autonomy, supported by targeted recruitment processes and training provision to enhance skills, with the system underpinned by performance-based rewards. Critically, though, these practices are not operated randomly or in isolation, but as 'mutually reinforcing systems' that serve to provide performance gains greater than would result from the 'sum of the effects of the individual components' (Harley 2005: 39). A similar categorisation is provided by Boxall and Purcell (2016: 189), who, like Harley, see HPWSs as a potential counter to Taylorist production forms, but include a job-enrichment or empowerment process embracing provision of means to undertake the job, motivation to do it and opportunities for advancement through organisational support and voice provisions (ibid.: 155). Under these favourable conditions, it is argued that employees become better prepared to make well-informed decisions and to undertake higher-level skills development, thereby receiving rewards commensurate with their inputs. Though the majority of commentators focus on the relationship between workers and immediate work environment as the source of raising performance through higher commitment, a wider definition of HPWS is offered by Wood through the extension of participation in decision-making to the organisation *as a whole,* though the scope and levels of participation are not elaborated on, other than specifying the possibility of direct or indirect approaches (Wood 2010: 409).

While there is general agreement over the intention and purpose of HPWS and some difference of view over possible participative levels covered by the system, more complex and contentious issues focus on which component practices are included in performance-seeking 'bundles' and on the strength and direction of their effects. Also, notwithstanding Wood's affirmatory comment (Wood 2010: 408) that HPWS has 'become a crucial part of management thought', the extent to which it is factually represented in organisational usage needs to be examined. Moreover, assessing HPWS outcomes is highly problematic because of the 'non-descriptive' nature of the terminology, the uncertainty of identifying relevant inputs and the lack of consensus on the meaning of 'high-performing' (Boxall and Macky 2014: 964). Legge's insightful interrogation of one authority's suggestion (Pfeffer 1994) 'that there is an identifiable set of best HR practices that have universal, additive, positive effects on performance' (Legge 2001: 24) forms a useful starting point for our enquiry. Her analysis suggests, as revealed by different studies, that it is indeed difficult to find one identifiable set of HPWS practices with these positive attributes.

An early analysis of five separate American studies by Becker and Gerhart (1996) found that 'of 27 practices included in these studies, not a single one is common to all five'. In addition Legge comments that of 15 practices 'identified in WERS ... 1998 ... only seven appear on the American list' (Legge 2001: 25). Perhaps a more significant problem in linking HPWS to performance is in identifying the nature of the interaction between the variables, the dynamics of which are compared to those in a 'black box', from which cross-sectional studies are ill-suited to derive causative relationships (Harley 2014: 88; Legge 2001: 28, 2005: 29–30; see also e.g. cautionary comments by Boxall and Macky 2014: 977 on their methodology). In other words, we have little idea of what is actually contributing to performance, or how factors are interacting to contribute to performance, however this may be defined and assessed. Even the role of the ubiquitous 'voice' is problematic as the 'evidence concerning the role of direct voice ... is limited and fragmentary ... that concerning representative forms of voice in HPWS is even more so' (Harley 2014: 90).

A further problematic is that the intermediary or mediating variable between high-performance work systems and actual performance is expressed through enhanced commitment. Therefore the introduction of the system is expected to have a positive commitment-inducing impact on employees, but, in addition to the difficulty of actually specifying commitment (to what?), some studies have pointed toward loose connections between HPWS and commitment and in particular to more pressurised work and to stress, adding some weight to Legge's contention that HPWS is in fact not commitment-seeking. Ramsay et al. (2000) conducted an analysis of the 1998 WERS and found an association between HPWS and heightened feelings of job strain as well as lower satisfaction with pay. Heightened pressure is reported in a number of surveys, but especially in case studies able to investigate employee responses to the interventions in greater depth (e.g. Danford 1998; Parker and Slaughter 1988). Data from national surveys of British workers in 1992 and 2000 analysed by White et al. (2003) found that some practices, including performance appraisal, group work and individual pay incentives, can adversely affect work–life balance for employees through pressures on the use of available time. These effects could, of course, be a consequence of enhanced voluntary work commitment impacting on free time, but longer-term consequences for both employees and their employers are unlikely to be beneficial (Cunningham et al. 1996).

Methodological issues are raised by a number of commentators, in particular the limitations of surveys in determining cause and effect. Legge (2001: 22), in her sustained critique of HPWS research, points out that 'different data sources ... generate different ... interpretations', with differences expressed both within quantitative analyses and between them and more intensive longitudinal case-studies. Among her criticisms of HPWS surveys she cites, in addition to the diversity of individual practices identified as 'high commitment' in different studies, problems in a practice's specification and measurement or even the lack of agreement on its positive or negative status in affecting performance (Legge 2001; Becker and Gerhart 1996: 784). An example here would be the inclusion of performance appraisal and performance related pay as commitment-inducing factors. Studies have shown that employees often associate these factors more with managerial control than with involvement or empowerment (e.g. Arthur 1994; Boxall and Purcell 2016: 76). Further critiques include the use of a single respondent (often an HR manager who can have responsibility for the system under investigation but may not be entirely knowledgeable about its grassroots implementation or objective about effects) in large-scale postal surveys of complex enterprises, which also casts doubt on interpretive and generalizable validity and reliability (Legge 2001: 26). More broadly for EPV, we can add the following: potential difficulties in establishing causality and interaction among a range of potential influences (the 'black box' factor); the problem of identifying suitable benchmarking dates; and the difficulty of specifying exactly what to measure (Wilkinson and Dundon 2010). Huselid's (1995) seminal study that associated the presence of specified practices with higher levels of both productivity and financial performance is not immune from criticism. Methodological shortcomings identified include: the difficulty of establishing causality through a cross-sectional survey approach; restricting investigation to commercial enterprises; including job analysis as a high commitment factor; and financial indicators that can only provide limited evidence of overall impact (Huczynski and Buchanan 2001: 686; Wood 2010: 420). In another influential study, Pfeffer (1998) concludes that a number of participative elements (some different from Huselid's) contribute effectively to organisational performance. In both these cases we should be aware of the danger of using 'crude short-term measures of profitability or efficiency for evaluating employee participation programmes [that] can lead to incorrect conceptualizations of cause and effect' (Gollan and Xu 2015: NP7).

Another relevant but rather neglected factor identified by Legge (2005: 31) when defining and evaluating performance is the influence of national culture and institutions. She contrasts the potential impact on people management of the 'patient capital' policies adopted in the coordinated market economy of

Germany with short-term profit optimisation and cost minimisation approaches that dominate free-market Anglo-Saxon economies and their constituent enterprises. It is in these economies that schisms between adopting commitment-seeking HPWSs and managing short-term labour costs can be most evident. This aspect is demonstrated in a national survey of New Zealand workers, in which Boxall and Macky conclude that two conditions are necessary for HPWS to be beneficial for employees: first, genuine enhancement of autonomy and personal control, underpinned by structural arrangements for communication, equitable reward and opportunities for development; the second condition relates to recognising and mitigating the potential damaging effects on employee welfare of work intensification and extensification (Boxall and Macky 2014: 976–77). As Danford et al. (2004) found in their aircraft industry study, these contrasting features of HPWS and intensification often accompany or follow organisational restructuring exercises, such as delayering and staff reductions. Boxall and Macky's findings also help to substantiate the claim made by Wood (2010: 414–15) that positive HPWSs comprise two different but supportive processes or systems, consisting of bundles of task-based practices backed by a supportive 'human resource' system that includes low-status differentials, comprehensive training and performance pay based on group performance. Wood presents a number of studies that demonstrate 'associations between measures of human resource management systems and performance' (ibid.: 420), which 'collectively are no better or worse than those of the high involvement management studies', indicating that positive impact can arise from alternative and probably combined sources, the dynamics of which are yet to be confirmed.

Evidence of actual take-up, usage and longevity of HPWS is also difficult to determine with confidence, owing to the different terminologies used and the varying pressures on organisations when deciding whether to invest in systems, with no guarantee of measurable return, especially during times of austerity. For this reason, it has been contended that HPWSs are less likely to be found in low-technology production and unsophisticated mass service provision, where minimising labour costs rather than developing human capital are paramount (Boxall and Purcell 2010: 41), or in labour-intensive sectors, where competitive advantage may be achieved through low-skill work and the availability of low-cost and easily replaceable labour, rather than through investment in advanced technology. Conversely, it has been argued (Harley 2014: 86) that HPWSs are more likely to be found in unionised workplaces and sectors where employers will be hoping to engage unions and their members in closer partnership for mutual gain (Danford et al. 2008; Liu et al. 2009). It may be expected therefore, that when enterprises are reliant on employees as a prime or even unique source for better quality or delivery of product or service, as seen in the resource-based view of strategic HRM (see Chapter 3), there is greater likelihood of investment in HPWSs. Reflecting on an earlier iteration of the WERS surveys (Cully et al. 1999), Legge reports 'the absence of any widespread, extensive adoption of HCM practices' in the UK or indeed in the USA (Legge 2005: 31).

Unfortunately, the authoritative WERS 2011 study did not directly investigate the incidence or effects of HPWSs in the UK, but there are a number of clues that suggest that the use of practices consistent with a high-performance approach has risen since Cully et al.'s 1999 report and has been sustained, despite the onset of recessionary pressures between the 2004 and 2011 surveys. On the other hand, policy changes, including the ICE 2005 regulations, have been implemented during the more recent period (see chapter 9), and these 'might have been expected to have more widespread influence on workplace practice' (van Wanrooy et al. 2013: 75). In the event, in 2011, a slightly higher number of managers than in 2004 reported that they consult employees on workplace changes that affected them, usually through direct rather than representative consultation. Employees, though, offered a less rosy picture: only a third reported that managers were good or very good at permitting them to influence decisions and 'only two fifths were satisfied with the amount of involvement they had in decision-making' (ibid.: 76). Recent analyses of coverage in different countries also report patchy deployment of *systems*, i.e. combinations of elements expected to act in a performance-directed synergistic fashion, coupled with the suspicion that from a practical point of view 'managers do not take it seriously' (Boxall and Purcell 2016: 77), unless they identify specific approaches compatible with their HR procedures, organisational culture and the markets which they serve.

Conclusions

Numerous studies do indicate the existence of positive links between HPWS and performance, though the complex dynamics and interactions between specific elements or between elements, culture and organisational structure suggest that it is difficult to identify or predict specific causes and effects. Generally, though, it seems, first, that high-performance bundles, supported by an HR infrastructure compatible with the organisational culture and appropriate to its operating strategy, are associated with positive behavioural effects, though a negative factor may be introduced through association between HPWSs and work intensification, extensification and stress (Carter et al. 2013; Esbenshade et al. 2016). Associations between HPWS and lean production models that have been identified as intensifying work indicate that these contingencies do occur. A second factor appears to be that identifying a direct link between EPV and HPWSs in supporting performance has not yet proven conclusive. Some commentators see EPV as an important catalyst for reinforcing the impact of HPWS, while others have failed to identify the mediating impact of voice practices, whether direct or indirect, on performance. Third, HPWSs (alongside sophisticated HR systems) are more likely to be found in high-tech and quality-based sectors and organisations, especially in large enterprises operating in more than one country. Finally, HPWSs are more generally associated with organisations that recognise trade unions, which by their nature tend to be large and often well staffed with teams of HR specialists. Nevertheless, we should bear in mind earlier findings, namely that pressures are being exerted on professional and high added-value employees to concede their expert or specialist autonomy in order to comply with managerial objectives that can undermine professional authority and may not be compatible with formal commitment-based HPWS policies. Moreover the presence of HPWS is somewhat patchy and enjoys only a limited presence in a large subset of organisations, including some SMEs and those sectors and enterprises adopting low-skilled policies or providing precarious employment conditions. Finally, and especially with respect to the UK, the seemingly intractable obstacle of weak productivity, the very problem that HPWSs might be expected to address, is still very much in evidence.

Chapter 7

Empowering and engaging employees?
Or simply reinventing the wheel?

Introduction

This chapter questions the extent to which empowerment and engagement resemble or diverge from earlier reciprocal 'be good to your employees and they'll be good to you' models. Twenty years ago, managerial enthusiasm for empowering employees received massive practitioner and, with reservations, academic endorsement (e.g. Scott and Jaffe 1991; Stewart 1994). Ten years later, employee engagement emerged as a prominent feature of the managerial lexicon (Alfes et al. 2010). Both practices contribute toward contemporary managerial enthusiasms for employee voice. These approaches have a common feature – they derive from management ambitions to use employee aptitudes to enhance their performance, either directly through extra effort or indirectly through commitment and other intangible qualities such as enthusiasm or, in management-speak, 'going the extra mile'.

Empowerment basically offers employees some discretion to make decisions without immediate reference to higher authority. Discretion is often cited as a positive attribute in making work more meaningful, conferring dignity and respect to employees, who respond positively through their enhanced contribution (Appelbaum 2002). Often this discretion is applied in order to satisfy customer or client wishes, which by so doing, channels positive feedback into intrinsic employee attitudes to work (Kazlauskaite et al. 2012). A practical example is provided by the Marriott hotel chain, which used a series of broadsheet newspaper advertisements to promote their unique service to guests by frontline staff, who were empowered to respond to reasonable requests on the spot. While employers and their advisers continue to advocate empowering exercises, academic research identifies problems both in concept and application. In particular, empowerment often accompanies or follows downsizing or restructuring, handing people more responsibilities ('empowerment') involving extra and extended effort, usually with no extra pay: the 'reward' is in the empowerment. Often training for new responsibilities has been found wanting. And when things go wrong, employers tend to be unsupportive of their staff, notwithstanding a nominal 'no blame' culture. Perhaps not surprisingly, independent employee surveys tend to offer less than enthusiastic support for these initiatives.

Employee engagement is in the same family of management-inspired initiatives, though underpinned by more elusive and complex definitions. Much favoured by the CIPD and consultancy firms, engagement seeks to generate a culture of close individual–organisation identification by creating a sense of mutual commitment whereby employees accept and believe in organisational goals, to which they are dedicated to contribute. Engagement variously embraces involvement in decision-making, employee voice and opportunity to develop in jobs, with employer concern for employee health and wellbeing acting as key drivers. The CIPD, an influential proponent, suggests that engagement is broader and deeper than simple job enrichment, employee satisfaction or motivational programmes, through aiming to combine commitment to the organisation and its values with a willingness to help out colleagues. Engagement is also defined as multidimensional, comprising (albeit somewhat vague) components of intellectual, affective and social engagement (Alfes et al. 2010). Engagement, therefore, presents significant claims; if they are upheld, it is not simply a case of reinventing the wheel.

Employee empowerment

There is little question that empowerment, as both a movement and a symbol, enjoys considerable elasticity. Thirty years ago, socialist writer and activist for workers' control, Ken Coates (1986), used 'Empowering People at Work' as the subtitle for a book aimed at presenting a charter for work based on international collectivism and solidarity in the face of the impending threats of economic liberalisation and globalisation. Today, we often see its intent with reference to achieving, within work and in society more broadly, freedom from restrictions imposed by misogyny, homophobia and racism (Kirton and Greene 2016; Rappaport et al. 1984). Disability campaigners have drawn on empowerment as a route towards achieving greater self-reliance and independence (Beirne 2006: 2). At another level, commercial ventures promote their products through instrumental empowering terminology: for example, Microsoft aims to 'empower every learner and every organisation on the planet to achieve more', while FLEX Automation claims that 'as a result of successful Digital Transformation, you will effortlessly empower your employees with FLEX to increase productivity within your workplace'. It is, however, with reference to work design that empowerment has attracted extensive academic and practitioner interest. But, in contradistinction to the above self-empowering ideologies and movements, it must first and foremost be borne in mind that in the employee relations context, 'it is employers who decide whether and how to empower employees' (Wilkinson 2001: 337).

In what ways does empowerment represent a departure from previous humanistic formulations to enrich jobs? We have shown that numerous neo-human relations prescriptions have advocated closely related remedies to steer work away from the enforced drudgery of Taylorism and Fordism by offering more task autonomy, sympathetic and supportive supervision and enhanced communication (Herzberg 1968; Wall et al. 2004). Arguably, empowerment aims to embrace these qualities but it also purports to offer opportunities to employees for initial and continuous training to help them adapt to new responsibilities (Stewart 1994); this training is coupled with a no-blame culture that treats operational errors as learning opportunities rather than disciplinary issues (Scott and Jaffe 1991). Possibly the most important question, one which earlier humanistic advocates had few ambitions to address, is whether empowerment does reallocate power to employees at the expense of their managers (Edwards and Wajcman 2005: 115).

This seems to be a strange proposition: if managers already possess power that they deploy for the common good of the enterprise, why would they willingly redistribute this, even if an act of power redistribution were conceptually or practically possible? On this question, Beirne, who has written extensively on the topic (Beirne 2006, 2013), harbours some doubts. Referring to the social theorist Stephen Lukes (1974), whose absolutist view suggests power is an indivisible resource, Beirne argues that empowerment serves as a screen, behind which its purpose 'is not to give power to employees but to take it away' (Beirne 2006: 10). Empowerment is a 'masquerade', wielded to steer greater control to management through the pretence of redistributing it. With this prospect, we return to the zero-sum world of Ramsay's 'cycles of control' where recalcitrant or assertive labour can be restrained or manipulated through involvement inducements. Beirne's doubts centre on whether power can indeed be treated in this restrictive zero-sum manner. Instead, he argues that power, from which empowerment practice flows, is subject to interpretation and negotiation and thereby not reducible to a 'one-way process' in which managers singularly act on their subjects, who respond passively and obediently. Conversely, he points out that employees are able to 'exercise agency and demonstrate their own ability to act, react, and interact with their working environment', with the important and well-recognised consequence that 'actors in subordinate positions are never wholly subservient or compliant' (ibid.: 11). From this perspective, offering greater discretion to employees through empowerment does little to diminish managerial control or authority. Indeed, it can reinforce both the authority and performance of management, but with the important caveat that this process need not fundamentally be at the expense of employees. Under market relations, employees would presumably prefer managerially sanctioned delegated task autonomy to the restrictive control associated with traditional authority relations, whose performance shortcomings were exposed so clearly by Walton (1985) in his persuasive empowerment-endorsing paper. Another important consideration that emerges from the empowerment literature is a possible distinction; on the one hand, empowerment can be seen as an intrinsic state of mind, a psychological state in which *feelings* of empowerment determine employee orientations to their work; conversely, this subjective perspective can be contrasted with a *managerial* dimension, which focuses on substantive sharing of informational resources and delegation of responsibilities and their observed effects (Conger and Kanungo 1988; Spreitzer 1995).

However power is perceived, the reality is that empowerment as a practical activity invariably emanates from management, whether as a standalone initiative or more generally as part of a broader agenda of direct involvement (Beirne 2013) or efficiency and cost-reduction drives (Psoinos and Smithson 2002). The relational aspect of power does imply, however, that employees, individually or collectively, have the potential to manipulate and possibly undermine managerial intentions. In technology-rich organisations, for example, strategic groups such as web designers possess latent power to utilise or withhold their knowledge through forms of 'silence' identified in Chapter 4. It could clearly be in the business interest of senior management to harness and develop this collective knowledge in pursuit of organisational objectives; one recognised approach could be individual empowerment or group processes enabled through teamworking (see chapter 8). But empowering employees is not the only option open to management: the power of hierarchy should be acknowledged in the potential deployment of those more restrictive approaches presented in chapter 1, in which expert power is made subservient to line authority by subjecting it to the same McDonaldised pressures of measurement and control as less higher-added-value occupations.

The analysis above suggests the following:

a   Employers can make strategic choices over whether to use empowerment or, when managing expert authority, decide that empowering approaches may not necessarily be the preferred option.
b   Empowerment has the potential to enhance the work experience of employees, and in so doing, can contribute positively to work performance.
c   Empowerment may not prove successful because of a lack of organisational support, such as training.
d   Empowerment, through its association with contemporary cost-cutting and efficiency exercises, may result in contingent performance gains but is recognised in negative affective terms by employees, including line managers charged with its implementation, as these may be implicated in introducing delayering exercises designed to engineer their own organisational superfluity.

Point (a) has been examined in some depth in earlier chapters, so the intention is now to look at evidence for the contrasting points (b), (c) and (d). Evidence regarding employees' felt experiences of empowerment has been mixed, and highly contingent upon organisational culture. In their study of HR managers in the top 450 British manufacturing companies, Psoinos and Smithson (2002) found that empowerment was positively associated with various informal indicators of improved performance, but continuing senior management commitment to the process and a receptive culture (managers' willingness or reluctance to let go, in particular) are essential. Also important for employees are their skill levels, training opportunities, the availability of information to support decision-making and the recognition of their contribution. Nevertheless, most of the companies studied had introduced empowerment as an instrumental accompaniment to a work-intensifying business change programme, including downsizing and delayering, in one case a reduction from seven to two levels of management, with the consequence, in the words of one manager, of 'a lot of empowerment on the shop-floor' (ibid.: 139). And, one might guess, a lot of extra effort as well.

Large-scale surveys covering over 200,000 American federal employees over a three-year period established direct links between empowerment practice, employee satisfaction, willingness to innovate and performance (Fernandez and Moldogaziev 2013). Empowerment was defined quite loosely as 'various practices' involving sharing of information, resources, rewards and authority. The study found that these empowerment practices were directly associated with performance gains, but also that empowerment was positively mediated by employee satisfaction, which also contributed to performance. Similar but weaker mediating effects were found for innovative practice. These two influences were identified in the study as 'key causal pathways by which empowerment practices influence behavioral outcomes' (ibid.: 490).

Stephen Wood, in a series of studies with various colleagues, has been consistent in his support for empowerment as an effective performance-enhancing instrument. Wall and Wood (2002) examined practice in 80 manufacturing enterprises in four countries and found that empowerment encourages employees to contribute ideas and to work more effectively in non-routine tasks (Huczynski and Buchanan 2013: 310). A later longitudinal study of senior managers in UK manufacturing (Birdi et al. 2008) found that empowerment and training impacted on added value and also that empowerment had a positive 'synergistic' relationship with other progressive HR practices. In their study, Wood and Ogbonnaya (in press) found that empowerment strongly influenced both satisfaction and wellbeing at work, with resultant staff morale a significant factor in enhancing performance, but these could all be offset by work-intensifying and cost-cutting measures.

Several factors appear to be relevant in linking empowerment to performance. First among these, as we saw with the Psoinos and Smithson (2002) study, is the role of management. When employees trust senior managers and these demonstrate open commitment to empowerment programmes that they themselves have launched, success is more likely. A study by Lorinkova and Perry (2014) showed that empowering leadership, defined as a strategy to 'share power' with subordinates, to give decision-making authority and to trust in the ability of employees to perform roles autonomously, is associated with positive employee attitudes through enhanced psychological empowerment.

Citing the (then) success of Japanese companies in gaining employee commitment, Walton (1985) specified job security as a key potential supportive factor toward employee embrace of empowerment, though Scott and Jaffe (1991: 48), possibly prefiguring the harsher flexible employment regimes to come, pointed out that empowering workers could provide them with the wider skills base necessary to enhance their employability in the open labour market. Other writers, notably Standing (2011: 61), argue that undermining job and employment security has simply acted to expand precarious work, providing a platform for greater managerial control and increasing intensification of work. Some studies have suggested, though, that line managers and supervisory staff who are faced with the practical implementation of empowerment may be less than enthusiastic with this responsibility, perceiving that lower-level empowerment may well function at the expense of their authority or even employment security (Hales 2000; Greasley et al. 2005; Denham et al. 1997).

By denying or downplaying these factors, empowerment exercises may face lack of enthusiasm, distrust, suspicion or even opposition from employees. Some may be fearful of extra responsibility, especially if the organisational climate is punitive rather than supportive (Cunningham et al. 1996; Johnson 1994). These obstacles are more likely when organisational employee-relations have a history of negativity and opposition. Empowerment has not been found to be a remedy for longstanding employee relations issues and could potentially exacerbate them through employee suspicion of what they perceive to be yet another management fad (Morrell and Wilkinson 2002). Research does reveal a number of contradictions between expressed and realised ambitions that have collectively led to characterisation of empowerment as a 'weasel word' (Collins 2000). For example, some studies have indicated little additional discretion offered to employees, while at the same time, strong managerial controls remain in place (Cunningham et al. 1996). Information provision and training essential for undertaking an enhanced role have been found to be limited or subject to tight budgets (Cunningham and Hyman 1999). Security, suggested above as a foundation for successful empowerment, is often not forthcoming (Edwards and Wajcman 2005: 142). There may also be negative associations between empowerment and emotional labour in the frontline delivery of direct services (Hochschild 1983). Cognitive (or emotional) labour is described by Berardi (2009, in Frayne 2015: 55) in terms of 'communication put to work', on the surface empowering, but systemically impoverishing, as personal communication becomes an 'economic necessity, a joyless fiction', even to the extent of eroticising client encounters in furtherance of commercial objectives (Ackroyd and Thompson 1999: 124). Finally, the association of empowerment with intensifying work regimes has also helped to undermine its credibility as a progressive HR force (Adler 1993; Beirne 2013: 7).

Academic and prescriptive interest in empowerment continues, though at a lower intensity than a decade ago. One explanation is that empowerment, originally defined as an end in itself, has gradually blended with more general interpretations of EI. Bowen and Lawler (1992), in an influential paper, suggested a three-tier hierarchy of empowerment, from suggestion schemes at the lower end to participation at the higher end, offering a 'sense of involvement ... in the total organization's performance'. Nevertheless, offering a 'sense' of empowerment does not provide material strategic input because Bowen and Lawler's prescriptions tend to involve routine involvement practices (share schemes, teamworking, etc.). The elasticity of empowerment is further demonstrated by Wilkinson's (2001) identification of its different forms and Edwards and Wajcman's (2005) absorption of empowerment into diverse EPV arrangements. A second explanation for the lower profile of empowerment is its identification with and contribution to contemporary management initiatives such as delayering, downsizing and restructuring (Grey 2009; Beirne 2013; Crowley et al. 2014). A third possibility is that empowerment has been superseded as a consequence of management and consultant enthusiasm to promote fresh-sounding involvement formulations such as employee engagement.

Employee engagement

Employee engagement is a problematic concept. At one level it can be seen as a throwaway line used by senior managers – 'we must engage our employees', in other words somehow gain their commitment, or 'we must engage with our employees', suggesting a shared work community. At the other extreme, a variety of intricate models, themselves consisting of complex components, have been formulated and presented as the 'true' engagement. Support for and discussion around employee engagement has emerged largely from and for policy interests, from established occupational bodies such as the CIPD and consultants eager to jump onto the latest EPV bandwagon, with some of them pushing their claims by deploying surveys and exploiting these with 'dubious constructs and measures' (Purcell 2014: 241). Academic interest has been stirred by the surge in political and prescriptive support, but although there is a substantial and growing body of empirical research, this has largely been found in business-facing surveys, meta-analyses (Bailey et al. 2015; Christian et al. 2011) and literature reviews (Saks and Gruman 2014), rather than studies of employees' lived experiences of engagement. Structurally, at least, engagement appears to be more multifaceted than empowerment, which can be stripped down to simply offering employees more informed influence at work. Indeed the apparent complexity of engagement may present a significant problem for its identity by obscuring what engagement actually is and what it purports to do. This is a widely recognised problem. Dromey (2014a: 7) notes a 'wide variety of approaches ... and indeed definitions of the term'. Truss (2012: 3) seeks more clarity over the meaning of the term to distinguish it from simply 'good management', a request made also by Saks and Gruman (2014). Guest (2014) points to the danger of engagement being reduced to the status of a fad and distinguishes between work engagement, which seeks to improve employee wellbeing, and organisational engagement, which focuses on organisational performance, two dimensions that operate 'in different worlds', each with different prescriptive and research agendas.

Purcell (2010, 2014) echoes concern for faddishness, but argues that evidence for strong positive links between engagement and both employee wellbeing and organisational performance are well established, though by directly incorporating engagement into high performance work systems, he risks further blurring the engagement focus as well as raising concern over explanations for its outcomes (see chapter 6). Purcell also expresses unease that employers could use engagement as a screen for work intensification (ibid.: 3; Rees et al. 2013). A hint in this direction is provided by one survey that included questions on employee willingness to work overtime or to take work home as an engagement indicator (Truss et al. 2006). A recent review found at least 13 different definitions of what the authors term a managerial 'buzz word', engagement being identified in some accounts with EI, employee commitment or organisational citizen behaviour, and distinctions being made in some versions of engagement as a psychological construct and in others as a behavioural component (Iddagoda et al. 2016; Gruman and Saks 2014). The boundaries of engagement are not necessarily restricted to the contributions of individual employees. Broader constructs have recently emerged to further blur its conceptual and practical focus, including team-based engagement (Costa et al. 2014) and collective organisational-level engagement (Barrick et al. 2015).

MacLeod and Clarke's (2009) 'highly influential' report (Dromey 2014a: 7) promoting engagement at the behest of the previous UK New Labour government was constructed from diverse empirical and conceptual sources from which emerges a detailed classification comprising four enabling components: strategic narrative; engaging managers; employee voice; and integrity. Together, these contribute to MacLeod and Clarke's definition of engagement as an approach 'designed to ensure that employees are committed to their organisation's goals and values, motivated to contribute to organisational success, and are able at the same time to enhance their own sense of well-being' (MacLeod and Clarke 2009: 9). The problem with this definition, as with others, is that it is of the "motherhood and apple pie' variety', with engagement simply addressing 'things that effective managers are already doing' (Truss 2012: 2). Truss avoids the generalisation trap but is also in an enabling mood, identifying six key facets of engagement. She first distinguishes between deep or *authentic* and surface-level or lip-service engagement. She then argues that engagement needs to be '*distributed*', i.e. shared and not imposed. The *architecture* of engagement needs to be designed for a specific purpose and potentially to extend beyond the workplace to suppliers and customers. Jobs themselves need to be *designed* in order to be engaging. Truss's next point aims to *differentiate engagement from EI*, though any distinctions tend to become blurred through an unfortunate and uncharacteristic descent into management-speak when distinguishing between 'zoned out', 'switched on' and 'tuned in' employees occupying different states of engagement and involvement. Finally, as an echo to empowerment's no-blame culture, Truss points to the positive implications of encouraging *risk* as part of the engagement enterprise. Again, these multiple components make the identification of engagement suspect and the evaluation of its impression questionable.

MacLeod and Clarke's four engagement enablers are worth examining in closer detail to reveal some of the fault lines identified above but also because a later attempt has been made to interpret and measure the impact(s) of the enablers. *Strategic narrative* is defined in terms of a strong and open culture offering employees 'a line of sight between their job and the vision and aims of the organization' (MacLeod and Clarke 2009: 31). This definition could of course represent the same vacuous words that constitute many organisations' aspirational but often derided vision statements. *Engaging managers* are identified as basically those who treat their employees well in terms of appreciation of efforts and support in their jobs. Again, it would be hoped that treating employees in these ways would be integral to *any* manager's job description. Voice ensures that employee views are consulted and that they 'make a difference'. Also, a strong communication culture supports and underpins voice processes (ibid.: 75). Here voice is identified as part of engagement, though of course, the converse view could be (and has been, as shown above) offered, that engaging with employees should be consistent with providing opportunities for expression of voice and participation. Finally, integrity is founded on openly endorsed values and behaviour that is consistent with values, leading to trust and engagement (ibid.: 33).

Dromey, on behalf of ACAS (the UK's Advisory, Conciliation and Arbitration Service), has analysed the contribution of these enablers using questions derived from the 2004 and 2011 WERS surveys. He found a number of interesting but also puzzling results. First, employee perceptions of the four enablers have improved since 2004, despite recessionary and volatile labour market conditions following the financial crash and economic uncertainty post-2008. Second, significant improvements were found in employee commitment, effort and sense of achievement, 'often used as indicators of engagement' (Dromey 2014a: 5). Third, there were significant variations in expressed engagement according to sector, organisation size and employee group. One issue which is not considered is that the improvements in stated commitment and effort arose as a consequence of the lack of security felt by growing numbers of people still occupying established but potentially vulnerable posts (Gallie et al. 2017). Further questions emerge when Dromey assesses different management approaches to employee engagement. Inexplicably, meetings with senior management, common in many workplaces (van Wanrooy et al. 2013: 64), were associated with increase in the voice index, especially if some meeting time was reserved for two-way communication. This finding contrasts with others. For example, Baddon et al. (1989: 189) describe their experiences of all-employee meetings held in a local theatre with the chairman and group managing director of a major brewery, in which 'state of the nation' presentations were made at quarterly intervals. Attendees were invited to raise questions or comments but rarely did and the popularly applied label for these meetings was the 'Doom and Gloom show', which was especially relevant when meetings were held prior to pay negotiations, as senior executives were keen to use the meeting to dampen employee expectations on profits or sales in order to pave the way for modest pay settlements. Though no surveys on employee attitudes were conducted on the impact of these meetings, the impression given was one of appreciation for some (paid) time away from the workplace, sprinkled with a healthy dose of cynicism, especially from the union representatives. Similarly, at a software company studied by Baldry and his colleagues and populated by highly educated and articulate engineers, full meetings were convened twice yearly, addressed by the chief executive. There were few contributions from the assembled staff, prompting one manager in the audience to comment to the researchers that 'the managerial style is control', with another adding that the 'owners have had a problem letting go' (Baldry et al. 2007: 93).

Another interesting aspect of plenary meetings is that such initiatives were reported in WERS 2011 as being substantially more widespread in the public sector, whereas public sector employees score lower on the engagement enablers than their counterparts in the private sector (Dromey 2014a: 24). In addition to all-employee meetings, Dromey also examined the value of other common involvement techniques often associated with engaging employees through voice enhancement. The findings were surprising. Meetings with line managers were associated with a lower voice index than the absence of meetings. The presence of joint consultative meetings and other representative forums such as works councils were also associated with a lower voice index than their absence. Employee perceptions of voice were also lower when regular staff surveys were administered. Rigorous statistical tests in Dromey's study (ibid.: 33) and other studies reveal that 'having a meaningful job is the most important factor influencing levels of engagement. This is true of all types of worker in all kinds of jobs' (Alfes et al. 2010: 2). These researchers define meaningfulness in terms that employees believe their work is important and that they can 'make a difference', with a positive impact on other people or on society in general (ibid.: 23). In a development from earlier characterisations, Alfes et al. identify and analyse three distinct forms of engagement, comprising cognitive (or intellectual), affective and social dimensions. Intellectual engagement is defined as 'thinking hard about the job and how to do it better'; affective engagement is defined as 'feeling positively about doing a good job'; and social engagement as 'actively taking opportunities to discuss work-related improvements with others at work' (ibid.: 5). Another unusual aspect is that the researchers disaggregate engagement temporally, even down to a daily basis, which again raises questions as to the fundamental nature of engagement.

These different dimensions recall Herzberg's multiple investigations into intrinsic motivating factors and extrinsic hygiene factors, distinguished by asking open-ended questions to a wide range of employee types about when they felt good and bad about their jobs (Herzberg et al. 1959; Herzberg 1966, 1968). Intrinsic factors include very similar enablers to those identified in the studies by Alfes and Dromey, namely recognition, sense of achievement, responsibility, opportunities for advancement and competence enhancement. In her review of Herzberg, Wilson (2004: 149–50) identifies a number of critiques of his analysis and omissions, such as neglecting the importance of trust in management as a prime factor in predicting employee job satisfaction, charges that could also be directed at less sophisticated models of engagement. Edwards and Wajcman (2005: 128) also elaborate on the key function of trust in supporting EPV. Other critical questions about engagement present themselves. In reported engagement studies, there is very little discussion about any representation or participation gap, despite findings from the WERS survey that confirm that a gap affects at least a 'large minority of employees' and appears not to be diminishing (van Wanrooy et al. 2013: 66).

Similarly, there is very little reported role for trade unions in accounts of engagement, notwithstanding multicountry studies showing that both unionised and non-union employees welcome the opportunity to be represented by a trade union (Peetz and Frost 2007: 168). The 2011 WERS survey indicated an overall increase in job insecurity, especially for employees in workplaces adversely affected by the recession (van Wanrooy et al. 2013: 108–09), the effects of which, along with associated austerity measures, were still increasing during the 2011 surveys (ibid.: 11). Insecurity is closely linked to the widely endorsed flexibility projects of management, where employment security is compromised through combinations of time, numerical, functional and pay flexibility (White et al. 2004). As other writers have confirmed, it is very difficult for employees to feel engaged or to experience wellbeing when they encounter insecurity in their work and enjoy few opportunities for genuine influence to address this insecurity (Gallie et al. 2017). It is also recognised that stress at work has increased over recent years and it is reasonable to assume that this can at least be partially accounted for by work pressures, such as intensification, that have the capacity to neutralise or override the engagement practices of employers (Beirne 2013: 7). When one considers that the exchange aspect of engagement is usually emphasised by advocates, it is hard to see what employers are actually doing in order to support employee welfare, undermined as it is by work-time pressures, stress and growing insecurity. Madeleine Bunting, in a newspaper article, reflected on

> the total absence of social affirmation in ... working lives. [Workers] are cajoled, ticked off, hectored, humiliated and bullied by ... advisers, trainers, bosses and team leaders. In all these work relationships they cease to be people, simply units of labour to be bought and sold.
>
> (*Guardian* 2011)

Organisational commitment is suggested as one outcome of engagement (MacLeod and Clarke 2009) but commitment as a concept can be problematic and, by association, so can engagement. First, there is the question of commitment to whom or what? Researchers have identified commitment to employer (which seems to be consistent with the engagement literature), to the occupation, and also to the task itself (Baldry et al. 2005). These forms of commitment are not necessarily compatible with one another. Nurses or social workers can be committed to time-consuming patient or client care, whereas employers may focus on ensuring that quantifiable objectives, such as numbers assessed or seen, are treated as a priority in a cost-focused system (Hart and Warren 2015). Many organisations now operate performance-management regimes aimed at achieving specified and often quantified targets, one outcome of which has been to raise employee insecurities and levels of stress (Mather and Seifert 2011; Hart and Warren 2015). Second, a more conceptual problem is that commitment is more complex than that contained within a simple and singular 'commitment to employer' platform. Occupational psychologists have identified at least three forms of commitment, each with different implications for employee behaviour. These include normative (a sense of obligation to the employer), affective (emotional identification with the organisation) and continuance (a perceived need to stay with an employer owing to the high costs of leaving) commitment (Meyer and Allen 1991). Clearly, different forms can have different implications for engagement, however formulated. The most ambiguous obvious form is continuance commitment: employees may be 'committed' to an employer because they perceive limited availability of alternative employment options, but would this commitment necessarily translate into engaging behaviour, especially if employees feel pressured through circumstances to stay with an employer (Meyer et al. 2002)?

In summary, we can make the following points about engagement. In essence, engagement urges employers to treat their employees in a socially responsible manner (by communicating effectively with them) and to provide an environment of shared values and cooperation. Offering opportunities to express 'voice' is central to a number of models, an important objective being to offer meaning to people's working lives. At present, though, there are undoubtedly unresolved issues about engagement that possibly jeopardise its status as an established approach to employee management. First, there is no universal agreement on the meaning of engagement, which is not helped by a variety of definitions, boundaries and approaches. Second, some interpretations see engagement as distinct from EPV while others see it as integral to it. Third, psychological engagement is sometimes separated from its behavioural counterpart and, while performance and employee wellbeing are often afforded parity in stated objectives, it is the former that has attracted more employer attention. Fourth, some well-reported accounts classify enabling components, but on investigation, these appear to be little more than direction signals to stimulate positive employee attitudes and behaviour.

Similar questions could be raised for the different 'forms', such as cognitive, affective and social engagement, which again lack specificity and could simply act as metaphors for aspects of socially acceptable management practice or as disguises for hardening work regimes. Finally, on the basis of statistical analysis, many engagement studies do report positive associations between engagement and indicators of performance or orientations to work, but we are again faced with the problem of the 'black box' in that the dynamics of antecedents and consequences remain untested (Saks and Gruman 2014). Engagement, like empowerment, can be implicated in employee indoctrination, diminished control and work intensification (Rees et al. 2013), which may offer more plausible explanations for employee performance than naïve and potentially conflicting expressions of 'engagement'. Purcell (2014), in highlighting the conflict-free, individualistic focus and 'almost total lack of context in most studies of employee engagement' arrives at a more crushing conclusion, that engagement 'is taking us backwards to a dangerously simplistic view of work relations'. With these layers of uncertainty, engagement could not only face the fate afforded to the now largely forgotten managerial appetite for quality circles (Purcell 2010: 1) or business process re-engineering (Buchanan 2000), but could also risk falling into disrepute unless more objective and critical perspectives on its meaning and practice are delivered.

Conclusions

Empowerment and engagement have emerged in the past two decades as putative alternatives to tightly controlled Taylorist drivers of employee performance at a time of heightened commercial competitiveness and public sector cost-efficiency drives. Both have been associated with higher performance, though often accompanied by reduced staffing and job status or employment insecurity (Gallie et al. 2017). Consequently, positive performance associations are not necessarily explained through practical expression of feelings of empowerment or of engagement, but potentially through insecurity of tenure and pressures imposed by staffing reductions and tighter performance measurement systems. Though both practices can be compromised, empowerment involves a less convoluted link between practice and performance and, bearing in mind that work 'meaningfulness' appears to be the feature most highly desired, though rarely achieved, by employees (Fox 1980; Baldry et al. 2007), it has perhaps the greater potential to provide a visible route between what workers want and how they perform at the level of the task. Clearly, a favourable job environment in terms of cooperative organisational culture, protection of employee wellbeing and shared values is an important underpinning factor, but should be a feature of effective people management and, as several studies have emphasised, should also be supported through representative employee participation (Gallie et al. 2017; Freeman et al. 2007).

Chapter 8

What's not to like about teamworking?

Introduction

A major managerial thrust to EPV over recent decades has been provided by the promotion of teams. Practically, a number of directions can be identified: at one level teamworking can offer genuine attempts to provide innovative solutions through creative, collaborative and stimulating work in high-tech environments or interdependent and complementary functional areas, for example in healthcare (Dromey 2014b), though these initiatives can also be influenced by cost considerations. One consequence of the latter has been the extension of team-based lean management to sectors such as health services (Radnor et al. 2012) and to the public sector more broadly (Carter et al. 2011). At the other extreme, nominal teamworking is exploited as an artificial means to promote intra-firm competition (and enhanced indirect control through peer monitoring), for example among call-centre workers (van den Broek et al. 2004) and, infamously, in companies like Enron and in the finance sector, where pressurised internal team-based sales competition became highly dysfunctional for both clients and organisations. As with many EPV initiatives, research indicates that between these polar opposites there are many variations: further, there is no black-and-white outcome for teamworking or even a common definition. Context, such as in software, where multidisciplinary teams are the norm, and organisational or community culture are all-important. In appropriate conditions (senior management support; regular and continuous training; synergy with other progressive HR approaches; careful team selection, etc.), teamworking can offer and deliver benefits to clients, organisation and employees. In other cases, teams can become internally and competitively dysfunctional and potentially self-exploiting. In this chapter we review the evolution of teamworking and the circumstances and conditions where its implementation might affect team members and their performance.

Why teamworking?

Virtually every young person's CV will include words and evidence that attest to the candidate's qualities as a 'team player', recognised as the *sine qua non* of employability. In the same vein, pressurised by potential employers keen for colleges and universities to provide oven-ready graduates, most academic courses now endorse group-working and team skills as essential components of student performance and assessment (Andrews and Higson 2010). Located in the psychology of belongingness and social identity (Tajfel and Turner 1986), teams also have an instinctive positive appeal, as shown by the emotions associated with football clubs, who may have little or no connection with the communities they purport to represent. The team concept can even extend to the national level – such as in exhortation to 'Team GB' success in the 2016 Olympic Games, a 'rhetorical strategy' resonant of the corporate 'team spirit' and socialisation associated with Team Toyota or Nissan (Benders and van Hootegem 2000: 54). Some companies extend the team metaphor to emotionally bind workers to the mythical corporate 'family' (Casey 1995), as evidenced by the US Postal Service, whose attendees at an 'annual recognition conference' allegedly concluded proceedings with a mass rendition of the popular song 'We are Family' (Cederström and Fleming 2012: 45). Teams and teamworking also capture the popular imagination as positive examples of fruitful shared enterprise, in which personal ambition is sacrificed for the sake of collective, collaborative endeavour, as popularised by the slogan 'there is no 'I' in team'.

In hard commercial terms, managers are attracted to teams because they appear to offer an effective and efficient way of managing workers and monitoring their product or service outcomes. Support for teams as vehicles for organisational success comes from academic sources (e.g. Buchanan 2000), popular management and airport books (e.g. Peters 1989) and from consultants who construct their case on practical experience in advising corporate clients (Katzenbach and Smith 1993), though not necessarily to the benefit of team members. For instance, as an advisee, Ehrenreich (2009: 120–22) presents a bleakly negative view of the impact of team 'advisers' based on her personal encounters with them. Teams can also be integral in offering voice to employees through various degrees of autonomy, expressed differentially through high-performance work systems, empowerment and shifts to lean production (Marchington 2000). Experimental work has also been undertaken on the optimal composition of teams in terms of numbers. Some reports suggest no more than 25, but usually less than ten is regarded as optimal (Wilson 2004: 206); others have suggested limits of between eight and 20 members, a range sufficient to undertake a discreet part of the production process but not too large to restrict group decision-making (Nijholt and Benders 2010: 381). It has been argued that effective teams blend complementary occupational skills, defined by Fisher and Hunter (1998) as 'task' skills, with an appropriate balance of personal talents and aptitudes to optimise these, defined by Fisher and Hunter as 'relationship' qualities (ibid.). The best-known framework for designating team roles has been provided by Belbin from his longstanding observations of management training schedules (Belbin 1993, 2000, 2003). Ultimately, Belbin identified nine key roles, each of which he proposed can make a positive contribution to the team's efforts. These roles can be classified into three discreet functions, namely: action (shaper, implementer, completer–finisher), social (coordinator, teamworker, resource investigator) and thinking (plant, monitor–evaluator, specialist) (Huczynski and Buchanan 2013: 370).

As with Maslow's hierarchy of needs, Belbin's role classification has proved very attractive to practising managers and their advisers. Unfortunately, as with Maslow, there is very little evidence to support team-role theory. Organisational research has serially failed to identify specific contributions attributable to different roles or their links to performance (Senior 1997; Aritzeta et al. 2007). The number of identified key roles can vary upwards from just two, which by their generality can be fluid (Fisher and Hunter 1998). Furthermore, linking team performance directly to designated roles poses the risk of neglecting other factors that influence team performance, such as management support, levels of training and team stability and cohesion (Bushe and Chu 2011).

One problem is that conceptually, teams and teamworking are not easy to define. In preceding chapters we have examined various practices, such as empowerment and high-performance systems, introduced unilaterally by managers to achieve certain productive ends. Many management commentators would categorise teams in similar instrumental ways. Nevertheless, as Buchanan (2000: 28) neatly reminds us, the genesis of teamworking can be very different, occurring spontaneously or defensively and 'adopted by working people in what they perceive to be adverse working conditions'. The classic example was provided by coal-mining where multiskilled, self-selected and highly self-dependent teams formed autonomous work groups (AWGs) in order to exploit the automation that threatened to fragment existing social relations among the colliers (Dennis et al. 1969: 44). Very often, cohesive teams developed from shared community experiences, as in coal-mining, deep-sea fishing and shipbuilding, all typified by mutual work dependence and close interpersonal relations (Salaman 1974).

As is well known, the first systematic analyses of AWGs were conducted by members of the Tavistock Institute of Human Relations who developed their ideas through examining the most socially and economically effective ways for emergent production technology to be used (Trist et al. 1963). From this point, a change of direction for teamworking could be discerned, as it became increasingly part of management's project to enhance performance through humanising working conditions. Hence, teamworking found expression in quality-of-working-life movements in America and Europe, industrial democracy initiatives in Norway (Heller et al. 1998: 23) and Sweden, specifically at Volvo's Kalmar and Uddevalla plants (Berggren 1993). Though teamworking was alleged to offer advantages to workers through looser supervision and involvement in task decisions (Heller et al. 1998: 24), it became increasingly linked to its role in potential performance enhancement. Walton's (1985) 'commitment strategy' emphasised the growing accountability of teams for performance; as hierarchical organisational layers were stripped away, supervisors were counselled to become 'team advisers' or 'team consultants' to their erstwhile subordinates. Walton's approach was, of course, strongly influenced by that adopted in Japanese industry in the 1970s and 1980s, where teamworking was ubiquitous, highly diverse and integrated into organisational culture and practice (Benders and van Hootegem 2000). British productive efficiency was starkly exposed in Dore's (1973) much cited comparative study of British and Japanese factories, in which teamwork was prominent in Japan and supervisors acted as participative team members. Nevertheless, it should be remembered that other factors contributed to the superior performance of Japanese factories; it is also important for corporate policy-makers to recognise that identifying and applying a singular factor outside its cultural context is unlikely to lead to meaningful performance gains or employee endorsement (Sewell 1996; Oudhuis and Olsson 2015).

Managerial backing for teamworking became further established through its deployment in Western car plants desperate to match Japanese cost efficiency and product quality. The best known of various initiatives was the International Motor Vehicle Program from which emerged Womack et al.'s (1990) lean production thesis, for which multiskilled workers operating in teams provide the foundation. Advantages and shortcomings of lean have been assessed in chapter 6, but our perspective here is to consider the extent and role of teams operating within a lean framework.

Types of teams

From the 2011 WERS survey it is difficult to calculate the prevalence of teams in the UK. We know that team briefings are common: 40 per cent of all workplaces undertake briefings, with at least a quarter of the time allocated for questions (up from 37 per cent in 2004). We also know that 14 per cent (down from 18 per cent in 2004) of workplaces have 'problem-solving groups', but these figures are indicative rather than confirmatory of teams and team membership (van Wanrooy et al. 2013: 64). Harder data are available from the sixth European Working Conditions Survey or EWCS (Eurofound 2016b), based on interviews with 44,000 workers in 35 European countries. According to the survey findings, half of all employees in the EU's current 28 countries report that they work in teams that have common tasks and allow members to plan their work. The incidence of teamworking varies across Europe, with teamworkers representing less than 40 per cent of the workforce in Albania, Italy and Turkey, and in excess of 70 per cent in Sweden and the UK. Workers in healthcare are most likely to report teamworking (72 per cent) but it is also common among managers, professions and agricultural workers (about 70 per cent).

As well as deriving from different sources, analysis of team contribution is complicated by the diversity of team forms. Extrapolating from the Japanese model, Benders and van Hootegem (2000: 54–55) identify three different dimensions: the team as a 'collective spirit', representative of corporate identity and culture; second, as an integral and dominant feature of lean production; and third, as a basis for quality circles. In the West, the concept and expression of 'collective spirit' tends to fall on stony ground (e.g. Oudhuis and Olsson 2015) and quality circles are no longer common. Teamworking is highly likely to be found within lean processes, both in manufacturing and service sectors. Buchanan (2000) analysed team identity chronologically, recognising AWGs as catalysts for various quality of work life initiatives in the 1960s and 1970s. Multiskilled 'high performance' teams characterised the 1980s, operating under managerial direction; and the 1990s brought flatter, delayered organisational structures, with teams operating 'as a key component of the wholly fresh and innovative BPR package' (ibid.: 31). Enthusiasm for the BPR project has now largely diminished and been superseded by its ubiquitous leaner offspring.

A broader classification was offered by Sundstrom et al. (1990), who identified four types of functional teams. These include advice teams, such as the now largely defunct quality circles, who were tasked to advise their immediate managers of production problems. The second team type is the so-called action teams, which undertake brief repeated performances but with variations that call for discretionary action by team members, according to circumstances. The third identified type is project teams, often with multidisciplinary composition, exemplified in software (Baldry et al. 2007: 57–60), creative or healthcare projects (Gitell 2009). About a quarter of workers in teams across Europe work in 'matrix' arrangements, in which they can belong to several groups and may have more than one reporting line (Eurofound 2016b: 87). Edmondson and Nembhard (2009) examined the role of project teams in new product development and found that skilful management of the teams was associated with growth of project management and teaming skills, broader perspectives among members, construction of social networks and heightened boundary-spanning skills. Knowledge workers may appreciate the benefits of project teamwork because it can help them gain broader and progressive expertise upon which career advancement and involvement in complex projects may depend (May et al. 2002). While project teams are thus often associated with extending job latitude, this need not necessarily occur. Hodgson and Briand (2013) report the case of an ostensibly collegiate project management team in the creative gaming sector where control was strongly vested in the team leaders and democratic decision-making largely illusory. The fourth team type consists of production teams with shared output objectives. The amount of discretion or autonomy available to each team type varies according to management style, objectives, team composition and skill availability. Benders (2005) further identifies the high performance work team that shows little distinction between sociotechnical and lean variants, but as part of a broader high performance system, its specific contribution to performance would be difficult to ascertain (see also Buchanan 2000).

Globalised enterprises, spatially dispersed operations, cost considerations and advances in communication technology are leading to the emergence of virtual teams (Gilson et al. 2015). As yet, there has been limited research on these developments, though some commentators point to a continuum from 'real' team to 'virtual', suggesting that all teams are capable of sharing elements of both reality and virtuality, with the balance determined by factors such as immediacy, cost and strategic imperatives (Shin 2005). A study of virtual teams in Swiss multinational corporation ABC found the main challenges to virtual teams were in the complexity of leading the team, developing trust among team members and handling the virtual aspects of communication, especially across cultural boundaries (Oertig and Buergi 2006). There is little doubt, however, that with technological advances, deployment of virtual teams is likely to grow although, as Gregg (2011: 83) points out in her detailed and sensitive study of an Australian telecommunications company, teamworking through emails and social networks intrudes increasingly into all areas of work and domestic life, with the added risk that a 'workplace free of *any* face-to-face office collegiality presents its own kind of neuroses' (emphasis in the original).

What makes a team?

We have seen that teams can take different meanings, different sizes, different functions and different forms. From an organisational perspective, teams are usually constructed and maintained with the objective of addressing ways to optimise task performance. From this point of view, researchers have attempted to identify the chief characteristics of teams, with two of the most cited comprising seven (Mueller and Purcell 1992) and nine (Buchanan and McCalman 1989) respectively. As might be expected, these mostly overlap, with Mueller and Purcell's team characteristics being as follows:

- The team works on a common task
- The team has its own workspace or 'territory'
- Team members organise their own task allocations
- Members encourage and organise multiskilling
- The team has discretion over work methods and time
- The team has a leader or spokesperson
- Members can influence recruitment to their team

Buchanan and McCalman's two additional characteristics include: negotiated production targets and support staff 'on the spot' (Buchanan 2000: 30). Buchanan (1987: 40) also suggested that a team is largely 'self-regulating and works without direct supervision', while in an early study, Mueller (1994: 383–84) described a team as a 'group of people ... responsible for producing well-defined output within a recognizable territory, where members rotate from job to job, under a flexible allocation of tasks'. While teams can possess some or all of these characteristics, the defining characteristic of teams is the extent and depth of authority. It has been suggested that the more characteristics a team possesses, the higher its autonomy (Banker et al. 1996); but focusing exclusively on extent of authority carries the risk of neglecting depth, which identifies the 'embeddedness' or autonomy of teamworking within decision-making processes and is thereby a defining characteristic of EPV (Marchington 2005: 31–32).

The question of team autonomy

A central question is whether or in what ways teamworking provides for worker voice and participation. In particular, we need to enquire whether teams can make self-determining decisions or whether they are simply allowed some latitude in responding to management directives. One problem is apparent: teams differ considerably in size, composition and function. The other problem is how to measure autonomy. They may all be called 'teams', but what differentiates one team from another? Nijholt and Benders (2010: 381) suggest that 'autonomy exists when rights to decide about aspects of work are delegated to the team level'. There are real constraints, though, as 'aspects of work' lack definitional or empirical clarity and 'the organization sets the boundaries within which any employee, thus also a team member, may act' (Benders 2005: 56). Therefore, modification of hierarchical control, not its removal, provides the core feature of teams and teamworking. Within this framework, Banker et al. (1996) propose a continuum of autonomy, from those who self-manage and regulate their work down to 'traditional work groups', performing routine tasks under supervision, which suggests they are teams in name only (Marchington 2000: 64). Other writers examine the 'ideal' characteristics of teamworking noted above and define team autonomy according to the number of characteristics that are met in practice. Hence, Marchington (ibid.: 65) suggests that meeting all seven of Mueller and Purcell's characteristics would merit a 'high autonomy' rating on Banker et al.'s scale. A similar measurement approach was adopted in the pan-European Employee Participation in Organisational Change (EPOC) project, in which eight 'decision rights' (work allocation, scheduling, quality, time-keeping, absence control, attendance, job rotation and work coordination) were assessed, teams being defined as those enjoying at least four of the eight rights (Nijholt and Benders 2010: 378). One problem, as the authors concede, is that different researchers have identified different autonomy indicators, ranging from seven to 15, which undermines the validity of the autonomy construct. Also problematic is that deconstruction of each autonomy indicator can reveal a host of definitional and measurement problems. The sixth EWCS found that team members decide on task allocation in just over half of cases, with higher levels (70 per cent and over) in traditionally socially liberal Denmark, Finland, the Netherlands, Norway and Sweden. Team members can nominate their leaders in 28 per cent of teams, again with higher levels in Northern Europe, and members can decide their own work schedules in 41 per cent of cases (Eurofound 2016b: 88).

Teams can, therefore enjoy varying degrees of autonomy and job latitude, though bounded by overall objectives and performance measures determined at higher levels of the enterprise. The managerial assumption is that teams encourage better performance through the synergistic effect of working together. Certainly there is evidence that teams can be associated with higher output or reduced costs, but the question of the dynamics underlying these effects needs to be considered. Do teams perform 'better' because of the socialising effects of working in a collaborative venture or because of the intensifying effects of working under pressure with reduced resources? Finally, do teams necessarily respond positively to what they might perceive as exploitative working conditions? Are there ways in which teamwork can be used to resist work intensification and management encroachment? There are a number of critical studies which argue that 'teamwork, while apparently empowering employees, generates new forms of control which assist management in extracting labour from employees via work intensification' (Harley 2001: 725).

Links between teams, performance and managerial direction and objectives are vital, as can be demonstrated by the Volvo experiments to humanise working conditions in vehicle manufacturing as a radical departure from Fordist assembly lines and Toyota's lean 'one best way' production schedules. Volvo had previously introduced limited teamworking at its Kalmar assembly-line plant in Sweden in the 1970s, but at Uddevalla in 1989, assembly lines were scrapped and teams were introduced that built whole cars using advanced technology, inspired by the supportive and idealistic company chair, Pehr Gyllenhammer, in cooperation with the relevant local trade unions. Gyllenhammer's vision was that there 'should be delight and pride in producing the car', helped by deploying 'the full potential of the employees, and the competitive advantage of good education, professional skills and an advanced form of work organization' (quoted in Sandberg 2007: v). Notwithstanding its use of advanced design and technology and its enrichment of work and workers (Sandberg 2007: 1), the Uddevalla plant closed in 1993 after less than four years of production, followed by the less innovative Kalmar plant a year later. The question of why these plants were closed is central to our thinking about the boundaries and potential of team autonomy. Though it seems clear that product quality was consistently high at Uddevalla and employee satisfaction at the plant improved, commercial problems still lingered. According to the New York Times (1991), Volvo also had pragmatic reasons for introducing advanced teamworking: to reduce absenteeism and labour turnover. It was claimed that absenteeism was high because of the high proportion of women workers (about 40 per cent), many taking primary responsibility for domestic arrangements. Further, excessive labour turnover was experienced because of low rates of unemployment (encouraging job mobility), coupled with a traditionally generous state benefits system. For the same reasons, recruitment to the Uddevalla plant was difficult (Sandberg 2007: 5). Nevertheless, these operational obstacles were reduced during Uddevalla's period of team production. The problem, though, was one of economics and company politics. In the early 1990s, Volvo had excess capacity, was experiencing losses and its least productive plants were said to be at Uddevalla and Kalmar; they therefore had to close. The New York Times (1991) claimed that it took 50 labour hours to build a car at Uddevalla, compared with 37 at Kalmar and, ominously, just 13.3 hours under Toyota's lean production regime, prompting James Womack, co-author of *The Machine that Changed the World*, to comment to the newspaper: 'Uddevalla is not in the ballpark. It's not even in the outer parking lot of the stadium. Frankly it's a dead horse.' This was a sentiment strongly held by Peter Wickens (1993), who as personnel director of Nissan UK, was intent on establishing lean production facilities at the company's Sunderland plant.

Sandberg (2007: 4), in his seminal studies of Uddevalla, arrives at more nuanced conclusions for the plant's closure. Rather than the productive failure of teamworking, the enterprise fell victim to the relative small size and limited corporate influence of the plant (and that of Kalmar), but more ominously, to the global production strategy pursued by Volvo in partnership with Renault, in which innovative but minority teamworking ideas were in unequal competition with traditional and lean production techniques. Berggren (1994) arrives at similar conclusions, claiming that the experiment 'did not fail' since measures of quality and productivity were high and equal to those of Volvo's more traditional Gothenburg operations (see also Nilsson 1994). He argues that, with excessive capacity, poor sales and Sweden's faltering economy in the early 1990s, the plants were vulnerable to pressures from Renault's senior managers seeking to implement a more traditional, uniform and control-sensitive production policy. Moreover as a 'pure final assembly' operation requiring shipment of car bodies 100 km to the plant, Uddevalla was at a decisive political disadvantage in the ensuing 'power games' over cost savings, especially as the unions on Volvo's board were not interested in defending progressive teamworking that was not available to their own members in the larger and more traditional Gothenburg plants (Berggren 1994: 119). Ultimately, managers in global organisations tend to look for standardisation in their operations, which allows productivity comparisons and gives them the means to minimise costs in highly competitive markets. At the same time, unions tend to focus on optimising employment and remuneration for their members and to pay less attention to humanising the workplace, especially if they are persuaded that such experiments can be detrimental to overall performance and possibly company viability. The concept and practice of progressive teamworking therefore suffered major setbacks with closure of the two plants; lean production has since been ascendant. Nevertheless, teams also form the basis for lean operations, though some argue that, through association with Taylorist management techniques, the meaning of teams in terms of job autonomy is stretched to insignificance in such cases (Wilson 2004: 212).

Teams and lean

The Toyota-derived lean system, as portrayed by Womack et al. (1990) for auto manufacture, consists of an integrated system with low inventory and buffers, replenished through just-in-time deliveries; continuous improvement in waste reduction, efficiency and quality (*kaizen*); and the transfer of a 'maximum number of tasks and responsibilities to those workers actually adding value to the car on the line' (ibid.: 99). Responsibility for delivering lean production rests on the shoulders of 'dynamic' teams that lie at 'the heart of the lean factory'. The promise for teamworkers under lean was clear: an assumed end to the rigidity of Taylorist control, the space afforded to enjoy reasonable autonomy over work schedules and opportunities to deploy wider ranges of skills (ibid.: 100–03; Townsend 2007). The benefits for employers were equally clear: higher quality, lower labour costs through streamlined production, with no scope for work with little direct added value, and the ability to compete internationally. Two issues clearly stand out: first, are lean teams Taylorist or counter-Taylorist? Second, what are the performance implications of lean teams?

As we have established above, *all* teams and teamworking are subject to managerial controls, though not all face direct Taylorist control. Nevertheless, the evidence for lean does appear to incline towards direct control. The Toyota approach, on which much of lean thinking is based, is strongly geared to continuous improvement, which in turn is based on adherence to so-called standard operating procedures that specify uniform task routines to be followed by all teams (Benders 2005: 61) through job standardisation, although workers are able to improve the procedures by applying their workplace experience and knowledge and then restandardising procedures in the practice manuals. In this sense, team autonomy under lean – at least in vehicle manufacture and associated sectors – is highly constrained (Danford 1998). A history and detailed examination of lean as experienced by workers in a vehicle manufacturing company is presented by Stewart et al. (2009); the dominant impression is one of managerial control by stealth over the team and its efforts (Stewart and Martinez Lucio 2011). First, we note that team leaders, appointed by the company, were afforded considerable influence over the team's activities, a similar conclusion to that reached by Delbridge et al. (2000). Though, as Thursfield (2015) has also noted, team leader interventions can be resisted, there is constant tension from 'speed-ups, destaffing, job loading and reduced job cycle times', over which team members have little discretion (Stewart et al. 2009: 76). Second, core teams were put under pressure by increased levels of outsourcing (ibid.: 83), as part of a 'major management tool in the political economy of neo-liberalism' (ibid.: 202). Third, lack of team control was linked to reports of 'stress, overwork, dissatisfaction with work and the employment regime more broadly' (ibid.: 203). Clearly, these accounts from workers point to a restrictive and Taylorist regime of tight control and denied autonomy, aspects of which have been shown even more dramatically in lean processes adopted in the Indian auto industry (Monaco 2017; see chapter 11).

Basically, lean production is based on the idea of 'getting more from less', with less often translating into reduced staffing; so it is perhaps not surprising that lean principles have now entered into areas of public services where increasing costs of capital equipment in healthcare (Moody 2014), coupled with political austerity measures, have led to pressure to achieve efficiency savings (Pollock 2004). Healthcare is therefore one sector which has experienced extension of lean teams though, as Purcell (2014) notes, a range of approaches have been adopted in recent years in National Health Service (NHS) trusts to enhance patient care through engagement with employees. The NHS is a massive organisation, employing over a million people, occupying literally hundreds of different jobs and with high trade-union presence and density. Joe Dromey, head of policy and research for the IPA, an independent not-for-profit think-tank campaigning for EPV, was commissioned to undertake comparative in-depth research in eight NHS trusts, chosen on the basis of their reputation for high employee engagement. Dromey (2014b) found that these 'high performing' trusts shared a number of positive characteristics, none of which appeared to involve lean processes. The main positive factors were:

a   supportive, visible and strongly communicative senior leadership
b   line managers who are supportive of staff
c   strong employee voice, embracing devolved decision-making to the frontline, and employee say 'over both how they do their jobs and how their services are delivered'
d   appropriate structures, culture and enthusiasm for working in partnership alongside recognised trade unions

Underpinning all these features, Dromey found a strong set of lived values where mutual trust stands out, also 'developed in partnership with employees' (ibid.: 5).

The report points out that virtually all NHS staff work in teams; findings concerning teams and teamworking were unequivocal: in contrast to 'pseudo' teams, 'real' teams not only have high levels of employee engagement, but in the words of one senior manager, 'teamwork saves lives'. 'Real' teams were defined as those where 'team members have a set of shared objectives, where team members meet to discuss the team's effectiveness, and where team members communicate closely with colleagues to achieve the team's objectives' (ibid.: 18). Detail from one of the case studies, at Frimley Park Hospital NHS Foundation Trust, provides the context for effective teamworking:

Line managers and team working at Frimley Park Hospital NHS Foundation Trust

There is a clear understanding of the importance of effective people management at Frimley Park. Although the trust performs very well in terms of engagement overall, they are forensic in looking at engagement on a team by team basis to see where there may be gaps. According to Eleanor Shingleton-Smith, where teams are less engaged, the difference is usually the manager.

There is a strong focus on what Eleanor called 'the nuts and bolts of good people management.' Line managers are offered support to ensure they are all capable of engaging with their staff including a year-long Managing People programme. Managers are encouraged to hold regular team briefings to feed key messages down to their staff and involve them in discussions about the priorities and challenges both for the team and for the trust as a whole. Regular face-to-face communication between employees and their immediate manager is seen as vital in engaging staff, ensuring they feel listened to and valued. Appraisals are also seen as particularly important in building engagement; helping employees understand their role and identify what support they need.

There is also a very strong sense of team working at the trust. Several employees talked about the 'Frimley family'; the sense of common purpose and mutual support that there is at the trust. Andrew Morris described how they have tried to 'instil in people that if you work as a team, you get better results. People rely on one and other.' Again, this comes out in the staff survey with the trust coming 4th out of 141 trusts in terms of effective team working. The sense of strong team working is seen as being supported by effective line management, good appraisals and inclusive team briefings.

(Dromey 2014b: 19; reproduced with permission from the IPA)

This study has been considered at length as it demonstrates that there are very real alternatives to lean in healthcare, and that lean cannot necessarily be translated successfully from the manufacturing industry to public-service sectors (see chapter 6). The Dromey study confirms the importance of 'real' teamwork in driving performance outcomes, of team leadership and of organic links between teams and other facets of people management, such as training and non-punitive appraisal systems (see also West et al. 2006). Nevertheless, there is considerable pressure to introduce lean working in the NHS because, according to the policy director of the NHS Confederation, it offers 'staggering improvements in quality and efficiency' (Jones and Mitchell 2006: 2). This rhetoric is highlighted by a review of the outcome of introducing lean in a pathology department, where there was a reported 70 per cent reduction in steps needed to undertake most tasks, 40 per cent reduction in floorspace and up to 90 per cent reduction in the time taken to do the pathology job – 'and all achieved with less ... staff' (ibid.: 22). They conclude with the upbeat comment: 'The Lean message is 100 per cent positive. Lean can improve safety and quality, improve staff morale and reduce costs – all at the same time' (ibid.: 23). There have been less evangelistic accounts of lean in healthcare and, while most of these do point to limited improvements in throughput, they are circumspect about lean's potential and few identify the dynamics through which improvements take place. One recent meta-study review of 243 articles indicated that no definitive conclusion over positive impacts can be drawn without further in-depth research (Andreamatteo et al. 2015). A more dramatic conclusion was provided by two academic health professionals who argue that

> [t]here is scant evidence that re-engineering health care services in line with industrial models increases their efficiency. Indeed, reducing the richness of healthcare to impoverished snippets of work may add to the problems of hospital misadventure and inefficiency rather than solve them.
> (Winch and Henderson 2009: 28)

Indeed, studies of lean in services such as healthcare tend to point toward work intensification as the vehicle for enhanced performance. Hence Kumar (2010) and Moody (2014) show that increased competition in private healthcare in the USA has led to the widespread adoption of lean working, accompanied by work standardisation, monitoring and growing work intensification. According to Moody, the 'enormous work pressures on its [the hospital's] workforce' has led to one, perhaps unexpected, development, namely, the growth in healthcare unionism (ibid.: 20). In these sectors and in public services generally, where lean working has proliferated, lean has been associated with work degradation, removing, rather than enhancing, discretion (Carter et al. 2011). In their UK research of 20 case-study organisations covering both private and public sectors, Burchell et al. (2002) found that teamworking is commonly introduced as part of a programme of delayering and restructuring, often leading to work intensification and heightened stress for team members. Others argue that within service work, lean is associated with almost no expression of voice, to the extent that 'some forms of work organization, especially the lean teams, cannot be considered to be teams at all' (Procter and Benders 2014: 300).

Conclusions

The problematic status of teamwork is revealed by the EWCS description of it as a 'double-edged sword' for employees because of its combination of positive and negative aspects. On the positive side, teamwork offers opportunities to learn new things, to apply ideas and enjoy mutual support, especially in what the report terms 'autonomous' teams. The negative side is found in its potentially emotionally draining and intense nature and the possibilities of internal conflict, especially in the same autonomous teams that offer the most benefits (Eurofound 2016b: 88). There is, though, little doubt that teams and arrangements for teamworking will continue to form a dominant part of managerial ideology and practice for the foreseeable future. All varieties of teams appear to offer performance advantages, whether located in service provision or in manufacturing. Teamworking is found in both developed and developing economies. Some teams are valued and appreciated by their members for the opportunities they provide for mutual learning and support, as well as enhancement of work experience; under favourable conditions, some allow a measure of worker agency (Stewart et al. 2009: 210–11; Hudson 2002). Crowley et al. (2014: 499) arrived at similar contextual conclusions in their examination of 204 workgroups, arguing that under supportive management regimes, 'workers prefer peer surveillance to traditional hierarchical control, and they enjoy the feeling of being part of, rather than subject to, the authority structure of an organization'.

Value appears to be especially prominent for teams composed of knowledge and creative workers, who in any event are liable to enjoy a measure of responsibility and autonomy that is unlikely to be undermined by team formation, even if this is accomplished under the direction of more senior personnel. As we have seen in the case of lean, one objective and outcome of team creation can be to re-engineer work in order to pursue efficiency gains, often in association with staffing reductions. While these arrangements can lead to enhanced task autonomy, this is usually bounded by tight procedures, surveillance and performance monitoring, which together can allow for little meaningful expression of voice. So-called teamworking is common in call centres but, as research has established, such teams often simply represent a convenient way for spatial control over work and an efficient technique to organise workers, who enjoy little in the way of 'creative and synergistic interaction' with colleagues (Baldry et al. 2007: 65; see also Townsend 2007, who examined peer control as a form of discipline in call centre teamworking). For practitioners, there will be attractions in lean teams, but it should be borne in mind that performance increases linked to work intensification may be of limited duration and do little to build the consensual forms of successful collaborative endeavour identified by Dromey in his healthcare case studies.

Chapter 9

Collective participation

Introduction

Previous chapters have focused largely on EPV approaches established or stimulated by management. These initiatives include mainly individualised or team-based involvement projects with any joint decision-making restricted to making suggestions to improve performance. Initiatives that have originated from workers, such as autonomous work groups, have either been replaced by more management-supportive approaches or been converted by management into team-based instruments designed to optimise performance rather than to provide opportunities for collective or oppositional expression of voice.

An alternative tradition to EPV is founded on collective employee-inspired participation (Hyman and Mason 1995). Collective participation is usually channelled through elected representatives and for this reason is often described as indirect or representative participation, with processes that include collective bargaining, consultative arrangements and works councils, worker-directors and social partnership. Participative intentions emerge from 'a collective employee interest to optimize the physical, security and aspirational conditions under which employees are contracted to serve' (ibid.: 29). They may also be supported by sympathetic governments, which are usually social-democratic (or, historically in the UK, Labour) in character and can act in association with other countries, for example within the EU. Worker-inspired initiatives aim to regulate labour market relations through collective representation, and consequently can be opposed by employers, their supporters and governments who believe that regulation restricts free operation of labour markets. From a theoretical perspective, collective participation derives from pluralist constructions of employment relations, while involvement is more closely aligned to unitarist ideas. Traditionally, trade unions, as representatives of the pluralist tradition, have provided the principal means through which collective participative action is undertaken; it is in countries where trade unions have been seriously marginalised that managerial involvement is currently most pronounced. One sign of declining union influence is diminishing union density; as we saw in chapter 4, this trend has been strongly marked in the UK and other market-orientated economies. In the UK in 1979 more than half of all employees were in a trade union; by 2016, density had declined to 23.5 per cent. It is, therefore, with collective bargaining in the UK that we begin our investigation into representative participation. Nevertheless, there are countries in Europe, including Germany and France where, irrespective of low union density, union participation in joint decision-making, notably through sectoral collective bargaining, is still prevalent. Coordinated market economies typically employ a range of mutually reinforcing collective participative approaches, though occasionally these can obstruct each other. One consequence of this complexity is that it is difficult to identify the impact of specific factors or the ways in which they interact to influence decisions.

The decline of collective bargaining in the UK

Collective bargaining, or joint regulation of terms and conditions of employment, enjoys a long history, stretching back at least to the end of the nineteenth century. It involves employers dealing directly with trade unions that they recognise as partners in 'the negotiation and continuous application of a set of rules to govern the substantive and procedural terms of the employment relationship' (Windmuller 1987). It is therefore principally a rule-making process that 'determines and regulates, in varying degrees, the terms on which individuals will be employed' (Salamon 1999: 305). Bargaining thus potentially deals with broader issues than pay alone and has for many years occupied a central place in debates over participation, industrial democracy and governance. Hugh Clegg was an influential contributor to a pluralist tradition that argues that conflicting sectional interests over employment are both natural and healthy, the essential requirement being to identify appropriate ways to regulate the conflicting interests of employers and employees. For this, trade unions occupy a fundamental role in maintaining democracy at work, 'as the guardian of the collective bargaining function upon which this industrial governance model is established'. Trade unions are therefore 'industry's opposition – an opposition that can never become a government' (Clegg 1985: 84). This permanent state of opposition, of course, raises serious questions about the democratic character of collective bargaining (Blumberg 1968: 144), an issue that becomes more pertinent when one considers the relative ease with which the 'loyal opposition' has been displaced in the UK and other countries in recent years. While many countries have legal backing for bargaining activities, in the UK, the tradition has been one of voluntary bargaining free from legislative control, arising mainly through union fears of having their protective functions compromised. As Richard Hyman points out, this fear extended to rejection of alternative forms of participation in management decision-making, which British trade unions saw as the responsibility of management (Hyman 2003: 46). The role of unions was to use collective bargaining to defend worker interests and to ensure that management decisions were not to the detriment of their members.

In the UK at least, collective bargaining has therefore been the preferred instrument of EPV for a confident and dominant trade union movement, a process that traditionally enjoyed broad governmental support (Brown et al. 2003). Collective bargaining is, however, now a minority practice: WERS studies estimate that about 70 per cent of employees were covered by bargaining arrangements in the 1970s and early 1980s, but this had declined to around 23 per cent by 2011. While bargaining coverage stagnated in the private sector at around 16 per cent between 2004 and 2011, the drop in the public sector was dramatic, from 68 per cent in 2004 to 44 per cent in 2011 (van Wanrooy et al. 2013: 79). At the same time, the scope of bargaining, namely the range of items negotiated between employers and unions, also narrowed in the private sector, while remaining constant in the public sector. What explanations can be offered for the unprecedented decline and fall of collective bargaining?

Clearly, the underlying factor in the decline of both union density and bargaining coverage is the UK's political commitment to liberate product and labour markets from 'rigidities' or obstacles to their operation. The aims of trade unions to set common pay levels for their members are perceived as such an obstacle, as could be the means by which unions pursue their objectives. Legislation from the 1980s has therefore restricted union scope to take industrial action by requiring postal ballots, prescribing limitations to numbers of pickets, outlawing secondary picketing and permitting employers to sue unions for damages incurred through unlawful industrial action (Pyper 2017). Much of this earlier legislation remains on the statute books and other restrictions have been added, culminating in the 2016 Trade Union Act enforced 'to protect people from undemocratic industrial action' (DBEIS 2017b). During their sustained period in office, between 1979 and 1997, Conservative governments also encouraged senior managers to take a hard line against unions in key sectors such as steel, car manufacturing, and, most infamously, coal-mining. Arguably, it was the defeat of the previously unassailable miners following their year-long strike in 1984/5 that did most damage to labour movement confidence (MacIntyre 2014). Privatisation was also adopted as a free-market policy instrument and, though union membership levels have remained relatively stable in previously publicly owned sectors (Arrowsmith 2003), other public-sector policy initiatives, such as outsourcing and contracting out services, have undoubtedly had an adverse effect on union recognition and activity (Huws and Podro 2012). The decline of manufacturing employment in the UK, coupled with exporting industrial jobs to lower-cost countries (Hardie and Banks 2014), has accompanied growth in service sector employment, which now represents 80 per cent of UK employment (ONS 2011), much of it in growth areas where union membership and activity are low, such as software (Hyman et al. 2004), retail and hospitality (Tait (2017).

Moreover, establishments are becoming smaller, which militates against union organisation; new or existing employers opening on 'greenfield' sites also tend to eschew union recognition (Brown et al. 2003: 201). Employer avoidance, antagonism towards and derecognition of trade unions became increasingly common from the end of the 1980s (Gall and McKay 1999; Gall 2004b; Dundon 2002), a trend that has unquestionably been exacerbated by the recession (Visser 2016), though mitigated by provisions of the 1999 Employment Relations Act that allowed unions to apply for statutory recognition. Initially, this act led to a large number of agreements, but latterly these have dwindled (Wright 2011). Van Wanrooy et al. (2013: 99) attribute some of the decline in collective bargaining over pay in the public sector to the increased use of Pay Review Bodies, which make independent recommendations to government on pay for about a quarter of public sector employees, including doctors, nurses and teachers. Low rates of inflation, providing little scope for union negotiations, have also influenced collective bargaining and, indirectly, the attractiveness of trade unions to employees, who weigh up the cost of union subscriptions against membership benefits.

So, if collective bargaining is in long-term decline in the UK, what is replacing it in terms of EPV? Though there has been an increase in non-recognition and derecognition, the main way in which employers have restricted collective bargaining and union influence more broadly has been the increased use of direct and individualised involvement practices and the expansion of HR techniques generally. Chapter 3 indicated the rise in briefing groups, which had as one of their objectives the replacement of lay union representatives by supervisors and line managers to be the main conduits of information to subordinates. Employee pay reviews based on appraised performance are now commonplace (van Wanrooy et al. 2013: 98) and can reduce the scope for setting common terms and conditions through negotiation as well as promote a counter-ideology to collectivism, based on individual reward for individual contribution. PRP and employee share schemes, both of which influence overall remuneration, are established under unilateral management control and are also common, especially in larger enterprises (ibid.: 96).

Collective bargaining experience in Europe

The law in the UK traditionally abstains from involvement in collective bargaining but instead offers trade unions immunities from restriction of trade when engaging in collective bargaining. The experience in mature European economies is rather different and founded on legislated protection of union activity that is treated as 'a component of human rights' (Block and Berg 2010: 194). Moreover, within the EU, the 1992 Maastricht Treaty's Social Chapter ensured that both employers and unions were allocated a formal role in EU policy-making, which also helped to safeguard the status of unions as a 'social partner' and the integration of collective bargaining into national, sectoral and organisational regulation and outcomes (ibid.: 197). Another important factor is the type of bargaining that is protected. One form may involve multiple employers covering specific sectors or groups of workers. A similar approach, termed centralised bargaining, can negotiate terms nationally for whole industries (Doellgast and Benassi 2014: 229). Both approaches aim to distance collective bargaining from the enterprise, where workplace representation is provided for by works councils (Rigby et al. 2009). An important implication of broad-based bargaining is that negotiating coverage is not necessarily dependent on union density. Both France and Germany have low (by UK standards) union density. In France in 2012, density was a mere 7.7 per cent, a drop of just 0.3 percentage points from ten years earlier, but through industry-wide agreements, bargaining coverage was maintained at 90 per cent. In Germany union density in 2013 was 17.7 per cent, a ten-year drop of 5.3 percentage points and coverage around 60 per cent (OECD and Visser 2016), though some estimates of coverage are lower (Dribbusch and Burke 2012). Nevertheless, union density shows a consistent pattern of decline in almost all developed countries over the past 20 years, although these trends vary significantly across Western countries, with few signs of precipitous decline among coordinated market countries, in contrast to more volatile liberal market economies (Schnabel 2013). In other words, the sometimes predicted extinction of trade unions is unlikely to occur while unions and collective bargaining are offered state protection.

Despite long-term governmental support, there has been concern among policy-makers and employers in many mainland European countries that centralised and sectoral collective bargaining systems fail to provide sufficient flexibility for companies to be competitive in global markets. As a consequence, there has been an 'overall shift towards flexibility, erosion and fragmentation of collective bargaining throughout Europe' (Eurofound 2015b: 49), including the two dominant economies of Germany and France. In Germany, neoliberalisation was initially implemented through the so-called Harz reforms of the labour market, aimed at encouraging greater employee tractability, increasing pressure on unemployed people to take jobs and, although there was little legislative activity directed at trade unions, some erosion and fragmentation of collective bargaining was initially evident 'through local concession bargaining, entailing deviations from collectively agreed industry standards' (Lehndorff 2009: 26). The German economy, which had been in decline following the financial crisis, revived dramatically as a result of the subsequent easing of neoliberal policies and the introduction of 'crisis corporatism' that provided government backing to collective bargaining at different levels and 'tripartite coordination at all levels' (Lehndorff 2011). In these processes, the unions have shown that their role in providing collective voice can prove beneficial not only to their members, but to the performance of the sector and economy. Nevertheless, the prospects for collective bargaining remain uncertain and rely on state support for sustenance. Recent research by Addison et al. (2017) found continual decline in sectoral bargaining and a 'declining share of establishments (and workers) having sectoral bargaining *and* works councils' (ibid.: 223, emphasis in original). They also found little evidence of an increase in firm-level bargaining. The authors conclude that there are signs of erosion of the dual system and 'scant evidence of (union) revitalization from below' (ibid.: 224).

In France, collective bargaining has a long and complex history and one that may experience new restrictive directions with the election of liberal-minded President Macron (L'Obs 2017b: 65–68). Basically, bargaining can be undertaken at national level, where all employees are covered, at industry or sector level and at company or establishment level. Industry-level bargaining can take place at national, regional or local levels (Fulton 2015). Collective bargaining first received legislative support in 1950. Twenty years later cross-industry or interprofessional bargaining was introduced. The Auroux reforms, in 1982, required companies to negotiate pay and working time at company level and thoroughly reformed the system of employee participation to offer broader employee representation at workplace level (Gumbrell-McCormick and Hyman 2010: 297). Between 2004 and 2008, further legislation was passed to facilitate company-level agreements over pay and working time but also to strengthen bargaining at national level, requiring the government to consult with employers and unions over proposed changes to industrial relations, employment and training (Fulton 2015). There is little doubt that in the last few years, with governmental support, company bargaining has attained higher status with a requirement to cover a wide range of topics including pay, working time, organisation of work and equality issues. Unions at company level can also review training provision and, where needed, negotiate over redundancies (Milner and Mathers 2013). Despite state support, French unions face a number of obstacles. The swing to a more liberal industrial policy agenda and the state-sponsored shift to workplace bargaining include some topics, which, through adapting labour law at workplace level, can be detrimental to employees. Union influence has also been threatened by the growth of casualisation and the adoption of restructuring HRM techniques (Salmon 2011) to create 'a sense of atomization and powerlessness that erodes union ability to formulate collective responses' (Milner and Mathers 2013: 127).

Different directions? Joint consultation in the UK and Europe

With collective bargaining apparently in long-term decline in the UK, are there other procedures of collective representation that may be more acceptable to the parties? A historically preferred approach for managers, joint consultation, (JC) is also under challenge from individualist involvement (Holland et al. 2009). JC has a long history in the UK and has traditionally drawn management support because, unlike collective bargaining, it does not formally invoke joint regulation or derogation of managerial prerogative. JC typically involves committee discussions between management and employee representatives over managerial intentions or actual initiatives, to which employee representatives are invited to respond, without enjoying the authority to contest management plans. However, informal bargaining can enter the JC system at times of high employment and union assertiveness. This was the case in the 1960s with the evolution of the so-called 'two systems' of industrial relations, a formal centralised procedural system agreed by the parties, supplemented by an informal system in which lay union representatives exploited consultative processes to broaden the scope of collective bargaining at workplace level to include items and issues that were formally part of management's responsibilities (Donovan Commission 1968). Steps were taken to restore managerial control and, with the subsequent decline of trade unions, the informal system became increasingly marginalised. Though JC is a collective representative process, representatives need not be union activists or members; companies with no union recognition agreements often adopt consultative arrangements, potentially to provide barriers to union entry.

Surprisingly, perhaps, consultative forums have been in decline in the UK, a reflection of managerial preferences to dispense with representative participation in favour of individualised involvement. The WERS data show that 8 per cent of all workplaces had a JC committee (JCC) on site in 2011, indicating little change from 2004. For workplaces employing more than 50 employees, the figures were 13 per cent in 2011 compared with 14 per cent in 2004 (van Wanrooy et al. 2013: 61). The figures are important because new consultative regulations were introduced in 2005 requiring the establishment of a JCC under specific conditions for enterprises with over 150 employees; this was extended to those with 50 employees in 2008.

The ICE regulations, based on an EC directive, for the first time provide employees with a statutory right to request the establishment or alteration of arrangements to inform and consult them about significant organisational issues. However, employers only need to act if ten per cent of employees request to opt in to the statutory procedures (Cullinane et al. 2015). According to government advisory service ACAS, a negotiated agreement should set out issues to be discussed and when and how often discussions should take place. The provisions contained in the ICE regulations set out the main generic topics for consultation. These include: the economic situation of the company; employment prospects; and decisions likely to 'lead to substantial changes in work organization or contractual relations', decisions which should be agreed between the parties (ACAS 2017). Obvious questions are: first, whether these regulations have led to broader use of JCCs or equivalent forums, and second, the nature of their impact. WERS data indicate an increase in JCCs in medium-sized enterprises with between 100 and 249 employees, from 9 per cent in 2004 to 18 per cent in 2011, suggesting some legislative impact. However, for larger enterprises there were observable declines in all organisation size categories employing above 250 employees, leading the authors to question the impact of the regulations on JCC growth. Conversely, decline in JCC was evident prior to the establishment of the regulations, suggesting that they may have helped to reduce, if not arrest, this decline. Also, there was no noticeable increase in the frequency of meetings between the two surveys (van Wanrooy et al. 2013: 61–62).

One possible reason for the modest take-up may be the difficulty for employees, especially if they are not union-organised, to act on the 'opt-in' mechanism. This difficulty was demonstrated by Cullinane et al. (2015) in the Irish context, which has similar voluntarist traditions and neoliberal policies as the UK, and is also subject to the same EC information and consultation directive. They researched a US-owned non-union manufacturer with three sites in Ireland, focusing on its main production site, employing nearly 3,000 people. The researchers found that despite valid opt-in procedures the 'regulatory pathway is porous and non-union employers can elude its ambit', concluding that the 'likelihood of successful opt-ins under the regulations in the non-union sector will be low' (ibid.: 23).

Resistance by management to the principle of consulting with employees was starkly demonstrated in an earlier research project conducted by Taylor and his colleagues in 2009. Bearing in mind that the regulations were designed to inform and consult employees about significant organisational issues, there was reasonable expectation that issues such as redundancies would fall readily into this category of 'significant'. Taylor et al. examined use of the ICE regulations during restructuring and redundancy proceedings in six companies in four key sectors: vehicle manufacturing, financial services, electronics and aerospace engineering. Their findings were uniformly negative. Five companies failed to consult employees over future employment and, in three, union participation was opportunistically displaced through non-negotiating consultation arrangements. In all cases ICE-inspired mechanisms failed to provide 'added levels of representation either to complement unions, or to fill the 'representation gap' left by declining membership' (Taylor et al. 2009: 44). Their critique also implicated the then UK government's commitment to a liberal market agenda in watering down the directive and the CBI's resistance to European social partnership or stakeholding as factors in encouraging employers to manipulate the regulations to their best advantage.

A recent analysis by Hall et al. (2015) draws on WERS data and case studies to indicate substantial problems with both the regulatory design and enforceability of the ICE regulations. In particular, they identify key EPV weaknesses: first, the 10 per cent threshold to initiate opt-in procedures is compromised by union estrangement from the process and the inability of non-union employees to mobilise and activate their rights to consultation. The authors then define the regulations as 'peripheral', leaving scope for employers either to do little or to impose only limited consultation procedures, potentially favourable to their needs. Hall et al. note that recognising these weaknesses there is some pressure for regulatory reform at EU level, but whether these will be of any benefit to UK employees will, of course, be determined by governmental employment policies following the UK's planned departure from the EU. Bearing in mind the UK's continuing strategies aimed at removing 'imperfections' in the labour market, union weakness and continued adherence to workplace individualism, the outlook for regulated consultation rights in the UK does not look promising.

Works councils and codetermination: the experience of Europe

It is important to note that the regulations that receive faint support from employers and the state in the UK merely aim to promote formalised information and consultation provision. On the other hand, many (largely) continental European countries have gone down the route of works councils and codetermination (Gumbrell-McCormick and Hyman 2010). The strategic importance of the codetermination process to EPV is demonstrated by its definition as 'an institutional process of employee information, consultation and *decisionmaking* in the management of an establishment' (Michel 2007: 3, emphasis added), though degrees of codetermination vary and in the case of France are highly circumscribed, formally (Gumbrell-McCormick and Hyman 2010: 297) and informally, through employer intransigence, notably in the service sector and in small enterprises (Rigby et al. 2009). Gumbrell-McCormick and Hyman contend that many Western European works councils are united through common early twentieth-century ambitions to regulate conflict between capital and labour and, through these objectives, offer voice to workers and provide for an employee stake in society (Gumbrell-McCormick and Hyman 2010: 302). As commentators (e.g. Nienhüser 2014: 248; Budd and Zagelmeyer 2010: 495) point out, diverse European works council models are legislatively equipped to support participation (albeit potentially by vetoing management plans) in workplace-level decision-making and hence form part of the codetermination process. Nienhüser is specific in his definition of a works council: it is an 'institutionalized, representative body' established to represent 'the interests of all employees of a company to its management' (see also Rogers and Streeck 1995). Works councils do not include: direct or individual involvement; worker-directors; or, because they operate at workplace level, supra-establishment EWCs (see chapter 10). They can also be identified by the broad scope of topics in which they are mandated to participate. Nienhüser identifies three long-standing models of works council, based on whether the council alone represents workplace employee interests or whether council and union operate in the same establishment, but with different responsibilities: (a) single-channel representation by a non-union body (Germany), (b) single-channel representation by a union body (Sweden), and (c) dual-channel employee representation (France). Gumbrell-McCormick and Hyman (2010: 302) also point out that councils vary in composition, member selection, powers and in their links 'to other industrial relations institutions', notably collective bargaining. In France, for example, the works council can submit resolutions to the annual general meeting of the board of directors, thereby requiring shareholders to consider worker representative proposals. The works council can also delegate members to attend board meetings (Conchon 2015). Coverage in different countries does vary, depending on their trigger mechanisms and levels of employer and state support: about 10 per cent of companies in Germany (representing approximately 40 per cent of employees), 63 per cent in Sweden (80 per cent of employees) and 81 per cent in France, where 'a works council must be established independently of the employees' will' (Nienhüser 2014: 254). In all cases, the larger the establishment, the greater the likelihood of a works council.

We noted above that the original objectives of works councils were threefold: to regulate conflict, provide a societal stake for employees and offer voice to employees. To these we can add a fourth, from the employers' perspective, namely to contribute directly or indirectly to organisational performance. Gumbrell-McCormick and Hyman note a number of potential structural constraints in achieving the first three objectives. Of considerable importance is the cooperation of the employer, the level of which can be difficult to assess (Gumbrell-McCormick and Hyman 2010: 303). Though formal sanctions against recalcitrant employers may be available, deployment by bodies authorised to action them can be questionable. Further questions have been raised regarding the representativeness as well as the independence and motives of council members, who may find themselves in 'deeply ambiguous' positions when responding to contrasting demands of their members, union and employer. Globalisation, mergers, organisational and employment restructuring have all led to a situation of greater precarity for works councils (ibid.: 308).

Nienhüser provides an excellent summary of research on works councils, dividing studies into two distinct traditions. First, he identifies mainly qualitative studies looking at the work undertaken by councils, the conditions under which members serve and social relationships between the interested parties. Second, there have been mainly German quantitative studies examining the impact of councils on measures of performance. Recent research by Jirjahn (2010) cited by Nienhüser (2014: 258–59) suggests positive links with performance but the identity of 'blackbox' moderator variables is as yet uncertain. Further, there also appear to be positive associations between councils, pay, labour turnover and the deployment of progressive human resource policies. Unfortunately, there has been little research to indicate the strength, depth and impact of employee voice associated with works councils or the ways in which council voice articulates with collective bargaining or other aspects of codetermination to influence employer behaviour. There are justifiable fears that in the prevailing climate of recession, austerity and ever-heightening competition, employers may attempt to use councils to promote plans to reduce employment costs.

Supervisory boards and codetermination

When Theresa May was appointed to the British premiership following the political upheavals of the referendum vote to leave the EU, one of her first pronouncements was to advocate greater enterprise accountability and in particular the appointment of employee board directors to counter toxic governance in well-publicised companies. Arguments have also been raised against the harmful effects of the dominant UK short-termist model of favouring shareholder primacy and consequent neglect of other stakeholders (Williamson 2013; High Pay Centre 2013). Following pressure from employer bodies, May's apparent commitment to board democratisation was quickly and quietly rescinded. This was not the first time that board membership for employees had been advocated and rejected in the UK. In the 1970s, in the wake of the EC's 1972 directive on participation and the height of policy interest in developing forms of participation as a means to democratise work and to improve economic performance, the Bullock Commission, established by the then Labour government to recommend appropriate representative systems for the UK, advocated in its majority report (Bullock Report 1977) the establishment of a system of worker-directors, sitting in parity with company directors on a single (unitary) board in large private-sector enterprises. The plan met with immediate and sustained opposition from the CBI, employers generally and a number of influential trade unions, concerned at their possible collusion with management and potential conflicts of interest in representing their members, though the TUC was, and continues to be, a strong supporter of worker-directors (Williamson 2013). The tone and vigour of opposition can be appreciated from a contemporary CBI publication:

> It is quite clear that no Government should contemplate bringing in legislation based on the majority Bullock Report. Surveys of public opinion show there is no popular support for it; the unions are divided; the owners and managers are united in opposition.
>
> (CBI 1977: 18)

Blessed with such an endorsement, the proposals were first diluted and then dropped entirely by the incoming Thatcher administration. The CBI's negative views of worker-directors appear to be little changed today (Financial Times 2016). Objections to worker-directors are not difficult to find. There are claims that decision-making will be slowed down (Vogel 2007); worker-directors do not possess the expertise of trained and qualified executives (Markey et al. 2010: 246); there may be risks of confidentiality leaks (O'Kelly 2005); and concern that employee representatives may seek to protect vested interests (ibid.; Kluge 2005). Also, some trade unions continue to harbour doubts about a potential impact of worker-directors on their traditional oppositional roles (Williamson 2013: 27).

In many European countries, however, employee representation on supervisory boards is an integral statutory element of codetermination and of the social model generally. Further, there are, especially in large German companies, formal organic links between works councils and supervisory boards. Perhaps surprisingly, in the European Economic Area, as many as 14 countries have rights to board-level employee representation in both private and public sectors, on either two-tier or unitary boards, and another five have limited participation rights. Twelve countries do not have either of these rights, including the UK

(Conchon 2015). The regulations over rights to board-level worker representation vary widely from country to country and national legislation has often been subject to change, especially in recent years. In response to financial crisis and recession, some governments have introduced privatisation plans, which can lead to a reduction in board-level representation in countries such as Ireland, where state-owned enterprises have adopted the worker-director route.

The German system is the best known and forerunner of worker-director programmes in Europe. It is also the model that has been most comprehensively studied and provides a firm basis for examining the critiques raised in the UK. Corporate governance in Germany, as in many European countries, is based on a two-tier board system consisting of management and supervisory functions, with employees represented at the supervisory level. According to Addison and Schnabel (2009), the supervisory board has four key functions:

a   approve management board membership.
b   monitor the management board.
c   codetermine business operations.
d   examine annual company accounts.

The authors identify three different models of company-level codetermination, namely (ibid.: 4–5):

a   the original full-parity seat allocation for the coal and steel industries established by the 1951 Codetermination Act, which also allows for agreement by employee representatives in the appointment of a Labour Director to the management board
b   'almost-equal or quasi-parity representation' for businesses with more than 2,000 employees (1976 Codetermination Act)
c   one-third representation in companies with 500–2,000 employees (1952 Works Constitution Act)

Figures from the Hans-Bökler Foundation show a steady decline in parity board representation in companies with over 2,000 employees, from 767 in 2002 (Addison and Schnabel 2009) to 640 by the end of 2013 (Mitbestimmung in Deutschland: Daten und Fakten 2014).

Addison and Schnabel undertook a comprehensive review of German worker-director research. Early studies on financial performance were inconclusive, possibly through methodological shortcomings, but later studies were more rigorous. FitzRoy and Kraft (1993) examined cross-sectional data for 112 companies in 1975 (prior to the 1976 legislation which provided quasi-parity codetermination) and 1983, which allowed time for the law to bed in. The conclusion was that the shift from one-third to quasi-parity determination 'might have measurable private costs' in terms of productivity loss. A later revision (FitzRoy and Kraft 2005) of their analysis indicated that the switch to quasi-parity had in fact raised productivity (Addison and Schnabel 2009: 13, 19). A study by Schmid and Seger (1998), conducted in 160 large companies, found an 18 percent decline in share prices. A subsequent study by Gorton and Schmid (2004) analysed cross-section time-series data in 250 companies over the five-year period between 1989 and 1993 and found 'serious consequences for shareholder wealth' and possible signs of protecting staffing levels (Addison and Schnabel 2009: 16).

Later studies (Renaud 2007; Kraft and Ugarković 2006; Fauver and Fuerst 2006) have generally been more positive in identifying favourable, albeit modest, productivity, innovation and profitability effects of introducing quasi-parity codetermination. In addition, Fauver and Fuerst found positive contributions between board-level representation and board-level decision-making. Notwithstanding these mildly encouraging outcomes, there remain residual tensions among the social partners, with employer organisations favouring a mandatory one-third representation (Addison and Schnabel 2009: 24) and trade unions tending to advocate consolidation of worker-directors by reducing the threshold company size stipulated in the 1976 legislation. The government, whilst keen to maintain the stakeholder model, is sensitive to the impact of competitive tensions arising from globalisation and seeks ways to counter its recessionary effects on mature economies like Germany.

One shortcoming of the quantitative studies reported above is that qualitative issues, such as the impact of codetermination on corporate governance, tend to be neglected whereas, in the light of trenchant critiques of British business practice and very public management scandals, codetermination could provide a strong (but unlikely) rationale for consideration in economies like the UK. Several studies from other Northern European countries, including Sweden and Denmark, have indicated strong satisfaction from all the social partners with worker-directors, in both unitary and two-tier boards. There has been little evidence of confidentiality leaks, promotion of sectional interests against those formally vested in the board, or problems associated with lack of organisational or financial expertise (Markey et al. 2010: 247). Employee directors appear to be effective intermediaries between management, unions and employees, though there have been suggestions that their influence is mainly restricted to personnel issues (Carley 2005). However, anecdotal evidence drawn from a number of interviews with worker-directors in Germany indicates a wider and sometimes strategic role for employees on supervisory boards, including in discussions over senior executive remuneration (High Pay Centre 2013).

Partnership at work: a tale of two systems

A form of representative participation that is well grounded in continental Europe, but relatively new to the UK, is partnership or, as its established counterpart is more commonly known on mainland Europe, social partnership. Essentially, the concept is based on achieving and sustaining mutual advantage through stakeholder cooperation, rather than through zero-sum negotiation-based confrontation. Recognising the relative weakness of employees in their dealings with employers, the mature economies of continental Europe are typified by 'highly developed systems of labour market regulation and social protection' (Hyman 2005: 12) that form the basis for the European social partnership model. Regulation, as we have seen, consists of an integrated system of collective bargaining (historically conducted at arm's length from the workplace), workplace works councils and, in many countries, worker-directors that often act within a broader corporatist framework involving employers, unions and state (Doherty 2011). Together, these processes provide a sense of stability and entitlement to employment relations in Europe by articulating a genuine collective voice for employees. Nonetheless, there is little doubt that the system is under threat from governmental responses to globalisation (often under employer pressure), compounded in recent years by economic recession. Reduced union density and collective-bargaining coverage have been experienced in most countries and the incidence of atomised plant or workplace bargaining has grown, leading to the concomitant growth of concession bargaining (Ebbinghaus 2002). Some governments have counter-responded by drawing back from deregulatory policies or, in some cases, adopting active measures designed to offer a degree of protection to employees by reinforcing the framework of social partnership (Lehndorff 2012).

The reactive role of the government in Ireland's experiment in social partnership is instructive. The Irish industrial relations system has for many years followed the competitive Anglo-Saxon format, yet, in the shadow of severe recession in the late 1980s, it introduced and successfully maintained a centrally coordinated social partnership approach for 20 years, during which the economy flourished. Partnership only collapsed following the 2008 financial crisis. Voluntary agreements over a wide range of labour market and welfare issues were achieved through negotiations between the government and the main confederations of unions and of employers. Faced with the consequences of the financial crisis, the government imposed pay cuts in the public sector, leading to disagreement and subsequent government withdrawal from the partnership (Doherty 2011: 373–75). The collapse of partnership was attributable to a number of factors: unlike some European models, it had no statutory base; also, the structure was held together by pragmatism, with no underlying ideological support, and when the economic crisis struck, the erstwhile partners went their separate ways (ibid.: 384). Reflective research by Valizade et al. (2016) suggests that workplace partnership in Ireland was influenced by trust in employment relationships, which acted as a mediating variable on partner interactions. Hence, high-trust relationships were a significant factor in consolidating the early viability of partnership, but, as we have seen, relations built on trust are difficult to establish and sustain in the present economic climate.

This experience raises the question of whether an embedded form of social partnership is compatible with a neoliberal approach to economic management.

The partnership approach that emerged in the UK in the late 1990s was arguably highly pragmatic in application and limited in ambition. For employers, it was seen as representing a means to securing better performance, while for unions, where they were recognised, partnership represented an opportunity to maintain an active workplace presence through closer collaboration with employers at a time of considerable labour movement fragility (Terry 2003a). The newly elected Labour government adopted partnership to bridge its twin ambitions of supporting trade unions that had helped the party into power, while signalling to employers and managers that the new government was 'open for business' (Johnstone 2014: 319). It should be noted that partnership in the UK, in common with other Anglo-Saxon countries, focuses on the workplace. It also complies with voluntarist traditions, which means that the government's role is merely to encourage or offer support, but with no direct intervention in the process (Samuel and Bacon 2010). Hence, there is no legislation that governs workplace partnership in the UK. These different perspectives mean that, as Johnstone points out, defining, interpreting and evaluating partnership is uncertain, with the term remaining 'conceptually ambiguous and contested' (Johnstone 2014: 311). A further difference from the predominantly Northern European model concerns the role of trade unions. Decline in union presence in the workplace left scope for employers' organisations, government and policy bodies to opportunistically promote workplace partnership, with or without a trade union role. As a consequence, definitions of workplace partnership such as those by the IPA (1997) and TUC (1999) tend to contain admirable mutual gain principles but come over as bland pronouncements demanding little strategic action and offering scant opportunity for measurement of effect (see Johnstone 2014: 312; Samuel and Bacon 2010).

It has been suggested that 'ideal-type' partnerships could impact on managerial prerogative by extending joint decision-making into areas of employment security as a quid pro quo for more flexible working, though partnership critics like Paul Thompson (2003) doubt whether, in prevailing economic conditions, employers would be able to commit to reciprocity or to undertakings that they might subsequently be unable to uphold. Bearing in mind the concomitant use of partnership in the public domain, alongside widespread adoption of new public management practices, it is not unreasonable to suggest that Thompson's doubts are well founded. If we add that partnership has also been said to draw upon commitment-directed high-performance techniques (Johnstone 2014: 313), it seems that, a priori, employers are well placed to take advantage of the project (Kelly 2004).

Irrespective of these reservations, between 1990 and 2007, some 248 partnership agreements were signed, covering about a third of employees in the public sector, but only 4 per cent of private-sector employees, according to studies by Bacon and Samuel (Bacon and Samuel 2009; Samuel and Bacon 2010). These authors examined 126 partnership agreements, with the majority covering health and social work (39 per cent) and public administration (20 per cent).

Findings show that few agreements contain IPA or TUC principles and most only 'have modest aims'. Also, most agreements were 'substantively hollow and procedurally biased'. Finally, these studies found that typical agreements did increase union involvement, though this was less evident in the private sector. Also, agreements showed little ambition to make mutual gains, possibly reflecting long-standing distrust between the parties, borne of traditional adversarial industrial relationships in the UK. The authors conclude that the voluntarist and non-statutory status of partnership is unlikely to lead to an extension of 'fairness at work' (Bacon and Samuel: 443–46).

Research by Oxenbridge and Brown (2004) in nine organisations also revealed valuable insights. They distinguish between 'robust' and 'shallow' partnerships, the former having high union density, collectively negotiated pay and well-established workplace representation. Some union representatives pointed out that in these situations, both formal and informal flows of information from management were increased and provided more regularly, and, in certain cases, the arrangements helped develop more substantial consultation procedures. There was also evidence of mutuality, as unions offered flexibility in return for job security. For critics of partnership, mutuality could extend to union collusion in restructuring, managing redundancies and cooperation in efficiency exercises. The lesson seems to be, though, that in the absence of supportive legislation, partnership is most likely to prove successful in the presence of strong trade unions and receptive employers, a situation that has become far less common since the research was carried out. Dangers to union independence were illustrated in Tailby et al.'s study of an NHS hospital trust and a number of private-sector manufacturing establishments (Tailby et al. 2004). In the trust, government targets and the means of achieving them appeared to form the motive for partnership for senior management. The study suggested that for HR managers, partnership was intended to be restricted in scope and employed instrumentally in pursuit of imposed targets. There was no enhancement in joint decision-making and danger of estrangement of unions from their membership, a situation also found in the manufacturing establishments where partnership appeared to implicate union officials in management processes, thereby distancing employees from their paid representatives.

An earlier study by Taylor and Ramsay (1998) demonstrates that union fears of partnership may not be unfounded. The authors focus on an in-depth case study of a national supermarket chain and the trade union it recognises. Faced with growing competition in the retail sector, the company was intent on introducing restructuring initiatives; to this end, it sought to agree a mutually beneficial national partnership agreement with the union, whose officials signed the agreement expecting that the union's existing status and interests would at least be protected. Within two years management had seriously compromised the agreement by bypassing the union, blocking union membership access to new company recruits, restricting union representative facilities and opening union-free new stores (ibid.: 129). Moreover, work intensification, diminished security and managerial aggression towards employees led to growing discontent, not only with the company but also with the union that had collaborated with it in establishing the partnership.

Conclusions

The reality is that even at their peak in the early 2000s, partnerships only ever achieved minority status in the UK, especially in the private sector. Those that do exist 'too often fall short of their rhetorical promise', according to Taylor (2004). The same writer harboured hopes that partnerships represented 'the beginning of a new kind of employment relations' (ibid.: 16) but, as he acknowledges, this depends to 'a very great extent on the initiative and support of employers' (ibid.: 12), which, as we have seen, has not always been forthcoming. Partnerships in other Anglo-Saxon countries appear to experience similar vulnerable and ill-defined positions, in contrast to EU countries, where a tiered, regulated and consolidated system of partnership and representative participation is evident. While respecting the voluntarist traditions on which UK employment relations are constructed, a number of commentators (e.g. Terry 2003a; Samuel and Bacon 2010) lament the lack of supportive legislation, without which workplace partnership is always vulnerable, especially with union density declining, bargaining becoming ever more restricted and increased prominence of individualistic involvement and HR practices.

As Oxenbridge and Brown (2004) note in their study, robust partnerships are associated with strong and active union presence, bargaining legitimacy and participation in workplace decisions, all of which are currently threatened. The recession has clearly compounded partnership vulnerability, especially as one of the main mediating variables, mutual trust, is at risk in highly competitive conditions. In their study of a large multinational engineering company, Butler et al. (2011) found that partnership was more likely to survive under recessionary conditions when management could be trusted, the competitive strategy was based on quality and innovation and trade unions had a solid presence. Under prevailing economic conditions, it is therefore questionable how robust surviving partnership arrangements are. Dobbins and Dundon (forthcoming) go further, describing sustainable labour–management partnership as a 'chimera', 'an illusion and figment of aspirational theoretical imagination', because of: managerial inability to maintain workplace bargains under neoliberal conditions; voluntarism failing to provide a positive context for workplace mutuality; and workplace mutuality being compromised by the power of competitive global economic forces and multinational organisations. As well as partnership, other forms of collective representation are vulnerable and for the same reasons, even in those countries where representative procedures are more heavily regulated and protected. As coordinated market economies come under increasing pressure to liberalise their systems, one outcome, the effects of which are already being experienced, will be concomitant pressures on governments to loosen regulatory regimes. Nevertheless, traditions of regulation, established union presence at different levels and statutory protections have served to protect employees in coordinated market economies rather better than those in marketised Anglo-Saxon ones.

In this chapter we have been able to see more clearly the origins and causes of the representation or participation gap in the UK. Collective bargaining has been marginalised and reduced in scope with the decline of trade unions and governmental support. Collective bargaining has not been supplanted or supplemented by more collaborative systems of participation. Joint consultation appears to be in long-term stasis or decline and European-derived consultative regulations and partnership initiatives have rarely been triggered, bypassed by employers or reduced to near insignificance in terms of employee influence, even over matters of prime concern to them. Employees are thus increasingly dependent on channelling their voice through employer-designed and operated involvement schemes, aimed at enhancing employee performance, but in reality these do little to raise either workplace satisfaction or productivity. There is, however, one other European-derived representative initiative whose impact remains to be evaluated, namely European Works Councils, which are considered in the following chapter.

Chapter 10

Internationalisation and the impact of European Works Councils

Introduction and background

For the past 50 years the European social agenda has struggled to provide an appropriate regulatory platform to give its citizens adequate protection from increasingly unable, internationalised and competitive market forces. The *World Investment Report* (UNCTAD 2016) provides an insight into the shifting complexities of international corporate identity and structure and the difficulties faced by employees and their representative bodies in monitoring and influencing enterprise decisions. Some '40 percent of foreign affiliates worldwide have multiple "passports"' and these complex ownership chains have 'multiple cross-border links involving on average three jurisdictions'. Moreover, the 'larger the MNE, the greater the complexity of their internal ownership' (ibid.: 8). The report also shows that recovery in foreign direct investment (FDI) has been strong since the financial crisis and 'buoyant' mergers and acquisitions (M&As) 'tilted FDI patterns towards developed economies' (ibid.: 1). The pace of FDI shift in Europe has quickened considerably: in 2013, inflows into the region totalled 323 billion dollars. In 2015, the figure was 504 billion dollars. Outflows increased from 320 billion dollars in 2013 to 576 billion in 2015 (ibid.: Table 2). According to the Institute for Mergers, Acquisitions and Alliances, in 2016, there were about 45,000 M&As worldwide, 18,000 across Europe and 3,500 involving the UK (IMAA 2016).

In these circumstances it is not too surprising that numerous EU attempts to deliver European-wide integrated systems of representative participation have faltered in the face of concerted opposition from multinational interests (Beirne 2013: 149). From the 1990s, worker vulnerability intensified as transnational companies operating across the single European market became increasingly dominant and numerous, with decision-making affecting workers in different countries often made at head offices distant from the reach of employees and localised participative systems. Lack of common regulatory provisions encouraged some companies to engage in internal competition and to transfer their operations to countries with minimal employee protection and low labour costs in a process of 'social dumping' (Alber and Standing 2000). From these tensions emerged the idea of 'Social Europe', with its Charter and Action Programme promising a platform of basic pan-European employment rights.

The main aim of the Charter was to provide means for employees to gain rights to information and representative participation at supranational level in organisations operating in Europe, irrespective of company head office location. The first European Works Council Directive offering European-level information and consultation rights for companies with operations within the EU (and later the European Economic Area, EEA) came into force in 1994 following considerable controversy and some hostility from non-European companies affected by the Directive, fearful that transnational representative participation would impinge on managerial decision-making (Sloan 1998). Politically opposed to the perceived anti-liberal thrust of Social Europe, the UK was originally not party to the Directive, having opted out of the European Social Chapter, but when the opt-out was revoked following the election of a Labour government, the UK became subject to the Directive in 1997. Later EU enlargement in 2004 extended the Directive to eight accession states of Central and Eastern Europe, followed by Romania and Bulgaria in 2007.

The Directive offered both hope and concern. For trade unions, there was the hope that participation could become more centralised to match that of corporate decision-making, with the possible opportunity to extend cross-national collective bargaining, precisely the fear entertained by many transnational companies (Hall and Marginson 2005). Business also expressed concern at the potential loss of managerial privilege and subsequent impact on decision-making through delays or through representatives defending and promoting collective employee interests, to the possible detriment of shareholders (UNICE 1991). Managerial unease was also voiced at potential public exposure of confidential commercial information by workplace representatives or union officials (ORC 2003; Laulom and Dorssemont 2015). More than twenty years of experience have led to numerous studies of EWCs but, before analysing their reported practice and effects, we first detail their institutional structures, regulatory procedures and incidence.

Forms and processes of EWCs

Companies with at least 1,000 employees, and 150 in two or more EEA states, are eligible to establish appropriate information and consultation arrangements. In August 2016 there were 1,101 currently active EWCs or their equivalents, representing about half of all eligible companies (Conchon and Triangle 2017). Nearly half the EWCs are Article 6 variants, regulated by the original 1994 Directive and the 2009 Recast Directive. A significant minority (39 per cent) of existing councils are pre-Directive EWCs, signed before 22 September 1996 and therefore not fully covered by the EU Directive of 1994 and the 2009 Recast (De Spiegelaere and Jagodziński 2015). Pre-Directive status was established under Article 13 of the 1994 Directive and provided exemption to those enterprises in which 'an agreement, covering the entire workforce, providing for the transnational information and consultation of employees' existed prior to the Directive's 22 September implementation date (Hall and Marginson 2005: 205). Subsequently, organisations were required to follow the Special Negotiating Body (SNB) whereby a procedure for establishing an EWC or its equivalent can be initiated through a request by a minimum of 100 employees from at least two sites or through management action.

The main provisions of the original directive included (Cressey 1998: 68):

- an annual joint meeting with management, to provide information on group performance including business prospects and financial situation, investment plans and employment situation;
- provision for 'timely' consultation on management proposals with potential 'serious consequences' for employees, although final decisions rest with management;
- a minimum of three and maximum of 30 EWC members, with at least one representative from each national establishment; EWC members are required to inform establishment-level representatives of information provided and consultation outcomes;
- EWC expenses to be met by central management.

EWCs are established through agreement between the parties, and these can be renegotiated under the following conditions: in the context of new legislation; to amend existing rights; or to reflect company changes. Renegotiation has been most common in the older pre-Directive councils in order to bring them closer in line with contemporary requirements. About 240 EWCs have been dissolved, most (about three-quarters) as a result of merger or acquisition. In recent years, about 25 new EWCs have been established each year. The majority of EWC bodies have been set up in the metals (373), chemicals (190) and service (239) industries. Notwithstanding original concerns, 151 EWCs are established in companies with headquarters in the USA, and about one-fifth are headquartered in Germany. Just eight have their head offices in new member states, with five of those based in Hungary. De Spiegelaere and Jagodziński also report that nearly half of EWCs are based in large enterprises employing more than 5,000 employees and a similar proportion are highly internationalised, operating in at least ten European countries (De Spiegelaere and Jagodziński 2015: 18).

An important feature of EWCs is that the Directive affords some structural and procedural flexibility, based on national and organisational conditions, providing that minimum statutory requirements are met. As Ramsay (1997) noted, this flexibility can, of course, influence both the structure and the practices of the EWC and these need to be evaluated through empirical research. As indicated above, from the start, EWCs were seen as potential threats for managers or supports for trade unions and employees and latitude in their application may have diverse effects. We first assess early research and subsequent critical narratives that helped to inform the 2009 revision of the Directive, and then review its provisions before examining research findings following the redraft.

Early research on EWCs

As might be expected from such a potentially far-reaching European initiative, there has been no shortage of research studies. Findings from early research on EWCs were extensively analysed in a comprehensive review by Müller and Hoffmann (2001). They examined the background tensions and inevitable compromises required; the application of EWCs was bound by national systems of participation and inevitably had far-reaching implications for practice. In terms of analysing practice, the studies reported by Müller and Hoffmann were somewhat exploratory because many EWCs were in their early stages and 'still finding their feet' (ibid.: 122). Nevertheless, differences in practice were already beginning to emerge: 'Some EWCs act as clearing houses for information, providing at most strategic impulses for IR [industrial relations] at lower levels', while others have taken on the role of peak negotiator in company-level industrial relations: some 'go well beyond the formal provisions laid out in the actual agreements, other EWCs do not amount to much more than an annual sales briefing' (ibid.: 122). Differences were ascribed to the influence of different national employee relations systems and traditions (Streeck 1997), location and dominance of headquarters (Hall et al. 2003) and a general failure to harmonise representation in favour of individual company voluntarism (Müller and Hoffmann 2001: 106). These different tensions divided commentators between 'Euro-pessimists' and 'Euro-optimists'(Waddington 2003c; Whittall 2000). The pessimists suggest that the weight of evidence mitigated against the development of a Europeanised system of employment relations because of the institutional obstacles presented by the diverse national regulatory systems that together help to prevent an 'effective supranational regime of social regulation' (Dolvik 1997: 17). Euro-optimists, on the other hand, look to previously unobtainable rights and opportunities for pan-European collaboration that could serve as catalysts for the development of a genuine multilevel system of European employment relations (Müller and Hoffmann 2001: 110).

What does emerge from early studies is that threats to management hegemony from the European project have generally failed to materialise. Both quantitative research (mainly surveys) and qualitative case studies have been conducted. Surveys are especially useful in signalling the main contours of EWC experience while case studies show in more depth the individual characteristics and performance dynamics of the councils.

One empirical problem has been that the contribution of EWCs to management objectives has not really been effectively studied. As Müller and Hoffmann (2001: 77–91) point out in their review, research into the implications and benefits for management has largely been cursory and speculative. Studies to that date largely assess potential opportunities for management to incorporate EWCs into their HRM policies and organisational culture. The extent to which these 'opportunities' had been translated into practice was very much unknown, and arguably remains unknown today. For example, Boxall and Purcell's (2016) major source book on strategic HRM scarcely mentions EWCs. Nevertheless, the bulk of the early research *suggests* that management does envisage advantages in terms of exchanging views with employee representatives (Eurofound 2015c), which can serve to capture cooperative and organisational cultural benefits. Not surprisingly, Müller and Hoffmann conclude their review with a strong plea for more integrated research into management, HRM and EWCs.

Bearing the above caveats in mind, Wills' 1999 study of UK-owned enterprises examined 17 companies that had established EWCs. A high proportion of these had been established under the initiative of management, which had been 'proactive in shaping EWCs to their advantage' (Wills 1999: 25). The majority of management respondents cited communication as a prime motive for EWCs that were treated as a 'mechanism to foster identity with the corporate mission, to widen understanding of the management process and to improve communication' (ibid.: 28–29). Wills summarised the process as a "new arm to corporate communication" that is "likely to strengthen on-going processes of 'top-down co-ordination and convergence' in managerial practice" (ibid.: 33). Several other surveys identified by Müller and Hoffmann indicated that irrespective of whether managers actually benefited from EWCs, they were happy to establish them on the grounds that they could anticipate communicative or symbolic gains (Weber et al. 2000) from them and little in the way of losses.

American companies tend to adopt an adversarial approach to employee relations, Japanese companies a paternalistic or bureaucratic cooperative culture; therefore these and other non-EEA based companies generally have different employee relations traditions from the European social model from which EWCs were derived and were initially, at best, hesitant towards the prospect of imposed communication and consultation procedures. An interesting study of management attitudes in Japanese transnational companies was offered by Nakano (1999), who conducted a survey of 14 senior human resource managers, mainly based at European head offices of their transnational enterprises. The managers tended to concur that the main function of their EWC was to enhance dissemination of company information, to exchange views with employee representatives and to promote a spirit of cooperation. Further, managers were consistent in their view that EWCs were unlikely to undermine managerial authority, though some thought that employee expectations for influence may be raised and that centralised EWCs may not be compatible with decentralised and divisionalised corporate structure, though of course most decentralised companies retain strategic and financial decision-making at head office level (Bartlett and Ghoshal 1989). A survey of 24 major transnational companies, largely of US and Japanese origin, also reported largely positive outcomes from the establishment of EWCs, though managerial commitment to the consultative process varied from compliance, in a minority of cases, to fuller endorsement on the grounds that the EWC adds (unspecified) value to the company, though the EWC did not necessarily represent a significant element in the strategic development of the enterprise (ORC 2003).

The views of employee representatives and trade unions tended to diverge from the management perspective of moderate or anticipated satisfaction. Lack of control over the agenda and questionable quality of information dissemination and consultation were specific issues Waddington identified in his 2003 review of representative views in six countries, with country of origin of transnational enterprises being a major factor influencing EWC practice (Waddington 2003b: 321). Representatives from less socially regulated UK and Ireland expressed more support for EWC processes and outcomes than representatives from Northern Europe, owing to the lack of formal information and consultation procedures in their home countries. Similarly, UK and Ireland-based companies tended to be criticised for the narrowness of their agenda and quality of information.

A number of case studies were also published in the early years of the EWC project (e.g. Cressey 1998; Whittall 2000). These, and other, studies confirm that external factors such as national systems of employee representation, along with company and sector characteristics, help to shape EWC practice. Also important are levels of representative training and degrees of member cohesiveness (Waddington 2003c: 305). Though not generalisable, case studies also tend to present a similar picture where management controls the EWC procedure and manipulates subsequent practice to its advantage. Tony Royle (1999) analysed the establishment of an EWC in the McDonald's Corporation, the universally recognisable fast-food retailer, headquartered in the USA and known in management circles for its less than welcoming attitude to trade unions. Royle's intensive study extended over a period of six years and included 150 interviews conducted in the UK and Germany. The company had opted for an Article 13 agreement, providing it with the freedom to negotiate the framework for information provision and consultation directly with its employee representatives. The resulting EWC was a joint body, consisting of senior European executives of the company sitting with their employee counterparts, the majority of whom were salaried managers rather than the hourly paid staff that make up the vast bulk of employees at the company. Royle points out that the agreement lacked the support of unions, who were effectively frozen out of the establishment process from the beginning. The consequence was that rather than representing 'a vehicle for employee rights', the subsequent McDonald's body was 'just another method of 'getting the [corporate] message across''. On the basis of his analysis of the company, Royle concurs with other commentators who distinguish between EWCs as 'active institutions', established with functional and independent employee representation, and bodies where the EWC is merely 'symbolic', with 'little or no influence over management decisions' (ibid.: 343). In the McDonald's case, other potential serious hindrances were also apparent. Representative pre-meetings were precluded, apparently on cost grounds; agendas were largely determined by management; independent union representation on the council was restricted; management permission was required to introduce support from outside experts; there was little opportunity for representatives to feed back information to employees; finally, franchise outlets were not covered by the EWC, leaving some 200,000 employees with no effective EWC representation (ibid.: 344).

Wills (2000) also undertook a detailed case study of a single EWC that had been in existence for three years. The manufacturing company studied was the result of a three-way Anglo–French–USA merger in the early 1990s, operating in a competitive market, which led to constant restructuring and reorganisation, resulting in significant job reductions and turnover of chief executives. UK EWC representatives felt increasingly frustrated at their impotence in responding to these events because of inadequate consultation and the apparent inability of the EWC to influence managerial decisions due to a lack of coordinated activity among the representatives. The study cites a comment from the then political secretary of the European Trade Union Confederation (ETUC), which indicates that this was not an isolated instance: 'All too often, company management merely sees the EWC as a body that can be used to legitimise decisions that have already been taken. The chance for dialogue with workers' representatives is not used' (ibid.: 102).

Revision of the Directive and the 2009 Recast

Experience from the early years of the EWC project demonstrates the difficulties in reconciling a pan-European policy approach with employee participation processes that are directed and operated through national systems of employment relations. Considerable divergence, whether at national or enterprise level, is evident in practice, leading to mounting frustration of trade unions and their coordinating bodies at the inability of EWCs to engage transnational management in joint decision-making. Managers, meanwhile, continue to control the purse strings and the contributions of the EWCs (Gilson and Weiler 2008). The early research findings indicate that the original directive exposed shortcomings for employees and unions that their representatives would like to formally address at EU level. These shortcomings were further confirmed during the 2008 economic crisis that pushed many international companies into restructuring operations but with variable contributions from their EWCs. The European Commission was committed to review EWCs under Article 15 of the 1994 Directive, starting within three years of the original 22 September 1996 vesting date of the Directive. As with the original directive, the social partners were unable to agree a timetable or rationale for Community action, with the ETUC's enthusiasm for revision contrasting with opposition from the employers' umbrella body, BusinessEurope (Laulom 2010).

The problems facing the employee side of EWCs are well rehearsed. First, at the start of the revision process, just over one-third of eligible companies, covering 60 per cent of employees, had established a council. Even by 2015, coverage of EWCs had yet to reach half of the eligible transnational corporate population. Coverage in the accession states is substantially lower: for example, although there are estimates of Polish EWC representatives in nearly 200 EWCs, not one council has been set up in Poland, despite the presence of multinational companies headquartered there that fall under the EWC Directive (Skorupińska 2015). Second, as we have seen from the above accounts, employee representatives, individual trade unions and the ETUC had expressed a number of reservations concerning the 1994 Directive. Fundamentally, while the Directive 'represented a major breakthrough in the development of transnational information and consultation, its pioneering approach of establishing the primacy of negotiated solutions in lieu of universally applicable rules left many gaps and loopholes' (Hoffmann 2015: 5). In particular, there were significant problems in achieving satisfactory articulation between national and European levels of participation. As Laulom and Dorssemont (2015) point out, EWCs deal with transnational issues but transnational decisions can have national consequences. Conversely, national decisions can impact on situations in other branches of a company's European operations and are therefore transnational in effect, if not in definition. Unfortunately, 'the 1994 EWC Directive (94/45/EC) remained silent about the relationship between national and European procedures for worker involvement' (Hoffmann 2015: 56).

Problems of EWC competence have been compounded by continuing complaints at enterprise level about the quality and timeliness of information provided by management and shortcomings in the consultative process. These weaknesses were especially noticeable during a period of commercial turbulence affecting so many enterprises and their employees (Waddington 2010; Mählmeyer et al. 2017), meaning that genuine transnational dialogue between enterprise partners has been seriously compromised. As the ETUC explained: 'The norm was for the EWC to be 'consulted' after management decisions had been finalized' (ETUC undated). Consequently, there have been frequent union demands for stronger definitions and for enforcement of information dissemination and consultation procedures. Many anticipated topics for information or consultation fail to appear as standing agenda items (Waddington 2003c). A third issue has been that of inconsistent training provision and funding that has varied across Europe. In some countries, unions have borne the full cost of representative training; in others, paid time off for training has not been guaranteed (Picard 2010). There have also been calls for more training provision in essential topics such as employment law and employment relations applicable in other member states (Waddington 2003c: 319). A more intractable problem has been that the original directive left individual member states to apply the information and consultation procedures most compatible with their systems and practices of employment relations, leading to inconsistent cross-national practice and the ability for the more economically dominant states to impose their preferred approaches to participation. This flexibility has also led to variations in the practices of different transnational enterprises, based on sector, national preferences and management strategies (Marginson et al. 2013). A further problem in some EWCs has been over access to external specialists and union officials to help support employee representatives (Royle 1999). Calls have further been made by the ETUC for the inclusion of franchise operations, such as those at McDonald's, to be included within the scope of EWCs (ETUC 2017).

There was considerable pressure at EC level to address these perceived shortcomings and to reform the Directive. Though revision was recognised as a priority by the EC, there followed protracted procedural delays, but agreement after 'a politically fraught exercise' (Jagodziński 2016) was finally secured between the EC and European Parliament and the 'definitive text' was adopted in May 2009 (Laulom 2010). The main direction of the redrafted Directive was to provide stronger terminological definitions; ensure the transnational competence of EWCs; provide for improved interaction between different levels of representation; anticipate an enlarged role for employee representatives and for trade unions; improve rules for establishing EWCs; and to provide for better EWC adaptation to correspond with major organisational changes. The redrafted Directive did not require renegotiation of existing agreements, though agreements that were signed between 22 September 1996 and 5 June 2009 would be subject to the new provisions from 6 June 2011 (ETUC undated).

Article 2.1.f of the redraft provided new definitions and requirements for information and consultation. Information from the employer must be disseminated to the EWC in time for representatives to acquaint themselves with the topic and to prepare an appropriate response for purposes of consultation. Article 2.1.g defines consultation as 'the establishment of dialogue and exchange of views' between EWC representatives and management, allowing sufficient time for meaningful dialogue with appropriate levels of management, but 'without prejudice to the responsibilities of management'. Article 1.4 relates to EWCs and their capacity to deal with transnational matters, defined as those that concern the effects of 'Community-scale' undertakings. Better interaction between levels of representation is promoted in a new rule requiring coordination between European and national levels of representation. Article 10 establishes the formal competence of the EWC to act as legal representative of the employees and conditions for provision of financial support if legal action is undertaken. There is also an obligation for representatives to communicate outcomes of information and consultation to the workforce. Article 10 also provides an unequivocal right for training of representatives to allow them to discharge EWC responsibilities. Article 5 itemises the facilities and role of trade unions, focusing expressly on the activities of the SNB, which should have access to experts in its negotiating responsibilities. With only small numbers of

EWCs being created annually, unions were keen to introduce provisions to facilitate the establishment of councils through SNBs, which now have more seats and are distributed more evenly to reflect the number of employees in each member state. The SNB is now entitled to hold both pre- and post-meetings following discussions with central management. Finally, in case of merger or acquisition, the Recast Directive includes an enabling clause for EWCs to adapt in order to be consistent with the corporate profile of the restructured enterprise.

EWC experience following the 2009 Recast

In an examination of the impact of the Recast, longitudinal research up to 2012 in ten major EWCs (including Air France KLM, Bayer, Unilever, and British Airways) concluded that the impact of the Recast was 'minimalistic' (Eurofound 2015c: 72). Union-commissioned analysts have not been overly impressed by the Recast. Laulom (2010), writing in the immediate aftermath of the redraft and in the context of heightened organisational restructuring activity following the global economic crisis of 2008, did find a number of 'technical improvements' to the original in: (a) strengthened access for the parties to information required for commencing EWC negotiations, (b) improved worker representation, and (c) better definition of the content of the agreement. Nevertheless, she remains critical of the Recast because of persistent ambiguities concerning the competence of EWCs, largely derived from lack of consensus among the European social partners in redrawing the Directive (ibid.: 207). First, there appears to be ambiguity over whether the EWCs can only deal with transnational issues. Second there appears to be confusion over the timing of information disclosure and consultation, which on one hand needs to take place prior to decision-taking, but on the other should not slow down the process of decision-making. Third, Laulom claims that 'the problem of the relationship between national and European procedures remains entirely unresolved' (ibid.: 208), despite this being one of the central aims of the revision. She also believes that the revisions would be unlikely to promote the expansion of EWCs, a proposition which appears to have been borne out by subsequent experience: the annual rate of new EWCs creation to 2015 is little changed from previous years (De Spiegelaere and Jagodziński 2015).

An in-depth analysis of the redraft, prepared by Jagodziński on behalf of the European Trade Union Institute (ETUI) in 2015, similarly concludes that a number of difficulties concerning information and consultation rights and their enforcement still remain. As well as expanding on those noted above, Jagodziński also has concerns about the following: confidentiality issues potentially restricting effective participation by EWC representatives; the problem of 'copy-pasting' provisions to countries with different national systems of information and consultation; and the lack of sanctions on companies for infringement of the Directive (Jagodziński 2015). Equally trenchant critiques from union-based analysts are presented by Conchon and Triangle. While praising the Recast efforts to strengthen the 'formation, running and influence of EWCs' and efforts to anchor them in enterprise systems of employee relations (Conchon and Triangle 2017: 5), they also point out a number of failings, some of which have been empirically demonstrated. Notably, there is still a lack of clarity about possible sanctions for non-compliance, procedural issues concerning information and consultation and the 'transnational' character of EWC contributions. A damning limitation is that (still) 'consultation *hardly ever* takes place in the *majority* of EWCs which are, at best, information bodies' (ibid.: 6, my emphasis). Recent studies by Waddington et al. (2016), Voss (2016) and Pulignano et al. (2016) appear to add evidential weight to these allegations. Often when consultation does take place, it is at the same time as the information provision, leaving EWC representatives insufficient time to construct an effective response (*effet utile*) or to consult their members. A recent development not addressed by the Recast concerns the growing transnational identity of companies where patterns of ownership are becoming increasingly blurred through extended supply chains and equity buyouts. It appears that one of the original aims of EWCs, to provide transparency and a means for employees to secure access to organisational decision-makers, is still being compromised.

A major survey of over a thousand EWC agreements aimed to evaluate the effects of the Recast by explicit focus on the ways the revised terms were included in EWC agreements (De Spiegelaere and Waddington 2017). The main findings were that the Recast affected definitions of information and consultation, transnational competence and reporting back. There was also evidence of a 'learning effect' independent of the Recast in issues such as training, definitions of information, consultation and union roles from which EWCs can influence one another. The role of management in guiding EWC structure and practice was also prominent. The authors conclude that there were shortcomings to the Recast, specifically in its failure to sufficiently progress union involvement in EWCs. From the business side, however, projected concern that the Recast would prejudice commercial operations has not materialised (BusinessEurope 2008).

In fact, EWCs would appear to offer few drawbacks for employers and managers generally. From the early days, managers were exploring 'various devices' in order to contain any perceived negative impact of EWCs, such as controlling meeting agendas, allowing little time for consultation and directing any training toward 'safe' topics (Weston and Martinez Lucio 1997). More recently and positively, Vissols (2009) identified joint benefit from EWCs in a large-scale econometric study of the largest 600 listed European companies, of which 233 had an EWC. The study was carried out prior to the impact of the economic crisis and the Directive recast. Vissols estimates that EWCs have no negative impact on shareholders and a positive welfare effect on workers and managers. Specifically, he finds that managers tended to have a favourable view of EWCs, with two-thirds thinking that EWCs improved communications with employees and a similar proportion believing that employee commitment improved. Over a third considered that the effectiveness of the implementation of management decisions had improved, against 3 per cent who felt the opposite. Management fears about a deleterious impact on the speed of their decision-making do not appear to have been borne out, with over four-fifths considering that EWCs had no effect. In fact, 10 per cent believed they had a positive impact, against 9 per cent who were of the opinion that decision-making speed was negatively affected. In-depth case studies from Eurofound (2015d) also found that, to borrow language describing the role of shop stewards from an older industrial relations era, EWCs were more a 'lubricant' to management than an 'irritant'.

Conclusions

Diverse arguments have been presented for introducing collective EP, ranging from humanistic to economic and social perspectives (Knudsen 1995; Strauss 1998; Summers and Hyman 2005). From a specifically European viewpoint, Gold (2010) has identified company law rationalisation, prevention of social dumping, extension of worker rights and production efficiency as rationales for participation. However, the principal policy argument for EWCs is based on recognition that, in competitive product and service markets, employees of transnational enterprises are in a relatively weaker position than management to defend their interests or exert influence over the directions and decisions of companies. While a 'representation gap' has been identified at organisational and establishment levels, the evidence strongly suggests that this will be much wider across national boundaries. Internationalisation of trade, with distant and inaccessible head offices, compounded by private equity buyouts, frequent mergers and demergers and joint ventures, has inevitably magnified these participation problems for employees and the European labour movement. The question that follows is the extent to which EWCs have been successful in addressing the constraints faced by employees in transnational corporations and their representatives. The analysis presented in this chapter identifies a number of problems that persist despite EU attempts at resolution. The first concerns the proportion of eligible companies that have established EWCs. The overall figure has varied between a third and just under half, but in recent years the average number of new EWCs has been only about 25 a year, notwithstanding the improved protocols offered by the 2009 Recast. Also, about a fifth of EWCs have been dissolved, the great majority through company merger or acquisition, which contributes to the difficulty in identifying the fluctuating and sometimes evasive ownership of international capital. As most EWCs are initiated by employee request, we certainly need to know the reasons why employees are not making requests and what more could be done to stimulate the initiation and recognition process.

A second problem is that under management direction EWCs tend to be more inclined toward information provision and communication than consultation. Understandably, managers are keen to manipulate the EWCs to suit their strategic and operational needs, and evidence tends to show that they have largely succeeded in this ambition. Information is often provided with too little time for EWC representatives to collectively consider the contents, prepare a response or provide feedback to their constituents; hence consultation may become an empty exercise. In addition, consultation often takes place over decisions already taken rather than over management intentions or at different stages of decision-making (Conchon and Triangle 2017).

Third, there can be ambiguity over what constitutes a transnational issue and the competence of EWCs to deal with such issues. Despite the clarification offered by the Recast, an issue may not be regarded as transnational if its immediate impact is local, notwithstanding its potential subsequent cross-national relevance. Hence, a policy introduced incrementally by a company in country-by-country stages may potentially not be subject to EWC review, though the Recast does stipulate that matters that concern at least two member states should be regarded as transnational and therefore subject to EWC scrutiny.

Fourth, sanctions for breach are either not imposed or insufficiently robust to deter subsequent infringement. The Recast Directive did attempt to improve enforcement but, as noted by Jagodziński (2016), this attempt has not been reflected in revision of national legislation to support implementation, so that the Recast aim of offering 'effective, proportionate and dissuasive' sanctions is at risk of being negated through national indifference.

Also difficult to measure is the impact of EWCs on the 'representation gap'. Enterprise works councils such as those operating in Germany are associated with mutual benefits, though of course it can be difficult to identify the specific contribution of a single employment relations practice and, as Gumbrell-McCormick and Hyman have observed, even enterprise works councils 'are engaged in a complex and problematic balancing act' in representing their constituents, interacting with management and responding to the authority of their unions (Gumbrell-McCormick and Hyman 2010: 308). For their European counterparts, these dynamics are likely to be even more complex. At present, though, there is insufficient evidence to demonstrate how effective the wider constituency-based EWCs have been in closing representation gaps, though attitudinal studies at least suggest that participating social partners are not dissatisfied with the operation of EWCs, even if it is difficult to identify tangible benefits and effects on employee attitudes and behaviour remain to be tested.

Further, employers and specifically their influential representative bodies such as UNICE (later BusinessEurope), favouring and reflecting a largely neoliberal orientation, tend to contest moves to make EWCs more accountable to employees. The negotiations around the Recast Directive are a case in point: BusinessEurope preference for self-regulation took an oppositional and partly successful stance of resistance to both revising the Directive and introducing new legislation on the grounds of compromising local market responsiveness through imposed centralisation (De Spiegelaere and Waddington 2017). It is because of political manoeuvring and lobbying that discussions over changes to European legislation tend to be drawn out. EWCs represent only one element of Social Europe's objective to provide greater protection to increasingly vulnerable employees. Enterprise-level information and consultation committees and, in continental Europe, worker directors, were established to encourage a representative and a partnership approach to employment relations, clearly necessary at a time of enhanced competitiveness, global operations and increasing union weakness. Social Europe also aims to establish a common set of rights for employees, but the employer lobby, together with diverse neoliberal national ideologies, emphases and practices, combine to undermine progress in this direction, as we see with EWCs. For the UK, a new and potentially serious problem has arisen. It has been estimated that between 120 and 160 EWCs have been established in companies headquartered in the UK (De Spiegelaere and Jagodziński 2015: 16). Usually the EWC is established according to the law of the headquartered company but the fate of EWCs that have been established under UK law has become uncertain following the vote to leave the EU.

Chapter 11

Global markets and prospects for employee emancipation

The context for globalisation

Previous chapters described European responses to increasing commercial internationalisation, involving the development of integrated systems of indirect participation aimed at offering worker representatives greater access to and influence with decision-makers of transnational enterprises. Europe, of course, represents only a modest proportion of world trade, while globalisation implies that the whole world has become a single interdependent market for the exchange and free movement of goods, services and labour. This process has accelerated over past decades through the congruence of a number of factors. First, there was the shift to neoliberal economic policies initiated by the major economies of the West from the late 1970s, supported by growing financial, competition and labour-market deregulation. Second, global integration has been stimulated and buttressed by negotiation of free-trade agreements, such as the North American Free Trade Agreement. Third, we have witnessed the development of manufacturing technologies that encouraged employers to shift production to industrialising countries, where labour was both plentiful and cheap (Livesey 2017). Information technology (IT) has also simplified offshoring services such as call centres, enabling them to operate cheaply from countries like India (Taylor and Bain 2005). Foreign direct investment in the form of joint ventures, outsourcing and offshoring, helps transnational enterprises maintain their competitiveness and command over markets while contributing to deindustrialisation (and growing disenchantment) in higher-cost Western economies (Standing 2011: 31). Standing points out that rapid developments in IT and its ready transferability, combined with facilities for transfer costing and pricing, mean that economic actors quickly learn from one another in an ever-increasing spiral of adaptation to changing economic conditions and opportunities. At the same time, there is constant uncertainty: if labour and other resources become relatively expensive in one country, transfer to another is always feasible. As Standing points out (ibid.: 33), a naïve 'retreat into protectionism' to counter the impact of globalisation is not a realistic option in a worldwide competitive economy dominated by transnational company interests.

Though globalisation has affected all developing and developed economies, its impact has been most profound and visible in China and India, countries with massive worker populations, rapidly changing in terms of education, training and workplace experience. From the perspective of employee management, participation and voice, two relevant trends stand out. First, companies, whether indigenous, joint venture, or based on inward investment, are becoming more sophisticated in their approach and more quality-focused and their managers are increasingly exposed to Western ideas and practice, whether through education or through experience. A total of nearly half a million Chinese students chose to study abroad in 2015, with the USA the most popular destination, and 91,215 decided to study in the UK, often choosing business and management degrees at undergraduate or postgraduate levels. Also, as products and services have become increasingly high-tech, innovative and quality-focused (for example, Chinese-built Lenovo tablets and laptops regularly receive highly favourable reviews for quality and innovation), companies operating in these countries are likely to adopt more contemporary approaches to managing, motivating and retaining key staff, including providing wider scope for voice. These postulated shifts conform to a 'convergence' direction for management that indicates that, under globalised production pressures, contingent systems of management are likely to be adopted (Warner and Zhu 2002). Second, at shop-floor levels of the production process, companies operating in China and India (as well as other countries as diverse as Indonesia, Bangladesh and Romania) are attractive for cost and flexibility benefits they offer companies; for some kinds of work at least, there is constant pressure towards controlling and reducing costs, and specifically labour costs.

These pressures apply even within industrialised countries. In the USA, cost and control motivations have encouraged manufacturers to establish production facilities in traditionally poorly unionised, low-wage Southern states such as Tennessee (Volkswagen) and Mississippi (Nissan) where union recognition is being fiercely contested by employers (New York Times 2017). In newly industrialising countries, adverse working conditions may lead to forms of resistance on the part of workers through organised or, more likely, unofficial collective organisation and action against oppressive work regimes, actions that ultimately has the potential to influence international public opinion and government policy. For these diverse reasons, it is worth first examining the different trajectories of EPV in China and India as indicative of developments typical of newly industrialising economies.

China and voice

The People's Republic of China (PRC) was established in 1949 under single-party communist rule. Initial steps to liberalisation were taken by chairman Mao's successor, Deng Xiaoping, who in 1980 introduced 'open China' economic reforms based around special enterprise zones designed to offer trade and investment opportunities to overseas investors, avoiding the tight regulations and restrictions applied elsewhere in mainland China. These zones and subsequent free-market policies were founded principally on promoting manufacturing, which has been the engine for subsequent sustained economic growth. Government policy has since focused on maintaining centralised control alongside promoting continuing economic liberalisation, attracting inward investment and maintaining growth. As part of the liberalisation project since 1995, there has been a vigorous privatisation programme of state-owned enterprises, accompanied by phasing out lifetime work security, replacing fixed wages with individual performance-related reward systems (Warner and Zhu 2002: 31) and engagement in massive downsizing and redundancy programmes (Cooke 2005: 45–50). The country confirmed its growing embrace of economic free trade by joining the World Trade Organization in 2001. China has since become the second largest economy after the USA, with one of the world's largest labour forces. Its GDP growth, though high relative to other economies, has declined in recent years from 9.5 per cent in 2011 to 6.9 per cent in 2015 and 6.7 per cent in 2016; according to official figures, this represented the slowest rate of growth since 1990 (BBC 2017a).

With a huge and diverse workforce, convoluted economic history and social relations located in the contrasting philosophies of Confucianism and Maoism (Walder 1986; Danford and Zhao 2012), as well as the informal system of personal reciprocal relationships and obligations known as *guanxi*, it would be impossible to do justice to all the employee relations developments that have taken place in China. Nevertheless, certain trends can be identified. One is that aspects of Western-located EPV can be identified. First, though, there is considerable evidence, in Cooke's words, that HRM is 'taking root in China' following an uncertain period in the 1990s when Child (1996) argued that Western concepts of HRM were 'not found in Chinese enterprises. It [HRM] is represented neither in the structures of management nor, by and large, in its practices' (in Cooke 2005: 173). Nevertheless, under the influence of inward investment and joint ventures and growing exposure to Western approaches of management, ten years later, Cooke was able to argue that the picture appeared to have shifted toward more recognisable forms of HRM, at least for some, specifically technology-focused companies employing educated and skilled workers (Warner 1999). One development seems to be the growing – if problematic for cultural reasons (Cooke 2005: 178) – use of performance management, centred on performance appraisal. Commentators tend to identify appraisal as a form of individualised EI, comprising joint dialogue between manager and subordinate over performance as well as organisational and individual means for performance improvement and reward allocation. A survey by Lindholm (1999) of 604 host-country managers and professionals working in transnational companies in China found them to be satisfied with Western-style performance management techniques and the opportunities for two-way dialogue they present. A later review by Cooke (2009) confirms the considerable growth in HRM research in China based on her analysis of some 265 articles published in major journals between 1998 and 2007. Many of these articles demonstrate that Western-style HRM is becoming more prevalent, largely owing to the influence of transnational company presence.

Another early feature of HRM 'with Chinese characteristics' noted by Cooke is the concept of enterprise culture management (Cooke 2005: 179–85), a complex amalgam embracing, depending on context, elements of paternalism, continuous improvement, Taylorism, branding and ideological imprinting. Emphases vary according to type of institution. Those derived from state-owned sources tend to focus on encouraging the correct enterprise 'spirit', while newer high-tech companies lean more toward Western terminology and practice, including individualised EI schemes such as suggestion schemes. Between these two models are companies that borrow aspects of both. While the emphasis is on improvement through enterprise acculturisation, critics suggest that, in practice, this simply provides the means to encourage more intensified work practices (Rubery and Grimshaw 2003).

In China, EPV can derive from different sources for higher-added-value employees and in customer-facing situations, such as hotels. On one hand the cultural background may mitigate against decision sharing. Commentators have drawn upon the 'filial piety' expectations of the modern commercial enterprise associated with Confucian ideology, a hybrid model expressed in the 'HRM with Chinese characteristics' concept (Danford and Zhao 2012: 842). Littrell (2007: 89) quotes Louie (1980), an earlier authority on Chinese culture, who argued that such beliefs 'turn China into a big factory for the production of obedient subjects'. She also suggests that 'unquestioning obedience' has been reinforced through dominant Communist Party ideology. From this perspective, managers are not willing to delegate authority or even share information and neither would employees feel comfortable in accepting responsibility. An early hospitality-sector study suggested that cultural adjustments such as empowerment tended to be rejected by Chinese employees, distrustful of Western HRM practice (Pang et al. 1998). Other authorities have also questioned whether perceptions of losing managerial 'face' could inhibit the development of delegatory involvement initiatives (Earley 1997; Littrell 2002). Another factor that needs to be considered is the impact of regional differences in work values across China but, other than reviews of regional typologies, there has been little empirical data associating these with different perspectives on EPV. Also, of course, different regions have different patterns of state-owned enterprises and it is well established that these tend to be more paternalistic and less progressive in approach toward people management than the emergent private sector (Cooke 2005: 43; Warner 1999: 17).

Set against these cultural factors is the argument that organisations operating in international and customer-facing markets need to be sensitive to quality as well as cost issues and, in more advanced markets in particular, be capable of innovation and flexibility, all of which leads to a recognition that meek compliance to managerial diktat may well result in non-optimising behaviour and performance. Related studies have been conducted in both knowledge-intensive and service environments. One of the earliest was Warner's 1999 study of people management in computer hardware and software companies. The findings indicate a system in the process of evolutionary change, with continuity of 'patron–client' dependency coexisting with emergent sophistication in HRM increasingly emphasising a 'congenial work environment' (Warner 1999: 16) in companies dependent on graduate-level employees. These early manifestations of HRM and EPV have been followed by more sophisticated approaches to capture employee knowledge and creativity in those companies designing and delivering high-added-value products and services.

Hence, trends over time appear to be more positive: a 2003 study in a US-invested company shows that Chinese workers' reactions to EPV were generally welcoming and not dissimilar to those of their US counterparts in terms of enhanced levels of satisfaction. Further, provision of teamworking provoked a positive reaction from employees (Scott et al. 2003). More recent longitudinal studies by Littrell (2007) of local supervisory management in a hotel chain point to positive attitudes toward empowerment, in contrast to some Western studies of supervisors that have demonstrated resistance through fear of loss of prerogative or even of employment (see chapter 7). An interesting development has been the encouragement by policy makers, media and managers of (often selective) employee share allocations as a potential motivating instrument (Cooke 2005: 83, 2009: 24). First adopted in the early 1990s by smaller companies, their use has spread to state-owned enterprises and to larger private-sector companies. A study reported by Benson et al. (2000) found forms of share-based remuneration in half of the companies investigated. Probably the best known and certainly most far-reaching of the employee share schemes is operated by the telecommunications giant Huawei. The company was established in 1987 and within three years its founder and CEO, Ren Zhenfei, had established its first ESOP, making subsequent modifications to the scheme in 1997 and 2001 (Zhu et al. 2013). Huawei is now the largest telecoms company in China, with some 170,000 employees. Of these, more than 82,000 hold virtually all the company shares, apart from a residual 1.4 per cent held by the founder (De Cremer and Tao 2015a). The company employs people outside China, but these are not eligible to join the ESOP. The company stresses that its commercial success is attributable to its ownership structure and the culture underpinning it, based on Confucian values of equality, harmony and equity. Translated into practice these values stress the primacy of a 'customer first' approach; employee commitment founded on the ESOP scheme; and universal two-way communication (De Cremer and Tao 2015b). Zhu et al. (2013) conducted a comparative study of Huawei with its nearest competitor, ZTE, and found that in policies including proportions of graduates, high-quality training schemes and political links, the two companies were similar, yet productivity in Huawei was higher, because all China-based employees were eligible for shares in Huawei, but only senior executives had this right in ZTE.

It appears that HRM and its attendant individualised voice practices have established a firm foothold in China, especially in companies employing substantial proportions of highly educated and trained staff whom they wish to motivate and to retain. From the perspectives of this growing group of educated and well-connected employees an expectation is also arising of greater involvement in workplace decision-making; as we suggest below, this could in the longer term have implications for the democratisation of work and potentially for broader areas of civil society.

But of course, there is another side to the Chinese economic success story. The country's unprecedented growth has not been led only by strong investment and the encouragement of foreign direct investment. HRM practices in manufacturing industry have also been studied and show that the emphasis is rather more on exercising involvement, if at all, to directly encourage performance, while preserving managerial control. One study of electronics and clothing plants suggested a hard HRM approach to supervising employees (Morris et al. 2009), while a study of state-owned mass-production automotive plants identified a subdued labour force operating under a tight regime of control and discipline, with few opportunities for individual or, especially, collective open expressions of discontent, though there were signs of a 'latent oppositional stance' with future 'potential for more systemic industrial conflict' (Danford and Zhao 2012: 854). Krzywdzinski (2017) investigated factors shaping EI among production workers in the German, Brazilian and Chinese plants of a German automobile manufacturer. The Chinese plant operated as a joint venture and the researcher examined depth of involvement along four dimensions, namely, self-organisation in teams, opportunities for problem-solving, social involvement through participation in company activity, and communication. The involvement picture that emerged was mixed, though the emphasis was strongly on performance-improvement activity. Teams were not originally seen as a priority, possibly, according to German managers, because the Communist Party 'regards self-organization with mistrust' (ibid.: 336). Nevertheless, there was involvement both through teams and individual suggestion schemes in improvement activities, and team members were able to influence the selection of their leaders. Employee attitude surveys were conducted annually and results discussed between team leaders and members. Finally there were 'comprehensive social integration activities' (ibid.: 338), involving numerous performance-based competitions as well as social and family events. Hence, opportunities for expressing employee voice tended to be channelled toward enhancing performance and, with union focus also on increasing productivity, there was only 'weak representation of labour interests' (ibid.: 339).

From the above we see that for production workers, both in state-owned and private-sector enterprises, employee voice, where it exists, is strongly directed toward supporting a management agenda. Though there is a formal trade union presence, its role has been to support government and management policies, which typically centre around increasing productivity. With a central strategic role afforded to them, it is worth considering the role of official trade unions in more depth. Cooke (2005) provides an excellent summary of historical trade union structure and function. Historically, the only union recognised by the Communist government has been the All-China Federation of Trade Unions (ACTFU), to which all other unions were subordinated. As capital and labour interests are regarded as synonymous, there was no representative oppositional function for union officials, other than acting as an intermediary between Party and workers, leaving workers vulnerable to mass redundancy and unemployment in a context of accelerating state withdrawal from its previous welfare provision role. As in the West, union recognition and membership were lower in the private sector than in the state sector, and the support role of private-sector union representatives decidedly ambiguous. Cooke summarises the then EPV situation in China succinctly: 'there is no real 'partnership' between management and trade unions or 'employee voice' in the management–labour relations' (ibid.: 38). That was 2005; has the position altered in any way today?

Formally at least, little has changed. ACTFU is still the only legally mandated trade union and, despite the growth of enterprise unions, these must be affiliated to ACTFU through a formal hierarchy of local and regional union federations and as the Chinese Labour Bulletin (CLB 2017) points out, ACTFU remains under the broad control of the Chinese Communist Party. Collective bargaining is still 'at an embryonic stage', with no formal mechanism for conducting it. Strikes organised by unrecognised unions, however, are becoming more commonplace, though once settled, solidarity among participants tends to dissipate (ibid.). Nevertheless, with modernisation of the economy, more vigorous labour agitation for improvements in pay and labour standards are reported and, importantly, a more independent voice in decisions is being sought (Estlund 2013). Estlund notes the tentative steps taken by the ACTFU and enterprise unions to establish staff and workers' representatives congresses, approximate equivalents to company works councils in Europe, in order to express a more potent collective voice at workplace level. Though currently 'feeble' and 'ineffectual', Estlund considers that these bodies may offer potential for works council-style participation in China. In the meantime, enterprise unions, though proliferating, tend to enjoy only a limited role in promoting worker interests. Research in 12 foreign-invested manufacturing enterprises located in the Pearl River Delta region showed little threat to management: union leadership was dominated by managers and supervisors and the union role was largely confined to mediatory activity, as well as the more traditional union function of organising welfare and social events (Chan et al. 2016). One major contextual development is that multinational operations have proliferated in recent years through offshoring and outsourcing, with Foxconn probably the best-known and most notorious example because of its intensive and intrusive working practices, where the scope for any individual agency is tightly circumscribed and support from the official union federation unlikely (Chan et al. 2013; Lucas et al. 2013; Standing 2014). The beneficiaries are hi-tech corporations such as Apple, HP and Sony, companies for which Foxconn provides assembly services. But labour oppression in this company and in others, such as Walmart, has led to possibly unanticipated consequences, as collective opposition and adverse publicity have mounted (Cederström and Fleming 2012: 58–59).

Though active support of workers by an enterprise union is still a rare occurrence, a recent series of disputes made international headline news when the US conglomerate Walmart closed a store in Hunan Province without offering employees the required compensation, prompting a vigorous campaign on the workers' behalf by the enterprise union chairman, Huang Xinguo (CLB 2014). Unrest subsequently spread throughout the company's 400 stores in China, with workers using social media to gather sympathy and coordinate resistance against aggressive managers and 'union puppets' (New York Times 2016b). Growing unrest has prompted discussion of future directions for the labour movement and the government. The so-called 'dual role' of unions that helps enforce labour discipline and drive productivity while acting as members' representative is under scrutiny (Chan et al. 2016), prompting comparisons with the early days of trade union mobilisation in Western countries and the pressures leading to the New Deal in North America. A critical event was the strike by Honda workers in 2010 (Bradsher and Barboza 2010), which led to a 35 per cent pay increase and was followed by increased activism in other sectors. According to the Financial Times (2017b), there were 2,775 recorded strikes and protests in 2015 in China and 2,663 in 2016, almost double the number of 2014. The government has tolerated these actions because they are not politically motivated but aimed at securing better terms and conditions of employment. At the 2013 Work, Employment & Society (WES) conference, the director of a campaigning workers' rights movement stated his belief that growing unrest could represent the start of a movement to transform China 'slowly and peacefully from dictatorship into semi-democracy, and finally into a democratic country' (Network 2013). However, these views are not shared by all observers of Chinese employment relations. Speaking at the 2016 WES conference, Ching Kwan Lee was less sanguine about prospects for political change, claiming that the 'optimism that underlies the empowerment thesis has been misplaced' and arguing instead that union actions to secure higher pay are tolerated because they meet with Chinese government aims to foster growth through higher consumption. Nevertheless, she did see the growth of unofficial labour action, including collective bargaining with employers, as a positive rebuff to the official union network (Network 2016). A report by Hernández in the New York Times (2016a) suggests that a range of factors appear to be feeding into current worker unrest. One of these is the slowing down of the Chinese economy and its impact on factory closures and attempts by employers, including in the state sector, to cut costs by extending working hours, cutting pay and laying off staff. Other overseas-invested companies have relocated from China to Southeast Asia, putting additional pressure on employment. Another factor is that workers are becoming better informed and more adept at using social media to organise unofficial disputes, which has in turn led to vigorous responses from the authorities, especially when state or local officials have been the target of worker protests.

These accounts indicate that rather different trends in people management and EPV are emerging from China's rapidly evolving and diverse economy. For quality and technology-based production and high-added-value services, whether indigenous or overseas-owned, relatively sophisticated forms of HRM and individualised forms of EI are evident. In manufacturing, there are indications of 'soft' Taylorism in joint ventures and subsidiaries, where EI practices have been introduced with the aim of impacting directly on productive performance. Also, there is the 'hard' Taylorism found in many outsourced assembly units, where there is little or no management-instigated EI, and collective grievances and informal collective participation are being channelled increasingly through unofficial trade unions.

India and voice

Like China, for a country the size and complexity of India, it would be impossible to do to justice to the diverse manifestations of EPV in the confines of a single chapter. In order to assess the directions of voice and participation, two broad perspectives can be adopted: industrial relations to examine collective expressions of EPV and HRM for a more individualistic view. One aspect that is common to both is the influence of the country's culture. Amba-Rao et al. (2000) identified three dominant influences that have shaped India's organisations, values and behaviour; namely the traditional caste system, British colonisation and its lingering bureaucratic heritage, and, following independence, a broadly socialist ideology, which has diminished in recent years with government policy shifts to a less welfare-orientated and more liberalised, if unpredictable, open economy (*Financial Times* Guardian 2017a). These different cultural influences feed into Cappelli et al.'s (2010) somewhat uncritical presentation of 'The India Way' as a distinctive approach to management. Based on surveys and a series of interviews with leading Indian executives, the authors identify the India Way as a blend of four main principles, which they contend have the potential to exert the same global influence on performance as the 'Toyota Way' described in chapter 8 and in its national specificity could confound the convergence thesis examined earlier. The first principle is identified as 'holistic engagement with employees', in which people are treated as valuable assets; the second concerns operational flexibility and readiness to improvise in the face of new challenges; the third involves readiness to meet market needs; and the fourth is a broad societal purpose to industry and commerce (ibid.: 4). It is perhaps surprising that there is little or no mention of trade unions or representative activity in a book that extols the virtues of the 'societal benefits' and 'collective calling' of executive thinking (ibid.: 207).

In recent years the Indian economy has been notable for its growth rate, far exceeding that of most other industrialising or industrialised countries. In 2008, American GDP had grown 1.64 times its 1990 size, while Indian GDP had increased by a factor of 3.02. Even more spectacular figures are reported for FDI, both inward and outward, with inward FDI rising from $100 million in 1990 to $21.8 billion in 2007, while overseas investment rose from $2.5 million to $13 billion over the same timeframe. Similar astronomic trends were found for mergers and acquisitions (Cappelli et al. 2010: 209–11). Mergers and acquisitions touched $12.3 billion in 2008 and data for 2016/17 suggest a remarkable figure of $61.26 billion (IBEF 2017).

The impetus for expansion in economic growth came in the early 1990s with the introduction of governmental economic liberalisation coupled with policies to protect domestic industry, giving a significant boost to the development of the private sector. Growth rates have averaged 7 per cent over the past 20 years and India is now one of the world's largest economies, with a labour force of some 500 million people. Unlike China, where growth has been mainly secured from a base of low-cost manufacturing, in India there has been sustained growth in both the service sector (e.g. IT and software) and in high-tech outlets, where there were 1,400 start-up companies established in 2016 alone (NASSCOM 2017). Domestically, though India is not strong in manufacturing, it has been well served by its large reserve of well-educated and English-speaking young people who have given momentum to the development of the service and IT sectors (Bhattacherjee and Ackers 2010). The dominant objectives of employers in these sectors have been to motivate and retain young and potentially mobile employees, ostensibly through developing a 'fun' organisational ethos and providing multiple opportunities for social activities (Kuruvilla and Ranganathan 2010).

Research does confirm the problem of retention: tertiary educated employees tend to be ambitious for promotion, higher pay and opportunities to undertake more prestigious work. One study of domestic call centres found that while these provides employees with a source of entry into business process outsourcing, many were seeking openings to upgrade to higher-status international centres, such that average tenure in domestic centres was a mere 13 months (Taylor et al. 2013: 444). However, expressed experiences and grievances diverge sharply from the human asset rhetoric presented by Cappelli et al. for the India Way. In contrast to 'fun', this study identified numerous frustrations among employees and considerable managerial and supervisory pressure to meet imposed targets. Lack of voice was a common complaint, and fundamental concerns raised by employees were allegedly left unresolved by senior management, a grievance raised particularly by women, who expressed specific anxieties over employment and personal security. Taylor et al. found minimal employee discretion, 'unforgiving' supervisory control and regimes where workers were 'denied any voice, let alone meaningful representation' (ibid.: 450).

Earlier research conducted in international call centres, where better working conditions might be anticipated, instead showed 'relentless call-handling [and] extensive monitoring' compounded by 'denial of identity at the command of overseas clients … [that] may deepen worker dissatisfaction … and may contribute to emerging resistance' (Taylor and Bain 2005: 278). Noronha and D'Cruz (2009) reported similarly negative findings in their examination of tensions between professional identity and union consciousness among call centre staff. Interviews were conducted with agents in a number of international call centres. The agents worked in teams and were remunerated by salary and individual and team-based performance supplements. Stringent monitoring was the norm and permission was needed to leave a workstation, even for toilet purposes. Delays in returning after an official break – even by one minute – led to 'severe public reprimands by the team leader' (ibid.: 220). Failure to meet employer demands led to punishments ranging from warnings to termination. An earlier comparative study of performance appraisal, a form of two-way communication between individual employee and manager commonly used as the basis for performance-related supplements (Thompson 2009), found evidence of structural and procedural barriers to workforce empowerment, information sharing and participative decision-making in domestic Indian private and public-sector companies. These deficiencies in performance appraisal practice were less prevalent in transnational and joint-venture enterprises (Amba-Rao et al. 2000).

Not surprisingly, these conditions of highly restricted channels of individual voice have led to calls for greater employee protection, notably through collective organisation, though in India there remain serious obstacles to the development of trade union-based collectivism. For workers who regard themselves as professional, such as in IT and business-process outsourcing, there are ideological internalised constraints against union membership and activism on the grounds that professional work is not compatible with union association; there is also imposed pressure from employers against union membership (Noronha and D'Cruz 2009).

Nevertheless, trade unions in India have a long history. Unions have to be registered under the 1926 Trade Unions Act, as amended in 2001. In 2012 it was estimated that there were some 16,000 trade unions, divided along political lines and affiliated to a small number of central trade union organisations. The exact number of union members is uncertain, though the largest of the central trade unions, the Indian National Trade Union Congress, claimed some 33 million members in 2012 (Business Standard 2013). Union membership is estimated to have grown over the past few years despite employer opposition and the rise of the informal sector and contract work. Nevertheless, estimates suggest that the majority of Indians work in the informal economy and thereby outside the formal systems of industrial relations and collective bargaining. Hill (2009: 404) estimates that only about 7.6 per cent of the workforce are covered by the formal industrial relations system; for women, the situation is worse, with only 4 per cent engaged in the organised sector (ibid.: 407). There is little doubt that casualisation is on the increase, even in larger companies. In registered manufacturing, one-third of workers are contracted to agencies rather than enjoying permanent employee status (Chandrasekhar and Ghosh 2014); agency work represents significantly lower employment costs and fewer obstacles to managerial control. A further benefit for employers is that contract workers are unable to subscribe to unions, thereby also precluding them from effective political representation (Monaco 2017; Barnes et al. 2015): a case of voice denied on at least two counts.

The seminal industrial disputes that began in 2011 at carmaker Maruti Suzuki are worth considering in detail because they highlight many of the critical issues and obstacles facing advocates of EPV in a newly industrialising country. The disputes also seriously undermine the validity of an 'India Way' thesis constructed on the basis of Cappelli et al.'s characterisation of employees as 'valuable assets' with whom management are in 'holistic engagement'. Maruti Suzuki is one of a cluster of auto and component manufacturers located in the National Capital Region. It was originally under public ownership but the government sold its controlling interest to Japanese auto manufacturer Suzuki in 2002. To reflect the change of ownership, in 2007 the company's name was altered to Maruti Suzuki India Limited, or MSIL. The company was opposed to independent union recognition, instead establishing a company-controlled (or 'yellow') union. Operationally, lean production based on principles of continuous improvement, teamworking and just-in-time schedules was introduced; in practice, the lean regime led to complaints of harsh working conditions, discrimination between established and contract workers, refusal to recognise an independent union and collusion between company management and local authorities against workers. Following a flashpoint confrontation, there were occupations and walkouts, company lockouts, mass dismissals, suspensions and multiple arrests over a period of a year (Monaco 2017: 133). In 2013, an independent delegation from the New York based International Commission for Labor Rights travelled to India to investigate alleged maltreatment of workers and denial of union rights. The delegation gathered evidence from various groups, but not from management, who turned down several invitations to meet the visitors. The delegation found that workers had regularly raised concerns about working conditions and the precarious situation of lower-paid contract workers. As there had been no official response, the workers formed an independent trade union, the Maruti Suzuki Workers Union (MSWU) to act on behalf of workers in preference to the house union established by the company. However, MSIL refused to negotiate with MSWU. In 2012 another strike had erupted, allegedly ignited by oppressive supervisory behaviour, leading to violent confrontations. The delegation established that there had been significant violations of labour law by the company, denial of freedom of association and one-sided intervention by the police (International Commission for Labor Rights 2013).

In addition, Monaco (2017) insists that the case starkly demonstrates the sharp divide between the unitarist rhetoric of lean and the reality of everyday working conditions in the plant.

There have been demonstrations of both disquiet and suppression in other sectors. Research carried out in a production cluster in one of India's Special Economic Zones, involving mobile phone manufacturer Nokia and its component suppliers, including Taiwan-based Foxconn, found evidence of aggressive local management, ineffectual health and safety systems and growing numbers of precarious agency-deployed workers. While Nokia's employment relations were regarded quite favourably following the establishment of the Indian enterprise, the company had experienced three strikes in a year between 2009 and 2010, the first leading to the establishment of a union. This had left a bitter legacy among some sections of management, who were willing to take 'a vindictive stance' against workers wishing to enter into collective dialogue with the company (Cividep 2010: 26–27). The aims of Nokia's component suppliers such as Foxconn were more straightforwardly to 'create a vulnerable workforce without the capacity to bargain for their rights' (ibid.: 29). A research review by Singh and Saini (2016) of industrial relations in private-sector manufacturing organisations throws a light on challenges to both collective and individual forms of EPV. Following liberalisation of the economy, the authors note a rise in employer resistance to union recognition and collective bargaining, pursued (often vigorously) through anti-union strategies (Saini 2006). Work has also become more casualised and insecure. While there has been some shift to Western models of HRM and EI through performance appraisal and empowerment (Saini 2008), again these tend to be restricted in scope such that 'employee communication is mostly top down with limited involvement of workers in the form of suggestion schemes, quality circles etc. Limited information is shared with workers' (Singh and Saini 2016: 866).

The scope for expression of employee voice in India does nevertheless depend on context. The development of overseas and Indian multinational companies (MNCs) in IT services is growing rapidly. NASSCOM (2017) estimated that aggregate revenues of the Indian IT/BPO sector amounted to some $130 billion in 2014. The sector directly employed some 3.1 million people and indirectly another ten million in India alone. HRM in multinational companies is influenced by a range of external factors, such as country of origin and international strategy, as well as domestic cultural factors. It is well established that India has a high power-distance and entrepreneurial culture (Thite et al. 2014: 935), neither of which is compatible with managerial acceptance of independent employee voice. Nevertheless, the research involving interviews with 51 line and HR managers conducted by Thite et al. (ibid.) in high-tech MNCs, whose performance is dependent upon the flexibility, adaptability and creativity of well-educated employees, shows that managers are willing to 'let go' by offering some autonomy to staff in the service of clients. Earlier research in software companies confirmed that 'intellectual work needs an environment conducive to creative thinking' (Paul and Anantharaman 2004: 83). This research showed that, for software engineers, opportunities for personal career development, appraisal and training, which feed into these developmental processes, enhance organisational commitment. These employee expectations are very similar, if not identical, to those of software engineers in the UK (Baldry et al. 2007).

With India's economy increasingly reliant upon a young, well-educated and talented workforce whose expectations are inclining toward individual empowerment at work, it may be expected that, for this expanding cohort at least, Indian companies will increasingly adopt the rhetoric of 'employees first', with provision for expressing individual voice (Thite et al. 2014; Cappelli et al. 2010). Nevertheless, there are cultural, political and economic constraints that may hinder EPV progress beyond a limited number of high-added-value sectors. Collective participation, through independent trade unions in particular, faces numerous obstacles. Culturally, as we have observed above, India is strongly entrepreneurial, which suggests executive determination and single-mindedness but also paternalism (Cappelli et al. 2010: 77) or possibly a lack of tolerance toward interventions from lower hierarchical ranks in a society that has traditionally 'emphasized social hierarchy and obedience' (Cooke and Saini 2010: 393). We have also seen that, in the pursuit of economic performance in highly competitive domestic and international markets, employers can adopt vigorously confrontational stances against independently organised labour, and are often assisted by local authorities, and the police. This instability was noticeable in the highly publicised 2005 month-long strike and lockout at the Honda Motorcycle and Scooter company, which involved riot police, dismissals and arrests (*BusinessLine* 2005). In its evaluation of the MSIL dispute, the International Commission for Labor Rights did not mince words: 'The Police has transgressed its powers in ways that amount to gross and inappropriate interference in industrial disputes, and yet failed to act to protect industrial peace when it should have' (International Commission for Labor Rights 2013: 2). The Commission also established that the Labour Department of the State of Haryana 'both through its actions and its failure to act, violated several important, internationally recognised principles of trade union rights' (ibid.: 24), including India's own employment legislation. These and other disputes are reminiscent of the early struggles of the labour movement in America to become established in the face of concerted opposition by employers like Ford.

Conclusions

The world of work has been profoundly transformed in the past thirty or so years. Governments across the world have increasingly adopted neoliberal economic policies that encourage enterprise, deregulation and individualism. Companies have increasingly gained economic influence through free-trade agreements that give cross-national legitimation and expression to these liberalising shifts. In consequence, newly industrialising countries are engaged in fierce competition to attract and retain overseas investment through providing low-cost conditions for profitable production, which can also involve collusion between governments and both domestic and international corporations to suppress collective grievances against exploitation and human rights abuses. We have examined the profiles of the two most prominent developing economies, but tightly controlled manufacturing regimes are reflected in dramatic fashion in many others. Unions representing garment workers in Bangladesh's poorly regulated 4,500 garment factories face continual pressure and harsh repression from both employers and authorities wanting to protect an industry that provides 80 per cent of the country's export trade (Guardian 2016d). Denial of the fundamental right to healthy and safe working conditions, which unions across the world struggle to achieve, is a most obvious casualty of the lack of control that employees endure, as was shown so horrendously in the collapse of the Rana Plaza in 2013 and the deaths of over a thousand workers (Motlagh and Saha 2014). Many abuses have been reported through the media and by labour rights organisations such as the International Labour Organization (Mosoetsa and Williams 2012). Products sold by highly profitable, prestige-clothing companies can often be traced back to poverty wages and oppressive working conditions, while trade union activists can face dismissal, harassment and arrest if they oppose them (Lange 2010). For example, many high-fashion and costly garments are made in low-pay Eastern and Central European countries, such as Romania, and in these countries 'workers' rights and human rights are publicly a taboo and not protected at all' according to a Clean Clothes campaigner (Guardian 2017a).

In terms of the question of global convergence of employment practice, a number of common trends can be identified that involve reduced cost and deployment of flexible labour, though the manifestations and consequences of these trends vary from country to country. In the neoliberal economies of the UK and other Anglo-Saxon countries, these developments have been reflected in migration of production jobs to low-cost, low-regulation countries and service-sector jobs have become increasingly atomised and precarious. Both scenarios have implications for people management and especially for trade unions, whose role is extending to try to protect the difficult-to-protect and to mobilise the unorganised. Conversely, rapidly industrialising countries like China and India face other challenges: they are confronted by the prospect of accommodating and managing the 'expert authority' of growing numbers of young, educated and mobile staff, many of whom are located in technology and enterprise zone clusters, offering opportunities to share and compare common experiences and aspirations. The evolving nature of employment and potential development for EPV can be anticipated from the rise in research and development (R&D) expenditure: over ten years, between 2003 and 2013, R&D investment in China doubled, from 1.13 per cent to 2.08 per cent of gross domestic product, putting it ahead of the UK in relative terms (Livesey 2017: 93).

In these situations, individual voice programmes have been introduced by employers, with the aim of inducing motivation and enterprise commitment. Many of these individual and team-based voice initiatives derive from joint ventures and inward-investment projects or have been reproduced from these transnational enterprises by domestic companies. Nevertheless, in the areas of mass production, a collective voice struggles to be heard while employers and public authorities impose restrictive policies through concern that prospective or actual industrial disputes deter inward investors or can lead to higher and unpredictable labour costs and consequent corporate migration to more enterprise-friendly locations. Notwithstanding these constraints, independent unions are gaining a foothold; even monolithic governments like that of China are beginning to adjust (if not relax) their grip on industrial relations matters, on condition that the political integrity of the state remains unchallenged.

Chapter 12

An uncertain future?

Introduction: a contested past

The aim of this book has been to trace the rationale, evolution and impact of EPV. Early mass production raised contrasting aspirations for worker emancipation through ownership and control of the means of production competing with more modest ambitions for work reform through collective mobilisation and recognition of union legitimacy. One intention was to gain industrial influence to counter the alienating effects of Taylorist mass production and Fordist assembly-line manufacture. Eventual separation of political and industrial labourist objectives and subsequent dominance of the reform approach was reflected in union attempts to gain some control *over* work rather than control *of* work, which formed the prime objective of more radical political movements. In Standing's words: 'most twentieth century unions were attuned to the needs of industrial capitalism, not its overthrow' (Standing 2014: 134). Cognisant of the limited threat to the established order posed by unions, governmental policy in most Western industrialising countries shifted from outright hostility to reluctant concessions to union ambitions to improve workers' material conditions. Gradual statutory acceptance of unions and formal endorsement of their bargaining and consultative activities followed, alongside reformist political activity through the emergence and consolidation of social democratic and labour parties. Reaction to the changing industrial order by employers was mixed: some embraced unions and collective bargaining, albeit hesitantly, while others resisted through the development of early EI techniques, what Streeck (2016: 2) terms 'artful devices ... continuously reinvented' to motivate workers, or by more abrasive measures intended, as at the Ford Motor company in the 1930s, to physically suppress union influence and activity. Many of these same dynamics are evident today in newly emerging economies. While labour movement institutions and activities were generally successfully incorporated into the economic and political structures of mature economies in the years following the Second World War, neoliberal economic policies adopted initially in many English-speaking countries and spreading to others from the late 1970s, sent these established frameworks and procedures into precipitous fragmentation. Discouraged and threatened by state actions, organised collectivism has been increasingly undermined and frequently diminished by managerially imposed individualism, even within previously secure public sectors (Smyth 2017).

EPV: a troubled present

Presenting and analysing evidence for voice and participation is vital for understanding its impact, but at times we need to stand back and reflect on the experiences and absence of voice for those faced with the harshness of current realities. This experience is reflected in the despairing comments of an anonymous academic working in a prestigious Australian university, where under pressure from imposed austerity and neoliberal macroeconomic policy, management has adopted an overtly marketised model of operational control (*THE* 2017b: 43):

> As academics we are trained to be self-reflexive, critical thinkers ... yet when it comes to our own profession, we are among the most conservative, ineffectual and disorganized of workforces. ... we passively toe the line ... Yet if the system is so broken and dysfunctional, why not organize and protest against the policies that are to blame? The answer is simple, and it is one I am all too familiar with: our jobs. As an early career academic, I know that to put my name to this article, for instance, would risk my position and diminish my already slim chances of getting a tenured position ... Meanwhile established academics are conscious that they are among the fortunate few, so they rock the boat as little as possible for fear that that will no longer be the case come the next departmental restructuring and round of forced redundancies.
>
> Redevelopment, redundancies and inflated marketing spends are all the result of the same forces of economic rationalization that are eroding our educational system. And the bleak irony is that those same forces are also responsible for our inability to speak out against it.

The voice of precarious workers, even those providing essential services, can be effectively silenced through the vulnerability of their working conditions. Standing (2014: 169) reprises the words of a zero-hours care worker whose colleague complained about the common practice of not paying for time spent travelling to clients: 'One girl went down to eight hours a week when she asked about it. You cannot live on that. So we all keep quiet.' An imposed alliance of precariousness, obedience and silence seems to dominate the lives of increasing numbers of workers.

EPV has enjoyed a mixed history for workers with more established employment rights. Commitment-inducing efforts, along with cross-national transplanting of techniques such as lean production, have led to the growth of individualised EI, initiated and largely controlled by employers. As we have seen, there is little question that, in the contemporary economy, involvement enjoys considerable international support among employers through teamworking, share schemes, engagement and empowering exercises, diverse communication forms and in combinations of high-performance work techniques. Meanwhile, collective representation, for which employees and unions have long struggled, is under sustained pressure from the same political and economic forces.

Employees can appreciate and indeed derive benefit from individualised EI practices. Employers also profit from the contributions of satisfied workers. Employee satisfaction from the bonus effects of employee share scheme has been substantiated, but this does do not translate into a sense of ownership. Numerous studies point to positive productivity associations with profit sharing. Decent employers like the John Lewis Partnership demonstrate that, even in highly competitive and cost-sensitive conditions, employee satisfaction and performance can be maintained, though of course, these positive associations may also derive from lack of comparable alternative sources of employment. Teamworking too, as illustrated by the Frimley Park Hospital Trust example in chapter 8, can provide both enriching work and productive effectiveness. Numerous studies point to the importance of trust in the employer as a catalyst for engineering employee satisfaction and performance. Moreover, some surveys examining social attitudes to work detect little change in the relatively high levels of satisfaction with jobs expressed by workers since 2005. Nevertheless, warning signs are present: the proportion of workers regularly experiencing stress has grown from 28 per cent in 1989 to 37 per cent in 2015, with most stress experienced by professionals and other high-status respondents. Job security is universally seen as important but only two-thirds report that they have this (British Social Attitudes 2015).

Notwithstanding positive findings there are questions surrounding EI that remain to be answered. As many studies have shown, EI practices are rarely applied in isolation, so that it is operationally difficult to attribute effect. More worryingly, techniques such as empowerment and lean-based teamworking are often introduced alongside or subsequent to restructuring exercises, which often involve staff reductions and/or work intensification in an institutionalised process of 'programmed insecurity' (Sennett 2006: 187). Moreover, practices such as performance appraisal, performance-related pay and management communications may serve to reduce union attractiveness to employees and hence bargaining influence. Although these developments can inflate performance levels, at least temporarily, they are also associated with reports of increased stress and accumulating dissatisfaction. More insidious and potentially more alarming are the negative impacts of the surrender of control through deprofessionalisation among largely, though not exclusively, public-sector high-responsibility occupations, such as teachers and medical staff, as market-driven McDonaldisation is implemented by managers in a systematic process of cost-driven standardisation and commodification of professional work. Human costs in terms of wavering commitment, stress-related absence and work withdrawals impact directly on the communities that these professions aim to serve. At lower skill levels, use of surveillance and tight monitoring by electronic tracking used in clerical work, in distribution centres such as at Amazon warehouses and Sports Direct, and for delivery and lorry drivers, has become ubiquitous. For workers, the issue is one of being constantly observed and controlled, rather than securing a measure of autonomy. With more control over their work, employees could also establish clear dividing lines between work and domestic lives, but with increasingly sophisticated technological means of intrusive communication, allied with constant pressure on employees to 'go the extra mile' (Frayne 2015: chapter 3), work intensification and extensification are now commonly reported for all grades of work, with psychological and medical consequences of burnout and stress clearly apparent (Fleming 2017). One perhaps surprising defensive approach to regain autonomy at work has been adopted by health professionals who use exit in preference to voice by taking on agency work (NIESR 2017): ownership of scarce skills offers greater personal control over work and domestic life and less exposure to an oppressive work climate.

It should also be noted that while EI initiatives are common, especially in larger organisations, they have done little to address the negative effects of workplace inequality or to increase labour's share of national income, which has been in steady decline over recent years in OECD countries (UNCTAD 2012). Corporate governance has scarcely been touched by the surge of EI. Employees were powerless to prevent aggressive asset stripping at UK retailer BHS, which led to the collapse of the company and the ensuing destruction of thousands of jobs and pensions through the actions of owners who walked away financially unscathed (Fleming 2017: 69). Further, the participation gap, which serves as principal barrier to expression of employee interests and can be attributed to the decline of collective representation, shows few signs of closing; for increasing numbers of workers in insecure employment or dubious self-employment, there remains a chasm over which trade unions are desperately trying to construct bridges. For these diverse reasons and notwithstanding the plethora of involvement techniques, levels of productivity in the UK remain obstinately below those of competitor countries.

While the overall perspective presented in this book demonstrates that EPV at work falls somewhat short of the 'good work' criteria presented in the Taylor report (Taylor 2017), it is in the field of philosophy that the most profound critiques of contemporary employment practice can be found. In a study that contrasts the promise of modern autonomous work with its betrayal by corporate leaders and their followers, Ciulla (2000) examines the meaning of work for today's workforce as seen through the lens of classical and contemporary philosophy. She draws especially on Aristotle's view of what constitutes a meaningful life by contrasting the potential of work to its actuality, dominated by psychological manipulation to make people feel superficially good rather than constructing workplace relations based on fundamental principles of justice and honesty.

Political philosopher Elizabeth Anderson contests the idea that workers are free (i.e. have control) simply because they enter or exit work under their own volition, as this ignores the status of an employment relationship that she describes as a form of dictatorial government, in which workers are not merely governed but dominated by employers and their agents (Anderson 2017: xxii). She also points out that exercising autonomy is a 'basic human need', one that is denied by 'arbitrary and unaccountable authority possessed by managers' (ibid.: xvii). Nevertheless, this is mild fare compared to the nihilistic vision of work as a form of living death, emptied of all meaning and creativity, espoused by Fleming (2015, 2017) and by Cederström and Fleming (2012) in their polemical narrative *Dead Man Working*. While not underestimating the effects of direct and brutal control presented by Anderson, these authors focus their aim on the oxymoronic notion of 'liberation management', which basically assumes surreptitious control of the complete person, with comprehensive, enthusiastic but blinkered endorsement by workers themselves, who become wedded almost unknowingly to today's 'friendly capitalism' in a seductive but captivating embrace that extends well beyond Hochschild's notion of emotional labour. In all these accounts, involvement techniques are denounced for providing a surface veneer to underlying one-sided power relations, in which employees as resources are increasingly malleable and ultimately disposable.

EPV: an uncertain future?

From the preceding analysis, the original impetus for EPV to establish some control by workers over their work and working conditions a hundred years or more ago has splintered in different and sometimes competing directions, propelled variously by: continuing employee aspirations for workplace influence and the means to attain it; the requirements of governments to achieve productive economic performance while offering necessary protections to participants; and finally, the needs of employers to operate both effectively and efficiently in the face of increasing quality and cost pressures. The ascendancy of individualised management involvement approaches, especially in Anglo-Saxon countries and accession states, where neoliberal economic policies intolerant of market obstructions predominate, have led to 'the substantial collapse of a system of worker representation founded on trade unions and collective bargaining' in the UK (Heery et al. 2004: 1). While similar trends are evident in European economies favouring social partnerships, collective participation in these countries has tended to be more resistant to unitarist overtures. In emergent economies such as China and India, we see similarly restrictive pressures, reminiscent of the struggles of industrial unionism to become established in the early days of factory production. Across the world, the spectre of globalisation casts a shadow over workplace demands for safer and more secure working conditions, let alone a more established say for workers in organisational affairs. Though both positive and negative indicators for the future of EPV emerge from these different trends, under prevailing economic dogmas it is difficult to be sanguine about the prospects for collective representative participation.

Positive indicators

One positive sign is the growing acknowledgement among policy-makers and their advisors of the potential deprivations inherent in modern work. In the UK, unemployment has attained historically low levels (ONS 2017), at least according to official statistics (which have rather less to say about underemployment), but diminishing quality of work is also receiving recognition as demeaning to workers and damaging to economic progress and social justice. In the face of numerous adverse reports on the workings of the contemporary labour market, the British government appointed a review of modern working practices, chaired by Matthew Taylor (2017), who was commissioned to investigate and make recommendations for the government to act on, with the objective to make 'all work good work'. Using a model developed by the Institute of Employment Research at the University of Warwick, the report provided a vital service in identifying the main qualities that, in Taylor's view, constitute quality work. These can be summarised in terms of pay; employment quality; education and training; working conditions; work–life balance; consultative participation; and collective representation. Clearly EPV could have a role in supporting important issues such as pay and working conditions, but the actual processes for accomplishing this are dependent on establishing firm collective recognition and legitimating foundations, which are precluded in many cases by the participation gap identified by many studies. Hence, pay for workers (but not executives) has failed to keep up with inflation, training in the UK is widely recognised as deficient and often paid for by employees themselves, and working conditions, which cover, inter alia, autonomy, variety and intensity, have been demonstrated to be under continued threat in neoliberal economic policy conditions and the new public management practices that these conditions have promulgated. This report provides a valuable service in identifying the elements of quality work, but eschews comprehensive remedial treatment needed to confront exploitation, instead trusting to a pragmatic combination of 'the British way' of flexible labour utilisation, good management and responsible corporate governance to achieve improvements to deregulatory policies in which the same corporate interests have been complicit. It was, perhaps, unfortunate timing that fast-food chain McDonald's was cited in the report as a case study of presumed good management of flexible workers shortly before the Bakers, Food and Allied Workers Union prepared to take industrial action against the company for failing to deliver an end to zero-hour contracts amid claims of cuts to employee hours, hostility to union membership and bullying (BBC 2017b).

If a national debate that acknowledges current employment shortcomings and the reasons behind these can provide a step toward stimulating positive change, another positive indicator is provided by initiatives that affected parties are themselves willing and able to undertake. Trade union membership and activity has long been recognised as a cyclical process, usually operating in lagged response to changes in macroeconomic conditions. What has concerned many social commentators is that the elasticity that previously connected union health and influence with economic performance has been overshadowed over the past 40 years by progressive union decline and that unions have failed to respond to favourable shifts in the economic climate. Nevertheless, there are signs of possible change. We have seen, for example, that in the UK and other countries, unions are beginning to establish organising platforms for mobilising precarious workers; the recent success of a major union, UNISON, in reversing the imposition of industrial tribunal fees provided welcome positive publicity for the labour movement.

More systematically, there has been prolonged debate among analysts and commentators on how union presence and influence can be renewed or revitalised (Murray 2017; Tait 2017). Clearly, the definition of the effectiveness of activism depends on interpretations of union role and objectives, and these differ widely, both conceptually and prescriptively. Hyman (2001) presents three conceptual models; firstly, one based on pragmatic collective-bargaining articulation with market opportunities and typified by Anglo-Saxon unionism. A second is a more corporative-focused integration between politics and society, epitomised by Nordic practice. A third is a classical class-based oppositional approach informed by Marxist thinking. From a more prescriptive perspective, as part of a major national study on the future of work, Healy et al. (2004) presented a series of studies examining prospects for worker representation. Introducing the studies, Heery et al. (2004: 4) identified four revitalisation models, all demanding steps to either adapt to or challenge prevailing economic and political conditions; these can be further distilled into two generic models: organising and partnership. The former, more radical approach, strongly associated with the ideas of John Kelly (1998), argues that power resources can only be rebuilt 'through organising, mobilising and regaining power over ideas about injustice at work' (Ibsen and Tapia 2017: 180), while the partnership or mutual gains approach is based on its greater likelihood to meet approval from employers, government and potential members. There have been numerous opportunities to identify the success or otherwise of different renewal campaigns. Recent research has examined revitalisation strategies and outcomes in terms of union membership growth or stability; density; relative economic power compared to that of employers; political influence; improved internal governance; and member participation in union affairs (Behrens et al. 2004; Ibsen and Tapia 2017: 179–80). Reviewing these studies, Ibsen and Tapia are not convinced that unions anywhere are capable of reversing their decline without state support; this, as we have seen in previous chapters, is rarely forthcoming in a neoliberal, globalised climate (ibid.: 184). Other commentators are more sanguine about variants of the organising model. Heery, while recognising that its hopes 'have not been fully realized', nevertheless argues that the approach has registered 'major successes' and at least reduced the rate of union decline (Heery 2015: 558). In a case-study comparison of the two revitalising approaches, Badigannavar and Kelly (2011) undertook a range of interviews and a national survey of lay representatives from a public-sector union enjoying relatively high levels of membership; management support for a partnership model might be anticipated here. The union used both organising and partnership approaches in its membership and recognition drives. The study indicated that union revitalisation was better served through a coordinated rank-and-file organising approach than through partnership, where there was little evidence of union gains in terms of management access, reduced worker grievances or membership levels. The importance of political support to the partnership approach was further underlined when the American UAW union attempted, with employer support, to unionise auto manufacturer VW in the union-averse state of Tennessee. The recognition election failed, not as a result of employer opposition, but chiefly through external intervention and notably 'the Tennessee political establishment' (Silvia 2017: 23).

In his review of research covering 30 years of union renewal campaigns, Murray (2017) identifies four generic areas and associated obstacles facing unions in their revitalisation efforts. First, unions need to develop organisational strategies to match the many structural changes found in the contemporary networked and internationalised economy. Second, union structures and policies should be suited to the ambitions and needs of both existing and prospective members. Third, ways in which effective collective action can be mobilised should be identified. Rather than questioning the superiority of mobilisation or partnership models, Murray instead draws on research that identifies potential (or demonstrated) success according to context, such as the suitability of partnership where there is institutional stability for unions and collective representation. Indeed, there is support for the contention that union decline has been mitigated through statutory institutionalisation of industrial relationships in coordinated market economies, where social partnership between national and local government, employers and unions has acted against decline in the representative role of unions (Ibsen and Tapia 2017). Finally, Murray identifies challenges in extending union membership and protection to 'outsider' or precarious groups such as migrants and young workers but also notes the relative success of the union movement in widening its appeal to women and in attracting female union leaders through broadening campaign agendas.

One major structural change that can offer support to union renewal is the growth of women in paid employment. In some Northern European states, including the UK, female participation has reached levels of around 70 per cent, but rates are substantially lower in Greece and Italy. Nevertheless, gender inequality in many countries is still evident: women tend to be found in occupationally segregated low-pay, low-status and more vulnerable jobs and of course part-time work among women is prevalent across the EU (Kirton and Greene 2016: 16–17). In the UK, women are clustered in specific occupations such as caring, administration and sales and in public-sector roles in primary school teaching and nursing. There is also considerable vertical segregation with higher-status posts tending to be occupied by men. One outcome of these differences is the gender pay gap, which for the UK remains around an obstinate 20 per cent. With many women concentrated in the public sector, the impact of UK governmental austerity programmes has fallen disproportionately on them: over a quarter of a million women have lost their jobs in local government alone since 2010. Other issues of direct concern to both men and women include maintaining a balance between paid work and domestic responsibilities, although family care, whether of children or of older and infirm relatives, still tends to fall more on women than men (Crompton and Lynette 2006; Fujimoto et al. 2012) and continues to present stressful dilemmas for carers (TUC 2017b). Harassment, bullying and gender discrimination are also issues that persist and remain largely unresolved (Brunner and Dever 2014) and, in further demonstration of worker silence, often unreported (Young Women's Trust 2017). However, unions, frequently with women in the forefront, have become increasingly proactive in focusing their efforts in confronting gender-based disadvantage through internet and social media campaigns for equality and against discrimination, workplace-equality agreements, often secured through negotiation, and the presence and activities of equality representatives and committees (Kirton and Greene 2016). In many countries, women now represent a substantial and growing proportion of union membership, up to 55 per cent in the UK, leading to claims that women activists are helping to revitalise trade unions, even in countries like Poland, where considerable cultural barriers to women's accession to higher levels of union decision-making bodies are still evident (Mrozowicki and Trawińska 2012).

Clearly, labour generally and the union movement in particular are facing diverse and profound challenges from global political and economic alignments over which they have had little or no control. Nevertheless, the investigations of Murray and others indicate that unions across the world are facing up to challenges by identifying potential new constituencies and exploring ways in which they can serve member and societal needs in new and uncertain environments.

Negative indicators

Negative indicators for the future of EPV have been rehearsed in some depth in previous chapters. The prime negative factors constraining representative participation are of course the neoliberal project, globalisation and financialisation and their global consequences for labour market deregulation (Streeck 2016: 63). Neo-liberalism provides the driving force for the growing atomisation and precarity of working life, whether through the actions of mega-corporations which utilise the 'infrastructure of persuasion' to 'govern our lives' (Monbiot 2017: 2–3) or through capturing human capital theory to enforce the 'economic insecurity and disempowerment' (Fleming 2017: 174) of labour under the domination of 'authoritarian management systems" (ibid.: 207).

Hence, unconventional employment, sweatshop conditions and precariousness are forecast to grow among workers who are unable to enjoy the benefits of employment status, let alone a voice over their employment. Where EPV is sustained it is likely to be on management terms, concentrated among core employees, who may gain some added work satisfaction from superficial involvement schemes and extra remuneration provided through equity sharing programmes, but there is little evidence of greater sharing of wider organisational control even for more favoured high-added-value and professional employees. With reduced resources, trade unions will become more stretched, leading potentially to collaborative passivity or increasingly desperate aggressive action, though anti-union legislation, such as the 2016 Trade Union Act in the UK, may be passed to serve as a restraint. Another firmly established and growing phenomenon is the use of business models in public-sector management for services where professional and once autonomous work is increasingly subject to managerially controlled monitoring, targeting and outsourced precariousness. Under these combined pressures overlaid by diminishing trust in management, intensification and workplace-initiated stress have become significant and growing features of working experience.

The impact on the UK of leaving the EU

Finally, there remains, for the UK, at the time of writing, the question of the impact of leaving the EU on EPV. Following the historic 'leave' vote in June 2016, there has been sustained commentary and debate over likely economic and employment effects. Unfortunately, there have been few tangible developments that can give substance to potential impacts on the economy, employment relations and EPV. Fundamental yet unanswered questions relate to whether the exit from Europe will be soft or hard, the nature and duration of any transitional arrangements and the eventual jurisdictional authority of European law and regulations. A 'soft' exit is usually defined as leaving the EU but opting to stay in the single market and customs union. This would involve maintaining close ties with the EU and probably a degree of free movement of labour, possibly operated through membership of the European Economic Area (EEA). Remaining in the customs union would mean no border checks on exports, harmonised intra-EU tariffs and common import duties imposed for countries outside the EU. A 'hard' Brexit could occur if the UK leaves the EU with no deal in place and could involve a policy of restricting free movement of people. Trade with the EU would be conducted as with any other non-EU country, but could also involve mutual imposition of tariffs or other trade restrictions (Dunt 2017). A transitional or implementation phase is a temporary arrangement to be established from the time the UK formally leaves the EU until an expiry date agreed by both sides, but with the EU insisting on a maximum period of three years. A transitional phase enjoys wide support among the business and financial community because it would provide an interim period of economic stability.

Another serious uncertainty derives from employers' concern to maintain employment, especially in the event of a hard Brexit, which could affect the availability of highly qualified talent at one level but also of lower-skilled European labour in sectors such as agriculture, construction and hospitality. The impact of Brexit on employment law is also highly uncertain. One prime worry for the labour movement has been the potential adverse impact on workers' rights, which one prominent supporter argues was 'a major reason to quit the EU' for many 'anti-European ideologues' (MacShane 2017). Employment lawyers Taylor Wessing (2017) are more circumspect, pointing out that it is 'impossible to predict with any degree of certainty how the UK's employment laws may change' while making the strong point that recent UK employee protection law emanates largely from the EU, and that no responsible government would entertain a major repeal of laws that provide fundamental rights to its citizens. For similar reasons, the body representing HR interests in the UK, the CIPD, believes that basic protective employment law would be unaffected by Brexit. Nevertheless, from the perspective of employee protection, there are reasons to be sceptical. As Gumbrell-McCormick and Hyman (2017) demonstrate, working people have borne the brunt of neoliberal policies and Brexit is unlikely to alter this pattern, especially with a government determined to preserve employment flexibility. It should also be borne in mind that European initiatives such as the Working Time Directive have not been supported by British governments; as Standing (2014: 332) points out, control over working time is the primary issue, especially for those to whom it is denied, whether junior doctors or precarious workers. One fear expressed by the TUC is that statutory employment protection and worker rights could be replaced by government regulations without the intervention or even scrutiny of parliament (O'Grady 2017).

Rather different arguments, but similarly restrictive outcomes, might apply to Europe-derived consultation procedures. There is little evidence that employers see establishment-level consultation as threatening their interests, and they are therefore unlikely to campaign for their removal. The situation for EWCs could be more complex for, as MacShane (2017) points out, 'outside the EU, the two EU directives of 1994 and 2009 [see chapter 10] which provide the basis for EWC operations will no longer have legal force in Britain'. Even if the regulations were to be transposed into UK domestic law, they will no longer be contained within EU rule of law or the prerogative of the European Court of Justice (ECJ), whose jurisdiction has been opposed by the present UK government. Even here, recent policy statements over multilateral disputes have suggested greater UK accommodation to a future role for the ECJ (Financial Times 2017d). Nevertheless, British companies will not be able to escape an obligation to establish an EWC if EU conditions are met.

One potential damaging outcome would be the relocation by companies of their central management offices from the UK to an EU member state. Moreover, Gumbrell-McCormick and Hyman (2017) sound a number of warnings, especially in the case of a 'hard' Brexit, when British employee numbers would not count towards the threshold for establishing an EWC. UK-based firms would have to appoint a 'representative agent' from within the EEA, as would non-European companies with European head offices located in the UK. Those EWC agreements based on UK law might have to be completely renegotiated and British representatives might only be eligible for consultative rights.

Brexit policy is still evidently in its formative stages and its outcomes for employment and EPV remain uncertain. However, with continuing weak productivity, trade deficits may mount up and pressure on sterling increase. Post-Brexit trade treaties are unlikely to be favourable to the UK, which will be under competitive pressure from stronger economies, potentially leading to a downward spiral of weaker employee protections and labour vulnerability in the absence of the defensive shield provided by the EU. Labour cost pressures in turn could lead to work-intensifying efforts by employers, though for valued employees, these may be accompanied by involvement practices designed to encourage or manipulate worker performance.

Prospects for EPV

Over twenty years ago, under increasing economic, political and global pressures and uncertainties, we questioned the possible future directions of EPV (Hyman and Mason 1995). Other commentators and researchers have posed similar questions (e.g. Terry 2003b; Heery 2009; Budd 2014). The fundamental participation question posed at the beginning of this book was whether people have gained more or less control over their working lives. As we have shown, this question has been answered in mainly negative ways, largely as a result of seismic changes to the world's economy that few could have anticipated. Work has become increasingly insecure and, without employment security, establishing any sort of control over corporate governance or even over individual tasks becomes increasingly difficult. Also lack of security hinders the efforts of trade unions to organise and represent workers or, in their absence, those of workers to represent themselves. Hence, the participation gap remains and may even have widened, certainly so for masses of vulnerable and precarious workers. With the rise of globalisation, workers in developing countries are often employed in harsh and potentially health-threatening conditions with no guarantees of employment security. Footloose capital, with allegiance to no country, will continuously seek its optimal location in terms of cost benefit. In situations of insecure and Taylorised work conditions, unsympathetic governments and weak or oppressed trade unions, there are few opportunities for voice to be expressed. Even so, employers recognise that production is adversely affected without labour cooperation and in countries such as China and India, political resistance to collective activity is beginning to soften.

Another major issue in the wake of the Enron scandal, inadequate supervision of financial institutions, and the self-serving or aggressive management of companies like BHS, Sports Direct and Rolls-Royce is how to ensure more effective corporate social responsibility, a concern emphasized quickly and strongly by Conservative Prime Minister Theresa May in her accession to the premiership, but discarded equally promptly under pressure from employer organisations and business interests. In companies such as Sports Direct and Rolls-Royce, the appointment of individual employee representatives to main boards of directors has now been dropped or the process reduced to token exercises. Sports Direct are to allow a worker representative to *attend* its board meetings, a move largely dismissed as a public relations exercise. In an attempt to demonstrate more open corporate governance following a massive £671 million settlement on bribery and corruption charges, the Board of Rolls-Royce intends to introduce an 'annual general meeting' for employees, but has also dismissed plans to appoint a worker to its board (Guardian 2017b).

So, if the exercise of influence at any level within organisations is limited for employees, what are the prospects for the re-emergence of countervailing pressures for representative employee interests? Clearly, as we have seen, context is key. In European countries, even those with low union densities, where the social model is informed by 'fundamental values concerning the rights of employees to protection in their work against arbitrary treatment by employers' (Terry 2003a: 281), there have been more safeguards for employees through established statutory bargaining and consultative procedures. Even within the EU, however, a long-term shift to austerity inspired by neoliberal policy-making under tight disciplinary control from the European Central Bank (Streeck 2016: 162) is apparent, a process which some commentators claim could spell the end of the European social project, with potentially disastrous consequences for labour movement solidarity in Europe (Rustin 2016; Varoufakis 2016). In more liberal economies, the effects of this disintegration in terms of representative presence have been apparent for some time. In Paul Mason's (2015: 91–92) apocalyptic vision, the definitive objective of neoliberalism is 'the destruction of labour's bargaining power' by removing 'organized labour from the equation', a process from which Europe is not exempt.

Threats to workplace participation and the employment rights that serve to protect participation have understandably not gone unnoticed, and have been met by numerous proposals to counter labour weakness, which, as we have seen, spreads from the most vulnerable members of the work community to the 'just about managing', 'the squeezed middle class' and those with professional qualifications and specialised expertise. Graduates entering the labour force, burdened by heavy debts, may be disempowered by restrictions to their career choice and disciplined into silence to safeguard income and prospects. While challenges facing different groups vary, what unites them is the absence or weakness of collective representation at both workplace and political levels. In developed countries with established democratic political rights, diverse trends are appearing. On one hand, voting participation is in apparent decline, on the other the rise in populism, which some see as underlying nationalist decisions to leave the EU and election of President Trump, is attributed to a sense of disempowerment (Hanley 2016: 200). If this 'decline of democracy' (Chomsky 2017: 3) or democratic deficit is experienced at the political level, would more individual participative rights at work (e.g. through share schemes) have any meaningful impact on organisational behaviour in the absence of collective means of exerting pressure or, in Chomsky's words, would they simply serve to 'engineer the consent' of the governed to be governed (ibid.: 88)?

Recognition that work has become dysfunctional at so many levels and for so many people (and ultimately for their employers and the national economy) has led to numerous recommendations and exhortations for its reform. In the UK, the most recent were of course contained in the 2017 Taylor report, but this suffered from the implicit treatment of the modern workplace as a largely self-righting system, demanding minimal state intervention. Importantly, though, the report provides a vital service by identifying the main characteristics of 'quality work' and by the Taylor committee's stated ambition to provide this for all workers. Nevertheless, the question of 'how' remains open. Based on his searching 2011 analysis of the precariat, Standing (2014) presents his proposed citizens' charter, comprising 30 diverse and admirable articles, but offers little practical demonstration of how these can be implemented, monitored and, if necessary, enforced. Anderson (2017: 65) follows her incisive critique of modern employment practice by suggesting four 'general strategies for advancing and protecting the liberties and interests of the governed'. These embrace exit, reliance on the law, constitutional rights, and voice. She then demonstrates that, in the context of work, each of the first three are necessary to provide a 'minimal floor' but there is 'no adequate substitute for recognizing workers' voice', acting through the agency of collective bargaining or nonadversarial consultation (ibid.: 69–71). She also recognises that these processes are available to a diminishing proportion of the working population, at least in the USA. Commissioned by the Fabian Society, Tait (2017) suggests practical steps to stem union decline by establishing service links with potential members in low-density but fast-growing areas of the private sector. In their influential critique of societal inequality, Wilkinson and Pickett (2010: 256) make modest but achievable recommendations, based on extensive research from different countries, for ESO to be combined with 'participatory management methods' to achieve economic benefits such as productivity enhancement. Unfortunately, less is said about the *types* of participation or the impacts on employees themselves, but with the thrust of their argument directed toward *democratic* EO, the assumption must be of high allocations of employee shares, combined with means for collective employee control over work, which could also secure health and welfare benefits.

Closing the participation gap

A fundamental obstacle to be confronted in any attempt to close participation gaps is the likely continuation and possible consolidation of neoliberal political economy policy. Resistance to neoliberalism would involve significant political shifts that might only arise through the election of parties enjoying established grassroots popular support. Even here national level collectivist policies and anti-austerity measures would be confronted by a united front of employers and business-supportive political interests and, as was the case for Greece, by the authoritarianism and imposition of the dominant EU economies. Nevertheless, that political resistance to EU-backed austerity is possible has been demonstrated by Portugal's socialist government, which in defiance of EU strictures, implemented an interventionist programme 'reversing wage and pension cuts, halting privatisations and restoring collective-bargaining arrangements' – leading to a revival in economic growth (Finn 2017).

In the probable absence of socialist or openly worker-sympathetic governments, challenge from below or 'social solidarity, sacrificed in the globalization era' is perhaps a more realisable ambition that 'must be revived' (Standing 2014: 326) if the labour movement is to present transformative alternatives to current neoliberal doctrine. Some professions, wishing to protect their societal role as well as professional status, have started to question government efforts to impose managerial metrication and control. Often against political opposition and official union conservatism and apathy, employees such as doctors in training ('junior doctors') have risen up collectively in the UK to campaign against the unilateral imposition of employment contracts and conditions that they perceive to be damaging to the welfare of the public they serve. More broadly, professions and sympathetic commentators are beginning to dispute the impact of deregulation and austerity measures and the neoliberal values that underpin them on their autonomy and to highlight the threats facing publicly funded health and welfare systems (for higher education, see Smyth (2017) and Collini (2012); for health services, Pollock (2004); for public services generally, Toynbee and Walker (2017)). Nevertheless, cohesive coalitions and networks between public-sector professions, employees and other activist groups will be vital in order to confront liberal market doctrines and policies.

Outside of professions, there is ample evidence that employees have expressed interest in collective representation, though not necessarily through confrontation (Freeman and Rogers 2006). There is also evidence that representation can be linked to improved organisational performance because it encourages more effective people management and provides employees with constitutional means to receive and act on information through recognised consultative and negotiating forums. In many cases, establishing representative structures will be resisted by managers fearful of losing prerogative, which means that unions, in particular, need to seek ways of recruiting, enthusing and retaining members and using legislated opportunities, such as the 1999 Employment Relations Act, to secure recognition and bargaining rights. Successful campaigns for women membership and activism show that unions also need to become attractive to underrepresented groups, such as young people and those not in established full-time employment. Problems in recruitment, recognition and presence will be especially severe for employees in powerful transnational companies opposed to regulation. Political support, which is unlikely to be forthcoming from market-leaning administrations, would also be vital in reducing the threshold for triggering union recognition procedures and implementing ICE regulations. In Anglo-Saxon economies, which do not enjoy the statutory social protections found in more coordinated market economies, legislated policies that encourage and support union growth and activity are essential, but these are dependent on the election and subsequent actions of sympathetic political parties, who are likely to face antagonistic coordinated campaigns from those who, rightly or wrongly, consider their interests to be under threat.

The future of work

Prospects for EPV are heavily tied in with projections for future directions of work. With employers facing increasing commercial pressure to utilise flexible and performance-measured labour, the main directions for EPV growth in most countries are likely to be in individualised, employer-initiated voice mechanisms, employee share schemes and possibly a revival of consultative procedures. In the UK, this may happen under mild pressure imposed by ICE regulations or by voluntarily adopting similar non-confrontational participative measures to meet governmental policy guidelines for improving corporate governance. For employees and trade unions, the evidence suggests continuing pressure against more assertive participative representation, compounded by challenges posed by computerisation, surveillance and enforced flexibility and precariousness. These negative features could be moderated through increased mobilisation of precarious workers and by developing gendered activism at the workplace.

The impact of advances in technology on people's working lives has long been debated (Braverman 1974; Cooley 1987), though opinions vary from freeing humans from drudge work to capturing and exploiting the capabilities of workers, who increasingly perform under technology-based surveillance. Manifestations of human–electronic interaction are found in call centres (Taylor and Bain 1999) and through electronic point of sale (EPOS) performance monitoring in outlets such as supermarket checkouts (Lapido and Wilkinson 2002). A recent BBC documentary showed intrusive procedures installed in the industrial warehouses of companies like Amazon, where technologically timed retrieval systems monitor and minutely control the performance of despatchers (BBC 2013). Similar technologically driven management systems are used in the USA to measure and compare performance data of truck drivers and other workers (Levy 2015). These examples demonstrate a growing shift from direct control by managers to technological control, to the extent that today, 'digital Taylorism is pervasive' (Frischmann and Selinger 2016: 19). A much-cited article forecasts that in the near future, nearly half of US employment will be at risk of automation, with low-skill jobs most at risk (Frey and Osborne 2017). The implications for these workers could be severe, first because of the need for costly continuous learning and job retraining, potentially borne by recipients (West 2015), but also because of prospective transferability of computerised and robotised jobs to low-pay countries with weak labour controls. The negative implications for worker participation, whether through individual voice or collective representation, are obvious.

The global advance of precarious work has been well documented and shows few signs of diminishing. When this is combined with technology, for example in digitally mediated work such as parcel delivery services, questions of control and regulation become paramount. Recent reports and studies have highlighted the need for clearer definition of employment status and for forms of protective regulation suited to changing profiles of work (Taylor 2017; Coyle 2017; Stewart and Stanford 2017) but all recognise the difficulties in procuring employment regulation in economies increasingly driven by flexible and fluid working arrangements. Responses of trade union officials to these developments have generally been slow and accommodative, and the strongest opposition to casualisation expressed by new unions or active lay elements of established ones. Pressure on exploitative employers has sometimes been successfully applied through 'social movement' tactics, involving street protests and forms of informal resistance (Rogers 2017). It is clear that unions need to develop campaigns and approaches that welcome and support precarious workers if they are to develop the critical mass required to provide an effective voice against recalcitrant employers. The University and College Union (UCU) is one of the UK's largest. It points out that 46 per cent of universities and 60 per cent of colleges use zero-hours contracts and that 68 per cent of research staff are on fixed-term contracts. This situation has led the UCU to launch a national anti-casualisation campaign, successfully targeting specific locations, often in joint actions between union and students.

Ultimately, doubts surrounding a progressive role for EPV are unlikely to diminish in the foreseeable future in the absence of radical political change. With business interests exercising strong influence on political directions (Chomsky 2017: 2), there are few signs of shifts from austerity-driven free-market orthodoxy. Even the European social model, which has long provided a source of protective collective representation, is under scrutiny as individual countries such as France seek to pursue neoliberal routes of labour-market flexibility, though this is one country where union-led grassroots opposition is most likely to be effectively expressed. Within this broad political-economy framework, EPV policies adopted by individual organisations may show superficial variances according to interpretation of their needs but all will share the unifying characteristic of being informed by universal market demands. So high-added-value labour may on the surface be offered a range of commitment-seeking inducements to follow designated behavioural routes, but these will be underpinned by free-market ideology. Individual communication and consultation programmes may also be offered to wider sections of the workforce. However, under prevailing economic doctrines, unions experience political weakness and trade-union backed collective bargaining will continue to be faced by employer manipulation, avoidance or resistance. The century-long shift from ideas promoting industrial democracy, through radical worker control and union-driven pluralist opposition to current corporate hegemony has been gradual and, in democratic societies, never likely to be complete, but there are few signs that the direction of travel will be altered, let alone reversed.

References

ACAS (Advisory, Conciliation and Arbitration Service) (2017), 'Information and consultation of employees (ICE)'. www.acas.org.uk/index.aspx?articleid=1598.
Acker, J. (2006), 'Inequality regimes: gender, class and race in organizations', *Gender and Society*, 20(4), 441–464.
Ackers, P., Marchington, M., Wilkinson, A. and Goodman, J. (1992), 'The use of cycles? Explaining employee involvement in the 1990s', *Industrial Relations Journal*, 23(4), 268–283.
Ackroyd, S. and Thompson, P. (1999), *Organizational Misbehaviour*, London, Sage.
Adams, S. (1963), 'Towards an understanding of inequity', *Journal of Abnormal and Social Psychology*, 67(5), 422–436.
Addison, J. and Schnabel, C. (2009), 'Worker directors: a German product that didn't export?', IZA Discussion Paper No. 3918, *IZA, Institute for the Study of Labor*, Bonn.
Addison, J., Kölling, A. and Teixeira, P. (2014), 'Changes in bargaining status and intra-plant dispersion in Germany; a case of (almost) plus ça change?', IZA Discussion Paper No. 8359, IZA, Institute for the Study of Labor, Bonn.
Addison, J., Texeira, P., Pahnke, A. and Bellman, L. (2017), 'The demise of a model? The state of collective bargaining and worker representation in Germany', *Economic and Industrial Democracy*, 38(2), 193–234.
Adler, P. (1993), 'Time and motion regained', *Harvard Business Review*, January/February, 97–108.
Alber, J. and Standing, G. (2000), 'Social dumping, catch-up or convergence? Europe in comparative global context', *Journal of European Social Policy*, 10(2), 99–119.
Aldridge, M. and Evetts, J. (2003), 'Rethinking the concept of professionalism: the case of journalism', *British Journal of Sociology*, 54(4), 547–564.
Alfes, K., Truss, C., Soane, E., Rees, C. and Gatenby, M. (2010), *Creating an Engaged Workforce*, London, CIPD.
Allen, N. and Meyer, J. (1990), 'The measurement and antecedents of affective, continuance and normative commitment to the organization', *Journal of Occupational Psychology*, 63(1), 1–18.
Almond, G. and Verba, S. (1965), *The Civic Culture*, Boston, MA, Little Brown & Co.
Amba-Rao, S., Petrick, J., Gupta, J. and Von Der Embse, T. (2000), 'Comparative performance appraisal practices and management values among foreign and domestic firms in India', *International Journal of Human Resource Management*, 11(1), 60–89.

Anderson, C. (2010), 'Doing more with less? Flexible working practices and the intensification of work', *Human Relations*, 63(1), 83–106.
Anderson, E. (2017), *Private Government*, Princeton, NJ, Princeton University Press..
Andreamatteo, A., Ianni, L., Lega, F. and Sargiacomo, M. (2015), 'Lean in healthcare: a comprehensive review', *Health Policy*, 119(9), 1197–1209.
Andrews, J. and Higson, H. (2010), 'Graduate employability, "soft skills" versus "hard" business knowledge: a European study', *Higher Education in Europe*, 33(4), 411–422.
Angelis, J., Conti, R., Cooper, C. and Gill, C. (2011), 'Building a high-commitment lean culture', *Journal of Manufacturing Technology Management*, 22(5), 569–586.
Anleu, S. R. and Mack, K. (2014), 'Job satisfaction in the judiciary', *Work, Employment & Society* 28(5), 683–701.
Appelbaum, E. (2002), 'The impact of new forms of work organization on workers', in G. Murray, J. Bélanger, A. Giles and P. Lapointe (eds), *Work and Employment Relations in the High Performance Workplace*, London, Continuum, 120–149.
Appelbaum, E., Bailey, T., Berg, P. and Kalleberg, A. (2000), *Manufacturing Advantage: Why High-Performance Work Systems Pay Off*, Ithaca, Cornell University Press.
Aritzeta, A., Swailes, S. and Senior, B. (2007), 'Belbin's team role model: development, validity and applications for teambuilding', *Journal of Management Studies*, 44(1), 96–118.
Arando, S., Freundlich, F., Gago, M., Jones, D. and Kato, T. (2010), 'Assessing Mondragon: stability and managed change in the face of globalization', No. 1003, *Working Paper*, William Davidson Institute, University of Michigan.
Arrowsmith, J. (2003), 'Post-privatisation industrial relations in the UK rail and electricity industries', *Industrial Relations Journal*, 34(2), 150–163.
Arthur, J. (1994), 'Effects of human resource systems on manufacturing performance and turnover', *Academy of Management Journal*, 7, 670–687.
Ashburner, L. and Fitzgerald, L. (1996), 'Beleaguered professionals: clinicians and institutional change in the NHS', in H. Scarbrough (ed.), *The Management of Expertise*, Basingstoke, Macmillan Business, 190–216.
Atkinson, J. and Meager, N. (1986), *Changing Work Patterns*, London, NEDO.
Australian Bureau of Statistics (2017), *Characteristics of Employment*, Canberra, ABS.
Baccaro, L. and Howell, C. (2011), 'A common neoliberal trajectory: the transformation of industrial relations in advanced capitalism', *Politics & Society*, 39(4), 521–563.
Bach, S. and Winchester, D. (2003), 'Industrial relations in the public sector', in P. Edwards (ed.), *Industrial Relations: Theory and Practice*, 2nd ed., Oxford, Blackwell, 285–311.
Bacon, N. and Samuel, P. (2009), 'Partnership agreement adoption and survival in the British private and public sectors', *Work, Employment & Society*, 23(2), 231–248.
Baddon, L., Hunter, L., Hyman, J., Leopold, J. and Ramsay, H. (1989), *People's Capitalism? A Critical Analysis of Profit-sharing and Employee Share Ownership*, London, Routledge.
Badigannavar, V. and Kelly, J. (2011), 'Partnership and organizing: an empirical assessment of two contrasting approaches to union revitalization in the UK', *Economic and Industrial Democracy*, 32(1), 5–27.
Bailey, C., Madden, A., Alfes, K. and Fletcher, L. (2015), 'The meaning, antecedents and outcomes of employee engagement: a narrative synthesis', *International Journal of Management Reviews*, 19(1), 31–53.
Bain, G. and Elsheikh, F. (1976), *Union Growth and the Business Cycle*, Oxford, Blackwell.

References

Bain, G. and Price, R. (1983), 'The determinants of union growth', in W. E. J. McCarthy (ed.), *Trade Unions*, Harmondsworth, Pelican, 245–271.

Baldry, C. and Barnes, A. (2012), 'The open-plan academy: space, control and the undermining of professional identity', *Work, Employment & Society*, 26(2), 228–245.

Baldry, C., Bain, P. and Taylor, P. (1998), 'Bright satanic offices: intensification, control and "Team Taylorism"', in P. Thompson and C. Warhurst (eds), *Workplaces of the Future*, Basingstoke, Palgrave Macmillan, 163–183.

Baldry, C., Scholarios, D. and Hyman, J. (2005), 'Organizational commitment among software developers', in R. Barrett (ed.), *Management, Labour Process and Software Development: Reality Bytes*, London, Routledge, 168–195.

Baldry, C., Bain, P., Taylor, P., Hyman, J., Scholarios, D., Marks, A., Watson, A., Gilbert, K., Gall, G. and Bunzel, D. (2007), *The Meaning of Work in the New Economy*, Basingstoke, Palgrave Macmillan.

Bamberger, P. and Meshoulam, I. (2000), *Human Resource Management Strategy*, Thousand Oaks, CA, Sage..

Banker, R., Field, J., Schroeder, R. and Sinha, K. (1996), 'Impact of work teams on manufacturing performance: a longitudinal field study', *Academy of Management Journal*, 39(4), 867–890.

Barnes, T., Lal Das, K. and Pratap, S. (2015), 'Labour contractors and global production networks: the case of India's auto supply chain', *The Journal of Development Studies*, 51(4), 355–369.

Barney, J. (1991), 'Firm resources and sustained competitive advantage', *Journal of Management*, 17(1), 99–120.

Barrick, M., Thurgood, G., Smith, T. and Cartwright, S. (2015), 'Collective organizational engagement: linking motivational antecedents, strategic implementation, and firm performance', *Academy of Management Journal*, 58, 111–135.

Barry, M. and Wilkinson, A. (2016), 'Pro-social or pro-management? A critique of the conception of employee voice as a pro-social behaviour within organizational behaviour', *British Journal of Industrial Relations*, 54(2), 261–284.

Bartlett, C. and Ghoshal, S. (1989), *Managing across Borders: The Transnational Solution*, Boston, MA, Harvard Business School Press.

Bauman, Z. (2000), *Liquid Modernity*, Cambridge, MA, Polity Press..

BBC (2013), 'Amazon: the truth behind the click', 25 November. http://bbc.co.uk/programmes/b03k5kzp.

BBC (2017a), 'China's economy grows 6.7% in 2016', 20 January. www.bbc.co.uk/news/business-38686568.

BBC (2017b), 'McDonald's could face first UK strikes', 18 August. www.bbc.co.uk/news/business-40982955.

Becker, B. and Gerhart, B. (1996), 'The impact of human resource management on organizational performance: progress and prospects', *Academy of Management Journal*, 39(4), 779–801.

Beer, M., Spector, B., Lawrence, P., Mills, D. Q. and Walton, R. (1984), *Managing Human Assets*, New York, Free Press.

Behrens, M., Hamann, K. and Hurd, R. (2004), 'Conceptualising labour union revitalisation', in C. Frege and J. Kelly (eds), *Varieties of Unionism: Strategies for Union Revitalisation in a Globalizing Economy*, Oxford, Oxford University Press, 11–29.

Beirne, M. (2006), *Empowerment and Innovation: Managers, Principles and Reflective Practice*, Cheltenham, Edward Elgar.

Beirne, M. (2013), *Rhetoric and the Politics of Workplace Innovation*, Cheltenham, Edward Elgar.
Belbin, R. (1993), *Team Roles at Work*, Oxford, Butterworth-Heinemann.
Belbin, R. (2000), *Beyond the Team*, Oxford, Butterworth-Heinemann.
Belbin, R. (2003), *Management Teams: Why They Succeed or Fail*, 2nd ed., Oxford, Butterworth-Heinemann.
Bell, D. and Hanson, C. (1987), *Profit-sharing and Profitability*, London, Kogan Page.
Ben-Ner, A. (1984), 'On the stability of the cooperative type of organization', *Journal of Comparative Economics*, 8, September, 247–260.
Ben-Ner, A. and Jones, D. (1995), 'Employee participation, ownership and productivity: a theoretical framework', *Industrial Relations*, 34(4), 532–554.
Benders, J. (2005), 'Team working: a tale of partial participation', in B. Harley, J. Hyman and P. Thompson (eds), *Participation and Democracy at Work*, Basingstoke, Palgrave Macmillan, 55–74.
Benders, J. and van Hootegem, G. (2000), 'How the Japanese got teams', in S. Procter and F. Mueller (eds), *Teamworking*, Basingstoke, Macmillan Business, 43–59.
Benson, J., Debroux, P., Yuasa, M. and Zhu, Y. (2000), 'Flexibility and labour management: Chinese manufacturing enterprises in the 1990s', *International Journal of Human Resource Management*, 11(2), 183–196.
Berardi, F. (2009), *The Soul at Work: From Alienation to Autonomy*, Los Angeles, CA, Semiotext(e).
Berggren, C. (1993), *The Volvo Experience: Alternatives to Lean Production in the Swedish Auto Industry*, Basingstoke, Macmillan.
Berggren, C. (1994), 'The fate of the branch plants: performance versus power', in Sandberg, Å. (ed.) (2007), *Enriching Production: Perspectives on Volvo's Uddevalla Plant as an Alternative to Lean Production*, digital ed., Stockholm; printed ed. (1994), Aldershot, Avebury, 105–126..
Bergvall-Kåreborn, B. and Howcroft, D. (2013), '"The future's bright, the future's mobile": a study of Apple and Google mobile application developers', *Work, Employment & Society*, 27(6), 964–981.
Beynon, H. (1973), *Working for Ford*, Harmondsworth, Penguin.
Bhattacherjee, D. and Ackers, P. (2010), 'Introduction: Employee relations in India – old narrative and new perspectives', *Industrial relations Journal*, 41(2), 104–121.
Birdi, K., Clegg, C., Patterson, M., Robinson, A., Stride, C., Wall, T. and Wood, S. (2008), 'Contemporary manufacturing practices and company performance: A longitudinal study", *Personnel Psychology*, 61(3), 467–501.
Blanchflower, D. and Oswald, A. (1986), 'Profit-sharing: can it Work?', *LSE Discussion Paper* 255, London School of Economics, London.
Blasi, J., Freeman, R., Mackin, C. and Kruse, D. (2010), 'Creating a bigger pie? The effects of employee ownership, profit-sharing and stock options on workplace performance', in D. Kruse, R. Freeman and J. Blasi (eds), *Shared Capitalism at Work: Employee Ownership, Profit and Gain Sharing, and Broad-based Stock Options*, Chicago, IL, University of Chicago Press, 139–165.
Blasi, J., Freeman, R. and Kruse, D. (2013), *The Citizen's Share: Putting Ownership Back into Democracy*, New Haven, CT, Yale University Press.
Blauner, R. (1960), 'Work satisfaction and industrial trends in modern society', in W. Galenson and S. Lipset (eds), *Labor and Trade Unionism*, New York, Wiley.

Blauner, R. (1964), *Alienation and Freedom: the Factory Worker and His Industry*, Chicago, IL, University of Chicago Press..

Block, R. and Berg, P. (2010), 'Collective bargaining as a form of employee participation: observations on the United States and Europe', in A. Wilkinson, P. Gollan, M. Marchington and D. Lewin (eds), *Oxford Handbook of Participation in Organizations*, Oxford, Oxford University Press, 186–211.

Blumberg, P. (1968), *Industrial Democracy: The Sociology of Participation*, London, Constable.

Bowen, D. and Lawler, E. (1992), 'The empowerment of service workers: why, how and when?', *Sloan Management Review*, 33(3), 31–39.

Boxall, P. (2012), 'High performance work systems: what, why, how and for whom?', *Asia Pacific Journal of Human Resources*, 50(2), 169–186.

Boxall, P. and Purcell, J. (2010), 'An HRM perspective on employee participation' in A Wilkinson, P. Gollan, M. Marchington and D. Lewin (eds), *The Oxford Handbook of Participation in Organizations*, Oxford, Oxford University Press, 29–51.

Boxall, P. and Macky, K. (2014), 'High involvement work processes, work intensification and employee well-being', *Work, Employment & Society*, 28(6), 963–984.

Boxall, P. and Purcell, J. (2016), *Strategy and Human Resource Management*, 4th ed., Basingstoke, Palgrave Macmillan.

Boxall, P., Haynes, P. and Macky, K. (2007a), 'Employee voice and voicelessness in New Zealand', in R. Freeman, P. Boxall and P. Haynes (eds), *What Workers Say: Employee Voice in the Anglo-American Workplace*, Ithaca, NY, ILR Press, 145–165.

Boxall, P., Haynes, P. and Freeman, R. (2007b), 'What workers say in the Anglo-American world', in R. Freeman, P. Boxall and P. Haynes (eds), *What Workers Say: Employee Voice in the Anglo-American Workplace*, Ithaca, NY, ILR Press, 206–220.

Bozkurt, O. and Grugulis, I. (2011), 'Why retail work demands a closer look', in I. Grugulis and O. Bozkurt (eds), *Retail Work*, Basingstoke, Palgrave Macmillan.

Bradsher, K. and Barboza, D. (2010), 'Strike in China highlights gap in workers' pay', *China Labor Watch*, 28 May.

Brannen, P. (1983), *Authority and Participation in Industry*, London, Batsford.

Bratton, J. and Gold, J. (2012), *Human Resource Management: Theory and Practice*, 5th ed., Basingstoke, Palgrave Macmillan.

Bratton, J. and Gold, J. (2015), 'Towards critical human resource management education (CHRME): a sociological imagination approach', *Work, Employment & Society*, 29(3), 496–507.

Braverman, H. (1974), *Labor and Monopoly Capital*, New York, Monthly Review Press.

Brinsfield, C. (2014), 'Employee voice and silence in organizational behavior', in A. Wilkinson, J. Donaghey, T. Dundon and R. Freeman (eds), *Handbook of Research on Employee Voice*, Cheltenham, Edward Elgar, 114–131.

Briscoe, D., Schuler, R. and Tarique, I. (2016), *International Human Resource Management: Policies and Practices for Multinational Enterprises*, 5th ed., London, Routledge.

British Social Attitudes (2015), The 33rd Report, London, NatCen Social Research.

Brödner, P. and Latniak, E. (2002), *Sources of Innovation and Competitiveness: National Programmes Supporting the Development of Work Organisation*, Brussels, European Commission.

Brown, A., Charlwood, A. and Spencer, D. (2012), 'Not all that it might seem: why job satisfaction is worth studying despite it being a poor summary measure of job quality', *Work, Employment & Society*; 26(6), 1007–1018.

Brown, C., Reich, M. and Stern, D. (1993), 'Becoming a high performance work organization: the role of security, employee involvement and training', *International Journal of Human Resource Management*, 4(2), 247–275.

Brown, W., Marginson, P. and Walsh, J. (2003), 'The management of pay as the influence of collective bargaining diminishes', in P. Edwards (ed.), *Industrial Relations: Theory and Practice*, 2nd ed., Oxford, Blackwell, 189–213.

Brunner, L. and Dever, M. (2014), 'Work, bodies and boundaries: talking sexual harassment in the new economy', *Gender, Work & Organization*, 21(5), 459–471.

Bryson, A. (2004), 'Managerial response to union and non-union worker voice in Britain', *Industrial Relations: A Journal of Economy and Society*, 43(1), 213–241.

Buchanan, D. (1987), 'Job enrichment is dead: long live high performance work design', *Personnel Management*, May, 40–43.

Buchanan, D. (2000), 'An eager and enduring embrace: the ongoing rediscovery of teamworking as a management idea', in S. Procter and F. Mueller (eds), *Teamworking*, Basingstoke, Macmillan Business, 25–42.

Buchanan, D. and McCalman, J. (1989), *High Performance Work Systems: The Digital Experience*, London, Routledge.

Budd, J. (2014), 'The future of employee voice', in A. Wilkinson, J. Donaghey, T. Dundon and R. Freeman (eds), *Handbook of Research on Employee Voice*, Cheltenham, Edward Elgar, 477–489.

Budd, J. and Zagelmeyer, S. (2010), 'Public policy and employee participation', in A. Wilkinson, P. Gollan, M. Marchington and D. Lewin (eds), *Oxford Handbook of Participation in Organizations*, Oxford, Oxford University Press, 476–503.

Bullock Report (1977), *Report of the Committee of Inquiry on Industrial Democracy*, Chairman Lord Bullock, CMND 6706, London, HMSO..

Burchell, B., Lapido, D. and Wilkinson, F. (eds) (2002), *Job Insecurity and Work Intensification*, London, Routledge.

Bureau of Labor Statistics (1916), 'Profit-sharing in the United States', *Monthly Review*, 2(6), 46–48.

Burkitt, B. (1981), 'Excessive trade union power: existing reality or contemporary myth?', *Industrial Relations Journal*, 12(3), 65–71.

Bushe, G. and Chu, A. (2011), 'Fluid teams: solutions to the problems of unstable team membership', *Organizational Dynamics*, 40(3), 181–188.

Business Line (2005), 'Outsiders instigated labour unrest: Honda management', 27 July.

Business Standard (2013), 'Indian trade unions are getting bigger, coinciding with slowdown', 6 April.

BusinessEurope (2008), *Letter to EU Commissioners' Heads of Cabinets on EWCs*, Brussels, BusinessEurope.

Butler, P., Glover, L. and Tregaskis, O. (2011), '"When the going gets tough" … : recession and the resilience of workplace partnership', *British Journal of Industrial Relations*, 49(4), 666–687.

Cable, J. and Wilson, N. (1989), 'Profit-sharing and productivity: an analysis of UK engineering firms', *The Economic Journal*, 99, 366–375.

Cable, J. and Wilson, N. (1990), 'Profit-sharing and productivity: some further evidence', *The Economic Journal*, 100, 550–555.

Cahill, N. (2000), 'Profit-sharing, employee share ownership, and gainsharing: what can they achieve?', Research Series No. 4, National Economic and Social Council, Dublin.

Caldwell, R. (2011), 'HR directors in UK boardrooms: a search for strategic influence or symbolic capital', *Employee Relations*, 33(1), 40–63.

Callahan, E., Dworkin, T., Fort, T. and Schipani, C. (2002), 'Integrating trends in whistleblowing and corporate governance: promoting organizational effectiveness, societal responsibility, and employee empowerment', *American Business Law Journal*, 40(1), 177–236.

Campolieti, M., Gomez, R. and Gunderson, M. (2007), 'Say what? Employee voice in Canada', in R. Freeman, P. Boxall and P. Haynes (eds), *What Workers Say: Employee Voice in the Anglo-American Workplace*, Ithaca, NY, ILR Press, 49–71.

Cappelli, P., Singh, H., Singh, J. and Useem, M. (2010), *The India Way: How India's Top Business Leaders are Revolutionizing Management*, Boston, MA, Harvard Business Press.

Campolieti, M., Gomez, R. and Gunderson, M. (2011), 'What accounts for the representation gap? Decomposing Canada – US differences in the desire for collective voice', *Journal of Industrial Relations*, 53(4), 425–449.

Carley, M. (2005), 'Board-level employee representatives in nine countries: a snapshot', *Transfer*, 11(2), 231–244.

Carter, B. and Stevenson, H. (2012), 'Teachers, workforce remodeling and the challenge to labour process analysis', *Work, Employment & Society* 26(3), 481–496.

Carter, B., Danford, A., Howcroft, D., Richardson, H., Smith, A. and Taylor, P. (2011), '"All they lack is a chain": lean and the new performance management in the British civil service', *New Technology, Work and Employment*, 26(2), 83–97.

Carter, B., Danford, A., Howcroft, D., Richardson, H., Smith, A. and Taylor, P. (2013), '"Stressed out of my box": employee experience of lean working and occupational ill-health in clerical work in the UK public sector', *Work, Employment & Society*, 27(5), 747–767.

Carter, B., Danford, A., Howcroft, D., Richardson, H., Smith, A. and Taylor, P. (2016), 'Uncomfortable truths: teamworking under lean in the UK', *International Journal of Human Resource Management*, 28(3), 449–467.

Carter, N. (1990), 'Changing ownership: meaning, culture, and control in the construction of a co-operative organization', in G. Jenkins and M. Poole (eds), *New Forms of Ownership, Management and Employment*, London, Routledge, 323–340.

Casey, C. (1995), *Work, Self and Society: after Industrialism*, London, Routledge.

Cathcart, A. (2009), 'Directing democracy: the case of the John Lewis Partnership', unpublished doctoral thesis, University of Leicester.

Cathcart, A. (2013), 'Directing democracy: competing interest and contested terrain in the John Lewis Partnership', *Journal of Industrial Relations*, 55(4), 601–620.

CBI (1977), *In Place of Bullock*, London, Confederation of British Industry.

Cederström, C. and Fleming, P. (2012), *Dead Man Working*, Winchester, Zero Books.

Center for Advanced Human Resource Studies (2010), 'A China-based high-performance human resources system: a model for success', *CAHRS Research*Link No 10, ILR School, Cornell University.

Chan, A., Snape, E., Luo, M. and Zhai, Y. (2016), 'The developing role of unions in China's foreign-invested enterprises', *British Journal of Industrial Relations*, 54(1), 160–191.

Chan, J., Pun, N. and Selden, M. (2013), 'The politics of global production: Apple, Foxconn and China's new working class', *New Technology, Work and Employment*, 28(2), 100–115.

Chandrasekhar, C. and Ghosh, J. (2014), 'Contract workers in manufacturing', *Business Line*, 28 April..
Child, J. (1972), 'Organizational structure, environment and performance: the role of strategic choice', *Sociology*, 6(3), 1–22.
Child, J. (1996), *Management in China During the Age of Reform*, Cambridge, Cambridge University Press.
China Labour Bulletin (2014), 'Searching for the union: the workers' movement in China 2011–2013'.
Chomsky, N. (2017), *Who Rules the World?*, London, Penguin Books.
Chowhan, J. (2016), 'Unpacking the black box: understanding the relationship between strategy, HRM practices, innovation and organizational performance', *Human Resource Management Journal*, 26(2), 112–133.
Christian, M., Garza, A. and Slaughter, J. (2011), 'Work engagement: a quantitative review and test of its relations with task and contextual performance', *Personnel Psychology*, 64, 89–136.
Church, R. (1971), 'Profit-sharing and labour relations in the nineteenth century', *International Review of Social History*, XVI, Part 1, 2–15.
CIPD (Chartered Institute of Personnel and Development) (2017), 'HR professionalism: what do we stand for', January.
Ciulla, J. (2000), *The Working Life: The Promise and Betrayal of Modern Work*, New York, Three Rivers Press.
Cividep (2010), 'Changing industrial relations in India's mobile phone manufacturing industry', Centre for Research on Multinational Corporations (SOMO), Amsterdam .
CLB (Chinese Labour Bulletin) (2014), 'Taking a stand: trade union chairman fights back against Walmart', 24 June.
CLB (Chinese Labour Bulletin) (2017), 'Labour relations FAQ'. www.clb.org.hk/content/labour-relations-faq.
Clegg, H. (1985), 'Trade unions as an opposition which can never become a government', in W. E. J. McCarthy (ed.), *Trade Unions*, 2nd ed., Harmondsworth, Pelican, 83–91.
Coates, E. (1991), 'Profit sharing today: plans and provisions', *Monthly Labor Review*, 114(4), 19–25.
Coates, K. (ed.) (1986), *Freedom and Fairness: Empowering People at Work*, Nottingham, Russell Press.
Cole, G. D. H. (1957), *The Case for Industrial Partnership*, New York, St Martin's Press.
Collier, P. and Horowitz, D. (1989), *The Fords: An American Epic*, London, Futura.
Collings, D. and Wood, G. (2009), 'Human resource management: a critical approach', in D. Collings and G. Wood (eds), *Human Resource Management: A Critical Approach*, London, Routledge, 1–16.
Collini, S. (2012), *What are Universities for?* London, Penguin.
Collins, D. (1996), 'How and why participatory management improves a company's social performance', *Business & Society*, 35(2), 176–210.
Collins, D. (2000), *Management Fads and Buzzwords: Critical–Practical Perspectives*, London, Routledge.
Collinson, D. (1994), 'Strategies of resistance: power, knowledge and subjectivity in the workplace', in J. Jermier, W. Nord and D. Knights (eds), *Resistance and Power in the Workplace*, London, Routledge, 25–68.
Conchon, A. (2015), 'Workers' voice in corporate governance: a European perspective', Economic Report Series, Trades Union Congress (TUC), London.

Conchon, A. and Triangle, L. (2017), 'IndustriAll European trade union: Over 20 years of working with European Works Councils', *European Journal of Industrial Relations*, March.

Conger, J. and Kanungo, R. (1988), 'The empowerment process: integrating theory and practice', *Academy of Management Review*, 13(3), 471–482.

Conyon, M. (1997), 'Institutional arrangements for setting directors' compensation in UK companies', in K. Keasey, S. Thompson and M. Wright, *Corporate Governance: Economic, Management and Financial Issues*, Oxford, Oxford University Press.

Conyon, M., Peck, S. and Sadler, G. (2009), Compensation consultants and executive pay: evidence from the United States and the United Kingdom', *Academy of Management Perspectives*, 23(1), 43–55.

Cooke, F. L. (2005), *HRM, Work and Employment in China*, London, Routledge.

Cooke, F. L. (2009), 'A decade of transformation of HRM in China: a review of literature and suggestions for future studies', *Asia Pacific Journal of Human Resources*, 47(1), 6–40.

Cooke, F. L. and Saini, D. (2010), How does HR strategy support an innovation oriented business strategy? An investigation of institutional context and organizational practices in Indian firms', *Human Resource Management*, 49(3), 377–400.

Cooley, M. (1987), *Architect or Bee: the Human Price of Technology*, London, Hogarth Press.

Costa, P., Passos, A. and Bakker, A. (2014), 'Empirical validation of the team work engagement construct', *Journal of Personnel Psychology*, 13, 34–45.

Cotton, J., Vollrath, D., Froggatt, K., Lengnick-Hall, M. and Jennings, K. (1988), 'Employee participation: Diverse forms and different outcomes', *Academy of Management Review*, 13(1), 8–22.

Coyle, D. (2017), 'Precarious and productive work in the digital economy', *National Institute Economic Review*, 240(1), R5–R14.

Cranet (2006), 'Cranet survey: Comparative HRM, executive report 2005', Cranfield School of Management, Cranfield.

Cressey, P. (1998), European Works Councils in practice', *Human Resource Management Journal*, 8(1), 67–79.

Crompton, R. and Lynette, C. (2006), 'Work-life "balance" in Europe', *Acta Sociologica*, 49(4), 379–393.

Crowley, M., Payne, J. and Kennedy, E. (2014), 'Working better together? Empowerment, panopticon and conflict approaches to teamwork', *Economic and Industrial Democracy*, 35(3), 483–506.

Cullen, D. (1997), 'Maslow, monkeys and motivation theory', *Organization*, 4/3, 355–373.

Cullinane, N. and Donaghey, J. (2014), 'Employee silence', in A. Wilkinson, J. Donaghey, T. Dundon and R. Freeman (eds), *Handbook of Research on Employee Voice*, Cheltenham, Edward Elgar, 398–409.

Cullinane, N., Hickland, E., Dundon, T., Dobbins, T. and Donaghey, J. (2015), 'Triggering employee voice under the European Information and Consultation Directive: a non-union case study', *Economic and Industrial Democracy*, June, 1–27.

Cully, M., Woodland, S., O'Reilly, A. and Dix, G. (1999), *Britain at Work: as Depicted by the 1998 Workplace Employee Relations Survey*, London, Routledge.

Cunningham, I. and Hyman, J. (1999), 'The poverty of empowerment? A critical case study', *Personnel Review*, 28(3), 192–207.

Cunningham, I., Hyman, J. and Baldry, C. (1996), 'Empowerment: the power to do what?', *Industrial Relations Journal*, 27(2), 143–154.

Cushen, J. and Thompson, P. (2016), 'Financialization and value: why labour and the labour process still matter', *Work, Employment & Society*, 30(2), 352–365.

Czarzasty, J., Gavewski, K. and Mrozowicki, A. (2014), 'Institutions and strategies: trends and obstacles to recruiting workers in to trade unions in Poland', *British Journal of Industrial Relations*, 52(1), 112–135.

D'Art, D. and Turner, T. (2004), 'Profit-sharing, firm performance and union influence in selected European countries', *Personnel Review*, 33(3), 335–350.

D'Art, D. and Turner, T. (2008), 'Workers and the demand for trade unions in Europe: still a relevant social force?', *Economic and Industrial Democracy*, 29(20), 165–191.

Dahl, S.-Å., Nesheim, T., Olsen, K. (2009), 'Quality of work: concept and measurement', Working Papers on the Reconciliation of Work and Welfare in Europe, REC-WP 05/2009, RECWOWE Publication, Dissemination and Dialogue Centre, Edinburgh .

Danford, A. (1998), 'Teamworking and labour relations in the autocomponents industry', *Work, Employment & Society*, 12(3), 409–431.

Danford, A. (2005), 'New union strategies and forms of work organization in UK manufacturing', in B. Harley, J. Hyman and P. Thompson (eds), *Participation and Democracy at Work*, Basingstoke, Palgrave MacMillan, 166–186.

Danford, A., Richardson, M., StewartP., Tailby, S. and Upchurch, M. (2004), 'Partnership, mutuality and the high-performance workplace: a case study of union strategy and worker experience in the aircraft industry', in G. Healy, E. Heery, P. Taylor and W. Brown (eds), *The Future of Worker Representation*, Basingstoke, Palgrave Macmillan, 167–186.

Danford, A., Richardson, M., Stewart, P., Tailby, S. and Upchurch, M. (2008), 'High performance work systems and quality of working life', *New Technology, Work and Employment*, 23(3), 151–166.

Danford, A. and Zhao, W. (2012), 'Confucian HRM or unitarism with Chinese characteristics? A study of worker attitudes to work reform and management in three state-owned enterprises', *Work, Employment & Society*, 26(5), 839–856.

Dawson, C., Veliziotis, M. and Hopkins, B. (2017), 'Temporary employment, job satisfaction and subjective well-being', *Economic and Industrial Democracy*, 38(1), 63–98.

DBEIS (Department for Business, Energy & Industrial Strategy) (2017a), 'Trade union membership 2016: statistical bulletin', DBIS, London.

DBEIS (Department for Business, Energy & Industrial Strategy) (2017b), 'Trade Union Act measures come into force to protect people from undemocratic industrial action', DBEIS, London.

DBIS (Department for Business Innovation and Skills) (2016), 'Trade union membership 2015: statistical bulletin', DBIS, London.

DCMS (Department for Culture, Media and Sport) (2014), 'Attitudes towards equality', DCMS, London.

De Cremer, D. and Tao, T. (2015a), 'Huawei: a case study of when profit-sharing works', *Harvard Business Review*, 24 September.

De Cremer, D. and Tao, T. (2015b), 'Huawei's culture is the key to its success', *Harvard Business Review*, 11 June.

De Menezes, L., Wood, S. and Gelade, G. (2010), 'The integration of human resource and operation management practices and its link with performance: a longitudinal latent class study', *Journal of Operations Management*, 28(6), 455–471.

De Spiegelaere, S. and Jagodziński, R. (2015), 'European Works Councils and SE Works Councils in 2015', European Trade Union Institute, Brussels.

De Spiegelaere, S. and Waddington, J. (2017), 'Has the recast made a difference? An examination of the content of European Works Council agreements', *European Journal of Industrial Relations*, 23(3), 293–308.

Defourney, J., Estrin, S. and Jones, D. (1985), 'The effects of workers' participation on enterprise performance: empirical evidence from French co-operatives', *International Journal of Industrial Organisation*, 3(2), 197–217.

Delbridge, R. (1998), *Life on the Line in Contemporary Manufacturing*, Oxford, Oxford University Press.

Delbridge, R., Lowe, J. and Oliver, N. (2000), 'Shopfloor responsibilities under lean teamworking', *Human Relations*, 53(11), 1459–1479.

Dennis, N., Henriques, F. and Slaughter, C. (1969), *Coal is our Life: an Analysis of a Yorkshire Mining Community*, London, Tavistock Publications.

Denham, N., Ackers, P. and Travers, C. (1997), 'Doing yourself out of a job? How middle managers cope with empowerment', *Employee Relations*, 19(2), 147–159.

Devlin, S. (2016), 'Massive surge in London's gig economy', New Economics Foundation, London.

Dickens, L. and Hall, M. (2003), 'Labour law and industrial relations: a new settlement', in P. Edwards (ed.), *Industrial Relations: Theory and Practice*, 2nd ed., Oxford, Blackwell, 124–156.

Dickens, L., Hall, M. and Wood, S. (2005), 'Review of research into the impact of employment relations legislation', Department of Trade and Industry, Employment Relations Research Series No. 45, London.

Dobbins, T. and Dundon, T. (forthcoming), 'The chimera of sustainable labour-management partnership', *British Journal of Management*, Wiley Online.

Doellgast, V. and Benassi, C. (2014), 'Collective bargaining', in A. Wilkinson, J. Donaghey, T. Dundon and R. Freeman (eds), *Handbook of Research on Employee Voice*, Cheltenham, Edward Elgar, 227–246.

Doherty, M. (2011), 'It must have been love ... but it's over now: the crisis and collapse of social partnership in Ireland', *Transfer*, 17(3), 371–385.

Dolvik, J, (1997) 'EWCs and the implications for Europeanisation of collective bargaining', in J. Dolvik (ed.), *Redrawing Boundaries of Solidarity? ETUC, Social Dialogue and the Europeanisation of Trade Unions in the 1990s*, Oslo, Arena andFAFO, 381–391.

Donaghemy, J., Cullinanem, N., Dundion, T. and Wilkinson, A. (2011), 'Reconceptualising employee silence: problems and prognosis', *Work, Employment & Society*, 25(1), 51–67.

Donovan Commission (1968), *Royal Commission on Trade Unions and Employers' Associations, 1965–1968*, report, London, HMSO.

Dore, R. (1973), *British Factory–Japanese Factory: The Origins of National Diversity in Industrial Relations*, London, George Allen & Unwin.

Doucouliagos, C. (1995), 'Worker participation and productivity in labor-managed and participatory capitalist firms: a meta-analysis', *Industrial and Labor Relations Review*, 49(1), 58–77.

Dribbusch, K. and Burke, P. (2012), 'Trade unions in Germany; organisation, environment, challenges', FES Study, Friedrich-Ebert-Stiftung, Berlin.

Dromey, J. (2014a), 'MacLeod and Clarke's concept of employee engagement: an analysis based on the Workplace Employment Relations Study', ACAS, London.

Dromey, J. (2014b), 'Meeting the challenge: successful employee engagement in the NHS', IPA, London.

Drucker, P. (1961), *The Practice of Management*, London, Mercury Books.

DTI (Department of Trade and Industry) (2003), 'Review of the Employment Relations Act 1999', London.

Dundon, T. (2002), 'Employer opposition and union avoidance in the UK', *Industrial Relations Journal*, 33(3), 234–245.

Dundon, T., Wilkinson, A., Marchington, M. and Ackers, P. (2004), 'The meanings and purpose of employee voice', *International Journal of Human Resource Management*, 15(6), 1150–1171.

Dunn, S. and Metcalf, D. (1996), 'Trade union law since 1979', in I. Beardwell (ed.), *Contemporary Industrial Relations*, Oxford, Oxford University Press.

Dunt, I. (2017), 'Know your soft Brexit', politics.co.uk.

Earley, C. (1997), *Face, Harmony, and Social Structure: an Analysis of Organizational Behavior across Cultures*, New York, Oxford University Press.

Ebbinghaus, B. (2002), 'Trade unions' changing role: membership erosion, organizational reform, and social partnership in Europe', *Industrial Relations Journal*, 33(5), 465–483.

Economist (2013), 'Ranked and yanked', 16 November.

Edmondson, A. and Nembhard, I. (2009), 'Product development and learning in project teams: the challenges are the benefits', *Product Innovation Management*, 26(2), 123–138.

Edwards, P. and Wajcman, J. (2005), *The Politics of Working Life*, Oxford, Oxford University Press.

Ehrenreich, B. (2009), *Smile or Die*, London, Granta.

EIRR (1991), 'Survey of board-level employee representation', *European Industrial Relations Review*, 205, February, 20–25.

Eldridge, J., Cressey, P. and MacInnes, J. (1991), *Industrial Sociology and Economic Crisis*, Hemel Hempstead, Harvester.

England, J. and Weekes, B. (1981), 'Trade unions and the State: a review of the crisis', in W. E. J. McCarthy (ed.), *Trade Unions*, 2nd ed.; 1985, Harmondsworth, Penguin, 406–432.

Erdal, D. (2008), *Local Heroes: How Loch Fyne Oysters Embraced Employee Ownership and Business Success*, London, Viking.

Erdal, D. (2011), *Beyond the Corporation: Humanity Working*, London, Bodley Head.

Erdal, D. (2015), 'Employee-owned paper mill closes, with almost 475 jobs lost', *Coop News*, 2 June.

Esbenshade, J., Vidal, M., Fascilla, G. and Ono, M. (2016), 'Customer-driven management models for choiceless clientele? Business process reengineering in a California welfare agency', *Work, Employment & Society*, 30(1), 77–96.

ESOP Centre (2012), 'Analysis of the HMRC statistics on employee share schemes 2012', London.

Estlund, C. (2013), 'Will workers have a voice in China's "Socialist Market Economy"? The curious revival of the Workers Congress System', Public Law and Legal Theory Research Paper Series, Working Paper No. 13–80, New York University.

ETUC (International Trade Union Confederation) (2017), 'For a modern EWC directive in the digital era', Position paper, adopted at the ETUC Executive Committee, 15–16 March, Malta.

ETUC (International Trade Union Confederation (undated), 'The New European Works Council Directive ("Recast")'. www.etuc.org/IMG/pdf/CES-Depliant_The_New_Recast_Directive_def.pdf.

Etzioni, A. (1959), 'Authority structure and organizational effectiveness', *Administrative Science Quarterly*, 4(1), 43–67.

Eurofound (2011), *European Quality of Life Survey*, Dublin, Eurofound.

Eurofound (2012), *Fifth European Working Conditions Survey*, Luxembourg, Publications Office of the European Union.

Eurofound (2014), *Impact of the Crisis on Industrial Relations and Working Conditions in Europe*, Dublin, Eurofound.

Eurofound (2015a), *Third European Company Survey. Workplace Practices: Patterns, Performance and Well-being*, Luxembourg, Publications Office of the European Union.

Eurofound (2015b), *Collective Bargaining in Europe in the 21st Century*, Luxembourg, Publications Office of the European Union.

Eurofound (2015c), *European Works Council Developments Before, During and After the Crisis*, Luxemburg, Publications Office of the European Union.

Eurofound (2016a), *Fifth European Working Conditions Survey, Overview Report*, Luxembourg, Publications Office of the European Union.

Eurofound (2016b), *Sixth European Working Conditions Survey*, Dublin, Eurofound.

European Agency for Safety and Health at Work (2012), 'Worker representation and consultation on health and safety: an analysis of the findings of the European Survey on New and Emerging Risks', Luxembourg.

Fauver, L. and Fuerst, M. (2006), 'Does good corporate governance include employee representation? Evidence from German corporate boards', *Journal of Financial Economics*, 82(5), 673–710.

Fenby, J. (2015), *The History of Modern France: from the Revolution to the Present Day*, London, Simon & Schuster.

Fernandez, S. and Moldogaziev, T. (2013), 'Employee empowerment, employee attitudes, and performance: testing a causal model', *Public Administration Review*, 73(3), 490–506.

Fibírová, J. and Petera, P. (2013), 'Profit-sharing: a tool for improving productivity, profitability and competitiveness of firms?, *Journal of Competitiveness*, 5(4), 3–25.

Financial Times (2015), 'Top US bank executives abandon share sale taboo', 16 June.

Financial Times (2016), 'Cabinet split over plans to put workers on UK company boards', 11 October.

Financial Times (2017a), 'Investors in India await Modi's long-promised reforms', 16 January.

Financial Times (2017b), 'China labour unrest spreads to "new economy"', 2 February.

Financial Times (2017c), 'French business leaders urge Macron to prioritise labour reforms', 9 May.

Financial Times (2017d), 'Davis proposes post-Brexit dispute mechanism on EU relations', 21 August.

Finn, D. (2017), 'Luso-Anomalies', *New Left Review*, 106, July/August.

Fisher, S. and Hunter, T. (1998), 'The structure of Belbin's team roles', *Journal of Occupational and Organizational Psychology*, 71(3), 283–288.

FitzRoy, F. and Kraft, K. (1993), 'Economic effects of codetermination', *Scandinavian Journal of Economics*, 95(3), 365–375.

FitzRoy, F. and Kraft, K. (2005), 'Co-determination, efficiency and productivity', *British Journal of Industrial Relations*, 43(2), 233–247.

Flanders, A., Pomeranz, R. and Woodward, J. (1968), *Experiment in Industrial Democracy*, London, Faber & Faber.
Fleming, P. (2015), *The Mythology of Work: How Capitalism Persists Despite Itself*, London, Pluto Press.
Fleming, P. (2017), *The Death of Homo Economicus*, London, Pluto Press.
Flick, U. (2002), *An Introduction to Qualitative Research*, London, Sage.
Foley, J. (2014), 'Industrial democracy in the twenty-first century', in A. Wilkinson, J. Donaghey, T. Dundon and R. Freeman (eds), *Handbook of Research on Employee Voice*, Cheltenham, Edward Elgar, 66–81.
Fombrun, C., Tichy, N. and Devanna, M. (eds) (1984), *Strategic Human Resource Management*, New York, Wiley.
Fox, A. (1966), *Industrial Sociology and Industrial Relations*, Royal Commission on Trade Unions and Employers' Associations (Donovan Commission), Research Paper No. 3, London, HMSO.
Fox, A. (1974), *Beyond Contract: Work, Power and Trust Relations*, London, Faber & Faber.
Fox, A. (1980), 'The meaning of work', in G. Esland and G. Salaman (eds), *The Politics of Work and Occupations*, Milton Keynes, Open University Press, 139–191.
Franca, V. and Pahor, M. (2012), 'Influence of management attitudes on the implementation of employee participation', *Economic and Industrial Democracy*, 35(1), 115–142.
Frayne, D. (2015), *The Refusal of Work*, London, Zed Books.
Freeman, R. (2015), 'Workers ownership and profit-sharing in a new capitalist model?', Swedish Trade Union Confederation (LO), Stockholm.
Freeman, R. and Medoff, J. (1984), *What Do Unions Do?*, New York, Basic Books.
Freeman, R. and Rogers, J. (1999), *What Workers Want*, Ithaca, NY: Cornell University Press.
Freeman, R. and Rogers, J. (2006), *What Workers Want*, updated edition, Ithaca, NY, ILR Press.
Freeman, R., Boxall, P. and Haynes, P. (2007), 'The Anglo-American economies and employee voice', in R. Freeman, P. Boxall and P. Haynes (eds), *What Workers Say: Employee Voice in the Anglo-American Workplace*, Ithaca, NY, ILR Press1–25.
Frege, C. and Godard, J. (2010), 'Cross-national variation in representation rights and governance at work', in A. Wilkinson, P. Gollan, M. Marchington and D. Lewin (eds), *The Oxford Handbook of Participation in Organizations*, Oxford, Oxford University Press, 526–551.
Frey, C. and Osborne, M. (2017), 'The future of employment: how susceptible are jobs to computerization?', *Technological Forecasting and Social Change*, 114, January, 254–280.
Frischmann, B. and Selinger, E. (2016), 'Engineering humans with contracts', *Cardozo Legal Studies* Research Paper No. 493.
Fujimoto, Y., Azmat, F. and Härtel, E. (2012), 'Gender perceptions of work-life balance: management implications for full-time employees in Australia', *Australian Journal of Management*, 38(1), 147–170.
Fulton, L. (2015), 'Worker representation in Europe', Labour Research Department and ETUI. www.worker-participation.eu/National-Industrial-Relations/Across-Europe/Trade-Unions2.
Gale, J. (2012), 'Government reforms, performance management and the labour process: the case of officers in the UK probation service', *Work, Employment & Society*' 26(5), 822–838.

214 References

Gall, G. (2004a), 'Trade union recognition in Britain 1995–2002: turning a corner?', *Industrial Relations Journal*, 35(3), 249–270.

Gall, G. (2004b), 'British employer resistance to trade union recognition', *Human Resource Management Journal*, 14(2), 36–53.

Gall, G. (2016a), 'Theresa May, prime minister: the ball is in her court on workplace democracy', *The Conversation*, 13 July. https://theconversation.com/theresa-may-prime-minister-the-ball-is-in-her-court-on-workplace-democracy-62388.

Gall, G. (2016b) 'May's backtrack on workers on boards shows the old guard is still in business', *The Conversation*, 22 November. https://theconversation.com/mays-backtrack-on-workers-on-boards-shows-the-old-guard-is-still-in-business-69235.

Gall, G. and McKay, S. (1999), 'Developments in union recognition and derecognition in Britain, 1994–1998, *British Journal of Industrial Relations*, 37(4), 601–614.

Gallie, D. (2003), 'The quality of working life: is Scandinavia different?', *European Sociological Review*, 19, 61–79.

Gallie, D., Felstead, A., Green, F. and Inanc, H. (2017), 'The hidden face of job insecurity', *Work, Employment & Society*, 31(1), 36–53.

Gillan, S. and Starks, L. (2003), 'Corporate governance, corporate ownership, and the role of institutional investors: a global perspective', Working Paper No. 2003-2001, Weinberg Center for Corporate Governance, University of Delaware.

Gilson, C. and Weiler, A. (2008), 'Transnational company industrial relations: the role of European Works Councils and the implications for international human resource management', *Journal of Industrial Relations*, 50(5), 697–717.

Gilson, L., Maynard, M., Young, N., Vartianen, M. and Hakonen, M. (2015), 'Virtual teams research: 10 years, 10 themes and 10 opportunities', *Journal of Management*, 41(5), 1313–1337.

Gitell, J. (2009), *High Performance Health Care*, New York, McGraw Hill.

Glassner, V. and Keune, M. (2012), 'The crisis and social policy: the role of collective agreements', *International Labour Review*, 151(4), 351–375.

Glyn, A. (2006), *Capitalism Unleashed: Finance, Globalization and Welfare*, Oxford, Oxford University Press.

Gold, M. (2010), Employee participation in the EU: the long and winding road to legislation', *Economic and Industrial Democracy*, 31(4), 9–23.

Gollan, P. and Xu, Y. (2015), 'Re-engagement with the employee participation debate: beyond the case of contested and captured terrain', *Work, Employment & Society*, 29(2), NP1–NP13.

Gollan, P., Patmore, G. and Xu, Y. (2014), 'Regulation of employee voice', in A. Wilkinson, J. Donaghey, T. Dundon and R. Freeman (eds), *Handbook of Research on Employee Voice*, Cheltenham, Edward Elgar, 363–380.

Gomez, R., Bryson, A. and Willman, P. (2010), 'Voice in the Wilderness? The shift from union to non-union voice in Britain', in A. Wilkinson, P. Gollan, M. Marchington and D. Lewin (eds), *The Oxford Handbook of Participation in Organizations*, Oxford, Oxford University Press, 383–406.

Goodrich, C. (1920), *The Frontier of Control: A Study in British Workshop Politics*, New York, Harcourt, Brace & Howe.

Gorton, G. and Schmid, F. (2004), 'Capital, labor and the firm: a study of German codetermination', *Journal of the European Economic Association*, 2(5), 863–905.

Greasley, K., Bryman, A., Dainty, A., Price, A., Soetanto, R. and King, N. (2005), 'Employee perceptions of empowerment', *Employee Relations*, 27(4), 354–368.

Green, C. and Heywood, J. (2011), 'Profit sharing, separation and training', *British Journal of Industrial Relations*, 49(4), 623–642.

Green, F. (2006), *Demanding Work: The Paradox of Job Quality in the Affluent Economy*, Princeton, NJ, Princeton University Press.

Green, F. (2008), 'Work effort and worker well-being in the age of affluence', in R. J. Burke and C. L. Cooper (eds), *The Long Hours Culture: Causes, Consequences and Choices*, Bingley, Emerald, 115–135.

Greenberg, F. (1990), 'Employee theft as a reaction to underpayment inequality: the hidden costs of pay cuts', *Journal of Applied Psychology*, 75, 561–568.

Gregg, M. (2011), *Work's Intimacy*, Cambridge, Polity Press.

Grey, C. (2009), *A Very Short, Fairly Interesting and Reasonably Cheap Book about Studying Organizations*, London, Sage.

Grint, K. (2000), *The Arts of Leadership*, Oxford, Oxford University Press.

Gruman, J. and Saks, A. (2014), 'Being psychologically present when speaking up: employee voice engagement', in A. Wilkinson, J. Donaghey, T. Dundon and R. Freeman (eds), *Handbook of Research on Employee Voice*, Cheltenham, Edward Elgar, 455–476.

Guardian (2011), 'Hectored, humiliated, bullied: how women bear the brunt of flexible labour', 1 May.

Guardian (2015), 'Four in 10 new teachers quit within a year', 31 March.

Guardian (2016a), 'Long hours, endless admin and angry parents: why schools just can't get the teachers', 1 February.

Guardian (2016b), 'How Boots went rogue', 13 April.

Guardian (2016c), 'Is profit-sharing an economic plan that suits all Americans? Clinton says, yes', 2 October.

Guardian (2016d), 'Outcry as 1,500 Dhaka clothes workers sacked', 28 December.

Guardian (2017a), '"Made in Italy": the Romanian factory that produces Louis Vuitton's premium shoes', 17 June.

Guardian (2017b), 'Rolls-Royce calls its first staff AGM', 12 March.

Guest, D. (1992), 'Right enough to be dangerously wrong: an analysis of the *In Search of Excellence* phenomenon', in G. Salaman (ed.), *Human Resource Strategies*, London, Sage, 5–19.

Guest, D. (2014), 'Employee engagement: a sceptical analysis', *Journal of Organizational Effectiveness: People and Performance*, 1(2), 141–156.

Guest, D. and Peccei, R. (2001), 'Partnership at Work: mutuality and the balance of advantage', *British Journal of Industrial Relations*, 39(2), 207–236.

Guest, D. and Bryson, A. (2009), 'From industrial relations to human resource management: the changing role of the personnel function', in W. Brown, A. Bryson, J. Forth and K. Whitfield (eds), *The Evolution of the Modern Workplace*, Cambridge, Cambridge University Press, 120–150.

Guest, D., Peccei, R. and Thomas, A. (1993), 'The impact of employee involvement on organizational commitment and "them and us" attitudes', *British Journal of Industrial Relations*, 24(3), 191–200.

Gumbrell-McCormick, R. and Hyman, R. (2010), 'Works councils: the European model of industrial democracy?', in A. Wilkinson, P. Gollan, M. Marchington and D. Lewin (eds), *Oxford Handbook of Participation in Organizations*, Oxford, Oxford University Press, 286–314.

Gumbrell-McCormick, R. and Hyman, R. (2017), 'What about the workers? The implications of Brexit for British and European labour', *Competition & Change*, 21(3), 169–184.

Hales, C. (2000), 'Management and empowerment programmes', *Work, Employment & Society*, 14(3), 501–519.

Hall, M., Hoffmann, A., Marginson, P. and Müller, T. (2003), 'National influences on European Works Councils in UK- and US-based companies', *Human Resource Management Journal*, 13(4), 75–92.

Hall, M. and Terry, M. (2004), 'The emerging system of statutory worker representation', in G. Healy, E. Heery, P. Taylor and W. Brown, *The Future of Worker Representation*, Basingstoke, Palgrave Macmillan, 207–228.

Hall, M. and Marginson, P. (2005), 'Trojan horses or paper tigers? Assessing the significance of European Works Councils', in B. Harley, J. Hyman and P. Thompson (eds), *Participation and Democracy at Work*, Basingstoke, Palgrave Macmillan, 204–221.

Hall, M., Hutchinson, S., Purcell, J., Terry, M. and Parker, J. (2013), 'Promoting effective consultation? Assessing the impact of the ICE Regulations', *British Journal of Industrial Relations*, 51(2), 355–381.

Hall, M., Purcell, J. and Adam, D. (2015), 'Reforming the ICE regulations: what chance now?', Warwick Papers in Industrial Relations, 102, Industrial Relations Research Unit, University of Warwick, September.

Hall, P. and Soskice, D. (2001), 'An introduction to varieties of capitalism', in P. Hall and D. Soskice (eds), *Varieties of Capitalism: the Institutional Foundations of Comparative Advantage*, New York, Oxford University Press, 1–69.

Hamel, G. and Prahalad, C. (1994), *Competing for the Future*, Boston, MA: Harvard Business School Press.

Hanley, L. (2016), *Respectable: Crossing the Class Divide*, London, Penguin.

Hanson, C. and Watson, R. (1990), 'Profit-sharing and company performance: some empirical evidence for the UK', in G. Jenkins and M. Poole (eds), *New Forms of Ownership, Management and Employment*, London, Routledge, 165–182.

Hardie, M. and Banks, A. (2014), 'The changing shape of UK manufacturing', *Office for National Statistics (ONS)*, London.

Harley, B. (2001), 'Team membership and the experience of work in Britain: an analysis of the WERS98 data', *Work, Employment & Society*, 15(4), 721–742.

Harley, B. (2005), 'Hope or hype? High-performance work systems', in B. Harley, J. Hyman and P. Thompson, *Participation and Democracy at Work*, Basingstoke, Palgrave Macmillan, 38–54.

Harley, B. (2014), 'High performance work systems and employee voice', in A. Wilkinson, J. Donaghey, T. Dundon and R. Freeman (eds), *Handbook of Research on Employee Voice*, Cheltenham, Edward Elgar, 82–96.

Hart, S. and Warren, A. (2015), 'Understanding nurses' work: exploring the links between changing work, labour relations, workload, stress, retention and recruitment', *Economic and Industrial Democracy*, 36(2), 305–329.

Hart-Landsberg, M. (2017), 'Monopolization and labour exploitation', *Socialist Project e-bulletin*, 3 April.

Healy, G., Heery, E., Taylor, P. and Brown, W. (eds) (2004), *The Future of Worker Representation*, Basingstoke, Palgrave Macmillan.

Hebson, G., Rubery, J. and Grimshaw, D. (2015), 'Rethinking job satisfaction in care work: looking beyond the care debates', *Work, Employment & Society'* 29(2), 314–331.

Heery, E. (2009), 'The representation gap and the future of worker representation', *Industrial Relations Journal*, 40(4), 324–336.

Heery, E. (2015), 'Unions and the organizing turn: reflections after 20 years of Organising Works', *The Economic and Labour Relations Review*, 26(4), 545–560.

Heery, E., Healy, G. and Taylor, P. (2004), 'Representation at work: themes and issues', in G. Healy, E. Heery, P. Taylor and W. Brown (eds), *The Future of Worker Representation*, Basingstoke, Palgrave Macmillan, 1–36.

Heller, F., Pusić, E., Strauss, G. and Wilpert, B. (1998), *Organizational Participation: Myth and Reality*, Oxford, Oxford University Press.

Hendrym, C. and Pettigrewm, A. (1992), 'Patterns of strategic change in the development of human resource management', *British Journal of Management*, 3(3), 137–156.

Hermman, C. and Flecker, J. (eds) (2012), *Privatisation of Public Service Impacts for Employment, Working Conditions and Service Quality in Europe*, New York, Routledge.

Herzberg, F. (1966), *Work and the Nature of Man*, New York, Staples Press.

Herzberg, F. (1968), 'One more time: how do you motivate employees?', *Harvard Business Review*, 46(1), 53–62.

Herzberg, F., Mausner, B., Peterson, R. and Capwell, D. (1957), *Job Attitudes: Review of Research and Opinion*, Pittsburgh, PA, Psychological Service of Pittsburgh.

Herzberg, F., Mausner, B. and Snyderman, B. (1959), *The Motivation to Work*, New York, John Wiley & Sons.

Heyes, J. (2013), 'Flexicurity in crisis: European labour market policies in a time of austerity', *European Journal of Industrial Relations*, 19(1), 71–86.

High Pay Centre (2013), 'Workers on boards: interviews with German employee directors', London.

High Pay Centre (2014), 'The high cost of high pay: an analysis of pay inequality within firms', London.

Hill, E. (2009), 'The Indian industrial relations system: struggling to address the dynamics of a globalizing economy', *Journal of Industrial Relations*, 51(3), 395–410.

Hirsch, D. and Valadez Martinez, L.(2017), *The Living Wage*, Newcastle upon Tyne, Agenda Publishing.

Hirschman, A. (1970), *Exit, Voice and Loyalty*, Cambridge, MA: Harvard University Press.

HMRC (HM Revenue and Customs) (2017), 'Employee share scheme statistics for 2015–2016'. www.gov.uk/government/uploads/system/uploads/attachment_data/file/645176/ESS_National_Stats_Commentary_Document.pdf.

Hochschild, A. (1983), *The Managed Heart: Commercialisation of Human Feelings*, Berkeley, CA, University of California Press.

Hodder, A., Williams, M., Kelly, J. and McCarthy, N. (2017), 'Does strike action stimulate trade union membership growth?', *British Journal of Industrial Relations*, 55(1), 165–180.

Hodgson, D. and Briand, L. (2013), 'Controlling the uncontrollable: "agile" teams and illusions of autonomy in creative work', *Work, Employment & Society*, 27(2), 308–325.

Hodson, R. (2001), *Dignity at Work*, Cambridge, Cambridge University Press.

Hoffmann, A. (2015), Preface, in R. Jagodzinski (ed.), *Variations on a Theme: The Implementation of the EWC Recast Directive*, Brussels, ETUI.

Holbeche, L. (2009), *Aligning Human Resources and Business Strategy*, 2nd ed., Oxford, Butterworth-Heinemann.

Holland, P., Pyman, A., Cooper, B. and Teicher, J. (2009), 'The development of alternative voice mechanisms in Australia: the case of joint consultation', *Economic and Industrial Democracy*, 30(1), 67–92.

House of Commons (2012), 'The FSA's report into the failure of the Royal Bank of Scotland', Treasury Committee, House of Commons, London.

House of Commons (2016), 'Employment practices at Sports Direct', Business, Innovation and Skills Committee, Third Report of Session 2016–2017, House of Commons, London.

HR Magazine (2013), 'What can HR do to change the banking culture and rebuild trust?', 26 February. www.hrmagazine.co.uk/article-details/what-can-hr-do-to-change-the-banking-culture-and-rebuild-trust.

HSE (Health and Safety Executive) (2009), 'Good jobs', Research Report RR713, London.

Huczynski, A. and Buchanan, D. (2001), *Organizational Behaviour*, London, Prentice Hall.

Huczynski, A. and Buchanan, D. (2013), *Organizational Behaviour*, 8th ed., Harlow, Pearson.

Hudson, M. (2002), 'Flexibility and the reorganisation of work', in B. Burchell, D. Lapido and F. Wilkinson (eds), *Job Insecurity and Work Intensification*, London, Routledge, 39–60.

Hunt, N. (1951), 'Profit-sharing and co-partnership', *Methods of Wage Payment in British Industry*, London, Pitman & Sons, 130–145.

Huse, M. and Eide, D. (1996), 'Stakeholder management and the avoidance of corporate control', *Business & Society*, 35(2), 211–243.

Huselid, M. (1995), 'The impact of human resource management practices on turnover, productivity, and corporate financial performance', *Academy of Management Journal*, 38(3): 635–672.

Huws, U. and Podro, S. (2012), 'Outsourcing and the fragmentation of employment relations: the challenges ahead', ACAS (Advisory, Conciliation and Arbitration Service) Future of Workplace Relations Discussion Paper Series, London.

Hyman, J. and Mason, B. (1995), *Managing Employee Involvement and Participation*, London, Sage.

Hyman, J., Lockyer, C., Marks, A. and Scholarios, D. (2004), 'Needing a new program: why is union membership so low among software workers?', in G. Healy, E. Heery, P. Taylor and W. Brown (eds), *The Future of Worker Representation*, Basingstoke, Palgrave Macmillan, 37–61.

Hyman, R. (2001), *Understanding European Trade Unionism: Between Market, Class and Society*, London, Sage.

Hyman, R. (2003), 'The historical evolution of British industrial relations', in P. Edwards (ed.), *Industrial Relations: Theory and Practice*, 2nd ed., Oxford, Blackwell, 37–57.

Hyman, R. (2005), 'Trade unions and the politics of the European Social Model', *Economic and Industrial Democracy*, 26(1), 9–40.

Hyman, R. (2015), 'The very idea of democracy at work', *Transfer: European Review of Labour and Research*, 22(1), 11–24.

Hyman, R. (2016), 'Editorial', *European Journal of Industrial Relations*, 22(1), 3–4.

IBEF (India Brand Equity Foundation) (2017), www.ibef.org/economy/indian-investments-abroad.

Ibsen, C. and Tapia, M. (2017), 'Trade union revitalisation: Where are we now? Where to next?', *Journal of Industrial Relations*, 59(2), 170–191.

Iddagoda, A., Opatha, H. and Gunawardana, K. (2016), 'Towards a conceptualization and an operationalization of employee engagement', *International Business Review*, 9(2), 85–98.
Ikeler, P. (2016), 'Deskilling emotional labour: evidence from department store retail', *Work, Employment & Society*, 30(6), 966–983.
ILO (International Labour Organization) (2015), 'Trends in collective bargaining coverage: stability, erosion or decline', Geneva.
IMAA (IMAA Institute for Mergers, Acquisitions and Alliances) (2016), 'M&A statistics 2016'. https://imaa-institute.org/mergers-and-acquisitions-statistics.
International Commission for Labor Rights (2013), 'Merchants of menace: repressing workers in India's new industrial belt', ICLR, New York.
IPA (Involvement and Participation Association) (1997), *Towards Industrial Partnership: New Ways of Working British Companies*, London, IPA.
IPA (Involvement and Participation Association) (2011), *Rethinking Voice for Sustainable Business Success*, London, IPA.
Jagodziński, R. (2015), 'Conclusions', in R. Jagodziński (ed.), *Variations on a Theme: the Implementation of the EWC Recast Directive*, Brussels, ETUI, 179–191.
Jagodziński, R. (2016), 'European Works Councils at a turning point', New European Trade Unions Forum, London School of Economics, London. http://blogs.lse.ac.uk/netuf/2016/05/24/european-works-councils-at-aturning-point/.
Jefferis, K. and Mason, N. (1990), 'Financing worker co-operatives in EC countries', *Annals of Public and Co-operative Economy*, 61(2/3), 213–244.
Jirjahn, U. (2010), 'Ökonomische Wirkungen der Mitbestimmung in Deutschland: Ein Update', Working Paper No. 186, Hans-Böckler-Stiftung, Düsseldorf.
Johnson, P. (1994), 'Brains, hearts and courage: keys to empowerment and self-directed leadership', *Journal of Managerial Psychology*, 9(2), 17–21.
Johnstone, S. (2014), 'Workplace partnership', in A. Wilkinson, J. Donaghey, T. Dundon and R. Freeman (eds), *Handbook of Research on Employee Voice*, Cheltenham, Edward Elgar, 310–326.
Jones, D. and Mitchell, A. (2006), *Lean Thinking for the NHS*, London, NHS Confederation.
Jürgens, U. (1989), 'The transfer of Japanese management concepts in the international automobile industry', in S. Wood (ed.), *The Transformation of Work?*, London, Unwin Hyman, 204–218.
Kaaresmaker, E. R. and Poutsma, E. (2006), 'The fit of employee ownership with other human resource management practices: theoretical and empirical suggestions regarding the existence of an ownership high-performance work system, or "Theory O"', *Economic and Industrial Democracy*, 27(2), 669–685.
Kaaresmaker, E. R., Pendleton, A. and Poutsma, E. (2010), 'Employee share ownership', in A. Wilkinson, P. Gollan, M. Marchington and D. Lewin, *Oxford Handbook of Participation in Organizations*, Oxford, Oxford University Press, 315–337.
Kahn-Freund, O. (1983), in P. Davies and M. Freedland, *Kahn-Freund's Labour and the Law*, Hamlyn Lecture Series, 3rd ed., London, Stevens.
Kaine, S. (2014), 'Union voice', in A. Wilkinson, J. Donaghey, T. Dundon and R. Freeman (eds), *Handbook of Research on Employee Voice*, Cheltenham, Edward Elgar, 170–187.
Kakabadse, A. and Kakabadse, N. (2008), *Leading the Board*, Basingstoke, Palgrave Macmillan.

Kalleberg, A. (2011), *Good Jobs, Bad Jobs: the Rise of Polarized and Precarious Employment Systems in the United States, 1970s to 2000s*, New York, Russell Sage Foundation.

Kalleberg, A. (2014), 'Measuring precarious work', Working Paper of the EINet (Employment Instability, Family Well-being and Social Policy Network) Measurement Group, University of Chicago.

Kalmi, P., Pendleton, A. and Poutsma, E. (2004), 'The relationship between financial participation and other forms of participation: new survey evidence', Discussion Paper 3, Helsinki Center of Economic Research, University of Helsinki.

Kalmi, P., Pendleton, A. and Poutsma, E. (2005), 'Financial participation and performance in Europe', *Human Resource Management Journal*, 15(4), 54–67.

Karasek, R. (1990), 'Lower health risk with increased job control among white collar workers', *Journal of Organizational Behavior*, 11(3), 171–185.

Karasek, R., Baker, D., Marxer, F., Akibon, A. and Theorell, T. (1981), 'Job decision latitude, job demands and cardiovascular disease: a prospective study of Swedish men', *American Journal of Public Health*, 71(7), 694–705.

Karasek, R. and Theorell, T. (1990), *Healthy Work: Stress, Productivity and the Reconstruction of Working Life*, New York, Basic Books.

Katz, L. and Krueger, A. (2016), 'The rise and nature of alternative work arrangements in the United States', *The National Bureau of Economic Research* 1995–2015.

Katzenbach, J. and Smith, D. (1993), *The Wisdom of Teams: Creating the High Performance Organization*, Boston, MA, Harvard Business School Press.

Kaufman, B. (2010), 'SHRM theory in the post-Huselid era: why it is fundamentally mis-specified', *Industrial Relations*, 49(2), 286–313.

Kaufman, B. (2015), 'The RBV theory foundation of strategic HRM: critical flaws, problems for research and practice, and an alternative economics paradigm', *Human Resource Management Journal*, 25(4), 516–540.

Kaufman, B. and Taras, D. (eds) (2015), *Nonunion Employee Representation: History, Contemporary Practice and Policy*, London, Routledge.

Kay, J. (1993), *Foundations of Corporate Success: How Business Strategies Add Value*, Oxford, Oxford University Press.

Kazlauskaite, R., Buciuniene, I. and Tiurauska, L. (2012), 'Organizational and psychological empowerment in the HRM-performance linkage', *Employee Relations*, 34(2), 138–158.

Keep, E. and Rainbird, H. (2000), 'Towards the learning organization?', in S. Bach and K. Sisson (eds), *Personnel Management*, 3rd ed., Oxford, Blackwell, 173–194.

Kelly, J. (1997), 'The future of trade-unionism: injustice, identity and attribution', *Employee* Relations, 19(5), 400–414.

Kelly, J. (1998), *Rethinking Industrial Relations: Mobilisation, Collectivism and Long Waves*, London, Routledge.

Kelly, J. (2004), 'Social partnership agreements in Britain: Labor cooperation and compliance', *Industrial Relations*, 43(1), 267–292.

Kelly, J. and Gennard, J. (2007), 'Business strategic decision-making: the role and influence of directors', *Human Resource Management Journal*, 17(2), 99–117.

Kersley, B., Alpin, C., Forth, J., Bryson, A., Bewley, H., Dix, G. and Oxenbridge, S. (2006), *Inside the Workplace: Findings from the 2004 Workplace Employment Relations Survey*, London, Routledge.

Kessler, I. (2010), 'Financial participation', in A. Wilkinson, P. Gollan, M. Marchington and D. Lewin (eds), *The Oxford Handbook of Participation in Organizations*, Oxford, Oxford University Press, 338–360.

Kessler, I. and Purcell, J. (2003), 'Individualism and collectivism in industrial relations' in P. Edwards (ed.), *Industrial Relations*, 2nd ed., Oxford, Blackwell, 313–337.

Kirton, G. (2015), 'Progress towards gender democracy in UK unions 1987–2012', *British Journal of Industrial Relations*, 53(30), 484–507.

Kirton, G. and Greene, A.M. (2016), *The Dynamics of Managing Diversity: A Critical Approach*, 4th ed., London, Routledge.

Klikauer, T. (2013), *Managerialism: A Critique of an Ideology*, Basingstoke, Palgrave Macmillan.

Kluge, N. (2005), 'Corporate governance with co-determination – a key element of the European Social Model', *Transfer*, 11(2), 163–178.

Knudsen, H. (1995), *Employee Participation in Europe*, London, Sage.

Knyght, P. (2010), 'Auditing employee ownership in a neo-liberal world', *Management Decision*, 48(8), 1304–1323.

Kochan, T. (2007), 'Social legitimacy of the human resources management profession: US perspectives', in P. Boxall, J. Purcell and P. Wright (eds), *The Oxford Handbook of Human Resource Management*, Oxford, Oxford University Press, 599–620.

Kraft, K. and Ugarković, M. (2006), 'Gesetzliche Mitbestimmung und Kapitalrendite', *Jahrbücher für Nationalökonomie und Statistik*, 226(5), 588–604.

Kramer, B. (2010), 'Employee ownership and participation effects on outcomes in firms majority employee-owned through employee stock ownership plans in the US', *Economic and Industrial Democracy*, 31(4), 449–476.

Kranendonk, M. and du Beer, P. (2016), 'What explains the union membership gap between migrants and natives?', *British Journal of Industrial Relations*, 54(4), 846–869.

Kruse, D. (1993), 'Profit-sharing: does it make a difference? The productivity and stability effects of employee profit-sharing plans', W. E. Upjohn Institute for Employment Research, Kalamazoo, MI.

Kruse, D. (1996), 'Why do firms adopt profit-sharing and employee ownership plans?', *British Journal of Industrial Relations*, 34(4): 515–538.

Kruse, D., Freeman, R. and Blasi, J. (eds) (2010), *Shared Capitalism at Work*, Chicago, IL, Chicago University Press.

Krzywdzinski, M. (2017), 'Accounting for cross-country differences in employee involvement practices: comparative case studies in Germany, Brazil and China', *British Journal of Industrial Relations*, 55(2), 321–346.

Kumar, S. (2010), 'Specialty hospitals emulating focused factories: a case study', *International Journal of Health Care Quality Assurance*, 23(1), 94–109.

Kuruvilla, S. and Ranganathan, A. (2010), 'Globalisation and outsourcing: confronting new HR challenges in India's business process outsourcing industry', *Industrial Relations Journal*, 41(2), 136–153.

L'Obs (2017a), 'Loi travail: jusqu'où, le big bang?', No. 2745, 15–21 June.

L'Obs (2017b), 'Faut-il vraiment réformer le Code du Travail ?', No. 2748, 6–12 July.

Laaser, K. (2016), '"If you are having a go at me, I am going to have a go at you": the changing nature of social relationships of bank work under performance management', *Work, Employment & Society*, 30(6), 1000–1016.

Lampel, J., Bhall, A. and Jha, P. (2010), 'Model growth: do employee-owned businesses deliver sustainable performance?', Cass Business School, City University London.

Lange, J. (2010), *Human Resource Management in Indonesia*, Hamburg, Diplomica Verlag.

Lansley, S. (2015), 'Tackling the power of capital: the role of social wealth funds', Thinkpiece 81, Compass, London.

Lapido, D. and Wilkinson, F. (2002), 'More pressure, less protection', in B. Burchell, D. Lapido and F. Wilkinson (eds), *Job Insecurity and Work Intensification*, London, Routledge.

Laulom, S. (2010), 'The flawed revision of the European Works Council Directive', *Industrial Law Journal*, 39(2), 202–208.

Laulom, S. and Dorssemont, F. (2015), 'Fundamental principles of EWC Directive 2009/38/EC', in R. Jagodziński (ed.), *Variations on a Theme: the Implementation of the EWC Recast Directive*, Brussels, ETUI, 33–68.

Lawler, E. (1986), *High Involvement Management*, San Francisco, Jossey-Bass.

Legge, K. (2001), 'Silver bullet or spent round? Assessing the meaning of the "high commitment management"/performance relationship', in J. Storey (ed.), *Human Resources Management: A Critical Text*, London, Thomson, 23–36.

Legge, K. (2005), *Human Resource Management: Rhetorics and Realities*, Basingstoke, Palgrave Macmillan.

Lehndorff, S. (2009), *Before the Crisis, and Beyond: Collective Bargaining on Employment in Germany*, Geneva, International Labour Office.

Lehndorff, S. (2011), 'Before the crisis, in the crisis, and beyond: the upheaval of collective bargaining in Germany', *Transfer*, 17(3), 341–354.

Lehndorff, S. (2012), 'German capitalism and the European crisis: part of the solution or part of the problem?', in S. Lehndorff (ed.), *A Triumph of Failed Ideas: European Models of Capitalism in Crisis*, Brussels, ETUI.

Levine, D. and Tyson, L. (1990), 'Participation, productivity and the firm's environment', in A. Blinder (ed.), *Paying for Productivity*, Washington, DC, Brookings Institute.

Levy, K. (2015), 'The contexts of control: information, power and truck driving work', *The Information Society*, 31, 160–174.

Lewin, D. (2010), 'Employee voice and mutual gains', in A. Wilkinson, P. Gollan, M. Marchington and D. Lewin (eds), *The Oxford Handbook of Participation in Organizations*, Oxford, Oxford University Press, 427–452.

Lewis, J. (2002), 'Did HR fuel the demise of Enron?', *Personnel Today*, 19 March.

Likert, R. (1961), *New Patterns of Management*, New York, McGraw Hill.

Lindholm, N. (1999), 'Performance management in MNC subsidiaries in China: a study of host-country managers and professionals', *Asia Pacific Journal of Human Resource Management*, 37(3), 18–35.

Littrell, R. (2002), 'Desirable leadership behaviours of multi-cultural managers in China', *The Journal of Management Development*, 21(1), 5–74.

Littrell, R. (2007), 'Influences on employee preferences for empowerment practices by the "ideal manager" in China', *International Journal of Intercultural Relations*, 1, 87–110.

Liu, W., Guthrie, P., Flood, P. and MacCurtain, S. (2009), 'Unions and the adoption of high performance work systems: does employment security play a role?', *Industrial and Labor Relations Review*, 63(1), 109–127.

Liu, Y., Combs, J., Ketchen, D. and Ireland, R. (2007), 'The value of human resource management for organizational performance', *Business Horizons*, 50(6), 503–511.

Livesey, F. (2017), *From Global to Local: The Making of Things and the End of Globalisation*, London, Profile Books.

Long, R. (2000), 'Employee profit sharing: consequences and moderations', *Industrial Relations*, 55(3), 477–504.

Long, R. and Fang, T. (2013), 'Profit sharing and workplace productivity: does teamwork play a role?', Discussion Paper No. 7869, Forschungsinstitut zur Zukunft der Arbeit/Institute for the Study of Labor, Bonn.

Lorinkova, N. and Perry, S. (2014), 'When is empowerment effective? The role of leader-leader exchange in empowering leadership, cynicism and time theft', *Journal of Management*, 20(10), 1–24.

Louie, K. (1980), *Critiques of Confucius in Contemporary China*, Hong Kong, Chinese University Press.

Lucas, K., Kang, D. and Li, Z. (2013), 'Workplace dignity in a total institution: examining the experiences of Foxconn's migrant workforce', *Journal of Business Ethics*, 114(1), 91–106.

Lukes, S. (1974), *Power: A Radical View*, London, Macmillan.

Macduffie, J. (1995), 'Human resource bundles and manufacturing performance: organizational logic and flexible production in the world auto industry', *Industry and Labor Relations Review*, 48(2), 197–221.

McGregor, D. (1960), *The Human Side of Enterprise*, New York, McGraw Hill.

MacInnes, J. (1987), *Thatcherism at Work*, Milton Keynes, Open University Press.

MacIntyre, D. (2014), 'How the miners' strike of 1984–1985 changed Britain for ever', *New Statesman*, 11 June.

MacLeod, D. and Clarke, N. (2009), 'Engaging for success: enhancing performance through employee engagement: a report to government', Department for Business, Innovation and Skills, London.

McManus, S. and Perry, J. (2012), 'Hard work? Employment, work-life balance and wellbeing in a changing economy', in A. Park, E. Clery, J. Curtice, M. Phillips and D. Utting (eds), '*British Social Attitudes: The 29th Report*,' London, NatCen Social Research.

McQuaid, R., Hollywood, E., Bond, S., Canduekla, J., Richard, A. and Blackledge, G. (2012), 'Fit for work? Health and wellbeing of employee owned business', report for Employee Ownership Association, John Lewis Partnership and Employment Research Institute.

MacShane, D. (2017), 'European Works Councils: another Brexit victim', *Social Europe*, 5 January. www.socialeurope.eu/european-works-councils-another-brexit-victim.

Mählmeyer, V., Rampeltshammer, L. and Hertwig, M. (2017), 'European Works Councils during the financial and economic crisis: activism, stagnation or disintegration?', *European Journal of Industrial Relations*, 23(3), 225–242.

Marchington, M. (2000), 'Teamworking and employee involvement: terminology, evaluation and context', in S. Procter and K. Mueller (eds), *Teamworking*, Basingstoke, Macmillan, 60–80.

Marchington, M. (2005), 'Employee involvement: patterns and explanations', in B. Harley, J. Hyman and P. Thompson (eds), *Participation and Democracy at Work*, Basingstoke, Palgrave Macmillan, 20–37.

Marchington, M. and Wilkinson, A. (2005), 'Direct participation', in S. Bach (ed.), *Personnel Management: A Comprehensive Guide to Theory and Practice*, 4th ed., Oxford, Blackwell.

Marginson, P., Lavelle, J., Quintanilla, J., Adam, D. and Sanchez-Mangas, R. (2013), 'Variation in approaches to European Works Councils in multinational companies', *ILR Review*, 66(3), 618–644.

Markey, R., Balnave, N. and Patmore, G. (2010), 'Worker directors and worker ownership/cooperatives', in A. Wilkinson, P. Gollan, M. Marchington and D. Lewin (eds), *Oxford Handbook of Participation in Organizations*, Oxford, Oxford University Press, 237–257.

Marks, A. and Chillas, S. (2014), 'Labour process perspectives on employee voice', in A. Wilkinson, J. Donaghey, T. Dundon and R. Freeman (eds), *Handbook of Research on Employee Voice*, Cheltenham, Edward Elgar, 97–113.

Marsden, D. (2015), 'The future of the German industrial relations model', CEP Discussion Paper No. 1344, Centre for Economic Performance, London School of Economics, London.

Martin, R. (1968), 'Union democracy: an explanatory framework', *Sociology*, 2, 205–220.

Martinez Lucio, M. (2010), 'Labour process and Marxist perspectives on employee participation', in A. Wilkinson, P. Gollan, M. Marchington and D. Lewin (eds), *The Oxford Handbook of Participation in Organizations*, Oxford, Oxford University Press, 105–130.

Mason, P. (2015), *Postcapitalism*, London, Allen Lane.

Mather, K. and Seifert, R. (2011), 'Teacher, lecturer or labourer? Performance management issues in education', *Management in Education*, 25(1), 26–31.

Mather, K. and Seifert, R. (2014), 'The close supervision of further education lecturers: "You have been weighed, measured and found wanting"', *Work, Employment & Society*, 28(1), 95–111.

Mather, K., Worrall, L. and Seifert, R. (2009), 'The changing locus of workplace control in the English further education sector', *Employee Relations*, 31(2), 139–157.

May Yeuk-Mui, T., Korczynski, M. and Frenkel, S. (2002), 'Organizational and occupational commitment: knowledge workers in large corporations', *Journal of Management Studies*, 39(6), 775–801.

Meardi, G. (2007), 'More voice after more exit? Unstable industrial relations in Central Eastern Europe', *Industrial Relations Journal*, 38(6), 503–523.

Meidner, R. (1978), *Employee Investment Funds: An Approach to Collective Capital Formation*, London, Allen & Unwin.

Meyer, J. and Allen, N. (1991), 'A three-component conceptualization of organizational commitment', *Human Resource Management Review*, 1, 61–89.

Meyer, J. and Allen, N. (1997), *Commitment in the Workplace: Theory, Research and Application*, Thousand Oaks, CA, Sage.

Meyer, J., Stanley, D., Herscovitch, L. and Topolnytsky, L. (2002), 'Affective, continuance, and normative commitment to the organization: a meta-analysis of antecedents, correlates and consequences', *Journal of Vocational Behavior*, 61(1), 20–52.

Michel, H. (2007), 'Co-determination in Germany: the recent debate', Johann Wolfgang Goethe-Universität Frankfurt/Goethe University Frankfurt.

Michie, J. and Sheehan, M. (2005), 'Business strategy, human resources, labour market flexibility and competitor advantage', *International Journal of Human Resource Management*, 16(3), 445–464.

Middlemass, K. (1979), *Politics in Industrial Society: The Experience of the British System since 1911*, London, André Deutsch.

Miller, E. and Rice, A. (1967), *Systems of Organisation: The Control of Task and Sentient Boundaries*, London, Tavistock.

Mills, M., Blossfeld, H.P., Buchholz, S., Hofäcker, D., Bernardi, F. and Hofmeister, H. (2008), 'An international comparison of the impact of globalization on industrial relations and employment careers', *International Sociology*, 23(4), 561–595.

Milner, S. and Mathers, A. (2013), 'Membership, influence and voice: a discussion of trade union renewal in the French context', *Industrial Relations Journal*, 44(2), 122–138.

Mintzberg, H. (1990), 'The design school: reconsidering the basic premises of strategic management', *Strategic Management Journal*, 11, 171–195.

Mitbestimmung in Deutschland: Daten und Fakten (2014), Düsseldorf, Hans-Bökler Foundation.

Monaco, L. (2017), 'Where lean may shake: challenges to casualization in the Indian auto industry', *Global Labour Journal*, 8(2), 120–138.

Monbiot, G. (2017), *How Did We Get Into This Mess?*, London, Verso.

Moody, K. (2014), 'Competition and conflict: union growth in the US hospital industry', *Economic and Industrial Democracy*, 35(1), 5–25.

Moore, S. (2013), 'Ten years of statutory recognition: a changed landscape for UK industrial relations?', Centre for Employment Studies Research, University of the West of England.

Moore, S., McKay, S. and Bewley, H. (2004), 'The content of new voluntary trade union recognition agreements 1998–2002, vol. 1: An analysis of new agreements and case studies', Employment Relations Research Series No. 26, Department of Trade and Industry, London.

Morrell, K. and Wilkinson, A. (2002), 'Empowerment: through the smoke and past the mirrors?', *Human Resource Development International*, 5(1), 119–130.

Morris, D., Bakan, U. and Wood, G. (2006), 'Employee financial participation: evidence from a major UK retailer', *Employee Relations*, 28(4), 326–341.

Morris, J., Wilkinson, B. and Gamble, J. (2009), 'Strategic international human resource management or the "bottom line"? The cases of electronics and garments commodity chains in China', *International Journal of Human Resource Management*, 20(2), 348–371.

Mosoetsa, S. and Williams, M. (eds) (2012), *Labour in the Global South: challenges and Alternatives for Workers*, Geneva, International Labour Organization.

Motlagh, J. and Saha, A. (2014), 'The ghosts of Rana Plaza', *Virginia Quarterly Review*, 90(2), 44–89.

Mrozowicki, A. and Trawińska, M. (2012), 'Women's union activism and trade union revitalization: the Polish experience', *Economic and Industrial Democracy*, 34(2), 269–289.

Mueller, F. (1994), 'Teams between hierarchy and commitment: change strategies and the "internal environment"', *Journal of Management Studies*, 31(3), 383–403.

Mueller, F. and Purcell, J. (1992), 'The drive for higher productivity', *Personnel Management*, May, 28–33.

Müller, T. and Hoffmann, A. (2001), 'EWC research: a review of the literature', Warwick Papers in Industrial Relations, No. 65, Industrial Relations Research Unit, University of Warwick.

Murray, G. (2017), 'Union renewal: what can we learn from three decades of research?', *Transfer*, 23(1), 9–29.

Nakano, S. (1999), 'Management views of European Works Councils', *European Journal of Industrial Relations*, 5(3), 307–326.

NASSCOM (National Association of Software and Service Companies) (2017), 'Annual report', New Delhi.

National Center for Employee Ownership (2015), 'ESOPS by the numbers', Oakland, CA.

Network (2013), 'Chinese workers' fight will create democracy', British Sociological Association newsletter, Winter.

Network (2016), '"Misplaced optimism" about plight of Chinese workers', British Sociological Association newsletter, Autumn.
New Economics Foundation (2016), 'Deliveroo: the next battle for the gig economy', November.
New York Times (1991), 'Edges fray on Volvo's brave new humanistic world', 7 July.
New York Times (2001), 'Employees' retirement plan is a victim as Enron tumbles', 22 November.
New York Times (2016a), 'Labor protests multiply in China as economy slows, worrying leaders', 14 March.
New York Times (2016b), 'As employees battle Walmart, China warily holds its tongue', 17 November.
New York Times (2017), 'Racially charged Nissan vote is a test for UAW in the South', 2 August.
New Zealand Centre for Labour, Employment and Work Survey (2015), Victoria University of Wellington.
Nichols, T. and O'Connell Davidson, J. (1992), 'Employee shareholders in two privatised utilities', *Industrial Relations Journal*, 23(2), 107–119.
Nienhüser, W. (2014), 'Works Councils', in A. Wilkinson, J. Donaghey, T. Dundon and R. Freeman (eds), *Handbook of Research on Employee Voice*, Cheltenham, Edward Elgar, 247–263.
NIESR (National Institute of Economic and Social Research) (2017), 'Use of agency workers in the public sector', February, London.
Nijholt, J. and Benders, J. (2010), 'Measuring the prevalence of self-managing teams: taking account of defining characteristics', *Work, Employment & Society*, 24(2), 375–385.
Nilsson, L. (1994), 'The Uddevalla plant: why did it succeed with a holistic approach and why did it come to an end?', in Å. Sandberg (ed.) (2007), *Enriching Production: Perspectives on Volvo's Uddevalla Plant as an Alternative to Lean Production*; digital edition, Stockholm, 75–86.
Nixon, L. and Penfold, A. (2011), 'Growing HR influence in the boardroom', Korn Ferry Institute, Boston, MA.
Noronha, E. and D'Cruz, P. (2009), 'Engaging the professional: organizing call centre agents in India', *Industrial Relations Journal*, 40(3), 215–234.
Nowak, D. (2006), 'Doctors on strike: the crisis in German health care delivery', *New England Journal of Medicine*, 355(15), 1520–1522.
NPR News (2002), 'What Enron employees have lost', 22 January. www.npr.org/news/specials/enron/employees.html.
Nuttall, G. (2012), 'Sharing success: The Nutall review of employee ownership', Department for Business, Innovation and Skills, London.
OECD (Organisation for Economic Co-operation and Development) (1995), 'Profit-sharing in OECD countries', in *Employment Outlook*, 140–169. OECD.org.
OECD.Stat (2016), https://stats.oecd/Index.aspx?DataSetCode=UN_DEN 19.
OECD and Visser, J. (2016), ICTWSS database (Institutional Characteristics of Trade Unions, Wage Setting, State Intervention and Social Pacts, 1960–2010), version 3.0, Amsterdam Institute for Advanced Labour Studies.
Oertig, M. and Buergi, T. (2006), 'The challenges of managing cross-cultural virtual project teams', *Team Performance International*, 12(1/2), 23–30.
O'Grady, F. (2017), 'Why Brexit could put our employment rights at risk', *Guardian*, 4 September.

O'Kelly, K. (2005), 'A European project for employee board-level representatives: issues, roles and responsibilities', *Transfer*, 11(2), 221–230.
Oliver, N. and Wilkinson, N. (1992), *The Japanization of British Industry*, 2nd ed., Oxford, Blackwell.
ONS (Office for National Statistics) (2011), 'Census analysis', Office for National Statistics, London.
ONS (Office for National Statistics) (2016), 'International comparisons of UK productivity, first estimates: 2015', Office for National Statistics, London.
ONS (Office for National Statistics) (2017), 'Contracts that do not guarantee a minimum number of hours'. www.ons.gov.uk/employmentandlabourmarket/peopleinwork/earningsandworkinghours/articles/contractsthatdonotguaranteeaminimumnumberofhours/may2017.
ORC (Organization Resources Counselors) (2003), 'European Works Councils survey 2003', ORC Worldwide, New York.
Ouchi, W. (1981), *Theory Z: How American Business Can Meet the Japanese Challenge*, Boston, MA, Addison-Wesley.
Oudhuis, M. and Olsson, A. (2015), 'Cultural clashes and reactions when implementing lean production in a Japanese-owned Swedish company', *Economic and Industrial Democracy*, 36(2), 259–282.
Oxenbridge, S. and Brown, W. (2004), 'Achieving a new equilibrium? The stability of cooperative employer-union relationships', *Industrial Relations Journal*, 35(5), 388–402.
Paauwe, J. and Boon, C. (2009), 'Strategic HRM: a critical review', in D. Collings and G. Wood (eds), *Human Resource Management: A Critical Approach*, London, Routledge, 38–54.
Paauwe, J., Guest, D. and Wright, P. (2013), *HRM & Performance: Achievements & Challenges*, New York, Wiley.
Pang, C., Roberts, D. and Sutton, J. (1998), 'Doing business in China: the art of war?', *International Journal of Contemporary Hospitality Management*, 10(7), 272–282.
Parker, M. and Slaughter, J. (1988), *Choosing Sides: Unions and the Team Concept*, Boston, MA, Labor Notes.
Pateman, C. (1970), *Participation and Democratic Theory*, Cambridge, Cambridge University Press.
Patmore, G. (2010), 'A legal perspective on employee participation', in A. Wilkinson, P. Gollan, M. Marchington and D. Lewin (eds), *The Oxford Handbook of Participation in Organizations*, Oxford, Oxford University Press, 76–104.
Patterson, M., West, M., Lawthom, R. and Nickell, S. (1997), 'Impact of people management practices on business performance', Issues in People Management, London, Institute of Personnel and Development.
Paul, A. and Anantharaman, R. (2004), 'Influences of human resource management practices on organizational commitment: a study among software professionals in India', *Human Resource Development Quarterly*, 15(1), 77–88.
Peetz, D. and Frost, A. (2007), 'Employee voice in the Anglo-American world: what does it mean for unions?', in R. Freeman, P. Boxall and P. Haynes (eds), *What Workers Say: Employee Voice in the Anglo-American Workplace*, Ithaca, NY, ILR Press, 166–180.
Pencavel, J. (2001), *Worker Participation: Lessons from the Worker Co-ops of the Pacific Northwest*, New York, Russell Sage Foundation.
Pendleton, A. (2001), *Employee Ownership, Participation and Governance*, London, Routledge.

Pendleton, A. (2005a), 'Employee share ownership, employment relationships and corporate governance', in B. Harley, J. Hyman and P. Thompson (eds), *Participation and Democracy at Work*, Basingstoke, Palgrave Macmillan, 75–93.

Pendleton, A. (2005b), 'Sellers or keepers? Share retention in employee share option plans', *Human Resource Management*, 44(3), 319–336.

Pendleton, A., Wilson, N. and Wright, M. (1998), 'The perception and effects of share ownership: empirical evidence from employee buy-outs', *British Journal of Industrial Relations*, 36(1), 99–124.

Pendleton, A., Poutsma, E., van Omreren, J. and Brewster, C. (2003), 'The incidence and determinants of employee share ownership and profit-sharing in Europe', in T. Kato and J. Pliskin (eds), *The Determinants of the Incidence and the Effects of Participatory Organisations: Advances in the Economic Analysis of Participatory and Labor-managed Firms*, vol. 7, Oxford, Elsevier.

Pendleton, A. and Robinson, A. (2015), 'The productivity effects of multiple pay incentives', *Economic and Industrial Democracy*, 38(4), 588–608.

People Management (2016), 'Sports Direct condemned for "appalling" HR practices', 22 July. www2.cipd.co.uk/pm/peoplemanagement/b/weblog/archive/2016/07/22/sports-direct-condemned-for-appalling-hr-practices.aspx.

People Management (2017), 'Who needs staff? The decline of full-time employment', 25 April. www.peoplemanagement.co.uk/long-reads/articles/who-needs-staff.

Peters, T. (1989), *Thriving on Chaos: Handbook for a Management Revolution*, New York, Harper & Row.

Peters, T. and Waterman, R. (1982), *In Search of Excellence: Lessons from America's Best-Run Companies*, New York, HarperCollins.

Pfeffer, J. (1994), *Competitive Advantage Through People*, Boston, MA, Harvard Business School Press.

Pfeffer, J. (1998), *The Human Equation*, Boston, MA, Harvard Business School Press.

Picard, S. (2010) 'European works councils: a trade union guide to Directive 2009/38/EC', Report 114, ETUI, Brussels.

Pollock, A. (2004), *NHS plc: The Privatization of our Health Care*, London, Verso.

Poole, M., Lansbury, R. and Wailes, N. (2001), 'A comparative analysis of developments in industrial democracy', *Industrial Relations*, 40(3), 490–525.

Porter, M. (1980), *Competitive Strategies: Technologies for Analyzing Industries and Firms*, New York, Free Press.

Porter, M. (1985), *Competitive Advantage: Creating and Sustaining Superior Performance*, New York, Free Press.

Preminger, J. (2016), 'The contradictory effects of neoliberalization on labour relations: the health and social work sectors', *Economic and Industrial Democracy*, 37(4), 644–664.

PrintWeek (2015), 'Employee-owners count the cost as papermaker goes under', 5 May. http://printweek.com/print-week/briefing/1151212/employee-owners-count-the-cost-as-papermaker-goes-under.

Procter, S. and Mueller, F. (2000), 'Teamworking: strategy, structure, systems and culture', in S. Procter and F. Mueller, *Teamworking*, Basingstoke, Macmillan, 3–24.

Procter, S. and Benders, J. (2014), 'Task-based voice: teamworking, autonomy and performance', in A. Wilkinson, J. Donaghey, T. Dundon and R. Freeman (eds), *Handbook of Research on Employee Voice*, Cheltenham, Edward Elgar, 298–309.

Procter, S. and Radnor, Z. (2014), 'Teamworking under lean in UK public services: lean teams and team targets in Her Majesty's Revenue and Customs (HMRC)', *International Journal of Human Resource Management*, 25, 2978–2995.

Prosser, T. (2014), 'Financialization and the reform of European industrial relations systems', *European Journal of Industrial Relations*, 20(4), 351–365.

Psoinos, A. and Smithson, S. (2002), 'Employee empowerment in manufacturing: a study of organisations in the UK', *New Technology, Work and Employment*, 17(2), 132–148.

Pulignano, V., Turk, J. and Swerts, T. (2016), 'European Works Councils on the move: management perspectives on the development of a transnational institution for social dialogue', Centre for Sociological Research, KU Leuven, Leuven.

Purcell, J. (2010), 'Building employee engagement', ACAS Policy Discussion Paper, ACAS, London .

Purcell, J. (2014), 'Disengaging from engagement', *Human Resource Management Journal*, 24(3), 241–254.

Purcell, K. and Purcell, J. (1998), 'In-sourcing, outsourcing, and the growth of contingent labour as evidence of flexible employment strategies', *European Journal of Work and Organizational Psychology*, 7(1), 39–59.

Pyper, D. (2017), 'Trade union legislation 1979–2010', Briefing Paper No. CBP7882, House of Commons, London .

Radnor, Z., Holweg, M. and Waring, J. (2012), 'Lean in healthcare: the unfilled promise', *Social Science and Medicine*, 74, 364–371.

Ramsay, H. (1977), 'Cycles of control: worker participation in sociological and historical perspective', *Sociology*, 11(3), 481–506.

Ramsay, H. (1980), 'Phantom participation: patterns of power and conflict', *Industrial Relations Journal*, 11(3), 46–59.

Ramsay, H. (1983), 'Evolution or cycle? Worker participation in the 1970s and 1980s', in C. Crouch and F. Heller (eds), *Organizational Democracy and Political Processes*, Chichester, John Wiley, 203–225.

Ramsay, H. (1992), 'Recycled waste? Debating the analysis of worker participation: a response to Ackers et al.', *Industrial Relations Journal*, 24(1), 76–80.

Ramsay, H. (1997), '"Fool's gold?" European Works Councils and workplace democracy', *Industrial Relations Journal*, 28(4), 314–322.

Ramsay, H., Scholarios, D. and Harley, B. (2000), 'Employees and high performance work systems: testing inside the black box', *British Journal of Industrial Relations* 38(4), 501–531.

Rappaport, J., Swift, C. and Hess, R. (eds) (1984), *Studies in Empowerment: Steps toward Understanding and Action*, London, Routledge.

Rees, C., Alfes, K. and Gateby, M. (2013), 'Employee voice and engagement: connections and consequences', *International Journal of Human Resource Management*, 24(14), 2780–2798.

Renaud, S. (2007), 'Dynamic efficiency of supervisory board codetermination in Germany', *Labor*, 21(4/5), 689–712.

Rhenman, E. (1968), *Industrial Democracy and Industrial Management*, London, Tavistock.

Richardson, R. and Nejad, A. (1986), 'Employee share ownerships in the UK: an evaluation', *British Journal of Industrial Relations*, 24(2), 233–250.

Rigby, M., Contrepois, S. and O'Brien Smith, F. (2009), 'The establishment of enterprise works councils: process and problems', *European Journal of Industrial Relations*, 15(1), 71–90.

Ritzer, G. (1996), *The McDonaldization of Society*, Thousand Oaks, CA, Pine Forge Press.
Robinson, A. and Wilson, N. (2006), 'Employee financial participation and productivity: an empirical reappraisal', *British Journal of Industrial Relations*, 44(1), 31–50.
Roche, W. and Teague, P. ((2014), 'Successful but unappealing: fifteen years of workplace partnership in Ireland', *International Journal of Human Resource Management*, 25(6), 781–794.
Rogers, J. and Streeck, W. (1995), 'The study of works councils: concepts and problems', in J. Rogers and W. Streeck (eds), *Works Councils: Consultation, Representation and Cooperation in Industrial Relations*, Chicago, IL, University of Chicago Press, 3–26.
Rogers, K. (2017), 'Precarious and migrant workers in struggle: are new forms of trade unionism necessary in post-Brexit Britain?', *Capital & Class*, 41(2), 336–343.
Rose, M. (2003), 'Good deal or bad deal? Job satisfaction in occupations', *Work, Employment & Society*, 17(3), 503–530.
Rossman, P. (2013), 'Establishing rights in the disposable jobs regime', *International Journal of Labour Research*, 5(1), 23–40.
Royle, T. (1999), 'Where's the beef? McDonald's and its European Works Council', *European Journal of Industrial Relations*, 5(3), 327–347.
Rubery, J. and Edwards, P. (2003), 'Low pay and the national minimum wage', in P. Edwards (ed.), *Industrial Relations*, 2nd ed., Oxford, Blackwell, 447–469.
Rubery, J. and Grimshaw, D. (2003), *The Organisation of Employment: An International Perspective*, Basingstoke, Palgrave Macmillan.
Rustin, M. (2016), 'The crisis of neoliberalism in Europe', *Eurozine*, 11 July.
Saini, D. (2006) 'Declining labour power and challenges before trade unions: some lessons from a case study on private sector unionism', *Indian Journal of Labour Economics*, 49(4), 911–924.
Saini, D. (2008) 'Labour in the new industrial-relations era: global and Indian perspectives', *A. T. Business Management Review*, 4(2), 82–92.
Saks, A. and Gruman, J. (2014), 'What do we really know about employee engagement?', *Human Resource Development Quarterly*, 25, 155–182.
Salaman, G. (1974), *Community and Occupation: an Exploration of Work/Leisure Relationships*, London, Cambridge University Press.
Salamon, M. (1999), 'Collective bargaining', in G. Hollinshead, P. Nicholls and S. Tailby, *Employee Relations*, London, Financial Times, 301–331.
Salmon, A. (2011), *Le travail sous haute tension. Risques industriels et perspectives syndicales dans le secteur de l'énergie*, Paris, Desclée de Brouwer.
Saloner, G., Shepard, A. and Podolny, J. (2001), *Strategic Management*, New York, Wiley.
Samuel, P. and Bacon, N. (2010), 'The contents of partnership agreements in Britain 1990–2007', *Work, Employment & Society*, 24(3), 430–448.
Sandberg, Å. (ed.) (2007), *Enriching Production: Perspectives on Volvo's Uddevalla Plant as an Alternative to Lean Production*; digital edition, Stockholm.
Sandberg, Å. (ed.) (2013), *Nordic Lights: Work, Management and Welfare in Scandinavia*, Stockholm, SNS.
Sautner, Z. and Weber, M. (2009), 'How do managers behave in stock option plans? Clinical evidence from exercise and survey data', *Journal of Financial Research*, 32(2), 123–155.
Scarbrough, H. (1996), 'Understanding and managing expertise', in H. Scarbrough (ed.), *The Management of Expertise*, Basingstoke, Macmillan Business, 23–47.

References

Schmid, F. and Seger, S. (1998), 'Arbeitnehmermitbestimmung, Allokation von Entscheidungsrechten und Shareholder Value', *Zeitschrift für Betriebswirtschaft*, 68(5), 453–473.

Schnabel, C. (2013), 'Union membership and density: some (not so) stylized facts and challenges', *European Journal of Industrial Relations*, 19(3), 255–272.

Schuler, R. and Jackson, S. (1987), 'Linking competitive strategies with human resource management practices', *Academy of Management Executive*, 1(3), 207–219.

Schuler, R., Jackson, S. and Storey, J. (2001), 'HRM and its links with strategic management', in J. Storey (ed.), *Human Resource Management: A Critical Text*, 2nd ed., London, Thompson, 114–130.

Scott, C. and Jaffe, D. (1991), *Empowerment: A Practical Guide for Success*, Menlo Park, CA, Crisp Publications.

Scott, D., Bishop, J. and Chen, X. (2003), 'An examination of the relationship of employee involvement with job satisfaction, employee co-operation and intention to quit in a US-invested enterprise in China', *International Journal of Organizational Analysis*, 11(1), 3–19.

Scottish Review (2016), 14 November. www.scottishreview.net/KenethRoy93a.htm.

SenGupta, S., Whitfield, K. and McNabb, R. (2006), 'Employee share ownership and performance: golden path or golden handcuffs?', paper presented to the Labor and Employment Relations Association, Boston.

Senior, B. (1997), 'Team roles and team performance: is there really a link?', *Journal of Occupational and Organizational Psychology*, 70, 241–258.

Sennett, R. (1998), *The Corrosion of Character: The Personal Consequences of Work in the New Capitalism*, New York, Norton.

Sennett, R. (2006), *The Culture of the New Capitalism*, New Haven, CT, Yale University Press.

Sewell, G. (1996), 'A Japanese "cure" to a British "disease"? Cultural dimensions to the development of workplace surveillance technologies', *Information Technology and People*, 9(3), 19–29.

Shin, Y. (2005), 'Conflict resolution in virtual teams', *Organizational Dynamics*, 34(4), 331–345.

Silvia, S. (2017), 'The United Auto Workers' attempts to unionize Volkswagen Chattanooga', *Industrial Labor Review*. https://doi.org/10.1177/0019793917723620.

Singh, H. and Saini, D. (2016), 'Private sector manufacturing organizations and workplace industrial relations: towards a new employment relationship', *XVII Annual International Seminar Proceedings*, January, 850–873.

Skivenes, M. (2017), 'Explaining whistle blowing processes in the Norwegian labour market: between individual power resources and institutional arrangements', *Economic and Industrial Democracy*, 38(1), 119–143.

Skorupińska, K. (2015), 'Towards a Europeanization of indirect employee participation: Polish experiences', *Economic and Industrial Democracy*, online, 21 July.

Sloan, R. (1998), 'European Works Councils: moving forward with employee consultation', IPA, London.

Smith, P. (2015), 'Labour under the law: a new law of combination, and master and servant, in 21st-century Britain?', *Industrial Relations Journal*, 46(5/6), 345–364.

Smyth, J. (2017), *The Toxic University: Zombie Leadership, Academic Rock Stars, and Neoliberal Ideology*, Basingstoke, Palgrave Macmillan.

Sports Direct website (2017), www.sportsdirect.com/jobs/hr.

Spreitzer, G. (1995), 'Psychological empowerment in the workplace: dimensions, measurement and validation', *Academy of Management Journal*, 38(5), 1442–1465.
Standing, G. (2011), *The Precariat: the New Dangerous Class*, London, Bloomsbury.
Standing, G. (2014), *A Precariat Charter: from Denizens to Citizens*, London, Bloomsbury.
Stewart, A. (1994), *Empowering People*, London, Institute of Management/Pitman.
Stewart, A. (2012), 'Australian labour law in transition: the impact of the Fair Work Act', *New Zealand Journal of Employment Relations*, 37(1), 3–21.
Stewart, A. and Stanford, J. (2017), 'Regulating work in the gig economy: what are the options?' *The Economic and Labour Relations Review*, 28(3), 420–437.
Stewart, P., Richardson, M., Danford, A., Murphy, K., Richardson, T. and Wass, V. (2009), *We Sell out Time No More: Workers' Struggles against Lean Production in the British Car Industry*, London, Pluto Press.
Stewart, P., and Martinez Lucio, M. (2011), 'Collective narratives and politics in the contemporary study of work: the new management practices debate', *Work, Employment & Society*, 25(2), 327–341.
Strauss, G. (1998), 'An overview', in F. Heller, E. Pusić, G. Strauss and B. Wilpert (eds), *Organizational Participation: Myth and Reality*, Oxford, Oxford University Press, 8–39.
Strauss, G. (2006), 'Worker participation: some under-considered issues', *Industrial Relations*, 45(4), 773–803.
Streeck, W. (1995), 'Works councils in Western Europe: from consultation to participation', in J. Rogers and W. Streeck (eds), *Works Councils: Consultation, Representation and Cooperation in Industrial Relations*, Chicago, IL, University of Chicago Press, 313–348.
Streeck, W. (1997), 'Neither European nor Works Councils', *Economic and Industrial Democracy*, 18(2), 325–337.
Streeck, W. (2016), *How will Capitalism End?*, London, Verso.
Summers, J. and Hyman, J. (2005), *Employee participation and company performance: a review of the literature*, York, Joseph Rowntree Foundation.
Sundstrom, E., de Meuse, K. and Furell, D. (1990), 'Work teams: applications and effectiveness', *American Psychologist*, 45(2), 120–133.
Tailby, S., Richardson, M., Stewart, P., Danford, A. and Upchurch, M. (2004), 'Participation at work and worker participation: an NHS case study', *Industrial Relations Journal*, 35(5), 413–418.
Tait, C. (2017), 'Future unions: towards a membership renaissance in the private sector', Fabian Society, London.
Tajfel, H. and Turner, J. (1986), 'The social identity theory of inter-group behavior', in S. Worchel and W. Austin (eds), *Psychology of Inter-group Relations*, Chicago, Nelson-Hall, 7–24.
Taylor, M. (2017), 'Good work: the Taylor review of modern working practices', Department for Business, Energy & Industrial Strategy, London.
Taylor, P. and Ramsay, H. (1998), 'Unions, partnership and HRM: sleeping with the enemy?', *International Journal of Employment Studies*, 6(2), 115–143.
Taylor, P. and Bain, P. (1999), '"An assembly line in the head": work and employee relations in the call centre', *Industrial Relations Journal*, 30(2), 101–117.
Taylor, P. and Bain, P. (2005), 'India calling to the far away towns', *Work, Employment & Society*, 19(2), 261–282.

Taylor, P., Baldry, C., Danford, A. and Stewart, P. (2009), '"An umbrella full of holes?" Corporate restructuring, redundancy and the effectiveness of ICE Regulations', *Relations Industrielles/Industrial Relations*, 64(1), 27–49.

Taylor, P., D'Cruz, P., Noronha, E. and Scholarios, D. (2013), 'The experience of work in India's domestic call centre industry', *International Journal of Human Resource Management* 24(2), 436–452.

Taylor, R. (2004), 'Partnerships at work: the way to corporate renewal?', Future of Work Programme Seminar Series, ESRC, Swindon.

Taylor, S. (1998), 'Emotional labour and the new workplace', in P. Thompson and C. Warhurst (eds), *Workplaces of the Future*, London, MacMillan, 84–103.

Taylor Wessing (2017), 'Brexit: employment law and HR implications'. www.taylorwessing.com/download/article-brexit-employment-law.html.

Telegraph (2008), 'UBS: the crisis at the heart of the Swiss bank', 6 July.

Terry, M. (2003a), 'Partnership and the future of trade unions', *Economic and Industrial Democracy*, 24(4), 485–507.

Terry, M. (2003b), 'Employee representation: shop stewards and the new legal framework', in P. Edwards (ed.), *Industrial Relations: Theory and Practice*, 2nd ed., Oxford, Blackwell, 257–284.

THE (Times Higher Education) (2015), 'Bar work? You must be a barrister!', 12 March, 43–45.

THE (Times Higher Education) (2016), 'Went the day well?', 4 February.

THE (Times Higher Education) (2017a), 'Senior staff pay-offs 'must not reward poor performance', 12 January.

THE (Times Higher Education) (2017b), 'What lies beneath', 11 May.

Thite, M., Budhwar, P. and Wilkinson, A. (2014), 'Global HR roles and factors influencing their development: evidence from emerging Indian IT services multinationals', *Human Resource Management*, 53(6), 921–946.

Thomas, C. W. (2002), 'The rise and fall of Enron', *Journal of Accountancy*, 193(4), 41–52..

Thompson, M. (2009), 'Salary progression schemes', in G. White and J. Druker (eds), *Reward Management: a Critical Text*, 2nd ed., London, Routledge, 120–147.

Thompson, P. (2003), 'Disconnected capitalism: or why employers can't keep their side of the bargain', *Work, Employment & Society* 17(2), 359–378.

Thompson, P. (2011), 'The trouble with HRM', *Human Resource Management Journal*, 21(4), 355–367.

Thursfield, D. (2012), 'The social construction of professionalism among organizers and senior organizers in a UK trade union', *Work, Employment & Society*, 26(1), 128–144.

Thursfield, D. (2015), 'Resistance to teamworking in a UK research and development laboratory', *Work, Employment & Society*, 29(6), 989–1006.

Time Magazine (2001), 'Rank and fire', 11 June.

Toubøl, J. and Jensen, C. (2014), 'Why do people join trade unions? The impact of workplace union density in union recruitment', *Transfer: European Review of Labour and Research*, 20(1), 135–154.

Towers, B. (1997), *The Representation Gap: Change and Reform in the British and American Workplace*, Oxford, Oxford University Press.

Townley, B. (1999), 'Practical reason and performance appraisal', *Journal of Management Studies*, 36, 287–306.

Townsend, K. (2007), 'Who has control in teams without team-working?', *Economic and Industrial Democracy*, 28(4), 622–649.

Townsend, K. (2014), 'The role of line managers in employee voice systems', in A. Wilkinson, J. Donaghey, T. Dundon and R. Freeman (eds), *Handbook of Research on Employee Voice*, Cheltenham, Edward Elgar, 155–169.

Toynbee, P. and Walker, D. (2017), *Dismembered: How the Conservative Attack on the State Harms Us All*, London, Guardian Faber.

Trist, E., Higgin, G., Murray, H. and Pollock, A. (1963), *Organizational Choice: Capabilities of Groups at the Coal Face Under Changing Technologies: The Loss, Rediscovery and Transformation of a Work Tradition*, London, Tavistock.

Truss, K. (2012), 'Spinning plates and juggling hats: engagement in an era of austerity', CIPD, London.

Truss, K., Soane, E. and Edwards, C. (2006), *Working Life: Employee Attitudes and Engagement 2006*, London, CIPD.

TUC (Trades Union Congress) (1999), *Partners for Progress: New Unionism in the Workplace*, London, May.

TUC (Trades Union Congress) (2010), 'In sickness and in health? Good work – and how to achieve it', Touch Stone Extras, London.

TUC (Trades Union Congress) (2015), 'Workers' voice in corporate governance: a European perspective', London.

TUC (Trades Union Congress) (2016), 'Equality Audit 2016', London.

TUC (Trades Union Congress) (2017a), 'What have trade unions ever done for us? Ask 3000 workers at Sports Direct', Worksmart, London.

TUC (Trades Union Congress) (2017b), 'Better jobs for mums and dads: a TUC report'. www.tuc.org.uk/sites/default/files/Better_Jobs_For_Mums_And_Dads_2017_AW_Digital_0.pdf.

Turnley, W. and Feldman, D. (2000), 'Re-examining the effects of psychological contract violations: unmet expectations and job dissatisfaction as mediators', *Journal of Organizational Behavior*, 21(1), 25–42.

Ulrich, D. (1997), 'Human resource champions', in *The Next Agenda for Adding Value and Delivering Results*, Boston: Harvard Business School Press.

Ulrich, D. (1998), 'A new mandate for human resources', *Harvard Business Review*, 76, 124–134.

Ulrich, D. (2017), 'Your employees are the people who make you win', *People Management*, April, 40–41.

Ulrich, D. and Brockbank, W. (2005), *The HR Value Proposition*, Boston, MA: Harvard Business School Press.

UNCTAD (United Nations Conference on Trade and Development) (2012), 'Greater income share for labour: the essential catalyst for global economic recovery and employment', Policy Brief No. 26, New York and Geneva, December.

UNCTAD (United Nations Conference on Trade and Development) (2016), 'World Investment Report 2016 – Investor nationality: policy challenges'. http://unctad.org/en/PublicationsLibrary/wir2016_en.pdf.

Underhill, E. and Quinlan, M. (2011), 'How precarious work affects health and safety at work: the case of temporary agency workers', *Relations Industrielles/Industrial Relations*, 66(3), 397–421.

UNICE (Union of Industrial and Employers' Confederations of Europe) (1991), 'UNICE's approach to community action with regard to information and consultation', Position Paper, Brussels.
UNISON (2017), 'A massive win for our union and a massive win for all workers'. www.unison.org.uk/news/2017/07/massive-win-union-massive-win-workers/.
US Bureau of Labor Statistics (2016), US Department of Labor. www.bls.gov/cps.
Ussher, K. (2016), 'Improving pay, progression and productivity in the retail sector', Joseph Rowntree Foundation, York.
Valizade, D., Ogbonnaya, C., Tregaskis, O. and Forde, C. (2016), 'A mutual gains perspective on workplace partnership: employee outcomes and the mediating role of the employment relations climate', *Human Resource Management Journal*, 26(3), 351–368.
van den Blucke, F. (1999), 'A company perspective of financial participation in the European Union: objectives and obstacles', Research Centre for Financial Participation, Brussels.
van den Broek, D., Callaghan, G. and Thompson, P. (2004), 'Teams without teamwork? Explaining the call centre paradox', *Economic and Industrial Democracy*, 25(2), 197–218.
van Wanrooy, B., Bewley, H., Bryson, A., Forth, J., Freeth, S., Stokes, L. and Wood, S. (2013), *Employment Relations in the Shadow of Recession*, Basingstoke, Palgrave Macmillan.
Varoufakis, Y. (2016), *And the Weak Suffer What They Must? Europe, Austerity and the Threat to Global Stability*, London, Vintage.
Visser, J. (2016), 'What happened to collective bargaining during the great recession?', *IZA Journal of Labor Policy*, 5(9).
Vissols, S. (2009), 'European Works Councils: an assessment of their social welfare impact', Working Paper 2009.04, ETUI, Brussels.
Vogel, S. (2007), 'Social partners divided over issue of co-determination at company level', Eurofound. www.eurofound.europa.eu/eiro/2006/11/articles/de0611039i.htm.
Vos, K. (2006), 'Europeanization and convergence in industrial relations', *European Journal of Industrial Relations*, 12(3), 311–327.
Voss, E. (2016), 'European Works Councils assessments and requirements: report to the ETUC', ETUC, Brussels.
Waddington, J. (2003a), 'Heightening tensions in relations between trade unions and the Labour Government in 2002', *British Journal of Industrial Relations*, 41(2), 335–358.
Waddington, J. (2003b), 'Trade union organization', in P. Edwards (ed.), *Industrial Relations: Theory & Practice*, 2nd ed., Oxford, Blackwell, 214–256.
Waddington, J. (2003c), 'What do representatives think of the practices of European Works Councils? Views from six countries', *European Journal of Industrial Relations*, 9(3), 303–325.
Waddington, J. (2010), *European Works Councils and Industrial Relations: A Transnational Industrial Relations Institution in the Making*, London, Routledge.
Waddington, J. (2014), 'Trade union membership retention in Europe: the challenge of difficult times', *European Journal of Industrial Relations*, 21(3), 205–221.
Waddington, J., Pulignano, V., Turk, J. and Swerts, T. (2016), *Managers, BusinessEurope and the Development of European Works Councils*, ETUI Working Paper 2016.06, Brussels.
Wailes, N. and Lansbury, R. (2010), 'International and comparative perspectives on employee participation', in A. Wilkinson, P. Gollan, M. Marchington and D. Lewin (eds), *The Oxford Handbook of Participation in Organizations*, Oxford, Oxford University Press, 570–589.

Walder, A. (1986), *Communist Neo-Traditionalism: Work and Authority in Chinese Industry*, Berkeley, CA: University of California Press.

Wall, T. and Wood, S. (2002), 'Delegation's a powerful tool', *Professional Manager*, 11(6), 37.

Wall, T., Wood, S. and Leach, D. (2004), 'Empowerment and performance', *International Review of Industrial and Organizational Psychology*, 19, 1–46.

Walton, R. (1985), 'From control to commitment in the workplace', *Harvard Business Review*, March/April, 77–84.

Walton, R. and McKersie, R. (1965), *A Behavioural Theory of Labor Negotiations*, New York, McGraw-Hill.

Warner, M. (1999), 'Human resources and management in China's "high-tech" revolution: a study of selected computer hardware, software and related firms in the PRC', *International Journal of Human Resource Management*, 10(1), 1–20.

Warner, M. and Zhu, Y. (2002), 'Human resource management with "Chinese characteristics": a comparative study of the People's Republic of China and Taiwan', *Asia Pacific Business Review*, 9(2), 21–43.

Watson, T. (1996), 'Motivation: that's Maslow, isn't it?', *Management Learning*, 27(4), 447–464.

Weber, T., Foster, P. and Levent Egriboz, K. (2000), 'Costs and benefits of the European Works Council Directive', Employment Relations Research Series No. 9, Department of Trade and Industry, London.

Weitzman, M. and Kruse, D. (1990), 'Profit sharing and productivity', in A. Blinder (ed.), *Paying for Productivity: A Look at the Evidence*, Washington, DC, Brookings Institution Press.

Welford, R. (1990), 'The organization and behaviour of UK worker co-operatives: an empirical investigation', in G. Jenkins and R. Poole (eds), *New Forms of Ownership, Management and Employment*, London, Routledge, 303–322.

West, D. (2015), 'What happens if robots take the jobs?', Center for Technology Innovation, Brookings Institution, Washington, DC.

West, M., Guthrie, J., Dawson, J., Borrill, C. and Carter, M. (2006), 'Reducing patient mortality in hospitals: the role of HRM', *Journal of Organizational Behaviour*, 27(7), 983–1002.

Western, J., Haynes, M., Durrington, D. and Dwan, K. (2006), 'Characteristics and benefits of professional work', *Journal of Sociology*, 42(2), 165–188.

Weston, S. and Martinez Lucio, M. (1997), 'Trade unions, management and European Works Councils: opening Pandora's Box?', *International Journal of Human Resource Management*, 8(6), 764–779.

White, M., Hill, S., McGovern, P., Mills, C. and Smeaton, D. (2003), '"High performance" management practices, working hours and work-life balance', *British Journal of Industrial Relations*, 41(2), 175–195.

White, M., Hill, S., Mills, C. and Smeaton, D. (2004), *Managing to Change? British Workplaces and the Future of Work*, Basingstoke, Palgrave Macmillan.

Whittall, M. (2000), 'The BMW European Works Councils: a case for European industrial relations optimism?', *European Journal of Industrial Relations*, 6(1), 61–83.

Whittington, R. (1993), *What is Strategy and Does it Matter?*, London, Routledge.

Wickens, P. (1987), *The Road to Nissan*, Basingstoke, Palgrave Macmillan.

Wickens, P. (1993), 'Lean production and beyond: the system, its critics and the future', *Human Resource Management Journal*, 3(4), 75–90.

References 237

Wilkinson, A. (2001), 'Empowerment', in T. Redman and A. Wilkinson (eds), *Contemporary Human Resource Management: Text and Cases*, Harlow, Pearson, 336–376.

Wilkinson, A. and Dundon, T. (2010), 'Direct employee participation', in A. Wilkinson, P. Gollan, M. Marchington and D. Lewin (eds), *The Oxford Handbook of Participation in Organizations*, Oxford, Oxford University Press, 167–185.

Wilkinson, A., Gollan, P., Marchington, M. and Lewin, D. (2010a), 'Conceptualizing Employee Participation in Organizations', in A. Wilkinson, P. Gollan, M. Marchington and D. Lewin (eds), *The Oxford Handbook of Participation in Organizations*, Oxford, Oxford University Press, 3–28.

Wilkinson, A., Gollan, P., Marchington, M. and Lewin, D. (eds) (2010b), *The Oxford Handbook of Participation in Organizations*, Oxford, Oxford University Press.

Wilkinson, R. and Pickett, K. (2010), *The Spirit Level: Why Equality is Better for Everyone*, London, Penguin.

Williamson, J. (2013), 'Workers on the board: the case for workers' voice in corporate governance', Economic Report Series, TUC, London.

Willmott, H. (1994), 'Business process re-engineering and human resource management', *Personnel Review*, 23(3), 34–46.

Wills, J. (1999), 'European Works Councils in British firms', *Human Resource Management Journal*, 9(4), 19–38.

Wills, J. (2000), 'Great expectations: three years in the life of a European Works Council', *European Journal of Industrial Relations*, 6(1), 85–107.

Wilson, F. (2004), *Organizational Behaviour and Work: a Critical Introduction*, Oxford, Oxford University Press.

Wilson, F. and Nutley, S. (2003), 'A critical look at staff appraisal: the case of women in Scottish universities', *Gender, Work and Organisation*, 10(3), 301–319.

Wilson, N. and Peel, M. (1991), 'The impact on absenteeism and quits of profit-sharing and other forms of employee participation', *Industry and Labor Relations Review*, 44(3), 454–468.

Winch, S. and Henderson, A. (2009), 'Making cars and making health care: a critical review', *Medical Journal of Australia*, 191(1), 28–29.

Windmuller, J. (1987), *Collective Bargaining in Industrialized Market Economies: a Reappraisal*, Geneva, International Labour Office.

Womack, J. and Jones, D. (2003), *Lean Thinking: Banish Waste and Create Wealth in Your Corporation*, London, Simon & Schuster.

Womack, J., Jones, D. and Roos, D.(1990), *The Machine that Changed the World: The Story of Lean Production*, New York, Free Press.

Wood, S. (1993), 'The Japanization of Fordism?', *Economic and Industrial Democracy*, 14(4), 538–555.

Wood, S. (2010), 'High involvement management and performance', in A. Wilkinson, P. Gollan, M. Marchington and D. Lewin (eds), *The Oxford Handbook of Participation in Organizations*, Oxford, Oxford University Press, 407–426.

Wood, S., Niven, K. and Braeken, J. (2016) 'Managerial abuse and the process of absence among mental health staff', *Work, Employment & Society*, 30(5), 783–801.

Wood, S. and Ogbonnaya, C. (in press), 'High involvement management, economic recession, well-being and organizational performance', *Journal of Management*. https://doi.org/10.1177/0149206316659111.

worker-participation.eu (undated), www.worker-participation.eu/National-Industrial-Relations/Countries/France.

Working Lives Research Institute (2012), 'Study on precarious work and social rights: final report for the European Commission', London Metropolitan University.

Wright, C. (2011), 'What role for trade unions in future workplace relations?', ACAS Future of Workplace Relations Discussion Paper Series, London.

Yin, R. (1994), *Case Study Research: Design and Methods*, 2nd ed., Thousand Oaks, CA, Sage.

Young Women's Trust (2017), '1 in 8 employers admit workplace sexual harassment goes unreported', 4 September.

Zhu, Z., Hoffmire, James, Hoffmire, John, Wang, F. (2013), 'Employee stock ownership plans and their effect on productivity: the case of Huawei', *International Journal of Business and Management Invention*, 2(8), 17–22.

Author Index

Ackroyd, S. 71
Addison, J. 138–9, 145
Alfes, K. 116
Amba-Rao, S. 174
Anderson, E. 5, 186, 195

Bacon, N. 148–9
Baddon, L. 84, 86, 87, 115–16
Badigannavar, V. 189
Baldry, C. 23, 116
Banker, R. 126
Barnes, A. 23
Barney, J. 52
Barry, M. 5–6
Becker, B. 102
Beer, M. 51
Beirne, M. 109
Belbin, R. 121
Benders, J. 123–4, 126
Benson, J. 170
Berggren, C. 128
Blauner, R. 18
Blumberg, P. 4, 17, 18
Bowen, D. 113
Boxall, P.: on HPWS 95, 101, 104; on SHRM 49, 50, 51, 52, 53, 156
Bratton, J. 54
Braverman, H. 20, 61
Briand, L. 71, 124
Brown, W. 149, 150
Bryson, A. 55
Buchanan, D. 122, 124, 125
Bunting, M. 117
Burchell, B. 132
Butler, P. 150

Cable, J. 81
Caldwell, R. 55

Cappelli, P. 174–5
Carter, B. 23, 98–9
Cathcart, A. 91, 92
Cederström, C. 186
Ciulla, J. 11, 12, 16–17, 185–6
Clarke, N. 114, 115
Clegg, H. 135
Coates, K. 108
Collini, S. 31n1
Conchon, A. 41–2, 161–2
Cooke, F.L. 168–9, 172
Cotton, J. 4
Crowley, M. 133
Cullinane, N. 71, 141

Danford, A. 72, 104
D'Art, D. 73, 80
D'Cruz, P. 176
De Spiegelaere, S. 162
Defourney, J. 30
Dickens, L. 38–9
Dobbins, T. 150
Donaghey, J. 71
Dore, R. 123
Dorssemont, F. 159
Dromey, J. 115, 116, 130–1
Dundon, T. 6, 7, 150

Edmondson, A. 124
Edwards, P. 117
Ehrenreich, B. 121
Eide, D. 45
Erdal, D. 90
Esbenshade, J. 98
Estlund, C. 172
Eurofound 123, 126

Fang, T. 80, 81–2

Fernandez, S. 111
Fisher, S. 121
FitzRoy, F. 145
Flanders, A. 91–2
Fleming, P. 186
Fombrun, C. 51
Freeman, R. 64–5

Gennard, J. 55
Gerhart, B. 102
Glassner, V. 43
Gold, J. 54
Gollan, P. 36
Gomez, R. 5
Goodrich, C. 12
Gorton, G. 146
Greenberg, F. 72
Gregg, M. 125
Guest, D. 55, 113–14
Gumbrell-McCormick, R. 142, 143, 164, 192, 193

Hall, M. 141
Hall, P. 32
Hanson, C. 82
Harley, B. 101
Healy, G. 188
Hebson, G. 18
Heery, E. 188, 189
Heller, F. 4, 7
Henderson, A. 132
Herzberg, F. 17, 47, 116–17
High Pay Centre 93–4
Hill, E. 176–7
Hirschman, A. 5
Hochschild, A. 61
Hodgson, D. 71, 124
Hodson, R. 3, 15, 17
Hoffman, A. 155–6
Humes, W. 24
Hunter, T. 121
Huse, M. 45
Huselid, M. 101, 103
Hyman, J. 9, 15, 16
Hyman, R.: on Brexit 192, 193; on democracy 8; on role of state 40; on unions 135, 188; on works councils 142, 143, 164

Ibsen, C. 188–9
IPA (Involvement and Participation Association) 6

Jackson, S. 51
Jaffe, D. 112
Jagodziński, R. 161
Johnstone, S. 148
Jones, D. 97

Kaaresmaker, E.R. 83, 85
Kahn-Freund, O. 36, 45
Kakabadse, A. 94
Kakabadse, N. 94
Kalleberg, A. 68
Karasek, R. 26
Katz, L. 68
Kaufman, B. 53
Kay, J. 49
Kelly, J. 55, 189
Kessler, I. 80
Keune, M. 43
Klikauer, T 22
Kochan, T. 54
Korn/Ferry Institute 55
Kraft, K. 145
Kramer, B. 87
Krueger, A. 68
Krzywdzinski, M. 171
Kumar, S. 132

Lansley, S. 89
Laulom, S. 159, 161
Lawler, E. 113
Lee, C.K. 173
Legge, K. 53, 54, 95, 102, 103–4
Lewis, J. 56
Likert, R. 7
Lindholm, N. 168
Littrell, R. 169
Long, R. 80, 81–2
Lorinkova, N. 111
Louie, K. 169

McCalman, J. 125
Macduffie, J. 82
McGregor, D. 7
Macky, K. 104
McLeod, D. 114, 115
MacShane, D. 192
Marchington, M. 7, 46, 126
Maslow, A. 47
Mason, B. 9, 15, 16
Mason, P. 194
Mather, K. 24
Mayo, E. 47, 48

Meardi, G. 74
Meidner, R. 89
Michie, J. 51
Moldogaziev, T. 111
Moody, K. 132
Moore, S. 39
Mueller, F. 125
Müller, T. 155–6
Murray, G. 189

Nakano, S. 156
Nembhard, I. 124
Nienhüser, W. 142, 143
Nijholt, J. 126
Noronha, E. 176
Nuttall, G. 88

Ogbonnaya, C. 111
Oliver, N. 96
Oxenbridge, S. 149, 150

Pateman, C. 3, 15, 16, 91
Pencavel, J. 90
Pendleton, A. 18, 86–7, 90, 92
Perry, S. 111
Peters, T. 100
Pfeffer, J. 103
Pickett, K. 26, 195
Procter, S. 99
Psoinos, A. 110–11
Purcell, J.: on engagement 114, 119; on HPWS 95, 101; on SHRM 49, 50, 51, 52, 53, 156; on teams 125

Radnor, Z. 99
Ramsay, H. 15, 46, 91, 102, 109, 149, 154
Ritzer, G. 20, 21, 61
Robinson, A. 92
Rossman, P. 70
Royle, T. 157–8

Saini, D. 178
Samuel, P. 148–9
Sandberg, Å. 128
Schmid, F. 146
Schnabel, C. 145
Schuler, R. 51
Scott, C. 112
Seger, S. 146
Seifert, R. 24
SenGupta, S. 84–5

Sennett, R. 61
Sheehan, M. 51
Singh, H. 178
Smithson, S. 110–11
Soskice, D. 32
Standing, G. 166, 182, 192, 195; on precarious work 66–7, 69, 112, 183
Stevenson, H. 23
Stewart, P. 129
Strauss, G. 6
Sundstrom, E. 124

Tailby, S. 149
Tait, C. 195
Tapia, M. 188–9
Taylor, F.W. 47
Taylor, M. 187, 195
Taylor, P. 141, 149, 175–6
Taylor, R. 150
Taylor Wessing 192
THE(Times Higher Education) 23
Theorell, T. 26
Thite, M. 178
Thompson, P. 51, 54, 71, 148
Thursfield, D. 22
Townsend, K. 6, 71
Triangle, L. 161–2
Truss, K. 114–15
TUC (Trades Union Congress) 20
Turner, T. 73, 80

Ulrich, D. 54
Ussher, K. 27

Valizade, D. 147
van den Blucke, F. 84
van Hootegem, G. 123–4
van Wanrooy, B. 72, 137
Vissols, S. 162

Waddington, J. 157, 162
Wajcman, J. 117
Wall, T. 111
Walton, R. 96, 112, 122–3
Warner, M. 170
Waterman, R. 100
Watson, R. 82
WERS (Workplace Employment Relations Surveys) 19, 55, 58–9, 62n2, 117, 123
White, M. 102–3

Whittington, R. 50
Wilkinson, A. 4, 5–6, 7
Wilkinson, N. 96
Wilkinson, R. 26, 195
Wills, J. 156, 158
Wilson, F. 117
Wilson, N. 81

Winch, S. 132
Womack, J. 97, 123, 128
Wood, S. 101, 104, 111
Workplace Employment Relations Surveys *see* WERS

Zhu, Z. 170

Subject Index

abuse 17
ACTFU (All-China Federation of Trade Unions) 172
action teams 124
advice teams 124
Advisory, Conciliation and Arbitration Service (ACAS) 40, 140
affective engagement 116
alienation 19, 22
All-China Federation of Trade Unions (ACTFU) 172
all-employee meetings 115–16
Anglo-Saxon system 64–5
appraisals 59–60, 103, 131, 168, 176
Australia 41
autonomous work groups (AWGs) 122, 124
autonomy: and dignity 17; and professionalism 22–5, 31n1, 184–5; and satisfaction 21; of teams 126–8, 129

Baida Poultry 70
Bangladesh 180
behaviour, impact of ESO on 83, 84–5
beneficiaries of EPV: democratic values and 15–16; economic performance and productivity 26–30; employee dignity, satisfaction, health and wellbeing 16–26
best fit SHRM model 51
best practice SHRM model 52, 100
Better than Zero network 69
BHS 185
board membership: for employees 10, 35, 42, 143–5, 194; for HR specialists 55
Boots pharmacists 24–5
BPR (business process reengineering) 98, 124

Brexit 191–3
briefing groups *see* team briefings
British Social Attitudes surveys 19
Bullock Report 35, 144
business partner approach to SHRM 53–4
business process reengineering (BPR) 98, 124
BusinessEurope 164

CAC (Central Arbitration Committee) 38, 39
call centres 175–6
campaigning groups 67, 69, 198
Canada 41
casualisation *see* precarious work and workers
CBI (Confederation of British Industry) 40, 144
Central Arbitration Committee (CAC) 38, 39
centralised bargaining 137–8
China 167–74
CIPD (Chartered Institute of Personnel and Development) 56
CMEs *see* coordinated market economies
codetermination: in Germany 10, 33; and supervisory boards 10, 143–6; and works councils 10, 142–3
collective bargaining: in Europe 137–9; in UK 135–7
collective participation 29, 134; collective bargaining in Europe 137–9; collective bargaining in UK 135–7; future of 186–91; joint consultation 139–41; partial participation 16; partnership 146–50; supervisory boards and codetermination 143–6; works councils and codetermination 142–3; *see also*

European Works Councils; representation/participation gap; trade unions
combination of initiatives 30
commitment: and engagement 108, 118; and HPWS 102; impact of ESO on 84–5
commitment strategy 122–3
communication 58–9, 156
company-level bargaining 138, 139
competitive advantage 52–3
Confederation of British Industry (CBI) 40, 144
consultation *see* European Works Councils; joint consultation
contract workers 177, 178, 198
contractual equivalence 45
contradictions of EI 17
control: as central issue 1, 12; cycles of control thesis 46, 109; delegation of 21; and dignity 16–17; and EI 46, 184–5; health, wellbeing and 25–6; and lean teams 129; and managerialism 22–3; relationship with participation 31; and satisfaction 18; silence as form of 71–2; and technology 197–8
convergence of employment practice 167, 180
cooperatives 90–1
coordinated market economies (CMEs) 10, 32–3, 43, 135
corporate ethics 56–7, 62n1
corporate social responsibility 194
crises 35, 41; *see also* financial crisis; labour disputes
cultural context 97–8, 103–4, 123, 169, 174, 179; *see also* national context
cycles of control thesis 46, 109

defensive role of EPV 46–7
deferred profit sharing 79
degradation of work 20
delayering 111
Deliveroo 69
demand control model 26
democracy 8–9
democratic values: and employee-ownership 89, 91, 92; and ESO 86–7; link with EPV 15–16
deterministic approach to strategy 49–50
dignity 16–17

direct involvement *see* employee involvement
discretion 107, 112
discrimination 36–7
downward communication 28

earnings *see* pay inequalities
economic context 32–5; in EU 42–3; in India 175; and lean production 97; and partnerships 147, 150; and trade unions 76, 188; *see also* financial crisis
economic liberalisation 167–8, 175
education, management approach in 23–4, 31n1, 183
effects, link with participation 14–15, 16
EI *see* employee involvement
emergent economies *see* China; India
emotional labour 21, 61, 112
employee empowerment 107–13
employee engagement 88, 108, 113–19
employee involvement (EI) 15–16, 183–6; in China 171, 174; definition and characteristics of 12, 15, 58–60; and dignity 16–17; employee responses to 75; and future of EPV 191; management rationale for 15, 46, 58
employee ownership (EO) 77, 87–92
employee participation (EP) 1–2, 4, 9–12; *see also* collective participation; employee participation and voice
Employee Participation in Organisational Change (EPOC) 126
employee participation and voice (EPV): beneficiaries of *see* beneficiaries of EPV; collective participation *see* collective participation; current context 183–6; defining 3–6, 8–12; dimensions of 5, 8–12; empowerment 107–13; engagement 88, 108, 113–19; evolution of 3, 4, 8–12, 182–3; financial participation *see* employee ownership; employee share ownership; profit-sharing; future of 186–91; and future of work 197–9; global dimensions *see* globalisation; HPWS *see* high-performance work systems; and impact of Brexit 191–3; impact on performance and productivity 26–30; international context *see* internationalisation; link with democratic values 15–16; measuring 6–7, 78, 94; perspectives on *see* employees; government approaches;

Subject Index 245

management; trade unions; prospects for 193–6; teamworking *see* teamworking
employee representatives on EWCs 157–8
employee share ownership (ESO) 18–19, 77, 82–7, 170–1, 195–6
employees: board membership for 10, 35, 42, 143–5, 194; grievances in India 175–6, 177–8; in insecure work *see* precarious work and workers; resistance by 5, 71–2, 110, 196; role in EP 11; silence of 5, 71–2, 110, 183; and union density 65–6; views of unions 72–4, 75–6; *see also* labour disputes; satisfaction
employee–employer meetings 115–16, 194
employee–employer relationship 45, 186
employers: motives for EVP 45–6, 78, 80, 84; resistance to unions 11, 136–7, 177, 178, 179, 180, 182; response to evolving EPV 182; *see also* management
employer–employee meetings 115–16, 194
employer–employee relationship 45, 186
Employment Acts (1980s) 37–8
employment law *see* legislation
Employment Relations Acts (ERA) (1999 & 2004) 37, 38, 39, 137
employment security *see* job security/insecurity
employment status 67, 68, 69–70, 177, 198; *see also* job security/insecurity; precarious work and workers
employment tribunals 71
empowerment 107–13
enabling legislation 40, 78; *see also* tax incentives
engagement 88, 108, 113–19
Enron 56–7, 59–60, 85–6
enterprise culture management 169
enterprise unions 172, 173
enterprise works councils 164
EO *see* employee ownership
EP *see* employee participation
EPOC (Employee Participation in Organisational Change) 126
EPV *see* employee participation and voice
equity 72
ERA *see* Employment Relations Acts

ESO *see* employee share ownership
ETUC (European Trade Union Confederation) 158, 159
Europe: collective bargaining in 137–9; employee views of trade unions in 72–4; EPV in international context 152–3, 163; joint consultation in 139–41; precarious work in 68–9; prospects for EPV in 194; social partnership in 147; supervisory boards and codetermination in 144–6; UK exit from EU 191–3; works councils and codetermination in 142–3
European Commission (EC) 41
European Social Chapter 34, 153
European Trade Union Confederation (ETUC) 158, 159
European Union interventions: UK perspectives on 34; *see also* European Works Councils
European Union law 29; EWC Directives 153–5, 158–63
European Working Conditions Survey (EWCS) 123, 126
European Works Council Directive (1994) 153–5, 158–61
European Works Council Directive (2009 Recast) 153, 160–3
European Works Councils (EWCs): continuing problems of 163–5; early research on 155–8; forms and processes 153–5; impact of 2009 Recast 161–3; revision of 1994 directive 158–61; UK position 10, 34, 153, 165, 192–3
exit: from employment 5, 74, 75, 185; from EU 191–3
expectations, and satisfaction 18
expertise 56, 158, 160

FDI (foreign direct investment) 166, 175
financial crisis (2008) 42–3, 62n1, 147, 158
financial participation: employee ownership 77, 87–92; employee share ownership 18–19, 77, 82–7, 170–1, 195–6; and inequality 79, 83, 85, 86, 89, 93–4; profit-sharing 77, 78–82, 92–3, 94; range of 77–8; trade union views of 83, 84, 85, 94
financialisation 44n.1
FLEX Automation 108

246 Subject Index

flexibility 42–3, 61, 117, 192, 198; *see also* precarious work and workers
Ford Motor Company 11
foreign direct investment (FDI) 166, 175
Foxconn 172–3, 178
France 43, 79, 138, 139, 142
franchise operations 158, 160
free-riding 79
free-trade agreements 166

gainsharing *see* profit-sharing
garment industry 180
gender inequality 189–90
Germany: coordinated market in 10, 32–3; government approach in 41, 43; trade unions in 138; worker-directors in 35, 145–6; works councils in 10, 142–3, 164
gig economy 67, 68, 70
globalisation: context for 166–7; EPV in context of 35, 179–81; EVP in China 167–74; EVP in India 174–9; and future prospects for EPV 186–7, 193–4
GMB union 69
good employer ethos 40
good jobs 19–25, 187, 195
government approaches 9–11; and closing participation gap 196; and collective bargaining 136, 138, 139; encouragement 40, 79, 80, 83, 148; and European Union 41–3; legislation 33, 36–41, 78, 136, 139, 192; market economy context 32–6
Gyllenhammer, P. 127

hard exit from EU 191–2
Harvard model 51
Hawthorne experiments 47
HCWS (high-commitment work systems) 95
Health and Safety at Work Act (1974) 36
Health and Safety Executive 20
health and wellbeing: and control 25–6; and HPWS 102–3; and inequality 93–4; and insecurity 69, 117; and job quality 20; and lean 98–9
healthcare 130–2, 149
hierarchical relations 83; *see also* employer-employee relationship
high performance work teams 124
high-commitment work systems (HCWS) 95

high-involvement work systems (HIWS) 95
high-performance work systems (HPWS) 21, 105–6; concept of 95, 101–2; influence of Japanese lean 96–9; influence of people management 99–100; research on 100–5
Honda 173, 179
Huawei 170–1
human resource management (HRM): and EWCs 156; and HPWS 99–100; link with business strategy 48–57; trends in China 168–71, 174
human resource specialists, status of 54–7
humanisation of work 47–8

ICE *see* Information and Consultation of Employees
Independent Workers of Great Britain (IWGB) union 69, 76n1
India 174–9
'India Way' 174, 177
individualism 59
industrial democracy 8–9
Industrial Relations Act (1971) 37
industry-level bargaining 137–8, 139
inequality: and employee ownership 89; and ESO 83, 85, 86; gender inequality 189–90; pay inequality 79, 92, 93–4; problems related to 93–4; and profit-sharing 79, 93
information, withholding 71–2
Information and Consultation of Employees (ICE) regulations 29, 37, 140, 141
information provision 112; *see also* European Works Councils
information technology (IT) 124–5, 166, 175, 178–9
inputs, measurement based on 6–7
insecure work *see* job security/insecurity; precarious work
integrity 115
intellectual engagement 116
intensification *see* work intensification
International Commission for Labor Rights 177, 179
internationalisation 152; continuing problems of EWCs 163–5; early research on EWCs 155–8; European EPV in context of 152–3, 163; forms and processes of EWCs 153–5; impact

of 2009 EWC Recast 161–3; revision of EWC Directive 158–61
Ireland 147
IWGB (Independent Workers of Great Britain) union 69, 76n1

Japanese approach 96–9, 123, 128–9
Japanese transnational companies 156–7
JC (joint consultation) 139–41
JICs (Joint Industrial Councils) 35–6
job quality 19–25, 187, 195
job security/insecurity 30, 112, 117, 184, 193–4; *see also* precarious work and workers
John Lewis Partnership 91–2
joint consultation (JC) 139–41
Joint Industrial Councils (JICs) 35–6

kaizen 96, 97

labour disputes 35, 173–4, 177–8, 179
labour force, impact of Brexit on 192
lean production 96–9, 123, 124, 128–32, 177–8
legal compliance 29, 40, 164
legislation: as employer motive for EVP 45–6; impact of Brexit on 192; market context 33; method of implementation 39–40, 78, 80, 83; relating to trade unions 36, 37–9, 136, 137, 139; role and impact of 36–41
liberal market economies (LMEs) 32, 33
line management 50, 112, 130–1
Loch Fyne Oysters 89–90

Maastricht Treaty (Social Chapter) 34, 153
McDonaldization thesis 20, 22, 61
McDonald's Corporation 157–8, 187–8
management: appeal of teams for 121, 127, 129; critiques of 61–2; defensive motives for EVP 46–7; and employee involvement 12, 15, 46, 57–60; employee meetings with 115–16, 194; engaging managers 115; financial rewards 79, 85, 92, 93, 94; and humanisation of work 47–8; and joint consultation 139–41; legislative motives for EVP 45–6; as source of empowerment 109, 110; strategy and HRM 48–57; and transnational EVP 153,
155–7, 162–4; *see also* employers; line management
managerialism 22–5
manufacturing technologies 166
Marriott hotels 107
Maruti Suzuki India Limited (MSIL) 177–8, 179
Maruti Suzuki Workers Union (MSWU) 177
meaning of work 17, 185–6
meaningfulness 116
meetings 115–16, 194
mergers and acquisitions (M&As) 152, 163, 175
methodological issues: and financial participation 78, 94; and HPWS 102, 103; measurement of autonomy 126; measuring effects/outcomes 14–15, 28, 30; measuring EPV 6–7
Microsoft 108
migration: of jobs 166, 180, 181; of workers 74; *see also* relocation
mismanagement, and dignity 17
Mondragon 90, 91
motivations 47
MSIL (Maruti Suzuki India Limited) 177–8, 179
MSWU (Maruti Suzuki Workers Union) 177
multinational companies (MNCs) 152, 172–3, 178; *see also* European Works Councils

national context 20, 32–5, 103–4; *see also* cultural context
National Domestic Workers Alliance 70
National Health Service (NHS) 130–1, 149
National Labor Relations Act (Wagner Act) (1935) 36, 37
neo-human relations school 47–8
neoliberalism: and future of EPV 191, 194; and globalisation 166; impact on EPV 9, 11, 34–5, 42, 89, 182–3; resistance to 196
new managerialism 22–5
new member states (NMS) of EU 73–4, 159
New Zealand 41
newly industrialising economies *see* China; India
NHS (National Health Service) 130–1, 149

no-blame culture 109
Nokia 178
Nuttall Review 88

offshoring 166, 172–3
organisational strategy, and HRM 48–57
organising model of union revitalisation 188, 189
outcomes: and measurement 7, 28, 30; *see also* performance; productivity
outsourcing 67, 136, 172–3, 174
overwork *see* work intensification

part-time work 68
partial participation 16
participation gap *see* representation/participation gap
partnership 146–50; approach to SHRM 53–4
partnership model of union revitalisation 188, 189
pay inequalities 79, 92, 93–4, 190; *see also* financial participation
Pay Review Bodies 137
pay reviews 137
pensions 79, 86
people management, influence on HPWS 99–100
performance: and EI 171, 184; and EI in China 171; impact of empowerment on 111; impact of EPV on 26–30; impact of teamwork on 127, 130–1; and satisfaction 18; and strategic fit 51, 52; *see also* high-performance work systems; productivity
performance appraisal 59–60, 103, 168, 176
performance management 118, 168
performance-related pay 59, 60, 77, 103; *see also* employee ownership; employee share ownership; profit-sharing
pluralism 10–11, 48, 135
Poland 74, 159
political perspectives *see* government approaches
populism 195
power: in employment relationship 45; *see also* empowerment
The Precariat: A New Dangerous Class (Standing) 66–7
precarious work and workers 42, 66–9; future directions 191, 193–4, 198; in India 178; and unions 67, 68, 69–70, 189, 198; and voice 69–70, 183; women's position 190; *see also* contract workers; job security/insecurity
private sector 65–6, 136, 149–50
privatisation 83
production teams 124
productivity: definition and measures of 27; impact of EPV on 26–30; link with profit-sharing 80–2, 92–3; and motivation for EPV 34; and satisfaction 21; *see also* performance
professionals: and autonomy 22–5, 31n1, 184–5; resistance by 196; status of HR specialists 56
profit-related pay *see* profit-sharing
profit-sharing 77, 78–82, 92–3, 94
project teams 124
property protection 9
pseudo participation 15–16
public sector: collective bargaining in 136; engagement in 116; lean production in 98–9; managerialism and autonomy in 22–5, 191; partnership in 148, 149; resistance to neoliberalism in 196; teamwork in 129–32; union density in 65–6, 70

quality of working life 19–25, 187, 195
Quality of Working Life movement 47, 124
quality-based production 96–7

RBV (resourced-based view) of SHRM 52–3
recession 19, 117, 150
relocation: following Brexit 193; *see also* migration
representation/participation gap: causes 11–12, 151; closing 196–7; continuing 185, 193; and engagement 117; and EWCs 163, 164; and precarious work 67; and union density 66
representative participation *see* collective participation
required legislation 39–40
research and development (R&D) 180
resistance: silence as form of 71–2; to neoliberalism 196
resourced-based view (RBV) of SHRM 52–3

Subject Index 249

restructuring 15, 29, 107, 141, 149, 158, 184
retirement plans 79, 86
revitalisation of unions 188–90
Rhine model 33
Rolls-Royce 194

salaries *see* pay inequalities
sanctions 143, 164
satisfaction 18–19, 21, 66, 74, 111, 184
save as you earn (SAYE) plans 84
sectoral bargaining 137–8, 139
security *see* job security/insecurity
self-employed status 67, 68, 69
service sector 98–9, 136, 175–6
Share Incentive Plans (SIPs) 83, 84
share ownership *see* employee ownership; employee share ownership
Sharesave plans 84
SHRM *see* strategic human resource management
silence 5, 71–2, 110, 183
Social Chapter (Maastricht Treaty) 34, 153
social dumping 152
social engagement 116
Social Europe 153, 165, 194
social partnership 146–50, 189
social problems 93; *see also* inequality
soft exit from EU 191
Special Negotiating Body (SNB) 154, 160–1
specialists 56, 158, 160
Sports Direct 57, 69–70, 194
stakeholder economy 33
state: role in EP 9–11; *see also* government approaches
strategic choice approach 50
strategic human resource management (SHRM) 48, 49–57, 99–100
strategic management 50
strategic narrative 115
strategy: defining 49–50; link with HRM 48–57
stress 26, 98, 117, 184
subjective experience of empowerment 110–11, 112
supervisors 17, 170; *see also* line management
supervisory boards 10, 143–6
surveillance 185, 197–8
Sweden 97–8

task restructuring 29
Tavistock Institute of Human Relations 122
tax incentives 79, 80, 83
team briefings 62n3, 72, 131, 137
team leaders 129
team roles 121–2
teams: autonomy of 126–8, 129; characteristics of 125–6; and lean production 128–32; prevalence of 123; size of 121; types of 123–5
teamworking: appeal of 120–1; in China 171; defining 122; and empowerment 110; and lean production 97, 99; link with productivity 81–2, 184; rise of 122–3
technology: impact on work 197–8; *see also* information technology
temporary work 68–9
threat, and role of EVP 46
Toyota 97, 128–9
Trade Union Act (2016) 39, 136
trade union density 65–6, 74, 134–5, 138
trade union recognition 29, 33, 37, 38–9, 69, 70, 189
trade unions: declining influence in UK 134–7; and economic context 76, 188; EI as response to 46; employee views of 72–4, 75–6; and engagement 117; and evolution of EPV 3, 182; and financial crisis in France 43; future directions 188–90, 191, 195, 197; global context 172–3, 176–8, 180; and HPWS 104; legislation on 36, 37–9, 136, 137, 139; and partnership 148, 149–50; and pluralism 48; and precarious work 67, 68, 69–70, 189, 198; and protection of voice 71; resistance to 9–10, 11–12, 136–7, 177–8, 179, 180, 182; role of 134, 135; status in Europe 137–9; views of financial participation 83, 84, 85, 94; views of transnational EPV 153, 157, 158, 159, 160, 161–2; views of worker-directors 144; women in 70, 189, 190
training 109, 112, 159, 160
transnational companies 152; *see also* European Works Councils; multinational companies
transnational issues, and EWC competence 160, 164
trust 30, 117, 147, 150, 184

Subject Index

Tullis Russell 90
two-way communication 28

UAW union 189
Uber drivers 69
UK: approach to unions in 9–10, 11, 33, 35, 136–7; decline of collective bargaining in 135–7; employee board membership in 143–4; and EWCs 10, 34, 165, 192–3; exit from EU 191–3; joint consultation in 139–41; lean production in 98–9; legislation in 36, 37, 39, 136, 137, 192; liberal market in 33; partnership in 148–9; political perspectives on EPV 33, 34–5; precarious work in 67, 68; profit-sharing in 79
UNICE 164
unions *see* trade unions
UNISON trade union 71
unitarism 12, 34, 58–9, 84
Unite union 69
University and College Union (UCU) 198
upward communication 28
US transnational companies 156–8
USA: approach to unions in 9, 11; government approach in 41; lean production in 98; legislation in 36, 37; liberal market in 33; precarious work in 67, 68; profit-sharing in 79, 80; share schemes in 84

virtual teams 124–5
voice: concept of 5–6; for precarious workers 69–70, 183; role in engagement 115, 116; suppression of 71, 183

voluntarist approach 29, 37, 46, 78, 148, 150
Volvo 127–8
vulnerable workers *see* precarious work and workers

Wagner Act (1935) 36, 37
Walmart 173
welfare corporatism 96
wellbeing *see* health and wellbeing
WERS *see* Workplace Employment Relations Survey
whistleblowing 72
women: and equal pay 46, 190; position in labour force 189–90; in trade unions 70, 189, 190
work: future of 197–9; meaning of 17, 185–6; quality of 19–25, 187, 195
Work, Employment and Society (WES) conferences 173
work intensification: and dignity 17; and engagement 114; and HPWS 104, 105; and lean 132; and surveillance 185; and teamwork 127
work-life balance 102–3
worker cooperatives 90–1
worker-directors 10, 35, 42, 144–5
working time 192
Workplace Employment Relations Survey (WERS) 19, 55, 58–9, 62n2, 117, 123
works councils 10, 138, 142–3, 164, 172; *see also* European Works Councils
World Investment Report 152

zero hour contracts 68, 70, 183, 198